ROBERT FROST HIMSELF

ROBERT FROST
HIMSELF

Stanley Burnshaw

George Braziller   New York

For Leda

CONTENTS

III. FROST'S LAST FIVE YEARS AND "THE HOLTS," 87

IV. THE FABRICATION OF THE "MONSTER" MYTH, 210

Thompson to Donoghue: "I'll tell you the REAL truth about that monster" (1957) • Thompson's birthday paean to Frost (1959) • The Frost-Thompson relationship: 1939-1963 • "The first downward trend from which it can never recover" (1953) • "I really don't care whether I ever see him again, alive or dead" (1963) • Editing *Robert Frost: The Early Years* • Thompson and a book-reviewer create the "monster" myth (1970) • Thompson suffers cerebral hemmorrhage (1971) • Winnick's account of the making of *Robert Frost: The Later Years* (1977) • *New York Times Book Review* prints protest letters • "Discovering" and examining Thompson's unpublished "Notes on Robert Frost" • Pages 966-1464 inexplicably missing • "Notes" compared with the published biography • Thompson's problems with Kay Morrison • "Frost and Elinor Frost: psychotics; Carol, Irma, Lesley, insane" • Thompson and "facts" • Ten other portrait books on Frost • His *Complete Poems: 1949* replaced by Lathem edition • Protests • Eliot: "verse is itself a system of punctuation"

V. TOWARD THE "KNOWABLE" FROST, 241

"It's 'temper' I have to watch" • Ciardi sees Frost plain • "Revelation" • Public performer • "Subtlest and most elusive poet" • Elinor Frost portrayed • Frost as parent • Family tragedies • "Survivalist" • New living arrangements • "just seeking, questing" • Teaching career: 1906-1912; 1917— • Educational "heresies" • Conversationalist • The "individual" and "self-cultivation" • Unfinished letter to Norman Thomas • Jealousy, "a passion I approve of" • "You've got to score" • Tutored in self-promotion • A "public self" • Friendships • Encouraging, aiding, praising other writers • Frost's "problem behavior": eight examples • Racist? • Mythologist? • "It's a funny world" • "Outer seriousness: inner humor; outer humor: inner seriousness" • Play • Dramatic and open-ended poetry • Statements on poetry • The "sound of sense" • Emblemism, not symbolism • "trip the reader head foremost into the boundless" • Being "rightly taken" • Mind, science • Limits of human thought • Contrarieties • "I *am* the conflicts, I *contain* them" • "All truth is a dialogue" • Thoughts on religion • "something" • James and Bergson • "There is such a thing as redemption" • "Form: everybody's sanity to feel it and live by it" • Momentary stays against confusion • Nine "givens" of Frost's existence • "The Draft Horse" • A gathering of lines of verse • "There are roughly zones. . . " • "Neither Out Far Nor in Deep" • Acceptance

ILLUSTRATIONS

following page 54

Facsimile of "Provide, Provide"

following page 176

Robert Frost as senior class poet • Elinor White • Frost in England • The poet at his writing desk • The Frost family in Bridgewater • Frost in Washington • Bread Loaf Writers Conference • Frost playing baseball • Frost with his dog Gillie • Frost with the Morrisons • Frost's 80th birthday party • At John F. Kennedy's inaugural • Frost resting in a field

PREFACE & ACKNOWLEDGMENTS

Robert Frost's presence had filled my life from my fifteenth year—first through poems, then a few friendly letters, climaxed by a weekend visit with him in Vermont in 1929 and followed by talks, letters, exchanges of books, advice, comments, and "words" through friends. Then the unforeseeable happened when, in joining the staff of Henry Holt in 1958, I became Frost's companion and editor. His death in 1963 could not take him out of my life—to the contrary, as the picture of Frost changed for the worse in the eyes of former admirers. Any day now, I felt certain, someone properly informed would come forward to right the wrong the detractors had done, wipe away the biases, add the missing essentials, and restore for the world the person he really was.

"When one writes about Frost," says Randall Jarrell, "one feels lamentably sure of how lamentably short of his world one is going to fall"—and in writing of random parts of our numberless hours together, these words proved dismayingly true. There is nonetheless comfort in keeping in mind, with Reginald Cook, that "in talking" the poet "rambled" about all manner of things "with impunity," whereas "in writing he was all for neatness, order, form." Yet the rambling might, without any warning, break into streams of words that, once they were heard, would stay with his listener forever—which explains why the *Christian Science Monitor* could state that Cook's *Dimensions. . .* "allows us to hear Frost's conversation with impressive fidelity." With his repetitions included, for as early as 1915 he had felt constrained to explain, "I must say some things over and over" and hint at the reason why.

I have been especially fortunate when reading the early drafts of "The Last Five Years. . . " in gaining access to many letters and notes—including a large correspondence with Dudley Fitts—and to calendars kept by Kathleen Morrison and Frost himself. For enabling me to verify dates, I am much indebted to Edward Connery Lathem, of the Dartmouth College Library, who has been more zealous and thoughtful in giving me all kinds of help than words of mine can describe.

In the course of writing this book, I have benefited from the knowledge, counsel, and understanding of four men in particular: Wade Van Dore, author of *Robert Frost and Wade Van Dore: The Life of the Hired Man*; Roy H. Winnick, for his detailed and moving account of the "making" of *Robert Frost: The Later Years, 1938-1963*; Alfred C. Edwards, the Executor of the Estate of Robert Frost; and Hyde Cox, co-editor of *Selected Prose of Robert Frost* and long-time friend of the poet. To each of them I extend my profound gratitude as I do, as well, to many friends and students of Frost for their contributions, large and small, parts of which may appear on the pages that follow: Gay Wilson Allen, William Arrowsmith, Jacques Barzun, Joseph Blumenthal, Mrs. Reuben A. Brower, Sterling Brown, Arthur Casciato, the late John Ciardi, Marcella Cisney, Peter Davison, Henry Dierkes, Denis Donoghue, Leon Edel, Robert Elias, Richard Ellmann, Robert N. Ganz, Dr. Jack Hagstrom, Donald Hall, Milton Hindus, Sholom Kahn, Frances Keegan, Mrs. Judith Kranes, Kathleen Morrison, Henri Peyre, Richard Poirier, Burton R. Pollin, William H. Pritchard, Luciano Rebay, Franklin Reeve, Rabbi Victor Reichert, Christopher Ricks, Edward Schuh, Harvey Shapiro, Donald Sheehy, William A. Sutton, Robert Thomason, Theodore Weiss, Richard Wilbur, and Robert Zaller.

Finally, I am privileged to express to Louise Waller and Deirdre Mullane thanks of a special order for all they have done to better this book in their role as editors.

Formal acknowledgment for gracious permission to quote from a number of sources appears on the copyright page.

S.B.

April 1986

ROBERT FROST
HIMSELF

I

TO THE READER

An "acute discomfort in biography arises," says Denis Donoghue in a recent essay, "when the biographer, in the course of his research, changes his attitude toward his subject.

> Sometimes the change is benign. There are charming instances in which a biographer, starting out in a fairly disinterested spirit, gradually takes on the lineaments of his subject, as a biographer of Samuel Johnson might become Johnsonian. But sometimes the change is dreadful. I assume that the late Lawrance Thompson undertook the biography of Robert Frost on the spur of admiring him, but it is clear that after a while he came to loathe him. When I met Thompson in Dublin, it was evident that the biography would be a work of riddance, if not a labor of hate. Perhaps he should have disqualified himself, like a scrupulous judge, the case being what it had become.[1]

Donoghue and Thompson met toward the close of the "good will" visit made by Frost to the British Isles for the State Department, May 19–June 20, 1957. Frost died on January 29, 1963, and within four years the first volume of Thompson's official biography appeared. *The New York Times* daily reviewer welcomed it warmly. But the sec-

---

[1] *The New York Times Sunday Book Review*, March 11, 1984, p. 32. See also below page 210. A number within parentheses—for example, (210)—refers to a relevant passage in the text.

3

ond volume brought a changed response from the same critic, Thomas Lask:

> It may be an exaggeration to say that a reading of this second volume of Robert Frost's biography [*The Years of Triumph*] will permanently chill your enthusiasm for the poet's work, but it is not that much of an exaggeration. The mind and the character of the poet revealed here are so unattractive, nay repellent, that long before the end, the reader will wonder whether Mr. Thompson realizes what he is doing. What Frost would have thought of such a performance can scarcely be imagined this side of Vesuvius. In his private life, violence in thought and expression was a function of his being. But I'm sure that a reading of this book would have stunned him into a New England stillness. Years of triumph, the author calls them. With such triumphs, disasters are unnecessary.
>
> *August 11, 1970*

Two days before, *The New York Times Book Review* had gone even further. The critic, though deriding Thompson's "crudeness" of mind and intellectual shallowness and then accusing him of "criminal blandness"—even worse, of "hiding behind an affectation of fairness"—ended by swallowing him whole. Close to the start of her strange performance, she advised her readers that Frost was no less than "a monster of egotism" who had left "behind him a wake of destroyed human lives" (219f.).

This, the nation was told by its most influential review, is the same Robert Frost only recently hailed (1963) as America's "national bard," its "laureate," "the best-loved poet in the country." From north to south, east to west, newspapers, radios, television programs announced in fervid statements the death in his eighty-ninth year of "the sage," "the seer," "the public man that the nation adored."[2]

Had countless millions been deceived: critics and readers, presidents and "unofficial spokesmen," audience members and intimates? By what superlative sleight of hand had Frost defrauded his worshippers? Nowhere else in the annals of literature has so marked a change of the public heart been recorded. In terms of effect upon readers, one might think of Poe and the injuries done to his reputation

---

[2] The sources of words or phrases quoted appear in the Reference Notes section. A double asterisk (**) always refers to the Reference Notes.

by Rufus Griswold. Two days after the poet's death on October 7, 1849, this assumedly friendly biographer and literary executor launched a prolonged attack on his memory, in the course of which he besmirched Poe's name and alienated Poe's friends. Though many years passed before the misdeeds were fully exposed, Griswold's manifest hostility almost at once evoked indignant replies, and, within six months, was followed by one irrefutable answer.**

No such efforts were made to protest Thompson's charge against Robert Frost as a person. And that countless people who read the reviews of *The Years of Triumph* or learned of its monstrous portrayal changed their minds about Frost for the worse, there can be no doubt. How could it fail to have happened? Volume Two, after all, was the work of the man whom the poet himself had chosen, and the writers assigned to review it must have been judged by their editors as dependable critics. But what of the quiet minority—friends of Frost: young, middle-aged, older, who had known him in *person,* some for a few, some for a great many years? To assume that their silence spelled assent would be false. But why, then, no protests?

Explanation calls for more than a simple answer. For one thing, three or four recent, respectively different portrayals of Frost were available to all who cared to read and compare; yet *all* the reviewers of Thompson's work wholly ignored their existence—from ignorance? Laziness? Biased intent? Reginald Cook, for long the Director of the Middlebury College Bread Loaf School of English, whose association with Frost had begun almost fifteen years before Thompson became the official biographer, had published a critical description of the poet as person and writer, including some records of conversations and speeches, most of them having been picked up *viva voce* from the poet "by listening thirty years." Cook's *The Dimensions of Robert Frost* had come out in 1958, a year after Sidney Cox's *A Swinger of Birches,* a portrait based on a forty-year-long relationship, with many quotations from their talks. Next to appear was a book by Elizabeth Shepley Sergeant, a *New Republic* war correspondent and author of essays on writers: *Robert Frost: The Trial by Existence* (1960), the first full-length biography. Finally, seven months after the poet's death, the long-awaited *The Letters of Robert Frost to Louis Untermeyer* appeared. At once both the record of a fifty-year relationship and a portrait of a man and his mind, the book presented "the speculations and activities, the large theories, the small irritations, and, perhaps most surprising to many readers, the extraordinarily playful spirit of a

5

great poet." With the help of the editor's background notes, the *Letters* provided "a gradually unfolding and unguarded autobiography." All four books portray distinctively different Frosts, the first, second, and last growing out of far greater intimate knowledge than Thompson possessed.

But of larger importance—with none of the authors had there been a question of trust or of anything vaguely approaching the grave interpersonal anguish that deepened throughout the last ten years of the Thompson-Frost relationship. I refer—phrasing it cautiously—to the growing loss of mutual trust and to Thompson's admitted animus. The existence of these problems and their force in shaping the portrait drawn by *The Years of Triumph* played no traceable part in any review. These facts inevitably lead to a question: Were reviewers unaware or—worse—unconcerned that such hostility problems existed between the two men? It seems obvious that those unaware or unconcerned were in no position to gauge the dependability of Thompson's interpretations.

More than a few friends of Frost had been worried about the increasing tension between biographer and poet. Yet so long as the latter elected to hold to the arrangement with Thompson, they could do nothing but wait and wish for the best. Nor did they have any means for resolving the problems. Tension already had grown too deep to be lessened by any efforts toward truce. For the first time, in 1959, Frost admitted as much to me, with an imprecation that also bespoke his acceptance of how things stood: "I'm counting on you to protect me from Larry. Remember!"

Why did he call upon me? Where did I stand in relation to Frost and the man now holding the reins? To attempt to reply, I must go back sixty years to the days when I first encountered Frost as a living presence through *New Hampshire,* and responded with a schoolboy's piece that appeared in a well-known journal which Frost could have missed. What matters is not *my* account but the truth about Frost as I saw it and see it now, and not only out of our lengthy association and numberless talks in the last five years of his life but equally out of my striving for tenable answers in the decades that followed his death.

II

ROADS TAKEN AND
NOT TAKEN

How I first got hold of Untermeyer's *Modern American Poetry,* in my
high school days, I am not quite sure, but I vividly recall flipping the
leaves till they happened on Robert Frost's poems. I had the uncanny
feeling that I'd known them before. "Mending Wall," "The Tuft of
Flowers," "The Runaway," "Birches"—they were not only
wonderfully strange but also oddly familiar. I knew this landscape of
Frost's, his trees, his fields; but the words were about my landscape
too, the world where I'd lived my childhood years: springs, autumns,
winters in the hills of Westchester County; my summers in Belgrade,
Maine, just north of Boston.

Untermeyer offered in three packed pages much that I wanted to
know of the life of this California-New England poet who had
worked as a factory bobbin boy, made shoes, edited a weekly, tried in
vain for eleven years to wrest a living out of his rocky New
Hampshire farm, turned to teaching, then made up his mind to risk a
change, sailing to Britain in 1912 with his wife and children. Writing
with unconcealed delight at the turn in luck that greeted Frost in
London after twenty years of total neglect as a poet, Untermeyer described the publication there of Frost's first books in 1913 and 1914 (*A
Boy's Will, North of Boston*), as well as the fame that awaited him on
returning home in 1915. The editor's insights into the poet's achievement, whatever limits in depth and range they may show today, more
than fulfilled the needs of my untrained mind. In any case the poems

themselves were what mattered. And within two years of this first encounter with Frost, I had bought all three of his books including his recent *Mountain Interval* along with the 1920 *American Poetry Miscellany* and its 1922 issue. Avid to read as much as I could of the moderns in English, I had also plunged into Untermeyer's *Modern American and British Poetry* (1922). It brought me closer to Frost's own views of his art. On "realism,"

> he is quoted as "once having said," the one who offers a good deal of dirt with his potato to show that it is a real one; and the one who is satisfied with the potato brushed clean. I'm inclined to be the second kind. . . . To me, the thing that art does for life is to strip it to form.

At the time I had no idea of the crucial part that "form" would play in the life and writing of Frost. Or the third essential (often repeated) tenet of his poetics: the "sounds, the delicate accents of speech," with which the editor closed his introduction:

> Frost's lines disclose the subtle shades of emphasis and expression in words, in the rhythms and tones that call to life a whole scene *by presenting only a significant detail* [italics mine]. "If I must be classified as a poet," Frost once said, with the suspicion of a twinkle, "I might be called a Synedochist; for I prefer the synedoche in poetry—that figure of speech in which we use a part for the whole."

By now I was starting to feel at home with this strange great poet, for great he most certainly was to me, though at times perplexing and strange. There were passages, even whole poems, that left me uncertain; others that lured me again and again in hope of finding their meanings. Of all his eighty-odd works I had read, most had been taking root in my mind and some I had learned by heart. Yet I wanted more. I began to frequent library periodical rooms, where I made the acquaintance of ponderous-looking quarterlies along with a score of slim little poetry journals. One of them, *The Measure,* published three of Frost's poems in August 1923. Months before, I had found what I guessed might become his most popular poem ("Stopping by Woods on a Snowy Evening") and eight weeks later, "Our Singing Strength," both in *The New Republic.* The *Yale Quarterly Review* offered

"To Earthward," "I Will Sing You One-O," and "Nothing Gold Can Stay." Hence, by the time *New Hampshire* appeared in November, I had read a third of its pages.

Having aged five months past the ripeness of seventeen years, I felt ready to look at the work with the eye of not only a poetry reader but a critic as well. And in fact I thought I knew more of what made up America's "poetic renascence" than anyone else in my sophomore class (at the University of Pittsburgh). I had read every essay and book I could find on the modern poets, also much of their verse, while exploring the libraries, and not only well-known figures—Robinson, Eliot, Pound, Aiken, Millay, H.D., *et al*. While writing verse of my own, I felt a part of this new and exciting "movement." I was reader, writer, observer—and inevitably also critic, "rating" this man or woman. But, alas, there was no one to hear me.

The moment had come to act, and *The Forum* provided the means. A well-respected monthly, it had just begun to invite its readers to offer book reviews, 300 words long, the best of which they would publish. Frost's *New Hampshire* seemed perfectly timed. Without even waiting to line up my thoughts, I dashed off a comment, referring to poems by name, kind, and performance, ending my praise with a call for "a local holiday." *The Forum* printed my words in its May 1924 issue and paid me $10. Three months later a professor unknown to me offered me half as much for permission to print my words in a college textbook for freshmen. With the *noblesse oblige* of a published critic still in his junior year, I consented. Meanwhile I was burning to know if Frost was aware of my tribute. I could think of no way of finding out. Nor did I learn till late: March 26, 1962, at his 88th birthday dinner.

Frost and poetry were the most important part of my days, especially after college. Daily from eight to five I worked at a white-collar job in a steel mill outside Pittsburgh, writing on gasoline-cracking equipment, smelting furnaces, concrete mixing, steel forms for subways, electric transmission towers. In the same months I published another *Forum* review (on Cummings' *Tulips and Chimneys*), and my verse was seeing the light in some of the little poetry journals. At about this time, with a long-standing fascination for book design and printing, I decided one day to issue my own magazine. I knew how to hand set type and I'd recently met a small-job printer who was more concerned with craft than with money. It cost about $15 for my brand-new font of "Caslon Old Style" cast by the Monotype firm, a wooden alphabet case, a composing stick, galleys, ink, roller, and brayer. Contributions arrived through the little-magazine network, and in April 1926 my *Poetry Folio* was born: four 9″ by 12″ pages on a bright white "Strathmore Laid paper," two type columns on each: critical prose on the opening page, verse on the inside spread, and both on the fourth.

I mailed one copy to Frost, another to Aiken, who sent me a noncommittal but warm reply that showed he had read it. To Frost I had sent a note explaining how I produced my tiny mixture of verse and prose. He wrote back saying he not only liked "the idea" of the *Folio* but also offered his thanks for receiving "such hand-set things," having "at one time threatened" himself to become a printer. I thanked him and apologized for having enclosed, uninvited, some of the verse I had written. His reply made me speculate. Both of us knew, it began, that all these poems were "poetical," then he went on to warn that anyone writing verse must recognize sooner or later the part played by chance in the making of poems. Was this a gentle letdown-by-consolation? A confidential confession? Neither or both? In time I mislaid the letter but some of its words were unforgettable: those that said it was "chance when the right subject and the right words come together. But you know all this." At the foot of the sheet he had added "Count on my friendship."

Months before, I'd received some excited notes from my summertime friend and college-mate Tony Kovner, now enrolled at Ann Arbor, where Frost was serving his final year as poet-in-residence. His daughter Marjorie's illnesses had kept him, on and off, away from the campus. He had just returned to fulfill his teaching commitment—meeting with twelve student writers—at the end of January, when the college's monthly, *The Inlander,* featured one of his still unpublished poems, "The Minor Bird." Tony sent me the issue, also a long account of a new acquaintance, Wade Van Dore, who had formed a special relationship with the poet.

Born in 1899 in Detroit, Van Dore had quit school in his sixteenth year, earning his keep by various jobs, from bookstore-clerking to gardening, as art apprentice, factory hand in a tractor plant, newspaper-mailer, etc., so as to give himself time for reading, writing, and music. Thoreau's writings had taught "the only acceptable way of living one's life." Hence his excited response on discovering Frost's new book of verse, *Mountain Interval.* Here was a living American author who seemed to share many of Thoreau's beliefs. Losing no time, he wrote to Frost, expressing his high admiration and also asking advice as to where he might work and live while getting to "learn the Frost country."

"First about Thoreau," read the letter of June 24, 1922, that came in reply. "I like him as well as you do. In one book (Walden) he surpasses everything we have had in America. You have found this out for yourself without my having told you; I have found it out for myself without your having told me. Isn't it beautiful that there can be such concert without collusion? That's the kind of 'getting together' I can endure." Frost went on to make a specific suggestion, which resulted in Van Dore's working part of the summer on the farm of one of the poet's friends in New Hampshire. Quite by chance one August day, Frost and Van Dore met at the Littleton railroad station. Not until three years later did they see each other again. By then Van Dore had traveled alone into Canada's wilderness, where he had lived before for a six-month stay.

With letters and poems, he had kept in touch with Frost, so that when he appeared at the poet's house in November, both were eager to talk. Frost spent much of the time on the young man's verse, reading at first to himself, then rereading aloud. When he came to the poem "Far Lake," he was startled enough to ask Mrs. Frost to join them both and hear it. He read it again and again, pointing to some of its "enviable felicities." Four or five later visits deepened the new relationship. "And now," said Tony's letter to me, "Wade will be going up north to live again like a hermit, but he may knock at your door without warning—that's how he is. Another thing, which you'll like: he's taken with *Poetry Folio*. Told me he might contribute. Hope I'll be sending you something of his for the second issue."

Publishing poems in my small magazine by a man who had won Frost's admiration excited me, yet something about Van Dore was oddly disturbing. My first few weeks at the steel mill outside Pittsburgh had made me aware that the earth was being menaced. Industrialism, pushing ahead inexorably, was to me the "enemy force." Luckily, there was one sure means for holding it back: banding all people together to salvage the earth. Automatically I became a "conservationist-communist"—for the obvious reason that once the earth was regained by the people, they would see to its safety. Though I made no move to bring on this change, visions of fear clouded my poems. Month after month, sketches in verse depicting the evils around me—from violation of the earth to the pain imposed on the lives of the people who lived in the steel mill's shadow. Late one night,

I saw the sketches fall into place, becoming an epic, a narrative, spiraling up toward a clarion call for defense. But the sketches reflected only my *public* outcry. The private one would be clustered in groups of lyric "excursions," away from the public theme. Thus would the public and private halves of my newfound vision mirror themselves in a book.

How, I wondered, thinking of Van Dore and his flight into Canada's wilderness, how could I countenance one man's selfish escape, leaving the earth to fend for itself unaided? Thoreau may have been sure he had found the one right way, but he lived at a time before the relentless assault of industry on the earth had begun. Yet, who was I to blame Van Dore, with my own escape in the offing? Soon—in May of the coming year—I would leave my job at the mill; compensation for finishing college at age nineteen: a year in Europe, paid in part by my father. One full *Wanderjahr,* then *status quo ante:* I would have to earn my way again; find a new place in the ranks that "battled for earth."

Sensible plan—irresistible! But when the twelve months ended, difficult to fulfill. Weeks passed, then months, until by chance a tabloid want-ad led me into a dull but bearable job. I was living now in the heart of my city of birth, where "remnants" of France troubled my nights and days. Not of its people, landscape, art, cathedrals, streets, but an indefinable strangeness in the air, borne—it seemed—out of smoldering centuries, cruel, bloody, or kind to a vanguard ever lost in pursuit of a vision. Touched by this air, aided by friends, books, and my own new eyes, I had found my way into strange new worlds. I had also come to learn the poets of Europe and to grasp much more than I'd known of English modernist verse, of its debt to France—Eliot's surely, and others'. Frost alone, for all he had found in the classics, was untouched by this new movement: so it appeared from a foreign shore. But now, with the publication of *West-Running Brook* in November, there was more to consider. Not that it offered any new strain or dimension. Frost's "darkness" had glowed before—"Home Burial," "A Servant to Servants," "Out, Out—" "An Old Man's Winter Night," others. By grouping eleven "grave" poems and naming them "Fiat Nox" ("Let There Be Night"), had the poet meant to turn readers to parts of his world they had failed to see? Did he hope to destroy for good the mindless view of the rustic bard who affirmed the complacent virtues, the simplicities, the comforting modes of feeling?

My friend Tony, freed from college, at home in New York, had been waiting to learn from a friend who had studied with Frost what she and the other disciples thought about *West-Running Brook.* Instead she wrote of Van Dore, who had driven to Florida, camped on a Naples beach, written some poems, and traveled north to spend three days with the Frosts, who were living in Amherst. April would find him back in Vermont for a five-month stay, helping to put the farm just purchased by Frost into suitable shape. "But don't be surprised," she added, "if suddenly he stops en route, knocks at your door, pays you a visit."

Which occurred at the end of the month, but instead of knocking at Tony's door, it was mine. We had much to discuss, and at last I was able to see the face of this unpredictable creature. To my pleased surprise, he seemed to know my essays printed in *Poetry* on French *vers libre,* also the "public poems" taken by *The American Caravan,* the new collection of verse, fiction, and drama by famous and unknown writers. Most of our talk centered on Frost, the summer to come, and the book of poems Wade was writing. Before he left for Vermont, I gave him my pamphlet of ten short poems (public and private) and a small book of prose I had written off "at one stroke" in a Paris hotel. As he studied the title—*A Short History of the Wheel Age*—I imagined him asking himself if this, like the public poems, was also a call for protecting the earth from civilization, which was how he'd have put it in terms of Thoreau.

Two months after he left, he wrote to me: "Come to Vermont for a weekend—late in July or any other days you can get time off from your job. Frost will drive to the station to meet you. Answer as soon as you can."

I hurriedly made my arrangements, sent Wade a note on the time and the hour, and, to be quite sure, named the station: South Shaftsbury. On the morning of August 1, 1929, I was on my way. After the stop at North Adams, the all but empty, broken-down coaches rattled along for what felt like hours.

I expected Wade to be there to introduce me. Frost, however, had come alone—purposely, I guessed—to size up the stranger. And the moment I settled beside him in his mud-spattered car, he held out a newly opened cigarette package. "Your brand?" he asked. I smiled, shaking my head. "Some of my New York friends smoke 'em," he added, starting the engine.

"I'm not surprised. They're fine Turkish tobacco—a bit expensive for . . ."

"What kind do *you* smoke?—You do. Don't you?"

I nodded. "Anything with Virginia in it if not too dry." I pulled out my pack of Old Golds. "These mostly. Will you try one?"

He chuckled, set both hands on the wheel, and looked straight ahead. We rocked along slowly over the rutted road. After a minute or two, he asked, "Have you been to Vermont before?"

"Never. But what I've seen so far reminds me of Maine." Trying to cloak my excitement with a nervous joke, I added that Vermont seemed similar to the landscape I'd glimpsed in his books.

He promised I'd see more of Vermont from the porch of the house they were living in, and The Gulley place, which Wade was putting into shape. We were now driving straight to the Shingle Cottage, not far from The Gulley.

The subject turned to poetry. Wade had told Frost I had written about free verse.

"Only the French variety—*vers libre*."

"Why ignore the English?"

I explained that at the University of Paris I happened to hear a French professor reading recent poems by a man named André Spire, free verse poems. I liked them so much that, after the hour, I started to put them in English. That very night I met the author at a party, and I asked him why he chose to write *vers libre*.

Frost waited for more.

Spire invited me to study with him, Thursday afternoons for about six months. He and his colleagues—scientists, not poets—had been able, he said, to *prove* that the lines of verse in French actually didn't depend on a fixed number of syllables but on stress; and that *meaning*—the sentence's meaning—always determined the stress. I had written about this for *Poetry*.

"Harriet Monroe's?" Frost asked. "I never knew that she was an expert in French."

"No need to be expert. My essays tell her all that she'd need. Once you're shown the differences between our languages, everything falls into place. Almost no French word has a tonic accent."

"For example."

"People speaking English always say 'ámorous,' but the French say 'amoureux'—three more or less equal syllables, except when a sentence's meaning puts the stress on the last."

"No tonic accent at all?" He glanced at me sharply. "I guess I ought to read what you've written. I may have some questions."

"Which I probably couldn't quite answer. All I intended to do was to cut through the blathering nonsense critics write, including your friend Amy Lowell." Even the diehards in France were forced to admit the validity of the new *vers libre*—though most of their best poets continued to write in traditional ways . . . I was just about to add "just as you've done." I waited, trusting that Frost would have listened between my lines. He showed no sign that he had. Raising his voice, he asked, "What about you? Do you write free verse?"

"I?"—I shook my head—"I wouldn't know where to end the lines."

"You know what I say? I should be as satisfied to play tennis with the net down as to write verse with no verse-form to stay me." The quip had become a byword but I wanted to hear him say it. Besides, I'd been talking too much. "Tennis with the net down." He smiled. "Do you play the game?"

"Every chance I can find. I'm a sort of tennis fiend."

"Singles or doubles?"

"Singles, unless I can't help it."

"What's wrong with doubles?" He glared suddenly, almost stopping the car.

"Nothing, I guess, except that you're always dependent on somebody else. I'd rather take the responsibility for winning or losing."

He thought a moment, nodded. "I guess I can understand that."

The car stopped. "That's what we call The Shingle Cottage." Pointing, he pulled up the brake. I followed him to the small frame cottage. Wade came out to greet us, and within minutes, we settled ourselves on the porch.

Frost emerged through a doorway. "Ginger ale?" Looking at me with the hint of a smile, "It's the strongest drink in the house."

Frost left us briefly, and Wade proceeded to ask the expected questions—the train, the trip from New York, Tony . . . Frost took some time before he returned with a large glass for each of us. For the first time I noticed the way his body moved—with the surefootedness of an athlete—agility he could summon at will.

He asked about my travels in Europe. Six weeks in England: May, June. Then at the end of the year, Italy: Genoa down to Capri and Pompeii. But the only countryside I came to know by foot was England's.

"My uncle was a walker when he wasn't practicing medicine. He had given me his Walking Society's maps. I was able to cross through farmfields covered with small wild poppies, away from the highways. Three days—to Brighton, something like sixty miles to the sea."

"It's a funny world. You were in France when we were in England. Maybe we passed each other all unknowing on a Paris street. We arrived in September."

I shook my head. "Oh, I'd have known from your pictures."

His daughter Marjorie wanted to live in France and learn to speak the language. She wasn't well, though well enough for sightseeing trips. He hadn't felt comfortable there, calling the French "a different race." He paused briefly. "I guess I say that because I've had friends in England. Have and had—had, almost from the start, when we came there in 1912. The first evening in London, we celebrated—Mrs. Frost and I—went to *Fanny's First Play*. We never wanted to *live* in the city. Long before we sailed we had set our hearts on the country. . . . When I first proposed England as the place to be poor and to write poems, Mrs. Frost cried, 'Yes, let's go over there and live under thatch.' "

From the way he had lifted his eyes as he talked, I felt he was "bounding away" from the present into the precious English past that had changed his life. I prepared myself—so had Wade, who sent me a telling glance—for a monologue of a kind I had never heard.

He was living again his days at "the Bungalow," twenty miles from London—a small, pretty stucco cottage in Beaconsfield. He described the grassy stretch in front, the gardens in back, strawberry beds, flowers—the place where Milton had finished *Paradise Lost*, not more than a mile or two from Gray's burial stone. From Untermeyer's anthology, I remembered the bare events of the London days that had changed the poet's career. Now I was hearing all that had really happened. London's literary world in the fall of 1912, I recalled, was a hot bed of poets—groups merging and dissolving overnight, the kind of literary turmoil that had been more or less the norm in Paris. But to hear it from Frost—what he saw in London was warfare. Writers taking positions: the old Guard at the Poetry Society versus Harold Monro, who edited its *Poetry Review*. He announced that the bookshop he owned would open on New Year's Day and that all *new* poets were invited. Another group, friends of Monro, who called themselves "Georgians" to impugn Victorians and Edwardians, included some well-known poets—W. W. Gibson, Walter de la Mare, Lascelles Abercrombie, Rupert Brooke. A fourth group welcomed T. E. Hulme for his emphasizing the image. Frank Flint was sympathetic, but Ezra Pound frankly and loudly declaimed his debt. Only vaguely aware of this state of war, Frost planned to attend the bookshop's New Year's opening—which actually occurred on the night of January 8th.

He arrived in a "more than usual" state of mind, for *A Boy's Will* was due to appear in April (1913). A London firm he had never heard of, David Nutt, had quickly accepted a manuscript almost entirely composed of poems that American magazine editors had rejected. Making his way through the crowd in the bookshop, Frost found a seat on a staircase. People about him were talkative, friendly, Flint in particular.

"He spotted me as American from my shoes and told me I'd better meet Ezra Pound, after he'd learned I was writing poems. Flint and I became friends. Pound—I had never heard his name before—was a *power*. He'd already published four books—paid $8 to have the first one printed. Flint told him about our talk and Pound gave him his calling card to send me, writing below his address 'At home—sometimes.' . . . I decided to do what Flint advised and pay him a visit. No sooner had I entered the room than he showed his rudeness. Why hadn't somebody sent him my book? We must rush right now to the firm and demand a copy—which is what we did. So the first copy of my first book was given to Ezra; they handed me the second." Frost laughed. "Typical Pound! But he hurried us back to his place and he started at once to read, after shouting 'Find yourself something—there!' A magazine, a book, so I wouldn't disturb him. But *he* was the one who interrupted. 'You don't mind our liking this?' he said. 'Oh no,' I answered, 'go right ahead and like it.' After a while he picked out the first few lines of 'In Neglect'—you know them?" Wade and I nodded.

He quoted: "They leave us so to the way we took, / As two in whom they were proved mistaken." Pound was pleased—also curious. Frost started to tell him part of the story behind the poem—troubles he'd had with his grandfather and uncle—money troubles. Pound listened with sympathy, then suddenly and brusquely, told him "to run along home" so he could start writing a review of the book for *Poetry*. "I made a mistake, thinking he'd take my family talk as the confidence that it was. Should have told him so, but it all happened so quickly. Before I left, he asked me to come back again; he wanted to take me to meet some poets, Yeats especially. Pound was working for him at the time. So off I went with two of his books—*Personae, Ripostes*. I suppose you know some of what followed though not the terrible part—what he said in *Poetry* of my having been disinherited, left in poverty by my grandfather and uncle. I began to wonder if Pound—with the best intentions—would do me more harm than good. . . . Never knew a promoter like that! I became pretty wary of Pound, even after he promised to take me to Yeats, who had said he wanted to meet me, that he greatly admired *my* work. Of course I was pleased, and I went with Pound to visit Yeats in his London rooms. He hadn't prepared me for all the darkness, curtains, candlelight—talk about ghosts, fairies, leprechauns. Yeats had become involved in psychical matters. It didn't take me long to get used to it all, and I started to talk about something I'd come to feel sure of. I said to Yeats I could tell from the way that the words of a poem behaved if the work had been done with one stroke of the pen, and I cited as one example his 'Song of Wandering Angus.' "

" 'Ah no, ah no,' he insisted. The song had been written 'in agony' at a terrible time. Not a word of the cause or the name of the lady—Maude Gonne, you know." It wasn't the visit he'd hoped for. Yeats was so drawn in by thoughts of his past that there couldn't be any real meeting between them, no connection. Before Frost left, Yeats asked him to come to his "Monday Nights," his regular weekly "at-homes." He went a couple of times. Nothing came of his hope for a close friendship.

Frost mentioned other friends he had made in the next few months—too many to talk about. Gibson, Abercrombie-Lascelles—"Did you know his first name rhymes with 'tassels'? Lascelles Abercrombie. But the one I miss the most died in the war. You must get to read his work—Edward Thomas." Frost left the porch. When he returned, he was carrying ginger ale—"strongest drink in the house" when he mixed it with rum.

I wondered what he would talk about next. Some of his listeners have strained to capture "his kind of talk." Most throw up their hands—even Gibson in "The Golden Room," writing of the August evening in 1914 in his "Old Nailshop," where he and his poet-friends and their wives, Edward and Helen Thomas, Catherine and Lascelles Abercrombie, Rupert Brooke, Elinor Frost

> talked and laughed; but, for the most part, listened
> While Robert Frost kept on and on and on,
> In his slow New England fashion, for our delight,

Holding us with shrewd turns and racy quips,
And the rare twinkle of his grave blue eyes . . .

And now he had started again, the one-way speaker nobody wanted to stop: taking us off into talk of people, books, events, speculations, tragedy, fortune, marking each with a word, a quip, a comment brief or long, with an obbligato of tone and gesture none might forget. His listeners were part of this presence in a bond of voice, tone, bodily motion, easeful-to-taut gaze of the eyes, between the poet who spoke and the one or the few who were there. Tape recordings could hardly give a sense of the humor or earnestness, of the shifting rhythms, the mimicking phrases, the frequent "Oh," "Sure," "See!" "You know," "Yeh-eh," "Yeh-eh," with their unmistakable messages. Now I was borne on a wave of friendliness flowing steadily—the low-pitched voice: soft, beguiling, bluff, mocking, brusque, as the thought required.

Every person he talked of opened a flood of connected thoughts that were vivid and sometimes elating to the book-filled mind of a youngster of twenty-three. Pound was still on his mind—the debt he owed, the deeply ambiguous feeling for the sometimes offensive "power." "Now he expected this 'Vurry Amur'k'n poet—that's what he called me to Alice Corbin at *Poetry*—to sit at his feet. . . . It didn't take long before we had quarreled and disagreed. But I'll always speak with praise of him for having been so quick and so kind—his haste to speak of my poetry. . . . A great promoter, Ezra! Soon he boosted the Imagist movement for all it was worth and *more,* but another promoter, Amy Lowell, took hold of it and Imagism came to be known as Amyism." Frost supposed Pound *did* something for Yeats—everyone thought so. And he was the first poet Frost ever sat down with to talk about poetry—Robinson's "Miniver Cheevy." " 'Miniver thought and thought and thought/ And thought about it.' Three thoughts would have probably passed, but the fourth made the intolerable touch of poetry . . ."

I knew Bynner's work, he supposed. From Bynner he skipped to Joyce, to Elinor Wylie, to Edna Millay, almost always making a comment—"She became too famous too quickly for her own good"—then added generous words on John Crowe Ransom. He had urged his publisher, Henry Holt, to issue Ransom's book. Somehow this led to Robert Bridges. He'd met the laureate by accident while visiting Lawrence Binyon. "Fine old boy, but he rides his hobbies. You know his greatest theory: that syllables in English have a fixed quantity. No denying," he stopped to make clear, "that vowels have length in English, but the accent of sense supersedes all other accent, overrides it, sweeps it away. Bridges would like English poetry to read as Latin poetry is read in the schools today. It was never read that way by the Romans. Even poets forget that words exist in the mouth, not in books." From the argument about syllable length, he turned to the plight of Latin and Greek teaching. And the subject of colleges brought recollections of Amherst, of a promising boy, a poet, who couldn't abide the rules. They hadn't allowed him time enough to browse about in books . . . the way he'd happened on Francis Thompson. "I was seventeen, a bobbin-cart pusher in a mill in Lawrence. I rode a train to Boston, stopped at the Old Corner Bookstore, picked up *The Hound of Heaven,* and started to read. I kept on reading. I had only money enough for my railroad ticket. I used it all to pay for the book and walked the twenty-five miles to Lawrence, reading the poem over and over." He stared ahead, pausing. "I wonder if they have that poem in the schools."

He turned to me suddenly: "Do you know him, Louis Untermeyer?" I shook my head. "He's one of the best." I wondered what he meant by "one of the best." Certainly not of the poets. Of poetry critics? Probably one of the best of friends, I decided, waiting for him to go on, for he must have known as much as anyone else of the tragedy. I had read the report two years before. Untermeyer's son, Richard, a nineteen-year old student at Yale, hanged himself. Frost surely had known the boy. I recalled one of his lines on the ocean that spoke of the "skin" of the water's surface. Frost was certain to speak of him, but instead he suggested I write to Louis, show him some of my work, and the *Folio*.

Once more, he shifted his thoughts. "*Walden's* one of the wonder books—so is *The Voyage of the Beagle* and *Robinson Crusoe*." I can't recall how Defoe led him to Shelley and of poets as the "unacknowledged legislators of the world." Shelley's extravagance brought up the dangers in adjectives, in exclamations, in words like "marvelous, wonderful, beautiful." This led him, after four or five comments, to what he described as "a memory of the Cliff House beach outside San Francisco" and to "Once by the Pacific," which was written before the war.

Soon after, Frost excused himself to pick up his wife at the station. Mrs. Frost, Wade explained, had been visiting with Marjorie, their youngest daughter, who was partway through a nurse's course at Johns Hopkins. "Traveling all day long by train—Baltimore to New York, New York to here." How many hours, he couldn't say. Nor did he need to after I looked at Elinor Frost as she stepped to the porch to greet us.

I had never seen so tired a human face, yet a delicate, carved beauty shone through the lines of weariness. She uttered some words of welcome, adding that much as she wanted to stay, it was better, she knew, to go to her room. We would understand. All that she said and did in the moments she spent in our presence seemed to me then—seems to me now—past portrayal. Graciousness over all, but touched with tenacity. An almost reluctant sweetness showed in the shape of her mouth, under a veiled sadness, yet the blue-black eyes when they turned your way looked *through* you. Was such surprising firmness tempered by reticence or was I imagining? I would never know, for I never saw her again. And those who did—sometimes often, sometimes close—draw a sketch of a self so finely spun in complexities of will and feeling as to make her mostly unknown.

The sky had darkened. Frost, suggesting supper, led us into the kitchen. "Ham? Bread? Butter? Raspberry jam?" he announced as he drew all four from the sidewall icebox. Frost kept talking all through the meal, but I cannot recall what he said. Wade finally spoke about plans for the coming day. Frost said nothing more than "We'll see," then excused himself and left the room. He was back in a moment to say that he'd better remain in the Shingle Cottage; Mrs. Frost "had things" to tell him. Wade and I would sleep at The Gulley, and wouldn't it be a good idea to go there now, get things set for the night? We would have a good visit tomorrow. Wade nodded, turned to me, but before I could answer his "Up to a bit of hiking?" Frost broke in. It was much too far to walk there now. We would go by car.

He let us out yards from the place that, a few weeks hence, would become the entrance door. Instead of saying goodnight, he called out, "Wade will make the breakfast and I'll be here at noon with lunch for the three of us."

Wade and I decided to tour the house in the morning, also to walk the woods and fields. Lighting a lamp, he led me into the future drawing room. My cot for the night had been spread with the white sheep blanket used on his wilderness trips. I put my few belongings aside, sat on the cot, and prepared for a long talk. We had not as yet exchanged ten words and my head was brimming with questions. Was

Frost such an unbelievable talker *always* or only when in the mood? Wade explained that he had been in the mood today, all right, but that he was also worried about his wife and daughter.

Marjorie was excited about her studies in nursing school, but Elinor often said "she gets so tired, it's a wonder the child can hold on"—she often used those words. Both of them worried about their children. Carol, they're sure, was a problem. We could see him tomorrow. He and his wife Lillian and their boy Prescott were a mile just south of the village, in the Stone House—only the lower part was stone, the upper timbered. The Frosts gave it to them six years ago as a wedding present. Wade and he were friends. Wade sometimes helped him on the farm. So did Frost.

Hiding a yawn, Wade nodded. "You won't need me to wake you. The sky will do it."

The morning brightness woke me, but I kept to the warmth of the cot till I heard a noise in the kitchen. Wade started talking about his book *Far Lake,* named for one of his wilderness places. Frost and he had studied most of the poems four years before in Michigan. Now they were working together again, page by page. Lesley, the eldest Frost daughter, a publisher's editor, assured them the book would come out next year if the manuscript arrived in time. Wade had added some poems and had made some revisions, of "The Echo" especially, one that Frost had urged him not to include. It belonged, said Wade, with another wilderness poem, "Man Alone," which Frost approved. But "The Echo," though revised, was "still defective." (At the time we talked, nobody could have foreseen that Wade's two poems would impel Frost to create "The Most of It," one of his greatest poems. Frost never mentioned the incident, so far as I know, but in Richard Poirier's words, "the similarities of circumstance and phrasing" are "extensive enough not to need comment"—or proof.)

Lounging outside in the sun, we rambled from subject to subject, leisurely. Why was this called "The Gulley House?"—because, said Wade, it stands in a hollow between two ridges, shielded by both from gales, northeast, southwest. Carol and Lillian's youngster gave it the name, which was near enough to "gulch," though Marjorie wanted it called "Nine Barns" for those it had had. Wade was to tear down the ones that blocked the truly spectacular view. From all I learned, it was hardly a modest farm for a man and wife—153 acres, about a third of it woodland, with a grove of white-paper birches I'd have to see.

The Frosts missed having a child around. They had told the Fresh Air Fund of *The New York Herald Tribune* they were ready to give a city boy or girl some weeks in the country. Their offer was quickly accepted. Frost drove ahead of time to the station. When he asked if his guest was tired or hungry, the little boy asked if the house "kept kosher." The two of them spent the better part of the afternoon hunting from town to town till they found a store that stocked the foods that the boy would eat. The Fund, of course, should have warned them. But the Frosts took it well and so did the boy. That autumn he sent them a New Year's card with some verse in Hebrew for "Thanks."

I asked if Frost had ever read my "Wheel Age" book—if he'd made any comment. Wade thought that he must have read some of it; maybe all. One morning Frost had said there wasn't much point in writing about utopias, any utopia. Wade noticed I hadn't brought even one of Frost's books for him to inscribe. He asked if I wanted to meet Lankes now or later. Either time, we'd find him working. He had twenty woodcuts to make for Lizette Reese's book *A Victorian Village*. He mused, "Lankes's a crank at times. Probably thinks I loaf too much. I don't mind. I like him. I lived in the northeast bedroom till he came. I gave it to him. It's the place with the best light, and he needs it."

I turned the conversation to Richard Untermeyer. Knowing that Frost and Louis had long been intimates, I thought that Frost would talk of the young boy's suicide, not act as though the tragedy had never occurred.

Wade started to explain that's "how Frost was"—he didn't talk about griefs—his own or others—almost never spoke of the closest friend he ever had, Edward Thomas, though he published a poem on him in *New Hampshire*. At first it was hard to believe how reticent he was—and the reticence extended even to shaking hands. Wade warned me not to be surprised if he only *waved* goodbye when I boarded the train.

We took a long stroll through the farm. Once outside under the gleaming sky, I found my bearings. Carol's house was less than a mile south of the village, The Gulley roughly the same distance east but only three-fourths of a mile by cutting through woods and fields. We were on our way toward the birch grove when Wade heard sounds of an engine. It was Frost's. Leaving the car where he'd stopped it the night before, he walked straight to the house, a large grocery bag under each arm out of which he produced a peck of fresh-picked string beans and three quarts of vanilla ice cream. Lunch was about to be served—on a wooden table under the windless light. Wade walked to the pantry for knives, forks, spoons, plates, and within ten minutes we were back to where we'd been the day before: "The Golden Room," listening "while Robert Frost kept on and on and on. . . ."

Names of people, of books, of poems I knew or had heard of filled my ears—Van Wyck Brooks, Alfred Kreymborg, James Oppenheim, Merrill Root, *The American Caravan, The Measure, Poetry* . . . Not a negative word from Frost: "all those people; friends of mine." I thought of ways to remember all that he said, the turns of phrase, the playfulness, the voice tones, the gesturing face. . . .

I was unaware that hours had passed when Frost announced quite suddenly, "Wade, I've a message I almost forgot." Mrs. Frost wondered if he'd care to help with some of the things in the Shingle Cottage in need of arranging. In the meantime Frost and I would talk and see a bit of the farm.

From his starting words, I assumed "our" talk would continue his own long monologue. I was wrong. Frost had questions—but first he offered a short apology: Mrs. Frost was sorry she couldn't have spent some time with us; hadn't felt up to it after the tiring day, all the worry about their youngest daughter. Her first four months at Hopkins had been hard, but ever since then she'd had high marks. "Nursing is what she says she wants to do. What about you? Wade told me something about your job. Is it bear-able?"

I answered as well as I could without going into minutiae. The work itself was easy, I said, and they treated me well. The head of the firm sometimes asked me to spend the lunch hour playing tennis at the nearby Armory. The wages were good but the hours impossible. Six days a week from nine till six; in November-December, till nine. I didn't need to add that I had almost no time left for reading and writing.

"You must have thought of looking around for a better arrangement."

"I've looked around, but the field I'm in is a jungle."

"Wade has it solved." Frost smiled. "At least for the present. Half of the year up north in Canada's wilderness, the other half back home, doing whatever he happens to find for pay. I talked with his mother. 'Wade has his place all to make,' I said. She knew what I meant: outside *her* home."

We walked uphill for a little while in silence. Frost pointed out what remained of the original nine barns on the farm. I looked and nodded.

He asked me about my home. I offered a hasty summary—where my parents were born, how and why they happened to come to New York, my father's career, teaching Latin and German and Greek in the city schools, writing his doctor's dissertation on Old Norse prose, finally turning to welfare work, founding a cottage-home in the country for 600 orphaned boys and girls for fifteen years, then running a large federation of welfare agencies. I had tried to enroll in a school for social work after college, but they wouldn't have me: too young.

"I'm thinking about your finding a job—something better."

I heard what he'd said about college teaching. I tried not to sound too apologetic. "I'm thinking about a teaching degree at New York University. I could go to class after work. Teaching French seems better to me than writing about men's fashions. I wouldn't earn nearly so much, but I'd have the time I need—and the summers too. . . . I wouldn't dare to teach poetry. I wouldn't want to teach literature. French is safer—something that's not too close to me."

"I don't suppose you've told all this to Wade, with his way of living. I'm glad you two are friends. I'm all for difference in people."

We walked slowly up toward a rise in the ground which gave me a fresh new sense of the landscape.

Frost launched into a list of tasks that would take up part of Wade's daylight hours for the coming weeks: tree planting—setting out elm and maple shoots and hundreds of red-pine seedlings—tree moving, trench digging, damming a stream, tearing down some of the barns, making the house livable. "As the barns come down, the view comes out." Frost pointed north. "Wade never seems in a hurry. It's a board at a time, when the mood comes over him." But the house itself, if all went well, would be ready soon, with much of the remodeling completed. Then Wade would go home to Michigan, wait for his book to appear. "Sometimes," Frost sighed, "he writes too much like me. Sometimes. But he has good poems that are all his own in the book we're reading together. He's a strange boy. I worry about him.

"Wade will go back to Kashabowie," Frost went on, "his settlement north of Superior, in the fall, and I shall have less to worry about." That ended the subject, I thought—mistakenly. "Wade has a good deal of the Wobbly in him—one of the reasons for Lankes's anger and jealousy." Didn't Frost know, I marveled, what Wade assured me: that the men got along well together; that Lankes had offered to illustrate Wade's book as a gift? Both things could be true, of course—the anger-jealousy and the friendly offer—but I was young enough at the

25

time to feel sure that something was wrong. I had been exposed—
without the slightest awareness—to one of the deep complexities of
the man beside me, for whom all "contrarieties" composed a true and
compelling part of reality.

I was also being taught—by indirection—more than a few rules on
writing. Some of them have stayed with me through fifty-five years,
though one of his urgent warnings—"When you put a book together,
always save a good many poems for the next"—I could never accept. I
was being allowed into his writing workshop—something I never had
hoped for—then suddenly, without warning, Wade returned to join
us. Nothing beyond the amenities of parting could follow—as they
had to, given the lateness of the hour and lengthy trip that awaited.
Soon Frost was taking us straight to the railroad. After my train departed, he said, he would drive to Carol's farm for a short talk. And
soon I would have to arrange for a longer visit.

We waited in the car till the smoking engine curved into sight. Frost
clung to the wheel. As Wade had guessed, he never offered his hand.
He waved, calling, "And the next time you come, we must have a
great meal together and some longer talks." I did my best to thank
him. I urged Wade, who kept to my side till the train halted, to stop in
New York in the fall for a good visit. "And the best of luck with your
book!" From the coach window, I watched till the mud-spattered car
swayed out of sight.

★ ★ ★

I could not know at the time how lucky I was to have been with Frost
in August of 1929; had I come a decade later, I'd have found a man
tried and ravaged by griefs. To the Frosts' household—as their intimates knew—sickness, worry, and death had seldom been
strangers. As early as 1900, in the fifth year of their marriage, they had
lost their first-born, Elliott, who would have been four years old.
Robert flailed at himself for not having summoned medical help in
time—God, by taking his son away, was punishing him. Elinor, silent
for days, at last let fly at him for his "self-centered senselessness" in
believing that any such thing as God or Divine Justice or a God's Be-
nevolent Concern for human affairs could exist; life, she declared, was
hateful, the world utterly evil. And yet, with a livelihood to be earned
and a fourteen-month-old daughter, Lesley, to care for, there could be
no choice. They went about their tasks, foundered in apathy. Robert's
body began to rebel; and although he ignored the recurrence of many

old ailments, one proved almost too hard to endure—the sneezing, coughing, and choking caused by the pollen dust. Meanwhile Robert's mother, who had formed part of the household, now suffering from advanced cancer, entered a sanitarium. She breathed her last two months after her grandson's death.

Since the early spring of their third year, the Frosts had been sharing a farm known as the Powder Hill House, three miles from Lawrence. The owner, who continued to live in some of the rooms, finally grew so annoyed with her tenant's late payments, as well as his failure to keep his chickens out of the house, that she served notice: They would have to leave by autumn. It was Elinor Frost who now took matters in hand. She went alone to speak to her husband's grandfather, and whatever her means of persuasion, she succeeded in winning his promise to purchase "the Derry farm" she had told him about provided, on careful inspection, it proved to be fairly priced. The thirty-acre New Hampshire farm had much to offer besides a shed, a barn, and a two-storey gable house that were new by comparative standards. The setting promised serenity, with hills that sheltered the dwelling, fruit trees, berry patches, pasture spring, west-running brook, hardwood grove, pasture lands. In October 1900, the Frosts moved into their newfound home, their household including 300 Wyandotte fowls. Robert, pleased though he was by the prospect, couldn't regard his grandfather's role without the bitter resentment that had marked his earlier request for aid, which the old man countered by offering money enough for a single year in which the poet would have to prove he could make his way as a writer or abandon it.

For the next six years he tried to earn his keep as a poultry farmer, while writing poem after poem for a literary world oblivious to his existence. Elinor, who had never concealed her disgust with housework, spent her days in bearing and rearing offspring. A son, Carol, their third, arrived in May 1902; Irma, thirteen months later; Marjorie, at the end of March 1905. Striving to gain a livelihood from New Hampshire farmland was trouble enough, without the successive trials brought on by sickness, and the annual hayfever illness, to say nothing of other discouragements that led the poet—possibly Elinor also—close to despair, or of Robert's nearly fatal siege of pneumonia, which had taken almost as high a toll of the wife who nursed him through to recovery while pregnant with their sixth offspring, Elinor Bettina. The infant died two days after birth. A grim account if taken for all that occurred in the lives at Derry. Not until forty years later would the world be told of the sunlit days, the joys, the delights, in the pages of Lesley Frost Ballantine's *New Hampshire's Child,* edited by Arnold Grade, and three years later, in the *Family Letters of Robert and Elinor Frost* (1972). All I knew of their lives had been gleaned from pieces and bits in concise accounts that dealt with the years of the poet's literary struggle before the miraculous change when he visited England. It was *this* Frost, the rugged, handsome, gracious, middle-aged man who had come through the storms and trials of both "inner and outer weather," to whom I had listened, hour upon hour.

A month after my visit, he wrote to John T. Bartlett, one of his favorite students from his Pinkerton Academy teaching years (1906–11) and a warm friend, who was now living in Boulder, Colorado. Mailed from Franconia, the Frosts' familiar New Hampshire retreat in the hayfever season, his letter provided a current account of the children:

> Marj is in hospital in Baltimore where she lay a hopeless invalid two years ago, now training to be a nurse. Lesley is in New York with her husband and baby. Carol is farming at the Stone House where you saw him. Irma is going to college at the Mass. Agricultural College next year with her husband and her baby. Her husband [John Paine Cone] has been farming near us but is turning to landscape architecture so called. We have three grand children in three different families. One of the three grand children starts school this year and so begins again the endless round.

On September 7th, the Maine State Hospital informed Frost that his sister Jeanie had died of natural causes. Two years younger than Robert, she had passed her fifty-third birthday. Carol, in response to his father's telephone call, drove at once to Franconia, then both went on to Augusta. The body was sent to Lawrence; father and son followed. They stayed until after Jeanie's remains had been lowered into the grave beside her mother's.

There had been no bond of love between brother and sister. In their childhood years, their mother had tried to keep them at peace with each other; but after her death the hostilities worsened. Yet even before, Jeanie's frequent fits of hysterical raving were beyond controlling, as was her later incredibly wild behavior in front of the young

Frost children on her Derry visits. Nevertheless with financial aid from her brother, she enrolled in 1916 at the University of Michigan and received her degree as a qualified teacher of languages. During these student days, however, she not only denounced America's part in the ongoing World War I but also proclaimed her love for the Kaiser, the German people, *and* the Communist-Socialist cause. When a mob was about to throw her into a pond for refusing to kiss the flag, she escaped, then fled by taxi fifteen miles to her brother's Amherst home, begging for help. Frost, sick with influenza, gave her some money but refused her demand that he find her a teaching position. Eighteen months or so later, he wrote to Untermeyer, "The police picked her up in Portland Maine. . . . She took them for German officers carrying her off for immoral use. She took me for someone else when she saw me." Her commitment to the state institution was sealed in May, and both Robert and Elinor visited her in the next nine years. "I must say she was pretty well broken by the coarseness and brutality of the world. . . . I am coarse for having had children. . . . She made a birth in the family the occasion for writing us once of the indelicacy of having children. . . . But it took the war to put her beside herself, poor girl." Her death as well as her life preyed on his fears, prone as he was to regard himself as ever in need of protection from situations and persons that he sensed might undermine his hold on himself (151).

Frost's *Collected Poems* appeared November 18, 1930, in his fifty-seventh year. Laudatory reviews by Genevieve Taggard and others more than made up for Granville Hicks's remarks in *The New Republic* which berated Frost for failing to write about Freud, industrialism, and the disruptive effect of science on modern thought. The book would receive the Pulitzer Prize and its author be made a member of the American Academy of Arts and Letters. On November 30th, the "London Letter" in *The New York Herald Tribune* declared the work to be "more sure of immortality than any other book of the last five years, whether published in England or America."

Two weeks later the Frosts rushed to their daughter's bedside in Baltimore. When at last her "puzzling" illness was diagnosed as tuberculosis, plans were made to send her at once to a sanitarium close to the Colorado home of the Bartletts. Not many months had passed before Marjorie's intimate friend, Carol's wife Lillian, was stricken with the same disease. Carol decided to sell his farm and drive with his wife and son to San Bernadino. En route they stopped at Boulder for a family reunion of sorts with Robert and Elinor and the now much improved Marjorie. And before the older Frosts set out for Amherst,[1] Carol had found the kind of home that he and his wife had hoped for, not far from his father's birthplace.

With some relief, the older Frosts made up their minds to buy a home of their own and they found one much to their liking: a large Victorian tree-shadowed house on Sunset Avenue. But soon after they made the move, Robert collapsed with a three-fold sickness: pneumonia, inflammatory rheumatism, nervous exhaustion. It was difficult not to relate the cause, at least in part, to the worries and fears of the year before and the added tasks he had shouldered to pay the costs incurred by his children's problems. Three weeks after taking to bed, he wrote to Untermeyer:

> I am so deeply smitten through my helm that I am almost sad to see infants young any more. I expect to look backward and see the last tail light on the last car. But I shall be going the other way on foot.
>
> Yet I refuse to match sorrows with anyone else, because just the moment I start the comparison I see that I have nothing yet as terrible as it might be. A few of our children are sick or their spouses are and one of them has a spouse still in college. I and my wife are not well, neither are we young: but we mean to be both better and younger for company's sake. . . .

Within a month Marjorie's news overjoyed her parents. She not only had made a splendid recovery but was now engaged to "a dear, kind, and considerate man . . . with beautiful ideals that she feared no longer existed"—Willard Fraser, whose interest in archaeology delighted her father. Moreover, the latest reports of Lillian's health were encouraging. But before the Frosts could meet this western half of their household, Robert had "work" to attend to: accepting three honorary degrees and producing a new Phi Beta Kappa poem, "Build Soil," subtitled "A political pastoral" (which Leftwing critics would read with especial relish four years hence).

Although the oncoming summer promised to more than make up

---

[1] In September 1926, Frost returned to Amherst College, which he served under varied arrangements until 1938. "During the winter, Professor Robert Frost will be in residence to conduct special classes in English and to hold informal conferences with students."—Amherst catalogue, 1926–27.

for the one before, it still confronted Frost with the heavy costs of his children's welfare. In practical terms: arranging additional lectures and readings. Two of the new commitments brought rewards of an unpredictable sort: a dinner in September with two leading scientists—the American physicist Robert Millikan and the British biologist J. B. S. Haldane—during which the three agreed then disagreed about metaphor, and a prankish contest of sorts with T. S. Eliot in Boston in mid-November (269f.).

Once again illness entered the house, this time when the family members arrived for the holiday season. Robert, the grippe's first victim, felt well enough to be up and around on Christmas. Then Marjorie took ill, then the maid, followed a day later by Irma and her husband John Cone, who had come with Jacky, their six-year-old son. A practical nurse took care of Marjorie, Irma, and John, while Elinor, devoting herself to Robert and Jacky, prepared the meals for the household. With the holiday ordeal over, Frost, relieved, turned to his many commitments. He hoped yet doubted that he and his wife could attend Marjorie's wedding in June at the Fraser home in Billings, Montana. The doubt was more than justified. After the round of readings—again undertaken to pay for part of his children's needs—he was taken ill. Frost had "been overdoing too much these last two years," his wife wrote to his publisher at the end of May, voicing her fear that now he was "in for real trouble." Through the next twelve months, ailments of various kinds made it all but impossible for him to fulfill his commitments. Even the summer escape to Franconia failed to afford the relief he had always known. For the first time, the Frosts gave serious thought to spending the harshest winter months in Florida, as his doctors advised. But not this year, for with Marjorie's expecting a child in the middle of March, Elinor decided to go to Montana to be on hand for the birth. All went well for eleven days after Marjorie Robin Fraser had entered the world: March 16, 1934.

But word that Robert was sick sent Elinor rushing back to Amherst, confident of their daughter's normal recovery. When two weeks later Willard telephoned to say that his wife was seriously ill with puerperal fever, the Frosts left for Billings as soon as they could. As they stood at her bedside, they were far from sure that Marjorie knew who they were. Weeks passed, the fever continued. When Frost learned that the Mayo Clinic had produced a possibly helpful serum, he hurried his daughter there by private plane, following with Elinor and Willard by car. On April 29th, Frost wrote briefly to Untermeyer: "We are going through the valley of the shadow with Marjorie." The tenth and final sentence: "You will probably see us home again whatever the outcome, but it will be months hence and changed for the worse for the rest of our days." On May 15th, he wrote again, from Amherst: ". . . The noblest of us all is dead and has taken our hearts out of the world with her. It was a terrible seven weeks' fight. . . . Marge always said she would rather die in a gutter than in a hospital. But it was in a hospital she was caught to die after more than a hundred serum injections and blood transfusions. . . . And here we are Cadmus and Harmonia not yet placed safely in changed forms." Elinor was unable to speak or write of her grief. When after forty days she wrote to Edith Fobes, she gave little more than the simple facts of the tragedy. And when she replied to her friend's letter, some ten weeks after Marjorie's death, her loss had deepened. "I long to die myself and be relieved of the pain that I feel for her sake. . . . I cannot bear it, and yet I *must* bear it for the sake of others here."

"Bear it" she did, her husband as well, sustained by their strong, dissimilar wills and to some degree, by the presence of (Marjorie) Robin, who was being cared for throughout the summer by Lillian at the Stone Cottage nearby. In early October Robert and Elinor took the infant to Rockford, Illinois, where the poet attended a friend's inauguration at the college. Robin went home with her father to Billings and in mid-October the Frosts returned to Amherst. Early the following month Elinor suffered an acute attack of angina pectoris. Even before she was out of danger, the doctor insisted for both their sakes that they flee the northern winter. Within a month they were on their way to Key West, to be joined there soon after Christmas by Carol, his wife, and son.

The winter retreat had been taken over by the Roosevelt government's administrator of public relief, the Key having gone into bankruptcy six months before. "A crown dependency," Frost named it in writing to Joseph Blumenthal, his friend and printer, whose views of the government's efforts to fight the Depression were at odds with his own. "I expected to find it a busted cigar town. It turns out to be a busted land-boom town—all cut up into speculator lots, with hardly a house on them." His antipathy to the Roosevelt regime had been deepened by what he had learned of "the drowning" three months before. Some two hundred men—war veterans—employed by the

Federal Emergency Reconstruction Act had lost their lives in a hurricane that struck at the Key West railroad span on which they were working. Frost and others, including Ernest Hemingway, viewed the disaster as having been made more tragic because of government negligence. While venting his opposition to the theories and practices of those in charge of the White House—notably in letters to friends who he knew considered him wrong—he began to work on an introduction to the autobiography by—of all people—an avowed socialist New Deal reformer: Sarah N. Cleghorn, a Vermont neighbor and friend.

Key West's "range of temperature is between 70 and 80," he wrote in a capsule description to one of his friends. "There are very few winter visitors. . . . We are on the point of the island exactly between the Gulf of Mexico and the Atlantic Ocean. The wave breaks 20 feet from our door. . . ." Despite the "balm of the air," the comfort, and quiet, Elinor remained unwell through most of their stay. They returned to Amherst in April, and as soon as his duties allowed, they were back in The Gulley. Frost went to work on an essay on E. A. Robinson, who had died on April 6, 1935, after reading the proofs of his book *King Jasper*. Elinor, who had planned to go to Montana in May to visit her granddaughter Robin, reconciled herself to a long postponement. Frost had consented, reluctantly, to take part in the Rocky Mountain Writers' Conference set for July. As the time for departure neared, he became extremely fearful, speaking his mind to Untermeyer: "Elinor is not fit for anything. She is trying to save up energy for a melancholy journey to the terrible scenes in Colorado and Montana. I am doing my best to dissuade her from such a pilgrimage. We can't have a soul in the house for a while. And I don't want to be away from her long at a time."

They set out late in July. She had already written to Joseph Blumenthal of the Spiral Press about a volume of poems written by Marjorie. "I should be so very glad to have the book by the middle of October." But months passed before he received the manuscript. The journey west demanded more than Frost had expected. He delivered three public lectures, and although he had many listeners and his new highly conservative political poem "To a Thinker" was roundly applauded, he also experienced moments of annoyance and disagreement. Meanwhile at Boulder, Elinor was enjoying her longed-for reunion with Robin, "the exceptionally bright, forward child," who became her charge throughout the Frasers' visit. After a troublesome

33

time with Witter Bynner in Santa Fe, redeemed in part by a warmly received poetry reading and an archaeological excursion into the desert, Frost returned to Vermont. One of the first tasks was to put into final form the poems for Marjorie's volume. Not until early November did the Spiral Press receive the text of *Franconia,* and not until 1936, two years after the daughter's death, would the private edition of 200 copies be ready.

Plans were already under way for the annual escape from the northern winter. Having once again agreed to join in the University of Miami's Winter Institute, Frost proposed that he and Elinor find a house in nearby Coconut Grove in time for the Christmas season. Before they left for Miami, three unusual invitations had come from Harvard. Frost accepted them all: to deliver in March the six Charles Eliot Norton lectures; in September, to recite both an ode for the Tercentenary celebration, and a poem for Phi Beta Kappa. A fourth event, of national import, lay in store: the publication in the late spring of his new volume of verse, *A Further Range.* He had already given much thought to its contents and sequence; also to the one to whom he would dedicate the book and the words of that dedication.

The Norton lectures were scheduled to start February 1, 1936. Frost, deeply concerned for Elinor's health, insisted on a postponement. But a month's delay failed to save her from coming down with a serious grippe. It took almost all of March for her to regain her strength. Frost, on the other hand, seemed to thrive; his Norton lectures attracted steadily larger crowds of highly responsive listeners. Before he was able to start his final performance, the unexpectedly large audience had to be moved from the thousand-capacity lecture hall to the college theater. "It is at least a question," wrote the Harvard *Alumni Bulletin,* "whether any such audiences as Mr. Frost has attracted have before gathered since the inauguration of the Norton chair."

Although the text had been stenographically recorded and placed in his hands, Frost shrank from the thought of making revisions. They were lectures, to be spoken aloud, directed to the *listeners'* response, and not designed for reading. He had, however, agreed—they would all be made available; but to put them into acceptable form would require time. Besides, he still had to write the Tercentenary ode and the poem for Phi Beta Kappa before September. He had also agreed to speak at the Bread Loaf Writers' Conference in August. Though far from eager to do so—he had been there twice before—the director,

Theodore Morrison, and his wife Kathleen had gone out of their way by arranging after each Norton lecture a small reception for him at their home. But the Middlebury College weekend proved far worse than expected, for the whole community knew of the many attacks that Frost and *A Further Range* were provoking from Liberal and Leftwing critics. Ultra-lavish expressions of sympathy at Bread Loaf were all he needed to make him suspect "the sincerity" of his consolers—Morrison included.

The effects of what he had suffered during the weekend gravely disturbed Mrs. Frost. With characteristic restraint, she expressed her fears in a letter to Edith Fobes, whose Franconia house they were living in for the twelfth hayfever season: "Robert is awake so late at night, and is apt to feel like a walk even after midnight, so he values the freedom to roam around the cottage very much. Especially this year, when he is having difficulty in even getting started on the poems. At least I am afraid he has hardly made a beginning."

An extremely severe attack of herpes zoster left him no choice but to give up all thought of writing the promised poems. On his doctor's orders, Elinor telegraphed Harvard. On her own, she wrote to Richard Thornton, head of the Trade department of Holt, to make him realize why any writing at all was out of the question till the "shingles"—notorious for the suffering it caused—had run its course: "He couldn't work anyway, the pain in his head was so acute," she underlined in her note of mid-September. Although within a fortnight, Frost seemed to be well enough to return to Amherst, another malady forced him back into bed. She canceled his November appearance at the American Academy of Arts and Letters in New York. Slowly but rather steadily he began to regain his health. In fact, some weeks before Christmas he declared himself both ready and eager to keep his engagement at the New School and to "have it out" with whatever Leftwing critics might challenge him from the floor.

Meanwhile plans had been made for the winter escape—this time to Texas—and on Christmas Day all the Frosts except Irma joined in a family dinner in San Antonio. Lesley and her daughter went on to Mexico City; Fraser back to Montana, leaving Robin in Lillian's care. Robert and Elinor rented a pleasant apartment. The months went by without incident and, so far as one knows, without the writing of poems. Frost was especially interested in the work of his forceful admirer Bernard deVoto and his controversial essays against the critics who wrote for the liberal Left. As editor-in-chief of the *Saturday*

35

Review, DeVoto was planning to publish a full-fledged essay against the poet's attackers. Frost persuaded his friend to delay the assault, while he turned to other concerns.

By April 1937 the Frosts had returned to Amherst with plans for a busy summer and fall, including at least five speaking engagements for October. The announcement of the Pulitzer Prize for *A Further Range,* though not unexpected, gave Frost the perfect occasion for playfully blaming Untermeyer: "I'm your bonfire that you started without a permit from the fire warden," his letter began, "[a]nd now look at it: it's got away from you, and if it gets into the woods not even the red-shirted fire-fighters of The New Republic will be able to put it out."

All seemed to be going well except for his sense of discomfort with his special relationship to Amherst College which he realized he would have to resolve in time. He would also have to give up the Fobes cottage that had been their home-away-from-home at hayfever times since 1925; its ever present reminders of Marjorie were too poignant to bear. Marjorie had always thought of Franconia as being "her place." The Frosts' search for a livable cottage ended with their purchase of two small houses in Concord Corners, Vermont, an all-but-abandoned village near New Hampshire. Shortly after returning for the fall semester in Amherst, Frost, at the doctor's insistence, drove his wife to a nearby Springfield hospital. On October 4th he wrote to Untermeyer:

I tried two or three times yesterday to tell you that Elinor had just been operated on for a growth in her breast. I doubt if she fully realizes her peril. So be careful how you speak in your letters. You can see what a difference this must make in any future we have. She has been the unspoken half of everything I ever wrote, and both halves of many a thing from My November Guest to the last stanzas of Two Tramps in Mud Time—as you may have divined. I don't say it is quite up with us. . . . She has come through the operation well, though there was delay over her for a day or so at the Hospital for fear her heart wouldn't stand the ether. Her unrealization is what makes it hard for me to keep from speaking to somebody for sympathy. I have had almost too much of her suffering in this world.

Ever yours,   R.

A note to his friend mailed the next day asked "Be easy on me for what I did too emotionally and personally." "Please burn [the letter]." Fortunately, metastasis did not occur. Fortunately also, within a month the patient was able to write to a friend, "I am gaining strength quite rapidly now, and have been out for a few drives, and a few very short walks. It seems grand."

Four weeks later she and Robert were on their way to Gainesville for the winter months, planning to live on the quieter second floor of the house that Lesley had found for herself and her daughters. Carol, Lillian, Prescott, and Robin completed the drive to Florida in time for a joyous Christmas dinner. "Everything went smoothly," Elinor wrote to Nina Thornton, and as for their choice of Gainesville, "We are very lucky this year. . . . The sun has shone every day but two since we came. . . . We have all been very well so far. I rest a great deal of course. . . . I hope the next three months will be as good as December. . . ."

On the afternoon of March 18th, Carol accompanied his parents on their final look at a house which all the Frosts had approved. It would serve as the permanent winter home for Robert and Elinor, both of whom enjoyed the prospect of being relieved of the annual search for a place to live. After driving them back to the house they shared with Lesley, Carol returned to his own. As she made her way up the stairs, Elinor suffered sharp pains in her chest. She considered them no worse than similar episodes which had come and gone, but Frost called a physician, who examined her at once. The report overwhelmed Frost, throwing him out of control into self-accusing. Luckily the doctor was still in the house when a second attack left Elinor unconscious. He revived her, ordered her husband not to enter the room, and shut her door. A third attack, he warned, was almost a certainty.

Elinor, having lived through the night, answered the doctor's questions. Frost could hear her voice as he walked the hall outside her room. Then she suffered the third attack that the doctor had prophesied. It was followed by several more. After surviving another night, she became so weak that when Frost was at last permitted to enter her bedroom, he couldn't be sure whether she was asleep or had fallen into unconsciousness. Death came when she ceased breathing on the third afternoon.

★   ★   ★

If by chance I had skipped the fifteenth page of *The New York Times* for March 21, 1938, Tony would have phoned with the news of Elinor's death. He and two of his writer-friends who had "studied" with Frost at Ann Arbor zealously followed the poet's career—as well as they could, through word-of-mouth, meetings, and numerous letters. All that I came to know of the last nine years of Frost's life, I owed to this Michigan network, except for book-note items and interviews with reporters that I happened to find in the press. Tony and I had, of course, been present at all his recitals at the New School and a few at other places. On each occasion, dozens of listeners ringed him in at the end to press him with questions, leaving him neither the time nor the heart to speak with whatever friends might be watching and waiting from the side. More than once, when I waved to him as I started to leave, he raised a beckoning hand, but the questioners tightened their ring.

My own affairs by now were strained by feelings of empty unease. True to what I had said to him of my future when he asked if my job was bearable, I had lost no time in enrolling for graduate study. New York University worked out an evening program by which I could earn the essential Master's degree within two years. The prospect of teaching French in a college with summers free, though less than enchanting, pleased me enough to shackle me to my studies. Besides, the chairman had said that my three-fourths written book on André Spire would fulfill the thesis requirement. The fall term went fairly well, then the ever-enlarging reading lists came to demand more time than my job-free hours allowed. I was nearing the point of dropping a course when sudden illness—my mother's—changed my plans. My weekly visits to Pittsburgh, starting early in January, continued through April, when cancer surgery ended her life. Almost at once my father's health gave way, and the visits resumed. By now I was much too far behind to continue my program. I would have to arrange some other escape from my labyrinth. But to hope to find a more bearable position was unthinkable in the wake of the recent Wall Street crash. People had been clinging to whatever jobs they had found, whether they liked or loathed them. Friends kept trying to make me aware of how lucky I was.

Chance, Frost had implied in a note on some poems I had sent him many years earlier, *had* to be taken account of for its role in all that happens. I would wait and hope—and use what time I had to polish the manuscript on Spire as well as my public-private steel-mill poems, some of which were already making their way into print in a magazine I'd discovered the week I returned from Europe. Walking New York's streets with the want-ad section clutched in my hand, I spied on a newsstand something I'd never seen, labeled in huge black type "The New Masses." I leafed through the pages and started to read. The butcher paper on which it was printed was all of a piece with its shrill contempt for the "haves" of society. One of its pages, however, spoke in a prose I had never before encountered. The author, Michael Gold, was also the editor, and his subject, an episode out of his life on the lower East Side. The story seemed to me to be out of place yet wholly in keeping with what *The New Masses* stood for, most of the pages dealing with strikes, factories, workers cheated of rights, greed, corruption, and so on. I read from cover to cover, forcing myself through poems I could hardly finish. To be sure, I still considered myself a "conservation communist," but here in this Communist monthly there was nothing that showed even passing concern for the safety of earth or the growing dangers that threatened it. Who were the readers? Hardly the people who slaved at machines, the "industrial workers," "shop stewards," and so on, all of whom appeared in heroical colors. I mailed some of my steel-mill poems to Gold. Three days later a letter arrived whose effect would set my course for the oncoming years. The poems were wonderful, great, he said, just what he'd wanted. He'd give them the space they needed, more than a page. And wouldn't I please come down to his office to get acquainted?

Meanwhile Marianne Moore had taken one of my private poems for *The Dial*. I thought perhaps I should send pages from both magazines to Wade, who might show them to Frost. Explanations would surely have to be made:

Don't be surprised, Wade, by the two enclosures. I believe I told you my book-long poem on the steel mill would also have lyric sections I call "Excursions," for that's what they are: purely private excursions away from the main—public—theme of the book, many of which seem totally unrelated to the awful life of the milltown employees . . . or "workers," as "The New Masses" calls them. By putting within the same two covers, private as well as public poems, I think I succeed in giving the two "divisions" of the writer's experience—my own, of course. No effort to be what some people call "objective." How can one be objective on such a subject? I'm telling you this in case you should talk to Frost. For all I know, he never looks at *The Dial,* though I haven't the slightest doubt it's the best in print. . . . Lucky for me Miss Moore accepted my "Blood" before its death-knell. Where are you now? Why hasn't Frost published even one poem in the magazines since *West-Running Brook?* Anything wrong? Wish we could have a long talk.

There was no reply, but Wade might have been off on a wilderness trip. Gold, on the other hand, was reachable. But—did I want to meet him? Why did half of myself, the Public Me that had seen "the way" out, keep apart from the people I seemed to belong with? What did I know of the steps they'd take to achieve whatever they prized? Dozens of placards announcing evening meetings of every kind and for every purpose pointed at me with accusing words. I found it easy to slip unobserved into a hall and hear the speakers explain "The Party's program on this issue." I found them hard to follow, being ignorant of the names they bandied about, as well as events that would strike a chord in most of the hearers.

But before too long I was able to follow the drift and to realize that a single power controlled each separate meeting: "The Party," officially The Communist Party of the USA (CPUSA). Its leaders' names and its office address were open secrets. I had only to read *The Daily Worker* to fill in gaps in my ignorance. And it took almost no time at all to see that my aims and those of The Party were not wholly the same. Nothing it ever proposed revealed the least concern with in-dustrialism's ruinous role except as it worsened wages, union rights, working conditions, and so on.

Would I have to decide on a choice? The question disappeared under deepening waves of people victimized by the ever enlarging Depres-sion. Breadlines, men on street corners peddling apples to passersby, endless lines of the unemployed, jerry-built "Hooverville" huts sheltering homeless people from the rain and cold—no one feeling the human pain that was spreading from north to south could question the need for help. Yet I knew from the little I'd learned about money, panics, and cycles that "the system"—despite the claims of Commu-nist experts—might recover enough in time to enable people to see the other priority: earth and its sound salvation. If earth and all it con-tained would at last belong to the people—as my steel-mill faith had reasoned with flawless logic—then my conservationist-communist faith could finally be fulfilled. I should have to cling to it silently while joining with all who wanted to do their best, in their limited ways, to help "the masses seize the world." For without my hidden private faith, what would arise from this triumph but a race not worthy to breathe the poisonous air that industrialism uncontrolled would bring to the world.

A vast cry from these cautious thoughts to the volume of Wade's poems. I received an advance copy early in autumn. At once I sent my congratulations; *Far Lake* seemed, at a first quick glance, all I had thought it would be. Meanwhile I looked for reviews. Of the three I found, two should have pleased him greatly. The one in *The New York Times Book Review* was sympathetic and positive; William Rose Benét, in the *Saturday Review,* wrote as a person truly moved by the poems. By contrast, *The New Republic* printed the kind of lifeless words that only a man who had never experienced closeness to the natural world might utter.

I received no reply from Wade, nor did he answer the letter I mailed after reading—again in *The New Republic*—an extraordinary judgment of Frost's *Collected Poems.* Although I already owned all that the work contained, I couldn't resist this handsome volume printed from plates prepared by the Spiral Press. Frost, I heard, was enormously pleased, naming himself "the best-printed American writer." Superlatives were not, however, always found in reviews of some of his books. Though widely hailed, Frost was far from being the best-perceived or best-understood of America's poets, as *The New Republic* of December 3rd made clear. The reviewer, Granville Hicks, had shown two years before (in an unsigned piece on *West-Running Brook*) a response to "Acquainted with the Night" that made his assignment to review the *Collected Poems* something I questioned. This poem "of deprivation" is one of a number of Frost's "close to terrifying poems about wandering off, losing the self, or belonging nowhere," as Richard Poirier says of "the plight" of the poem's speaker. No reader, I thought, would have found these words other than unexceptionable—except for Hicks, who had made the poem proclaim that "the time [and, by implication, also the world] in which he happens to live" does not matter to Frost. Obtuseness of a different sort—and within its larger range, even more impressive—marked his peculiar analysis of *Collected Poems.* After repeating what he had said before of "Acquainted with the Night," he offers a short interregnum of praise. Ready at last to bring his readers the light, he uncovers his list of prescriptions, adding that none of the remedies will be found in Frost. In fact the *Collected Poems* must be rated deplorable: It hasn't a single Freudian term or Freudian treatment of love. Also, one "looks in vain for evidences of the disrupting effect that scientific hypotheses have had on modern thought." Finally, Frost hasn't offered a single poem on industrialism. On the other hand, the penultimate paragraph sings a quite different tune:

> It remains to summarize briefly some of the things that can be found in Frost's world. For purposes of narrative verse he can find not merely pathos but also, because there are certain standards implicit in that world, something close to tragedy. He can find subjects for comedy there, dramatic conflicts, objects of natural beauty. He can treat abnormality and yet keep it in its place, or he can find a theme for as illuminating a commentary on failure as Robinson ever wrote. In the contemplation of nature he can, as scores of lyrics show, find the beginnings of paths that lead straight to the problems that have perennially perplexed the mind of man. He can, in short, find opportunity and stimulus to exercise to the full the poetic imagination.

But, he concludes, Frost "cannot contribute directly to the unification, in imaginative terms, of our culture."

Hicks's solution typified that of many reviewers opposed to the poet's politics. Frost hadn't any intention of hiding his views. He was quite as sure of the rightness of what he declared as were those who denounced him as wrong. Even with the delivery of his Phi Beta Kappa poem, "Build Soil: a political pastoral," at Columbia University (May 31, 1932), few people would understand what he thought. And not until it appeared in 1936 in *A Further Range,* did the poem reach thousands of readers—and enrage the Left.

Meanwhile Van Dore had finally done what Frost had been urging: "Go find a farm for yourself and I will pay for it." Franconia was too costly despite the Depression, and with Frost financially pressed by his children's needs, Wade limited his choice to a one-room house on an acre halfway between Massachusetts and Connecticut. Frost sent him more than the $100 it cost, invited him to live in The Gulley from autumn till spring, then spend some days at Amherst as his guest. Wade, I imagined, was deep in his second book, drinking the blessings of time—while I still waited for chance to help me out of my plight, which, owing to various small events, had become a bit better than bearable.

Through the little-magazine network, my world was beginning to widen. At a small reception given by Harriet Monroe for *Poetry*'s writers, I had met a score of poets some of whose work I knew—William Carlos Williams, Louise Bogan, Rolfe Humphries, Alfred Kreymborg, others. Nobody talked about politics, the Depression, the unemployed, the Left, the liberal journals, or what the state of the nation might do to writers—yet before very long, each would be trying to find a political stand. Humphries would cross my path in unforeseeable ways in another three years. Kreymborg had just selected my short ecological poem ("End of the Flower-World") for his soon-to-be-issued anthology *Our Singing Strength*. He had also read my Spire book and was writing an introduction, though publication plans were not yet made.

During one of my lunchtime breaks, while stopping to buy some pipe tobacco at a well-known drugstore at Eighth and Sixth, I picked up a book I had never heard of: *Poetry and Myth*. It was one of hundreds heaped on a table: "Remainders—10¢ Each." The writer, Frederick Clarke Prescott, was a Cornell professor of English and author of a pioneer essay, "Poetry and Dreams." One quick reading was all I needed to send me in search of his major work, *The Poetic Mind*. How had I missed this treasure? Why did no one I spoke with know it existed? What if I were to ask him to let me study with him?

I wrote a letter that said no more than I thought he needed to know of my background: the verse and prose I had published, names of journals, speculations about a thesis that relates creative processes to the so-called mystical experience. He replied at once. My subject, strangely, was one he had wanted to follow. If I were to make up my mind to come, "we could both explore it together." This was more than I'd wished for—more than enough to fend off friends who feared for my sanity. But before making the move, I should have to consider finances. Could I save enough for at least a year? If I started in June, by next September I might have $4,000. Where should I place the money? Banks, the experts said, were not to be trusted. Without telling anyone, I opened a private account with the government's Postal Savings. And after a month I was primed to defend my decision to quit my job. Tony had already known. Though teaching jobs were rare, he warned, "If you don't quit now, you never will. Besides, how does anyone know how long you can live this way, making twice as much as a full professor?"

I was now ready to ask two older judges: my father and Frost. I knew in advance how the first would reply: He coupled dire predictions with old reminders on the subtle dangers in teaching, yet if teaching was what I was *sure* I must do, then do it and God be with me! Frost's was a different response: "You know some of the things I say about college and teaching and education but let that pass for now because if you think that you can remake yourself as you want to in the academic matrix, then I'm all for going ahead with what you plan. You will want to think it over before you make the move, but don't think it over too much. Let me know after you make up your mind, and where you will stay. And whatever you do, count on my friendship."

The flawless golden brightness of the morning sky woke me suddenly. This was the moment: Sunday, October 1, 1932! In an hour or so, if I hurried, I could drive a part of the way toward my own Ithaca. I arrived early enough to rent a room in a faculty widow's house and take the ten-minute walk on the bridge past a waterfall onto the long broad quad. It was filled with giant trees—yellow, scarlet, crimson. To my right, miles off, Lake Cayuga's waters glittered in the late sunlight. At an angle across the hazy grass: Goldwyn Smith Hall, where Prescott would expect me in the morning.

The gray-haired, bare-as-bones, lanky, bespectacled man greeted me. "We can start unless you have questions." I shook my head. "Daring thing you've done! How shall we start?" Pause. "Any questions?" He seemed so ill at ease that I kept my eyes from his face. The dry silences separating each of his phrases invited my interruptions.

"Any question, you ask, Mr. Prescott? None except Professor Herbert Muller. I don't know the name of anyone else at Cornell."

"And how do you know Muller?"

"Friend of a friend."

"He expects you at the Faculty Club at noon. He's brilliant, gifted. Someone should get him started to write. Maybe you—by example. Your coming book on the French poet—when may I read it?"

"April. Possibly March."

Silence. His repeated wordless pauses started to worry me. "Is there anything I wrote that disturbed you?"

"On the contrary, *I* am the trouble. I can't get over what you've done, giving up everything you had in these fearful times just to come to study with me . . . Makes me ask if I'm worth it. You know, both of us might have been wrong. . . . I'm not a popular teacher. I bore classes with my hollow voice and pauses."

"I've hundreds of questions and not about poetry only."

He smiled, "You're a radical in politics." I nodded. "I'm a liberal, but we're closer than you think. It's a matter of tempo. A radical is a liberal in a hurry."

"Hurrying is sometimes necessary."

"Sometimes yes." He nodded. "Nobody plays the violin when his house is on fire."

"Many writers say that art is a weapon."

"Of course, as propaganda. Its effectiveness as persuasion depends on its merit as art. Your radical writer-friends have much to learn, from the subtle kind—Keats, Shelley; from Emerson's plain statement at times: 'Line in nature is not found' to 'a subtle chain of endless rings/ The next unto the farthest brings.' Or Hardy, thinking of Providence, coming back with his hands empty. Or, of course, Frost."

"Frost?"

He smiled gently: " 'Truth? A pebble of quartz? For once, then, something.' The speaker leaning at well curbs, looking down at the water. Why in a well? He heard that you might see things down there that are not to be seen elsewhere. Frost was a good classicist. He must have known what Democritus was supposed to have said: 'We know nothing of truth, because it lies at the bottom of a well.' Frost, of course, isn't convinced but he's driven; he *has* to look for whatever might lie beyond the sight and sound and touch of the senses. *Is* there something beyond, something more? Something within him feels that there must be more, or there may be more. You've read 'The Trial by Existence.' " He reached for Frost's *Collected Poems*. "The last four lines in the next-to-last stanza: 'And God has taken a flower of gold/ And broken it—' "

Someone was knocking. "Shall I open the door?"

He shook his head. "I suppose so. I removed my *Do Not Disturb* for fear it might keep you out. . . ."

My head buzzed as I went through the chores of paying fees and so on. But by noon "the Prescott effect" had diminished enough to make me think about Muller. I found him waiting outside the Faculty Club. Fifteen minutes of talk was enough to put me at ease. "And another thing"—he beamed—"You're now a registered guest here, which means you've the run of the place, though it's no great shakes as a club. . . ."

One evening at dinner, a friend of Muller's accosted me: "Sorry to hear you've embraced the hopeless Communist cause. Since you're such an avid admirer of Frost, tell us how you take that poem he read at Columbia?"

I didn't know what he meant.

"The end of May, for Phi Beta Kappa. 'Build Soil.' "

"Frost hasn't published a line in the last four years. It couldn't be very important. Occasional poems never are."

"True, but according to one of my friends who was there, this one's *very* important. It even outclassed Lippmann—brought down the house."

I wondered why. Muller, visibly impatient, burst out "I move this discussion be tabled till we read Frost's poem, if he hasn't destroyed it. He did that once with something he wrote to order."

My frustrated host had twitted me once before about Frost. Crowded inside the Faculty Club on election night, I watched with the rest while the numbers chalked on a blackboard kept up with the radio news. "How will you *really* feel if my Democrat wins—you *and* Frost?" He had stopped joking. "Don't you realize what you'll face? Roosevelt may give you much more trouble than your Marxist double-talk could possibly cope with."

"Trouble?" I raised an eyebrow. "What sort of mysterious trouble?"

"Don't tell me you haven't studied his program!"

"You mean his platform rhetoric for winning him votes? Please don't tell me that you *believe* he meant what he said."

"I do—obviously Frost does—and I think you had better do so also. Roosevelt's offered a dozen ideas that are really one: Saving the system you want to replace with you-can't-say-what. But how will you act if he really succeeds in helping the poor and the hungry, and the jobless, and the farmers? Will you fight him?—praise the virtues of suffering so as to hurry in your revolution? You'll be crucifying yourselves, if you do. You'll find yourselves caught in the futile position of taking ludicrous potshots at the White House. As for your cagey poet, Frost will be doing the same but for different reasons. Our fine Individualist poet in bed with Collectivist Marxists but refusing to talk to each other."

"You've gone insane, my friend." I smiled, untouched by his warnings.

After three or four months, with Prescott's help, I was well on my way to the answers I had hoped to find by coming here. With my thesis work under control, Prescott and I were able to talk for hours, exploring "meanings" and "intimations" in various works of which I was still unsure. What, for example, did Frost intend when he spoke of "the spirit" or "God" in "The Trial by Existence"? The table of contents in *A Boy's Will* offered a gloss: The youth, after resolving "to become intelligible, at least to himself, since there is no help else," sets out "to know definitely what he thinks about the soul." We agreed: Man's soul—whatever that means—descends from heaven only to learn that there's nothing on earth "but what we somehow choose" and that "the utmost reward/ Of daring should be still to dare." To Prescott this was not a religious work at all; it was really about behavior, guides for conduct. Free will with a touch of Emerson's insistence on "fatal courage," fatal because of the final words "bearing it crushed and mystified." So, living on earth was a trial: People would *have* to dare while armed with the power to choose. For me it was still unexplained except as a mythic challenge of resolution combined with acceptance of human puniness in facing the *All*—that is, the remaining mystery of what "God's" creatures are doing upon "His" earth.

The "Hundred Days" of the Roosevelt era were on everyone's mind, but for me the sudden arrival of *André Spire and His Poetry,* my first book, published in 1933, overshadowed all questions of politics. I sent a copy to Frost with a separate note. What would he make of this book, with its plain introduction and its earnest attempt to legitimate *vers libre?* He would probably skip them both to scan the translations, the book's best pages, though I knew what Frost had said about all translations. I hardly expected an answer but I trusted that Wade would reply. He and his wife had been asked to visit the Frosts at their house in Amherst. Though the poet had just returned from a tiring lecture tour, he spared no energy during his four-day talks with Wade in making him understand the cause of his fear of Roosevelt. In his public readings, he said, whenever appropriate, he did his best to promote the ideas he had written into "Build Soil." Hopeful that Wade might still be there in time to copy the poem and send it to me, I wrote by special delivery. My letter brought no response.

My last visit with Prescott took place the day before I left. Neither poets nor mystics troubled his mind but the years ahead for our country. Just how sure, he asked, was my view of the Marxist solution. "Not sure," I said, "that anyone *really* knows what to do but experiment. Roosevelt, I thought, had already helped, and this was only a start. What if Cermak, who took the assassin's bullet, had lived and Roosevelt had died? What if Hitler, now at the reins of Germany, were

47

to keep his promise to wipe out the Jews? Russia offered no hope, with its miseries after the Revolution, in spite of the glorious tales that the Communists told. But how could anyone finally *not* choose sides? I felt I knew where I'd have to go at the proper moment, for all Frost's warnings against the liberal-radical-socialist dangers to the individual person, his integrity, his courage, his faith in himself."

The dangers were real, Prescott thought. No one could wish them away. Nor did I want to. After all, I insisted, each of us was a *whole*— one individual whole, in spite of Eliot and all he said about splitting the self into parts—which set us off on a long discussion of the famous lines from "Tradition and the Individual Talent." Apart from its dubious prose, I argued, nothing he said seemed more than a wish—Eliot's wish for Eliot's private reasons. Prescott read the passage aloud and shrugged. "All that he says," I went on, "flies in the face of the organismic view of man. Only a person afraid of his passions could wish so hard to alienate the 'thinking mind' from the 'feeling body'— whereas for me they are plainly one; they were always one; and they must be one."

"I hope you will follow through the implications of what you've said, when you write your book, which you must." He paused. "Where, by the way, will you live? I may hear of a decent teaching job or want to send you a book or something."

"Maine for the summer. I've a cabin on one of the Belgrade Lakes. I'll send the exact address."

"I'm afraid I shall miss our talks. We should keep in touch. Spend less time on politics, more on your book." Pause. "Make sure to discuss your idea with Frost when you see him. Let me know what he says."

★   ★   ★

Prescott knew I planned to visit the poet on my drive back from Maine. And at Frost's invitation, I wrote early in August, asking that he name a date. He replied on August 22nd:

Dear Burnshaw:
 I am still here at South Shaftsbury later in the hay-fever season than I should be, but expecting to pull out for Franconia, New Hampshire by Saturday or Sunday. If you are travelling by car

couldn't you drop in on me there for a talk and a meal? The exact address to look for is the Fobes farm on Toad Hill. We could have a good time.

Ever yours,
Robert Frost

I answered at once, thanking him for directions. My summer cabin companion would not be alone in my absence. Tony and his wife would arrive for the last two weeks of August. Then we'd all drive back to New York, so that the working couple could be at their desks on time. It had all been carefully planned. But a second letter from Frost, mailed from Franconia, ended my hopes:

Dear Burnshaw:

Sickness again with us. I have hay-fever very hard from not having migrated soon enough; and my wife is worn out with the care of me and the others. So I wont promise anything in the way of a party. We can have our talk however—I dont want to miss that. And then if I feel up to it we can have a meal at some inn. You'll understand my inhospitableness.

Always yours,
Robert Frost

So much, then, for reading "Build Soil" and for learning what the poet hoped his poem would achieve. So much also for having him hear my "organismic" idea and its implications for writing.

I returned in early September; five months later I quit the part-time job I had luckily found to become a full-time editor of the weekly *New Masses*. To readers of a book on Frost, the details of how and why this occurred can hardly be relevant. Sufficient instead to recall that the Communist Party platform for the 1932 presidency had been warmly acclaimed by thousands besides a group of fifty-two highly publicized "professionals" who gave it their formal endorsement.** The Party's stated goals and plans were basically those of the newly created *Weekly*, which strove to attract readers of *The New Republic*, *The Nation*, and similar journals. It had one advantage, however: the support in a score of cities of "Friends of the *Weekly Masses*"—organizations closely linked to a national political party of well-disciplined members with clear, fixed-policy stands on every issue. Its only flexibility arose in its varied ways of response to the arts—my main, though not my sole, concern, for this was no usual job. We were four editors, each from a different world, transmogrified into a single organism striving to tell our truth, with a sense of elation in helping with all our power to alleviate suffering, wipe out corruption, and institute programs to better the lives of people. The heading of Michael Gold's *Daily Worker* column defined our aim: "Change the World"—the collectivist opposite of Frost's Phi Beta Kappa call for a "one man revolution."

Joseph North was the only one of the three editors[2] of the *New Masses* to whom I could speak candidly of the danger of a narrow, mechanical approach in reviewing fiction, poetry, and plays. I showed him Hicks's critique of Frost's *Collected Poems*. North loaded my arms with Marxist pamphlets "that should throw some light on the subject," while admitting that certain questions hadn't as yet been resolved. I found the writings as tiresome as those I had read when my Maine summer companion had tried to "instruct" me. All the guidance I needed to keep my thinking in line had come on its own from what I had learned of the system's collapse and Fascism's dangers. Besides, not a word of all I had written on politics or anything else had been editorially altered because of a "fellow-traveler's deviations," an indictment that would have caused my prose to be "corrected." Obviously there hadn't been any, a fact I impressed upon North. But the morning after our talk he was not to be found, and nobody knew "a thing" about his return. More than a month later he appeared without warning. "I haven't forgotten," he greeted me, "but give me a week to catch up." He laughed. "I can tell you've been getting along very well without me. See you tomorrow morning."

"Tomorrow morning," out of the blue of an April sky, came a dozen letters from chapter-chairmen of "Friends of the *Weekly Masses*." They had doubtless conspired together: "Members are getting tired of doing nothing but raising money and selling subscriptions. Show them proof you appreciate their existence by sending one of your editors here for a speech. If we know in advance,

---

[2] The other editors: Herman Michelson, Managing Editor, formerly the Sunday Editor of *The New York World;* Joseph North, political reporter and short-story writer; Joshua Kunitz, Russian literature scholar and former professor. Part-time editor Granville Hicks, charged with assigning books for review, currently a professor of English. I was the only staff member who was not a member of the Communist Party, then or ever.

we'll round up a very big audience. Answer quickly yes or no, but *better say yes! . . .*" Their words had been sent to the Business Manager, William Browder, brother of Earl, the Party's chief. He prepared a list of places and dates and rushed to our rooms, locking the door. "You're going to have to vote. Something important's come up." He read from the letters and waited, staring in turn at each of us. "I've typed up a list of chapters. Which of you will it be?" No answer. "If *you* can't decide, I will." Gazing at me, he grinned. "First lecture: Rochester, 8:00 P.M., April 27th. Ten days to get ready."

"I've never made a speech in my life. What would I talk about? How many days is this junket? Oh, it's crazy, crazy. Count me out." But my fellow editors, circling my desk, started to say what a joy it would be, watching springtime unfurl in the "real America" and meeting "real people, not just New Yorkers but farmers, factory workers, shop stewards, organizers. . . ."

The trip lasted through May. Bus travel had none of today's comforts, nor were the people any more real or different, except for a certain humorless political righteousness. Perhaps their annoying solemnity explained why I said, when a questioner asked what I thought about *Poetry,* "I'll answer by quoting one of Harriet Monroe's outstanding contributors," whereupon I pronounced the olfactory figure of speech he had used to describe *Poetry*'s "decadence." Part of the audience laughed, then I turned to the next questioner, mentioning a handful of poems by Fearing and Patchen—also by Richard Wright, whom I'd found at the John Reed Club in Chicago and urged to move to New York. The day before I had stood with the Midwest Chief of the Party where five of us counted the city's May Day marchers. We agreed: 36,000. "Fine. Now wire the *Daily Worker:* 110,000. The *Times* will say 20,000." I shook my head. "How can you squash a lie," he growled, "except with a bigger lie?—standard bourgeois procedure."

After returning to work, I found on my desk the July *Poetry* clipped with a note: "See editorial pages." One of my Midwest listeners, hearing the phrase about "decadence," had sent my "unprintable" words to the editor who tore me apart while defending *Poetry*'s "strictly neutral position." Unwittingly her article stressed the point I'd been trying to make: In these times of human suffering, to be neutral was irresponsible; ethically, one was forced to take sides and one *had* to work for solutions. I mailed my rebuttal at once. The ever-gracious Monroe thanked me and promised to print it as soon as she could, but to wait for months with her accusations unanswered was unthinkable. My reply appeared in our next issue, following a headnote:

> In May the author delivered a series of lectures in several midwestern cities. Harriet Monroe, veteran editor of *Poetry,* received a report from one of her horrified listeners, and in her July 1934 issue articulates this horror in the form of an editorial "Art and Propaganda." The following reply is as much a discussion of the problems involved as it is an answer to *Poetry*'s attack. In September *Poetry* will print in abbreviated form (owing to "space limitations") the reply which we publish in full.—The Editors

The controversy was far from our minds when Tony and I entered the New School's auditorium to hear Frost's reading. We thought it strange that he'd published nothing for more than three years, then suddenly two unforgettable poems this spring: "Neither Out Far nor In Deep" and "Desert Places." We knew that Frost had been making his views on politics more or less clear to his listeners, and some of our friends who had read "Two Tramps in Mud Time," in the *Saturday Review,* cited it as "the perfect example of where Frost" stood. We disagreed. The poem's speaker protested too much in the hope of convincing himself. "Where Frost stood" was a question for Frost to answer, establish, or intimate. No poet alive could be more elusive, though we granted from all that was argued about "Build Soil" that Frost's views were not our views and his faith—whatever it was—differed from ours. And in terms of political practice and program, we were probably on opposing sides.

Every seat in the hall was filled. Having come there early, we centered ourselves in row fifteen. People were growing restive: Frost was already ten minutes late. Finally his burly figure came striding slowly down the aisle to our right, his eyes peering from side to side. Suddenly he halted—near row fifteen. Gazing in my direction, he signaled with his hand. I nodded and smiled. He waited, apparently expecting me to move. He motioned again with his head, then wagged a beckoning finger. Apologizing to the people who rose to let me pass, I squeezed my way to the aisle.

"How have you been?" He beamed at me. "I was sorry you couldn't come to Franconia. I was hoping you would even after your letter. But tell me, how have you been?"

"Fine, fine," I replied hastily, feeling the dagger-like eyes of the audience.

"I've read what you wrote to Harriet." He continued to smile.

"*You* read it?"

"Read it all—her words against you and your reply. You got the better of the argument. I'm on your side."

"*You're* on *my* side?" I could hardly believe his words.

"I'm all on your side, all on your side." He glanced toward the platform. "Just wanted to see you and tell you. Glad you're here tonight." He shook his head, sighing. "I suppose I'd better get started." I nodded, still wondering. "We should see more of each other. Come up for a talk and a meal. But soon—I go to Florida because of the bug, you know."

"Oh, I will; thank you. I've lots of questions to ask."

He nodded, smiled, and made his way to the platform while I tried to spare the toes of the furious people who jostled me back to my place. He started to speak. I heard nothing, still overcome by our colloquy. "What did he say?" Tony pressed. I shaped my lips to make them say, "Later, I'll tell you later." He shrugged, forsook me for Frost.

From what Tony explained later, the speech had started much like the one recorded by Reginald Cook, "On Taking Poetry," which appeared many years after. But ten minutes or so into the talk I was able to concentrate on Frost's comments between his recitals of poems. He inveighed against "gangs." People, wherever he went these days, had been forming themselves into think-alike groups, and every member was letting "the gang he belonged to do his thinking for him" instead of trying to puzzle things out for himself. All Frost needed to hear, he said, were the first ten words, then he'd know which gang the person belonged to. It was that simple! "I'm all against gangs of thought"—I remembered the phrase. Before concluding the talk, he had somehow tied his opening theme to the one at the close: "You can tell from the way a person takes a poem how he takes himself"; but he phrased it in different words.

Three weeks later, thanks to a friend who happened to browse in a Cambridge bookstore, I chanced on "Provide, Provide." He had found the poem in a new little poetry journal, *The New Frontier*, produced by a former Frost student, Reuben Brower. My instant response was much like Jarrell's in "To the Laodiceans," and if only I had

set down my thoughts in advance of meeting with North, the outcome might have been different. The poem had made me decide to
confront him with "problems." North, an impassioned believer in
Communist policies, was a gifted writer of stories and a poetry reader
whose range would often amaze me, as had happened when, faced
with a jumble of papers, I muttered, "Order is a lovely thing," only to
hear him add, "On disarray it lays its wing." Who but North in this
secular Marxist universe would have learned by heart "The Monk in
the Kitchen" by the scarcely famous, deeply religious Anna
Hempstead Branch? He greatly admired the work of Frost, but before
attempting to show him "Provide, Provide," I discussed what I called
our dilemma. Except for a handful of poems—Fearing's "Dirge,"
Kalar's "Paper Mill," Patchen's "Joe Hill Listens . . ."—the verse of
the Left was a sad affair and the fiction not much better. North decried
my impatience. I felt sure, I said, there were vastly superior works
which we wouldn't even consider simply because their authors might
hold some political views that didn't *in every respect* conform to our
own.

"What are you trying to tell me?" He seemed a bit nervous.

"It's the writing alone that counts—stands or falls on its own, once
it's in print. We should think of it as an object, an object that will
better—enrich, deepen, or worsen—our sense of the world."

"You've something specific in mind?"

"Not right now—nothing like Sarah Cleghorn's." At once he
recited:

> The golf links lie so near the mill
> That almost every day
> The laboring children can look out
> And see the men at play.

"We couldn't print that, you know," I went on. "She's wildly in love
with Roosevelt, praises whatever he does, which, strange to say, didn't
keep Frost from writing an introduction to her autobiography—
though he's said to be just as anti-Roosevelt as she is pro. But that's
beside my point right now, which is this." I pulled from my pocket a
sheet with "Provide, Provide." I watched North's face. He read the
poem a second time, then a third. "We talk of 'the system,' " I said.
"There it stands in twenty-one bitter lines, with very much more."

Provide Provide

The witch that came, the withered hag,
To wash the steps with pail and rag,
Was once the beauty Abishag.

The picture pride of Hollywood.
Too many fall from great and good
For you to doubt the likelihood.

Die early and avoid the fate
Or if predestined to die late,
Make up your mind to die in state.

Make the whole stock exchange your own.
If need be, occupy a throne
Where nobody can call you crone.

Some have relied on what they knew;
Others on being simply true.
What worked for them might work for you.

No memory of having starred
Makes up for later disregard
Or keeps the end from being hard.

Better to go down dignified
With boughten friendship at your side
Than none at all. Provide, provide.

                    Robert Frost

PROVIDE, PROVIDE

The witch that came, the withered hag,
To wash the steps with pail and rag,
Was once the beauty Abishag,

The picture pride of Hollywood.
Too many fall from great and good
For you to doubt the likelihood

Die early and avoid the fate,
Or if predestined to die late,
Make up your mind to die in state.

Make the whole stock exchange your own.
If need be, occupy a throne
Where nobody can call *you* crone.

Some have relied on what they knew;
Others on being simply true.
What worked for them might work for you.

No memory of having starred
Makes up for later disregard
Or keeps the end from being hard.

Better to go down dignified
With boughten friendship at your side
Than none at all. Provide, provide.

                              Robert Frost

North said nothing. His eyes searched mine. "What would have happened if Frost had sent us that poem? Tell me!"

"*You* tell *me!*"

"I can only say what we ought to have done, but wouldn't have dared."

"Go on." He waited.

"Well, one of us should have called on Frost."

"And told him exactly what?"

"If I had gone, I'd have talked of the people in *North of Boston*— which, by way, was originally called *Farm Servants and Other People*. I'd have stressed their courage, scratching a living out of hopeless soil, surviving against the odds and succeeding. I'd have quoted 'The Tuft of Flowers' " . . .

"Men work together," he began, and finished the couplet: " 'Whether they work together or apart.' "

"I'd have stressed the fact that lots of his poems are concerned with the kind of people closest to those *we're* working to help. And then I'd have brought up 'Provide, Provide.' "

"That's all?" He smiled, eyebrow raised.

"No. I haven't been able to read 'Build Soil,' that everyone talks about. I'd have asked him to let me read it so at last I could see for myself what it *really* says. All we *know* are rumors, but we *know* he makes no secret of what he thinks of Roosevelt. Basically is it different from what we're doing? Frost is much too canny not to know that the whole New Deal is aimed at saving the system. That's one of the things I'd try to explore."

"What he thinks of the system?" North laughed. "He wants it just as it was."

"If things were fine as they were, how could he write 'Provide, Provide?' "

North looked straight ahead. "I can't answer that question right off. It isn't a *simple* poem."

"Mine isn't a simple question."

His suddenly changed tone told me he wanted our talk to end. "Keep that page," I said. "I've another copy. Read it again—and *think* about my question. It really matters to both of us. I'll be waiting to hear your answer."

I assumed he would take my proposal to one of the Party authorities and return with a ruling from Earl Browder or V. J. Jerome, the reigning Cultural Commissar. Broad changes in policy had been hinted at since the murder in early December of one of Stalin's trusted aides. Treason trials of famous "Old Bolshevik" heroes were held sometime in January. What the affair might do to the Party's "position," no one I questioned would talk about. Might the net effect be a change to a "harder" or "softer" line, or to neither? Having always been secretly bored by events in the Soviet Fatherland, I felt far removed from all that had happened in Moscow. I assumed that the victims were guilty of trying to seize the reins from the men they considered incompetent, wrong, or in other respects unworthy. Besides, I was mainly concerned with what *we* were doing about the Roosevelt programs.

To be sure, the *Masses* was obligated to make our readers aware that the government's acts were designed to salvage the system. Yet to write off Roosevelt as merely a "Social Fascist"—which we often did—was ludicrous, since none of his works could honestly be called even quasi-totalitarian. True, some acts seemed to verge on the dictatorial, but who were we to talk, who fell all over ourselves in extolling Moscow's dictatorship? Everyone knew that New Deal programs had helped all classes of needy people, from farmers to unskilled workers to writers and painters. "Labor's Magna Charta" was *Time* magazine's phrase for defining the government-backed guarantee of collective bargaining. But in spite of these startling achievements, the *Weekly Masses,* rather than giving the devil the due he had patently earned, nagged away at the negative—sounding at times uncomfortably like the diehards we mocked who cursed "That Man in the White House."

Days, weeks, more than a year had passed, and my strange new life so hopefully launched had become, like all other earthly blessings, unhappily mixed—joys, satisfactions, delights mingling with doubts, confusions, despairs. Yet the faithless moments loomed small in the growing brightness of a nation steadily rising out of its dark and pain. And then—all at once and without warning, an unbelievable change, decreed out of Moscow: a Franco-Soviet mutual military pact on May 2, 1935. Caught unaware, France's Communists suddenly heard themselves lauding the acts they'd been branding as vilely fascistic, while the all but incredulous faithful here hastened to plan a "United People's Front" to be made up of groups they had recently worked to condemn. I thought it too good to be true: Divisiveness replaced by a twofold striving to cut off the spread of fascism and help repair the broken-down "bourgeois system," with the Revolution shelved, at least *pro tem*. Months before the official work-with-your-former-enemy line, "The First Congress of American Writers" had sent out a call for its maiden gathering on April 26th. Had Frost, like all other leading writers, been invited?

Should I make an unannounced visit? There were things I was eager to discuss—*Panic*, Archibald MacLeish's "modern tragedy" about the system and the lively platform discussion I'd led in March after the curtain fall.** Had he known of *Waiting for Lefty, Awake and Sing!*, the *Living Newspaper* plays? How could these fail to excite the man who proclaimed that "everything written is as good as it is dramatic"? If I made the trip, I could talk of "Provide, Provide" and the plan I proposed to North, and learn Frost's reaction. Also, I had heard about Wallace Stevens' forthcoming *Ideas of Order*, which I planned to review. Were the Key West stories of Frost and Stevens valid? Had Stevens actually said that night, "The trouble with you, Robert, is that you write about subjects"; which Frost supposedly countered with, "The trouble with you, Wallace, is that you write *bric à brac*"? And finally—I could learn all about "Build Soil." I was also hesitant to visit a man who I'd heard inveighing against all "gangs." True, he had said he was on my side, "all on my side," but . . . ?

It was most unlikely that talking with Frost might have altered my view of Stevens or of what I should have to write of *Ideas of Order* and of *Pittsburgh Memoranda* by Haniel Long. Both men were accomplished poets and both revealed not only their troubled concerns but also a trust in the human imagination's ability to remedy man-made evils. They appeared to Long as the joint creation of all classes, which all classes would have to cure not by "any theory of the State" but by changing "the worst within ourselves." His mosaic of verse, stories, news, quotations imaged the hope for some new collective order. No such program was found in Stevens' *Ideas of Order*, which reflected its title. I paid due homage to *Harmonium*, his early book, to some fine new lines, and at least one remarkable poem; but the book as a whole was "the record of a man who, having lost his footing, now scrambles to stand up and keep his balance." I refrained from decrying his use of the fiercely offensive word "Nigger" in one of his titles. My review closed with a handful of temperate questions.

Six months later an editor of the forthcoming *New American Caravan* telephoned. "You've just been immortalized. Stevens has sent us a wonderful poem in reply to your essay—'Mr. Burnshaw and the

Statue.' The *Caravan* is sure to come out this fall and"—he laughed—
"with that purely non-political poem of yours included."

The call came at a time when I felt myself driven to make a decision.
Disagreements, differences in judgment, and numberless annoyances
led me to question my right to remain where I was. But whenever I
wanted to voice my doubt some emergency would force me to hold
my tongue. More than two years had passed since I took up my
editor's tasks. I had found almost no time at all for my private writing.
Worse, I had suddenly realized how the pressures of putting a news
magazine to press each Monday night of the year had narrowed my
view of the world. Could I willingly continue this treadmill regime? I
announced to North that I'd stay for two or three weeks so that one of
the other new editors could take on some work I had started.

He protested. Frost's new book, *A Further Range,* was being de-
layed till June. I was really concerned. "First, whatever happens, don't
let Hicks get his hands on it. Second, give me your word that you'll
personally read the review and approve it before it appears."

"Why don't we wait till we read the book—both of us? I'll call you.
Better still, get in touch with me so there won't be a slip up. I'm anxious to see the book. You should be too."

Especially after I read Frost's poem "To a Thinker in Office" in a
January *Saturday Review,* followed weeks later by a *New York Times*
editorial on an interview with Frost in the *Baltimore Sun,* in which he
had "bitterly condemned an alleged Administration policy of regarding farmers as possessors of what he called submarginal minds." He
produced a new poem, the report added, that "he indicated was written about the President." The verses were given in full, followed by:

> "Seriously though," said Mr. Frost, "I'm not horribly anti-
> Roosevelt. Henry Mencken bears down on the President pretty
> hard. Roosevelt is making his mistakes, just as we did. But I'm
> very much a country man, and I don't like to see city against
> country. And I can't stand coercion."

Not long after, he was said to have told *The Forum*'s editor that the
poem had been written before Roosevelt took office, that it was aimed
at "the despairers of the republic and of parliamentary forms of government"; also, that by adding to the original title ("To a Thinker")
the words "in Office," he had narrowed it to fit Roosevelt.

There was no gainsaying one point in the *Times* editorial: "If [Frost] implies that Mr. Roosevelt's thought is pedestrian, the implication is a compliment. A statesman who has his feet on the ground can't very well have his head in the clouds. So the poet contradicts himself." But in other places as well, I thought in rereading the poem. The speaker maintains:

> I own I never really warmed
> To the reformer or the reformed.
> And yet conversion has its place
> Not halfway down the scale of grace.

Not halfway? Where, then? Paradoxically—perhaps by design?—the gait of the poet-speaker seems no more sure than the thinker's, who believes that his shifting about constitutes "thinking." "No," writes Frost, "it's walking" and "Not even that, it's only rocking,/ Or weaving . . . back and forth."

Change in the *Weekly*'s editorship occurred in gradual stages. I continued to seek all possible means for talking with North about critics for Frost's new book, but no one could say where North was. From what I was able to piece together, nothing at all had been done or was planned to be done "for some time." In mid July, I quit the *Weekly*'s staff.

On July 20th, I left New York; three days before, General Francisco Franco had flown to Morocco, where he led a revolt against Spain's Republican government. Civil war had begun. The Popular Front of Communists, Socialists, and Liberals had recently won an election. Was this the price a country would pay when its legally chosen government sought to install the social reforms that its voters had authorized: a Rightist revolt? Perhaps the strength of the People's Front would prove weighty enough to subdue what was still but a single attack by the army. Spain had always lived outside the stream of the continent's history; it had even "escaped" the Renaissance. We should have to follow events, to hope and see.

Before leaving for Maine, I had read through *A Further Range* and three early reviews: Newton Arvin's (*Partisan Review*), Horace Gregory's (*The New Republic*), R. P. Blackmur's (*The Nation*). Though I knew they would have to be hostile, I expected to find, intermixed with negations, glimmers of critical insight. This was asking too much. Obviously, each reviewer had aimed at diminishing Frost as a poet: Arvin calling his work "expressive much more of the minor than of the major strain in Yankee life and culture," Gregory ranking him as "the last survivor of the Georgian movement in England," and Blackmur dismissing him as "an easy-going versifier" and not a true poet at all. Today these words seem absurd. *A Further Range* was one of Frost's greatest volumes, with ten or more of his finest poems, and certain reviewers who were unattached politically instantly saw its importance—Dudley Fitts, for example, pointed to Frost's "supremacy as a lyricist," and hailed *A Further Range* as "a book of the greatest distinction." Arvin, Gregory, and Blackmur as expected fixed their eyes on the few works of social concern, such as "Build Soil," "To a Thinker," "A Lone Striker"—undoubtedly *as poems* the worst in the book. Fitts, on the contrary, called attention to the best. And Wilbert Snow, free from political motives, remarked simply that "Some of [Frost's] philosophical and political humor does not seem to be very important; hence the volume is rather uneven . . . which is no more nor less than one might say about a volume of Tennyson or Browning, or even of Shakespeare's sonnets." All but one of the five reviews appeared in June. Not until August was I able to read the *Masses,* whose comments by Rolfe Humphries had the tired ring of the old-fashioned Communist line: "When you call Frost a reactionary—, or a counter-revolutionary—, you have, in essence, said it all." The same book that Humphries saw as "A Further Shrinking" exhibited "magnificent growth" to Merrill Root, his fellow-editor of *The Measure.* Frost, who had said that he never bothered to read reviews of his books, no longer pretended ignorance of what his critics were saying. "Abuse from The New Masses mass or mess," he wrote to Ted Morrison, "comes particularly hard in that I have twice been approached by them in private to come in and to be their proletarian poet." Had North been the secret emissary? Kreymborg, perhaps, on whom he could count as a friend? It was now too late to wonder if the caller had hoped to persuade the poet to change "Build Soil" or other offending poems.

No changes, so far as I know, had ever been made by Frost at the urging of others. Four years had passed before he decided to print "Build Soil"—against the advice of Elinor, who also "begged" him not to include "To a Thinker." Nothing would change his mind. And if he believed in the likelihood that the writer of a public poem tells more about himself than his subject, Frost should have welcomed the prospect. He wanted to make his position known. Eliot, his rival for critics' acclaim, had publicized his point of view "as classicist in literature, royalist in politics, and anglo-catholic in religion" eight years before. And the "Nashville Group"—Allen Tate, Stark Young, Robert Penn Warren, his friend John Crowe Ransom, and seven others—had been urging the South to reclaim its aristocratic culture by adopting the old small farm of the Middle South as the model for its economy—an approach Eliot warmly approved in *After Strange Gods*.** Frost offered no cure-all program of action. He did, however, propose definitive views which anyone reading "Build Soil" could find by looking above and below the lines. One could no more mistake Frost's attitudes than those of MacLeish, for example, in his anti-Marxist "Frescoes for Mr. Rockefeller's Radio City," with its "Lenin! Millenium! Lennium!" epigraph, published but two years before he became a *New Masses* contributor.

"Build Soil" was clearly an adaptation of Virgil's "First Eclogue," even to using its speakers' names: Meliboeus, a farmer, and his friend Tityrus, a poet-farmer. "Hard times have struck me," the first complains, have forced him to give up potato-growing for raising sheep. In asking advice from Tityrus, who lives "by writing/ . . . Poems on a farm and call[s] that farming," Meliboeus plays the questioner throughout the dialogue. And at first its almost 300 lines seem little more than a leisurely ramble. But further readings reveal some marked divisions.

In the first, Tityrus states that a poet dealing with politics must write of specific matters, only to hear Meliboeus complain that "The times seem revolutionary bad." Tityrus disagrees (53-66): all times seem bad. "Let newspapers profess to fear the worst"; as for himself, "Nothing's portentous, I'm reassured." When his questioner, unconvinced, inquires: "Is socialism needed?" he explains:

> We have it now. For socialism is
> An element in any government.
> There's no such thing as socialism pure—
> Except as an abstraction of the mind.
> There's only democratic socialism,
> Monarchic socialism, oligarchic—
> The last being what they seem to have in Russia.
> You often get it most in monarchy,
> Least in democracy. In practice, pure,
> I don't know what it would be. No one knows. . . .

And no one, Frost goes on, can, with reason, hope to oppose it; yet certain degrees and certain types do not deserve to be countenanced.

In answer to the sheep-grower's further prodding, Tityrus proceeds to discuss some specific questions (97-129). Ambition, greed, and ingenuity all should be held in check; but the third must be read ironically, for the author of "Kitty Hawk" and of "The Wrights' Biplane" could hardly oppose ingenuity, the outcome *par excellence* of the hazardous kind of freedom that "Build Soil" advocates. Yet Malcolm Cowley and other adversaries deafened their ears to the overtones (103-125): "Bounds should be set/ To ingenuity for being so cruel/ In bringing change unheralded on the unready"—on the other hand, even uncurbed ingenuity may produce results that bring more good than bad. Taking risks is not only part of existence but the price of all we achieve. We also must realize that ingenuity—

> Which, for no sordid self-aggrandizement,
> For nothing but its own blind satisfaction
> (In which it is as much like hate as love),
> Works in the dark as much against as for us.

Because ingenuity works for no end but its own, and is therefore wholly disinterested, we have to take care not to keep it from flourishing—the very thing, Tityrus fears, that a socialist system might do.

The poem's title comes to the fore in the final part, as Tityrus, "preaching on," stresses the need for cultivating the individual self as having much greater import than social engagement. A rich, salutary social existence cannot emerge *except* out of rich, salutary individuality.

> Build soil. Turn the farm in upon itself
> Until it can contain itself no more,
> But sweating-full, drips wine and oil a little.

"Build soil" not only on the farm but everywhere in all endeavors. For example:

> The thought I have, and my first impulse is
> To take to market—I will turn it under.
> The thought from that thought—I will turn it under.
> And so on to the limit of my nature.
> We are too much out, and if we won't draw in
> We shall be driven in.

In short, self-cultivation. And so Tityrus, bidding his friend to start in himself "a one-man revolution," watches him leave for home, where, free "from company" and alone, he will think things out for himself, come to his own conclusions.

In so earnest a poem, one hardly expects moments of humor. They appear throughout the dialogue—mild, mocking, slyfully teasing, farcical, some even aimed at the author himself. But for those who believed that the nation's surest hope was a Socialist future, jokes were beside the point. They were hardly inclined to savor the comic relief in a screed that mocked their faith—worse, that declared that the "one-man revolution" it called for was the only one worth having. Frost had indeed taken his stand: on the opposite side of the ideological barricades, firing against all Liberal-Radical-Socialist enemies, salvos of his conservatism. "His" should be stressed for its difference from other extant varieties.

Why had Frost overruled Elinor and published the poem? Why this need to publicize personal thoughts about government? From his own accounts of his early years, no one can doubt that Frost as a boy had imbibed politics with his father's beer. At the age of six he had watched while his hero, in top-hat and frock-coat regalia, rode off to the sounds of a loud brass band to serve as a party delegate to the Democrats' National Convention. Though a journalist by profession, William Prescott Frost, Jr., ate, drank, slept, and battled politics as long as his health allowed. He even ran for office (unsuccessfully) as the city's collector of taxes. When he died soon after, his son, then eleven, lost not only his idol but also a quick-tempered disciplinarian whose acts of bravado never quite left Robert's mind. Under so heady an influence, the boy couldn't fail to become a political animal and to think and talk like one throughout his life. Roosevelt's fight for the presidency was but one among many events that would "force" him to speak his mind.

Other writers, as noted, were having their say: the Agrarians in *I'll Take My Stand,* Eliot in *For Lancelot Andrewes.* In *After Strange Gods* the latter's antisemitic remarks made at the time of the Hitlerite terror startled a great many readers, as did certain statements by Yeats and Pound that sounded suspiciously Fascist. Frost's "Build Soil," however, which he read in advance of the national party conventions, was aimed directly at all he feared might ensue if Roosevelt were named to run for the presidency and his platform enacted.

Fear was the spur and its reason frankly stated as early as the pre-election program for the farms that alerted Frost to the possible dangers in store. What did he think they might be? First, the reformers who, convinced they alone possessed "the correction solution," would inflict it on others and force them to do their bidding. Second, "the easy despairers of the republic and of parliamentary forms" who appeared quite pleased to exchange them both for a socialist system. Third, his concern that our limitless freedom of speech might be deftly abused to usher in a dictatorship that would step-by-step deny it to all as treason. Fourth, his fear that a well-entrenched centralized government could gradually move us away from republican democracy into some kind of totalitarian existence. Fifth, and of equal importance, his profound belief that a "welfare state" would infantilize the individual.

Shades of Concord and Walden. Of Emerson, for example: "The less government we have, the better—the fewer laws, and the less confided power [*Politics*]." Or "Society everywhere is in conspiracy against the manhood of every one of its members [*Self-Reliance*]." Closer to Frost's concern were Emerson's words on "the masses" from *Conduct of Life:* they are "'rude, lame, unmade, pernicious in their demands and influence. . . . I wish not to concede anything to them, but to . . . divide and break them up, and draw individuals out of them." Whitman, the loud yeasayer of 1855, wrote in strikingly similar terms in his *Democratic Vistas* of 1871:

> I myself see clearly enough the crude, defective streaks in all the strata of the common people; the specimens and vast collections of the ignorant, the credulous, the unfit and uncouth, the incapable, and the very low and poor. . . . We believe the ulterior object of political and all other government . . . to be . . . but to develop, to open up to cultivation, to encourage the possibilities of all beneficent and manly outcroppage, and of that aspiration for independence, and the pride and self-respect latent in all characters. . . . I say the mission of government . . . is . . . to train communities through all their grades, beginning with individuals and ending there again, to rule themselves.

The first and last proposals are "strikingly similar": While differing with respect to means, their aims and faith are the same. Whitman could hardly have disagreed with Emerson's *Diary* note of 1840, that in all his lectures he "taught one doctrine, namely, the infinitude of the private man." Since such objectives cannot evade the pressures of social living, how can they be attained? Frost parts company with Whitman. "Keep off each other and keep each other off," "Build Soil" proclaims, not only on the farm but everywhere else.

"To build soil in all endeavors" presupposes a dependably stable and impersonal social system, which Frost in his view of history took for granted. Disbelieving in progress, he warned that: "We have no way of knowing that this age is one of the worst in the world's history. . . . Ages may vary a little. One may be a little worse than another. But it is not possible to get outside the age you are in to judge it exactly." Self-cultivation can be pursued without concern for the epoch in which one lives. Frost's cyclic view of history mirrors his faith in the innate capacity of people for self-renewal. Yet the proviso he failed to add to these words to Amherst students pulses throughout "Build Soil": The individual must not be interfered with by any outside force. Freedom is the pre-condition for self-cultivation.

When I finally read "Build Soil" I saw nothing wrong in its "call" provided our country's sickened condition were cured. Under the kind of pervasive Socialist change as I envisaged it, "self cultivation" could flourish in full. I had stated as much in my *Masses* essay on Edna Millay. "Communism is repugnant to me," she had cried; "I am intensely an individualist." My reply—that "socialism alone can bring genuine freedom for the individual"—should have concluded: "once any ruling dictatorship no longer is needed to guard the land from its enemies." This, at the time, was unquestioning Leftwing gospel and, given the Communist "truths" as purveyed by the Party, it seemed to make sense. To others it was both naïve and absurd. But the issue transcended Millay, Frost, Emerson, Marx, *et al.,* being deeper and vaster than those any program for governing people had ever confronted; for it lay at the core of what came to be, after eons of social existence, the uniquely human predicament. Whitman, facing the search for solutions, put it in simple words: "That is the same old question—adjusting the individual to the mass. Yes, the big problem, the only problem, the sum of them all."

Though many readers of "Build Soil" and other political poems in *A Further Range* pictured Frost as a rockbound New England conservative, a number of remarks in his letters and comments to intimates make such a portrait untenable. Did he think of himself as conservative? "No, I'm not," he insisted to Reginald Cook. "I'm more radical than they [the social thinkers] think. If I were one of the poor, I'd ruin the world to satisfy my needs." That this current scorner-of-socialism

65

once voted for Eugene Debs on the Socialist ticket for president is a well-known fact; and though some prefer to ignore it, it can hardly be viewed in a highly political man in his fourth decade as meaningless youthful caprice. Besides, *A Further Range* confounds oversimple judgments by poems such as "On Taking from the Top to Broaden the Base" and "Provide, Provide." Within five years Frost would be urging that unfair extremes be remedied for the sake of the "public health": "So that the poor won't have to steal by stealth, / We now and then should take an equalizer." Which differs little from what he had written to Untermeyer in the twenties: "Count me as in favor of reforming a whole lot of things downward." He would say very much the same at the end of his life in an unfinished letter to the head of the Socialist Party, Norman Thomas (259). He could also state other views on reform as such, at times raging against it ("It is not the business of the poet to cry for reform"); at others, defending it ("Sarah Cleghorn . . . [S]aint, poet—*and* reformer").

Readers may well begin to wonder "where Frost really stood"—as I had wondered two years before when, after reading my outspoken praise of the Left, he had taken pains to tell me he was "all on [my] side" (53). I had wondered also about his entreaty to Untermeyer: "Pity me for not knowing what would set everything right"; and later, after the 1936 election, at his telling his friend: "The national mood is humanitarian. Nobly so—I wouldn't take it away from them. . . . Life is like battle. But so is it also like shelter. . . . The model is the family at its best." Obviously these shifting attitudes had little to do with "mood." On July 3, 1961, at the end of a Bread Loaf lecture, he offered a prayer. Asking the audience to take seriously his well-known couplet ("Forgive, O Lord . . ."), he recited "another prayer. . .only this is as if I spoke to a star up there. That's the one"—he explained of "Choose Something Like a Star"—"[in which] I hate myself for being too much one way and then too much another through fifty years of politics."

No essay on Frost can fail to perceive, in this late confession, indications of the normative way in which he appeared magnetically drawn to the presence of conflict not only between "the good and the evil" but also between two or more "goods." Here lies the path to his widely discussed contrarieties. At the moment, however, a simpler question confronts us. Did he deem his political verse effective as action? As poetry? He scorns "O'Shaughnessy's poem ["Ode"] about us music-makers having built Nineveh and overthrown Babel [as work that leads] to nothing on the lower plane of politics," for there "On the lower plane of thought and opinion the poet is a follower." As for its worth as poetry, "Wordsworth and Emerson both wrote some politics into their verse. Their poetic originality by which they live was quite another thing." Why, then, did he strive so hard to make his views known to the world? Merely because, as the creature of politics his father had made him, he could never resist the excitement of parrying arguments?

What role, if any, did Elinor Frost play in her husband's politics? There are few sources to turn to, but those we have leave no doubt of the answer. According to Stearns Morse, a Dartmouth faculty member and a friend of forty years who owned a farm where the Frosts visited in 1933: "They feared and hated the New Deal; at least Elinor Frost did. . . . For a few moments she lost her taciturnity and inveighed against it bitterly, then retreated into her inner world, put on the mask of what I should call her masculine stoicism."

Five years later she wrote to her son-in-law, Willard Fraser:

[T]he awful state the labor situation is in, on the U.S. merchant ships . . . is entirely due to Roosevelt's encouragement of the C.I.O. [Congress of Industrial Organizations]. Many people have realized from the first that some of his advisors wished to ruin business, so the government could take it over and turn us into a state socialism. I think that event isn't far off.

Her strong Republican bias had been evident as early as Hoover's election, a decade before, Frost had informed Robert S. Newdick, who was writing the poet's biography. The work remained unfinished—Newdick died in 1939. Thirty-five years later William A. Sutton published the thirteen complete mini-chapters with 135 pages of research findings in *Newdick's Season of Frost*. Those on Elinor Frost include two pertinent items:

Even outsiders, Amherstites, could see the rift between them in politics—and his dancing to cover it up! But she went on clipping, clipping, relentlessly clipping, day after day after day—clipping all that damned FDR, nothing that was in his favor.

She hated FDR. A passion with her. Said she would kill him, if she had the strength. "Charlotte Corday?" asked RF, laughing, turning it off. But she didn't join in the laugh.

Morse observed that "Frost's political conservatism was to a great extent induced by his concern for his wife." Yet both Frosts had been reared on the Puritan work ethic and both shared a revulsion against the relief programs: The "demoralizing" effects of enforced beneficence, they feared, might well become a threat to the sturdy people who were proud to have "made it" on their own.

My wish for a long-delayed intimate talk with Frost now became impossible, pressed as I was with learning another profession, as editor and typographer of a newly organized publishing house, The Dryden Press. I heard, however, that Kreymborg had been asked to try to persuade Frost to endorse the published "call" to the Second Congress of the League of American Writers. As a trusted friend, Kreymborg, I thought, would be happy to bear my message along with the League's. The new "call," purged of all talk of a working-class revolution and the death of the social system, asked little more than support in its fight against war and Fascist repression. Kreymborg, who had refrained from signing the earlier call, would surely have rocked with delight in recounting to Frost his "enemy" Arvin's dismissal of Emily Dickinson as "a fantastic," of Whitman as "a bourgeois," along with Rolfe Humphries' characterization of Franz Kafka as at best "an obscure psychologist." When I asked Kreymborg about his discussions with Frost, he replied by changing the subject. Not that it mattered; I knew the result in advance. Nor could I possibly doubt that Frost, through his friend Bernard DeVoto, editor of the *Saturday Review,* would hear all about the Second Congress.

Soon after it opened, DeVoto challenged the signers to list the achievements of the First Congress, and James T. Farrell, eager to strike at the Left, wrote an "Interim Report on Its Results" which DeVoto delighted in publishing. Nearly a thousand people had to be turned away from the overcrowded Carnegie Hall when the Congress opened on the evening of June 4th. Some 358 delegates—of all political complexions—filled the stage. "The main attraction," as Arthur Casciato reports:

> was Hemingway, only recently returned from the battlefields of Spain. His supporting cast was impressive as well: MacLeish, the humorist Donald Ogden Stewart, and the journalist Walter Duranty. MacLeish, the chairman of the opening session, read dramatic messages of support from, among others, Albert

Einstein, Ernst Toller, Upton Sinclair, C. Day Lewis and Sylvia Townsend Warner. A preview of the film *The Spanish Earth* completed the spectacle. . . . [Y]ears later Matthew Josephson remembered it as "a festival in honor of the defenders of Spain."

Hemingway, arriving late, strode forward nervously "to talk on the problems of a writer in wartime." He had no need to stress the recent bombing of Guernica: "The Totalitarian fascist states believe in Totalitarian war . . . whenever they are beaten by armed forces they take their revenge on unarmed civilians. . . ." The applause at the end of his speech shook the hall. During the next two days the members discussed politico-literary problems and two nights later the Congress closed. No observer from within or without failed to fear that contention would plague the League and the People's Front.

It would take many shapes—between Stalinists and Trotskyists, between Communists and non-Communists, between naturalism and modernism, between a European and an American conception of the artist's role, between literature and politics. In its broadest sense, it was a conflict between art and life. Even the trends toward "americanization" and "internationalization" pulled the League in irreconcilable directions, stretching it thin between Moscow and America.

The last point was not lost on Frost or DeVoto, nor the role in the whole event of the Communist Party, which, as Hicks declared, "was leading the way," waving high the new slogan: "Communism Is Twentieth-Century Americanism."

Two months before, *A Further Range* had received the Pulitzer Prize. With the help of the Book of the Month Club, the new volume reached the poet's largest audience. And except for the Left, its achievement as art had been hailed by reviewers. In the same season, his publisher was planning to issue a book in *Recognition of Robert Frost;* and DeVoto, who the year before had proposed to attack Frost's attackers, now restated his offer. Frost had been doubtful; DeVoto had made no move. In January 1937 the poet changed his mind: "I am going to have you strike that blow for me now if you still want to and if you can assure your wife and conscience you thought of it first and not I." It appeared twelve months later in the guise of DeVoto's review of the *Recognition* volume. Ridgely Torrence, of *The New Republic,* wrote to Frost that he couldn't imagine how Arvin, Blackmur, and Gregory "would ever get up from the slaughterhouse floor."

DeVoto printed a letter defending Blackmur written by F. O. Matthiessen, a member of what Frost condemned as the "Pound-Eliot-Richards gang" at Harvard. Author of a book on Eliot and a critical study, *American Renaissance,* Matthiessen—in Poirier's words—was "a natural enemy" of Frost: "Combining a taste for difficult, culturally saturated literature on the one hand and, on the other, an announced sympathy for the political left and for the Soviet Union, he epitomized a new force in American cultural and academic life which brought Frost's literary position and the politics implicit in it into serious question." At the time of the Left attack upon Frost, it was clear to me, and some others who belonged to the Left, that these critics were simply incapable of reading Frost at what Poirier called "his already published best. They were locked into simplistic expectations and their reading yielded correspondingly simplistic results." From one point of view, their behavior struck us as blindly illogical; from another, it caused discomfiting doubts about their allegiance, for the poets they all but worshipped—Pound, Eliot, Yeats—stood for everything they professed to oppose in politics. I also came to doubt their critical competence in reading a poet whose subtleties called for more than their standard approach.

I tried to put the embroilments of Europe out of my mind as I made my way in this new profession of publishing. It could not be done. Every day Spain's plight was leading people I knew into risking their lives. One of the books I was editing closed with the thought that the future of man "lies somewhere between barbarism and the fantasy world portrayed in the H. G. Wells film, *Things to Come.*" I dashed off 2,000 words pointing to the line-up of "systems" in Spain—Fascist Right, Socialist Left, Democratic Middle—and the use of its lands as "a testing ground. Only in those political systems which welcome, or at least appear to welcome, the growth of the spirit of free inquiry," may we take some hope. I thought of sending it to Frost with a letter explaining all that had kept me from making a visit. But perhaps the noncommital Kreymborg had, after all, given him at least the sense of my message.

★   ★   ★

On the first day of spring, 1938, *The New York Times* announced the death of Elinor Frost. Where would the service be held? I had no way of knowing; no way of learning how Frost was faring. My best tie, Wade Van Dore, was unreachable. I considered doing what Frost had urged on me nine years before—"Write to Louis. Tell him I told you to" (20). My name would not be entirely meaningless; we had made an acquaintance by correspondence three years before which I mentioned to Christina Stead and William Blake while talking about an anthology they were completing. No one can say, I remarked, that your title isn't exact; on the other hand, *Modern Women in Love* might well catch the eye of the censors. "Simple enough," said Blake. "Just add a serious foreword by a well-known literary name. How about Louis?"

Untermeyer was more than willing, and his introduction proved to be all we needed. Blake delivered it by hand: "On time and with best wishes. Louis asks about you. I hope you don't mind, but Chris and I thought he should read your *Bridge*. We loaned him our galleys."

A thoughtful, generous comment about my play arrived in a letter which closed: "Please feel free to quote what you wish on the jacket." I replied with thanks and the hope that "we two might meet in the flesh some time." Within a month we were both surprised, hearing ourselves introduced to each other by Philip Van Doren Stern, our host at a fund-raising party. "Louis"—the name he insisted I use—had been working as general editor of the Armed Services Editions. At our first lunch he talked of his plans, his work, his divorce, his now uneasy relationship with the poet whose intimate friend he had been for thirty years. I had endless questions to ask about Frost, but Louis and I met only seldom. Our offices were far apart and both of us treasured our nights for reading and writing. With the move of The Dryden Press to West 54th Street, meeting for lunch became possible almost whenever we pleased—Louis' office was now but three blocks north. As special advisor to the head of Decca, a leading recording firm, he was carrying out his employer's "dream of bringing the living theater and the spoken word to the masses" by producing a series of plays and poems, as well as dramatized stories and legends. Louis was also part of a popular television program, "What's My Line?"

Soon he embarked on a freshly exciting private "career" with a new companion, Bryna Ivins, an editor of the teenager's Bible, *Seventeen*. After their Mexican honeymoon, while looking about for a country retreat, they discovered a handsome ancient house nestled between two giant maples close to the smallest pond in Connecticut, which they christened "Lake Inferior." My wife and I had a cottage thirty miles south; exchanging visits was easy and pleasant. The four of us were enjoying a warm relationship which would last for years even after we moved from the New York world.

The bond of trust and affection between Louis and Frost seemed as secure as ever despite the rift that the war had caused. Soon after Pearl Harbor, when Louis had joined the Office of War Information, he asked Frost to write a statement opposing fascism, or at least to add his name to a public appeal. Twenty years later Louis explained: "I should have remembered how much Robert had prided himself on being a 'separatist'. . . . I should have respected his private isolationism. . . . He wrote me a sad, intimate, rueful . . . letter-poem:

> I'd rather there had been no war at all
> Than have you cross with me because of it. . . .
> The army wouldn't have me at the front,
> And hero at the rear I will not be . . .
> I couldn't bring myself Tyrtaeus-like
> To sing and cheer the young men into dangers
> I can't get hurt in. . . .

But during the 1950s, Louis, while trying hard to be understanding, would sometimes sneer, "For all he cares, Europe can sink in the ocean." Frost was not alone in his fear that postwar Europe might drag us into its endless troubles. Yet a "One World" approach to the problems of all earth's nations was the only means, I believed, for achieving a bloodless solution—as a highly political person, Frost couldn't possibly justify his isolationist's stand in the wake of the world's most hideous war. "Why don't you telephone Holt," Louis suggested. "Ask Al Edwards [Holt's vice-president] to call you the next time Robert's in town. I know that he wants to see you."

What if he started to question me about Yalta? What I should really like to ask, I couldn't: how Frost had weathered the years since Elinor died. Louis' reluctance to elaborate kept me from pressing the subject, yet in time he told me all I might hope for—and more.

By June Frost had cut his ties with Amherst, resigned from the college, sold his fine Victorian house. Living for weeks in his son Carol's household convinced him that he had to strike out alone. He planned to stay at The Gulley. Late in July, Kathleen Morrison, whose husband directed the Bread Loaf summer Writers' Conference, drove to Vermont to leave a message for Frost: an invitation to teach through the last two weeks of August and to spend some time as the Morrisons' guest. At the specified day, Carol drove him to Bread Loaf to be greeted there by intimate friends, among them Louis, with whom he would share a cottage. On the evening that followed, Frost delivered one of the finest public talks he had ever given. It was also one of the darkest. For the next ten days his behavior troubled the people about him—his unpredictable moods, brilliant monologues, sudden departures from friends, long solitary walks to the mountains, not to mention his fierce declamations about his lifelong selfishness, his "badness." For the very first time this man whose tipple had always been ginger ale would accept whatever was offered—and quite on his own, down a tumbler of whiskey. This had occurred—according to one report—moments after MacLeish had delivered a lecture-poetry reading in the midst of which Frost's behavior stunned and embarrassed the audience. Luckily the evening closed with a friendly exchange between the poets. And early next day Frost, worried by his daughter Irma's recent behavior, drove to Concord Corners to visit her. Her hurtful conduct angered him so acutely that he left in the morning for Bread Loaf.

The Conference had ended, Louis explained, but the Morrisons stayed till classes began at Harvard. Kay Morrison had already arranged to be Robert's secretary-manager on a permanent basis. She quit her part-time publishing job, moved him into a Boston apartment, and planned a lengthy trip of poetry readings. Robert had been at Louis' farm in the Adirondacks. Two weeks later he wrote that he wanted to visit again. Louis quoted the letter from memory: " 'I've been crazy for the last six months. I haven't known what I was doing. I wonder if you have noticed and could tell me. That's what I'm coming over to find out.' By December the worst part of his long period of blackness was over. By then he'd delivered fifteen readings—and 'with perfect calm,' he wrote to Lesley. 'I shall never be the scared fool again that I used to be.' This from the man who had filled up his shoes with pebbles to lessen his terror in front of an audience."

Oddly enough, Louis and I rarely discussed a poem by Frost. It might have seemed as though our concern with the person meant more to us than his work. Untrue, of course. Yet the fullhearted, mostly accepting way in which he would talk of the poet struck me as past believing, for no one was more aware of the foibles, the failings, the real and imagined "badness" of Frost. No one was more dismayed by his separatist politics, despite the fact that their difference in viewing the world had long been assumed, each granting the other complete freedom to cling to his views.

For the next few years—after the blackness had ended—Frost lived in the Boston apartment with his new friend, Gillie, a Border collie from Martha's Vineyard. He was not very far from Harvard, which had made him the Ralph Waldo Emerson Professor of Poetry. He summered in Vermont on the "Homer Noble" farm he had recently purchased, 150 rolling acres in Ripton, with the Green Mountain National Forest bounding most of the land. Ted and Kay Morrison lived below in the farmhouse, Frost in the three-room cabin above, 200 yards to the north. In 1941 he moved to a two-story house at 35 Brewster Street in Cambridge, and in January he supervised the construction of a third, on the five acres he owned in South Miami: "Pencil Pines." Then he made still another change in his teaching career: this time (1943) to Dartmouth, which he would leave six years later for a life appointment at Amherst. The clutter of facts fled from my mind, but not my overall sense of the man: Working with luck and care, he had done his best with the one part of his life he could still control.

What of the other, the reachless parts where the griefs arise? As Louis made most painfully evident, Frost was able to do no more for his son Carol than he did in earlier years for his sister Jeanie. In their different ways, both, plagued by hallucinations and feelings of persecution, turned on the world. Jeanie, beyond all help, long ago had been placed in a state institution; but Carol seemed to be in control of himself despite his unwarranted fears for his wife, Lillian. In response to a plea she sent from her hospital bed in October 1940, Frost rushed to his son and grandson Prescott, now sixteen, at their home in the Stone Cottage. Carol promised his wife that, for all his talk, he would never give in to suicide. Frost, far from relieved, spent the whole of a desperate night trying to reason him out of his feelings of failure, rejection, hopelessness. Three days later Prescott telephoned: Carol had ended his life. . . . Two years before, death had taken Elinor; six years before, Marjorie. What might become of Irma, now in her thirty-eighth year? They had often argued so angrily—of her jealous marital clashes, physical ailments, bitter behavior, her fearsome condition of mind—that by now only to think of her was a grief. For the moment, Carol's death was enough to endure.

I wondered if talking with Van Dore could comfort Frost. Louis knew that Carol and Wade had been friends. They had talked and worked together all through the months when Wade was at work on The Gulley. Carol was growing and selling flowers, also running his farm. "Carol, they're sure, is a problem," Wade had said of the parents on the night I spent in Vermont. The words came to my mind. Neither Louis nor I was aware that Wade had bicycled 140 miles in a day, from Montreal to Sugar Bush, New Hampshire, "to be with Frost for a little while" in August of the year of Elinor's death. "All three days I was there, no one came near us," he recalled years later. "We talked and talked. I had to tell him all I knew about hosteling— my job at the time; and he in turn told me about James Stephens. He sent me back with a copy of The Crock of Gold. People talked of his mental stress after Elinor's death. I couldn't see any sign of it, but it may have been there."

In December 1942, Frost sent him a letter from Cambridge:

Perhaps if you knew exactly where I was, you would write and tell me where you are and then I might venture to send you for Christmas or somewhere near it a copy of my latest book. I trust you are happy in your life of a poet. It is some time since you came a-bicycling to see me. You must come again with your news. There is always more to the life of a poet than writing and publishing poetry. You have learned the serenity of that wisdom.

Months later the postman delivered an invitation from Ripton. "I've got an idea," it began. "Why couldn't you come up and help with our haying?" After explaining the "farm situation," the letter concluded: "We can arrange something for a few weeks' work probably and if we can't at least we can talk. I want to see you./ Affectionately/ R.F."

Wade arrived as soon as he could. Farming with Frost, he thought, might be accepted as war work, from haying and moving chicken coops to vegetable gardening and anything else that had to be done to keep up the farm:

Lunch and dinner were taken with Frost, Ted, and Kay at their house. During the day Frost and I worked or walked five or six

75

hours, and except when company came or he had to go out, Frost spent every long evening with me. Five nights a week we talked till 1 A.M. before going out to walk the dirt road and look up at the stars. He was almost constantly accompanied by his dog Gillie. They came close to closing the man–animal gap in communication. In fact, somebody said that Frost could talk "dog." . . .

On one of our outings with Ted and Kay, we drove as far up the side of Mt. Mansfield as we could, then walked the path to the summit. On adventures of this sort, Frost was really more of an observer than a walker, making minute observations of plants. Ferns especially stopped him. Their being related to prehistoric times and the formation of coal must have had something to do with it. I often thought of him as the "fern man" when we walked in the woods together.

A telegram which announced the death of his father arrived too late for Wade to attend the funeral. "Unfortunately," to quote from his letter:

the news arrived at the time when Frost began to suggest, and with profound delicacy urge, that I stay permanently as his helper and companion. The word "partner" (which he had used before) was breathed or sighed in my direction. I had neither the heart nor courage to ask him to clear his proposition of innuendoes and flatly put it before me. But the whole truth was that all would have been well, if I hadn't renewed my association with Erma, with whom I had been in love some years before. I was now as a house divided. Feeling honored and deeply touched by Frost's esteem and trust, I didn't feel I should say "yes" while afflicted with a mood of unrest. The best I could do was to say I would seriously consider the matter during the consoling visit I was going to make to my mother. Frost seemed to take it for granted that I would accept his proposal and return. . . .

He could not make the decision. He allowed matters to drift, torn as he was between his bond to Frost and desires that goaded him on toward complete freedom. He knew the depth of the poet's need never to be alone; that he often "escaped" to his presence, where he seemed fully at ease. But what, if unwittingly, he might fail Frost? Not long after visiting with his mother, he found himself at work in a local saw-mill, making window frames for war-time houses. Then a letter came from Ripton. Weeks before, he had mailed a poem to a magazine which, belatedly, sent him a check in payment. Frost wrote on the statement enclosed with the check:

> I opened this by mistake and was so glad it wasn't a bill I almost overlooked the fact that it was made out to you and kept it. Oh come on back farming and writing poetry.

The "latest book" mentioned by Frost in his note to Wade was the exceptionally well-received *A Witness Tree*. Mary Colum wrote in *The New York Times* that although many poems in his earlier books are as fine as those in the new volume, "few of them bear so strong an impress of the poet." To be sure, the opening lines could invite readers to regard the poems for whatever bearing they had on the life of the poet. I read *A Witness Tree* as I always read, from page one on, taking each of the poems as a work in itself. Later readings—over the weeks, over the years—might imply biographical tracings which, however much they could "fascinate," obtruded to some degree on the poem *qua* poem. All Frost's books had been marked by meaningful struc-ture, and although I had lacked the words to explain the especial sense of *A Witness Tree*, it was unmistakably present. And yet, what remained for me were a number of poems that might have appeared before, memorable in themselves, not in any way altered by those that preceded or followed—"The Most of It," "The Subverted Flower," "The Secret Sits," to name but three, and integral fragments in "I Could Give All to Time," "The Silken Tent," "All Revelation."

With *A Masque of Reason*, three years later, Frost confronted "ac-ceptance" through lines that critics found, for the most part, difficult or impossible to mean as the author meant them. The same held true of the complementary *Masque of Mercy* that followed (1947). Before I had read far into the first, I recalled John Keble's statement that if poetry "reveals the fervent emotions of the mind" it can do so "only under certain veils and disguises." The Anglican clergyman-Oxford professor-author-anthologist of *The Christian Year* (1827) had not been speaking of puns, parodies, barbed allusions, ironies, or the cun-ning at work in these dark-and-light-hearted masques, yet what could have served Frost so well to veil the ever-brooding concern with justice-and-mercy that would stay with him till his death.

I had read Frost's *Steeple Bush* early in April and, six months later Louis' carefully worded praise in the *Yale Review*. True, the new book's range was impressive—songs, soliloquies, seemingly whimsical lyrics, seemingly bitter conclusions. I could have skipped all but a handful of striking passages, one brief lyric ("The Middleness of the Road"), and the instantly hailed "Directive." Inevitably my first responses differed from what they are now after forty years of critics' "explainings." One of the earliest, Reuben Brower's, confirmed what I felt at the time as a "turning point in the poem and in Frost's poetry" because of "a number of things that happen in language and in feeling" after the halfway mark (lines 36ff.).

What would Louis reply if I asked his view of "Directive"? I decided not to inquire. By now I realized, with regret, how widely our tastes differed. At first I felt that his private views diverged from those in his many successive anthologies which displayed shifts in judgment that I *hoped* arose from his publisher's "urge" to provide teachers with poems they were "sure would work" with their students. And yet, Louis' enormous zest for change, his eagerness to welcome the new, his remarkable breadth of sympathy—all could have played some part. Nowadays he would often speak of himself—sadly, I thought— as a popularizer of poetry, at the very time he hoped that his modest forthcoming book, winnowed from hundreds of poems, would earn the acclaim he believed they deserved.

Our differences in responding to verse grew ever more unpredictable. We seemed to agree as much as we disagreed; nonetheless, the gap between our interpretations of "difficult" lines or phrases in works we admired was seldom unbridgeable. There were poems and parts of poems by Frost I had never quite grasped, and Louis, I guessed, had answers. I questioned him rarely, fearing his closeness to Frost would result in the kind of remarks that were currently damned as "biographical fallacies." Louis would *have* to read Frost's work in the light of his knowledge of Frost-the-person, and he surely had clues to the "difficult" private meanings that few other people possessed. How reconcile, if possible, our divergencies? How make of our close, ever warmer friendship all that we wished it to be?

One day at lunch he asked, "What's happened to all those promised productions of *The Bridge?*"

"Nothing so far," I said, "and probably never. A Negro as a *serious* quasi-hero doesn't appeal to playgoers, so the directors say. But of all the unexpected things, the one firm promise I had came from a Southern college. It's still pending."

"White, no doubt," he mocked. I nodded. "Don't, please," Louis said. "I'm serious. With all the reviews, nothing?" Again I shook my head. "I don't suppose you've heard from Robert."

"Not directly."

"What's that supposed to mean?"

"At the Christmas Modern Language meetings someone I knew, and you know him too from Bread Loaf—Walter Havighurst—walked toward our book display. His smiling expression surprised me. I must have peered at him quizzically, for he said at once, 'Surely I told you before—what Frost told me about your book?' 'Frost? He read it?'

"He was carrying it in his hand when I met him. He stopped, waved it high in the air; saying, 'Now here's a book with a real idea in it—a real idea.' " After catching my breath, I began to wonder if he'd said anything more?

"More?" Louis scowled. "That's the best review you could hope for. Robert knew it would reach you. Don't tell me you think that Havighurst was the only person he stopped to talk of a book he was *carrying* around!" He looked at me with annoyance. It seemed to be bitter, and left me staring. After a minute or two he quipped, "What else is new? . . . Now, seriously, you must be working on *something*." I managed a hasty sketch of an eight-part poem that would interweave parts of my steel-mill book with my "personal" verse of the last twelve years—to be ready, I said, in September.

I had spoken too soon. Months passed before it was finished enough to show to him and four other men who were just as likely to say what they thought: MacLeish, Horace Gregory, Mark Van Doren, and Hiram Haydn, who failed to persuade *The American Scholar* to print it in full. The response gave me the courage to do what I shouldn't have otherwise dared: dedicate the work to Frost. In May I mailed it to Ripton, with a letter saying I hoped he might grant permission in spite of the differences in our point of view. I probably added: "Some of your public statements that I've read since our last talk make me think that you put more trust in the strength of singleness than I'm able to do, which isn't to say that my trust is small or that you might not be quite ready to grant its limits." I had no way of knowing whether the package had reached him. I waited through June before giving up. Six weeks later his answer arrived:

Dear Stanley Burnshaw:

May June July and half of August. What must you have decided to sentence me to for neglecting your letter all that time. I wince to think. And it isn't as if it were just any ordinary letter of the kind I let pile up against me without qualms. No I would never have left yours unanswered if I had known I had it. But it got among a lot of things raked together from my two homes when I was in transition between them in the spring, and I've just now found it. I might never have. I'm that bad. I'm not defending myself. Neither am I boasting of my badness. I'm sorry. That's all.

Of course I should be proud to have a poem like that dedicated to me—if you haven't already given me up and dedicated it to some one else more deserving. At any rate, I am deeply moved that you should have thought of me. Moved, but amused that you should think you knew the final idea in my writing well enough to tell how it differs from the final idea in your own. You arent as young as when I first knew you, but you are still young.

Sincerely yours
Robert Frost

August 15, 1951

I lost no time in sending a copy to Louis, who lost no time in reminding me that "the tribute is all the greater since Robert is one of the world's worst correspondents."

Frost's last sentences led me to ponder both his letter and mine. He had never rebuked the "fellow feeling" lines at the close of his *Masque of Mercy*. Nor would I argue against his belief that "the best people rise out of their separateness." Neither point was at issue; nor the individual's freedom, though it might have to step aside at times—as in war—but then return after the threat had ended. The "answer" seemed to hover over the strength-of-singleness question—but how measure such strength? Its powerlessness against enemy force was irrelevant. What, in fact, did "strength of singleness" signify? Separateness, if drawn to extremes, meant aloneness; and Wade Van Dore, who had spent more hours than anyone else in close living with Frost, understood as no one else "his need to be never alone." Was the "final idea" in his writing kept from intrusive eyes in his revelational concealments? Did a "final idea" exist?

★   ★   ★

"I was lunching with Robert yesterday," said Louis, shaking his head. "Three teenage girls walked to our table, each with a notebook. 'Aren't you Mr. Untermeyer?' one of them asked. I nodded. 'We knew it was you. We watch you on Sundays on *What's My Line?* Please, will you give us your autograph?' I said 'Of course, but I'm sure you'd prefer my guest's. He's one of our country's most important writers.'—'Who is he?' she asked. 'Robert Frost, the poet.' 'Oh,' she replied, 'thanks, but we only collect celebrities.' "

I needed a moment before I could ask, "Did Frost say anything?"

"Nothing except, 'They're pretty girls, aren't they.' "

I had never looked at the program. "TV at its best," I was told and, as one of my friends said with a smile, "custom-made for Louis' verbal agility." People stopped him to ask if the show was rehearsed or "real, like it happened." Because of its high popularity rating, it was now commercially sponsored. He was now a "name"—not only to readers of poetry, books, and reviews. Things went riding on splendidly—then all at once letters were flooding the station: Untermeyer was a "pinko," "a stooge," "politically dangerous," "a Communist Party dupe". . . . The era of Senator Joseph McCarthy was reaching its height. Rightwing extremists "smeared" whomever they fancied as a "Red," a traitor, a fellow-traveler, and so on. Louis had made the mistake of attending a Conference for World Peace at the Hotel Waldorf-Astoria in the company of Albert Einstein, Thomas Mann, Charles Chaplin, Mark Van Doren, as well as various self-professing liberals. The producers of *What's My Line?* planned to wait for the storm to die; instead it became more menacing. Rightwing American Legionnaires, urged to write to the sponsor, peppered their accusations with patent lies. When the nervous producers proposed some ways for "clearing" his name, Louis resigned.

His plight was not unique. Countless careers were being destroyed by the witch hunt, working hand-in-hand with the House Committee on Un-American Activities and even the Attorney General. Victims were profoundly shaken, more than they knew, and traumatized in ways they could hardly suspect. In Louis' case, the experience threatened his deepest friendship. Throughout World War Two, the coolness between Frost and Untermeyer troubled them both till they found a *modus vivendi* (72). But their problems were now more acute. In December 1952, Frost decided to withhold his new Christmas

poem: "Does No One But Me at All Ever Feel This Way in the Least."
He waited until July 4th, then excused the delay with a note enclosed
with the folder: "This Christmas poem, though not isolationist, is so
dangerously near isolationist, it was thought better to send it out for
Independence Day instead of Christmas.—R.F./July Fourth/ 53." After some words of thanks and qualified praise, Louis' reply spoke his
mind:

> You ask: "Who are you to bring me to trial?" Who am I, indeed,
> who have not yet been brought to trial myself for once associat-
> ing with Jack Reed, now buried in the Kremlin, and Max
> Eastman, now buried in the Readers Digest. Of course that was
> almost forty years ago, but the smearing committees are practi-
> cally delving into prenatal associations. My friendly support of
> Wallace has been turned into charges of Communism; my
> lectures have been canceled; my books have been attacked,
> banned, and withdrawn. I'm lucky that I still have a garden to
> cultivate. I'm also lucky that I am allowed to keep on writing,
> especially since I am at work on the biggest book I've ever
> attempted: an account . . . of this century's hundred men and
> women who have influenced our thinking, affected our values
> and, in one way or another have changed the pattern of our cul-
> ture. Need I say that you will be one shining example?

Louis said nothing of Frost's reply—if he replied. Three months later,
however, his account of his recent hour with the poet said so much of
the "changed" Frost that the instant he left, I hammered a note to myself, while his words still rang in my ears:

> Just lunch with Louis, baring his soul about Frost, who "has
> come to close out the whole world and want to talk about noth-
> ing but himself."

> Some months ago Frost sent out a poem "Isolationist" to which
> Louis wrote a personal letter—"the first in which" Louis "ever
> said anything in disagreement with Frost." Said Louis: "I can see
> why you wish to take this position, but as for myself, I have al-
> ready been 'judged' — by the current McCarthyite campaign and
> hysteria,"etc. This was said "because Frost" had "written on the
> copy" to Louis, "But who are you to judge" or maybe "bring me
> to trial?" Louis' "long letter to Frost was never replied to."

At lunch with Frost on Monday this week, Louis greeted with "Shall we talk with him about it now?"—an "aside between Frost and Kay Morrison." Louis expected it to be about the matter of his letter, but it was instead "Frost's new idea about NORTH OF BOSTON, reissuing it with some new poems, so that people will think of Frost and North of Boston as they think of Thoreau and Walden."

General feelings of Louis: what is this, being a today to Frost? No. "Frost for the past ten years has become increasingly narrowed in interest. Will listen only to people who praise him or talk about his work. Has removed himself from the world. Tells Europe to go to hell. Screams with irony about 'Provide, Provide,' " etc. "Violent resentment that Louis wrote an article 3 yrs ago praising Auden." "Can't abide praise of other poets" etc.

Louis' worry: how to write the piece on Frost for the book he's doing for S&S. "Can't be honest." If he writes "one negative line, will never hear end of it."

Frost's "fantasy for Kay Morrison"—"go to South Sea Islands." "Is it a fact or real" "What happened to the Puritan?"

Looks as though a great friendship—Louis and Robert—is at its end because "of the end of Frost as a person."

Do I want to see Frost when he comes to New York?

Five months later, March 1954, after attending the eightieth birthday dinner for Frost, arranged at Amherst by colleagues and fellow-poets, Louis set down these words:

It has taken a long time for Robert to show his years, but now he begins to show them. It is not that he looks so old as that he seems weary with age or, perhaps, the age. The scar left by his operation [for a skin cancer] makes his cheek hollow; his walk is slow. But his talk—an occasionally interrupted monologue rather than a conversation—is lively and as peppery as ever. He liked my "remarks" at the dinner, which contrasted with the more formal tributes by Archibald MacLeish, Thornton Wilder, and President Cole of Amherst—George Whicher had died three weeks before the anniversary, and his speech (his last piece of writing)

83

was read by Curtis Canfield. "You know me better than anyone," he said when we were alone. "Al Edwards is still hoping
that you'll write my biography, and so do I. Most of the others
are writing theirs by wheedling little pieces out of other people."

We talked about how many of our fellow-poets—Robinson,
Masters, Lindsay, Fletcher, Amy Lowell, Sara Teasdale, Edna
Millay, Elinor Wylie, both Benéts—had failed to survive. "I
suppose there's something to the superstition that the good die
young—here we still are, me wicked at eighty and you unregen-
erate at almost seventy. I'm glad it isn't just the good poets who
die young! As I said at the dinner, poets die in different ways.
Most of them do not die into the grave but into business—which
you almost did—or into philosophy, one of the noblest ways to
die. It's the fear of being impractical that turns many people
against poetry, and sometimes turns the poet against himself. Often what begins more ethereal than substantial ends by being
more substantial than ethereal. . ."

The difference between the two portrayals of Frost—in November
1953 and in March 1954—needs no comment beyond the one implied
in Louis' own memoir: balance regained had come out of "curing"
himself by "a writer's therapy: his writing." At his wife's suggestion,
he was planning a book on the *Makers of the Modern World* while also
preparing his own *Lives of the Poets* and a new edition of *Modern American and Modern British Poetry* "in consultation with Karl Shapiro and
Richard Wilbur." But the task that excited him most was the invitation from Harvard to serve in 1955 as its Phi Beta Kappa poet.

After noting how well, through my six-week absence in Europe, the
Dryden Press had been getting along without me, I hit on a plan.
From October on: mornings at home, in my office the rest of the day.
Mark Van Doren warned me against expecting a miracle—"Smoke a
cigarette, read the papers, pick up a book—wait! and *don't be impatient!*" Sooner than I'd expected, pages were filling with words. Except for sporadic telephone calls, the morning hours were mine. To be
sure, the regular Christmas manuscript meetings and the spring
publications planning would suspend my program, but if all went
well, by the middle of March mornings again would be mine. Un-

foreseeable problems forced me back into *status quo ante* till June. How dependable, I asked, was this morning-free plan that promised so much? Ever more frequent telephone calls, printers' emergencies, out-of-town visitors—these and dozens of other intrusions ended my hopes. By March 1957, I was back to the nine-hour daily regime I had followed for twenty years.

The publishing world was becoming steadily and brashly more competitive, and with worse in view; bigness seemed a logical goal as the size of the book-buying public mirrored the baby boom. For a firm like Dryden, to survive meant choosing one of two courses: swallow up three, even four much smaller publishers, or invite oneself to be swallowed. The fact that the first would have to entail enlarged administrative burdens led me to favor the second. A cordial lunch with Alfred Knopf, at his invitation, ended with fruitless pleasantries, each of us having at heart the identical wish: "full" personal freedom.

The best prospect arose from a casual talk with the president of a booming competitor. For more than a year, he said, he'd been thinking of plans for our "working together." Was I ready to "talk figures"? We met with my auditor present. Meetings followed more meetings, then a joint commitment to try to arrive at a figure "fair to us both." But change would be out of the question until after the last of Dryden's new spring books had been published.

At this time, one of the principals of a large old publishing firm I had never considered—Holt—heard of my interest in selling. Knowing that he was Frost's publisher, I agreed to meet with him. After our self-introductions, I asked, "What makes a banker become a publisher, and of all things, poetry books?"

"What made a poet enter the book *business?*"

"Chance, I suppose, though I couldn't go on with the job I had. But tell me, which of the Holt editors works with Frost?" We were on our way—miles from the business matters he had come to discuss, and whenever he paused, I threw in another Frost question, which he seemed delighted to dwell on. Finally, he smiled. "We could talk all night about Robert, and we will—soon, I hope. But I'm making my train—New Canaan." He was suddenly brisk. Nothing any other firm could offer could come even close to what he would do. Second, he knew I'd find the place to my liking. I'd be "welcomed with open arms by all of us, Robert included." And the president, Rigg, knew all about my books. He added more of the same; then cut himself short.

"We must all meet together quickly—you, your auditor, myself—tomorrow. I'll study the figures at home on the weekend."

Meetings—once more—followed by meetings, in a building opposite Holt, at the office of one of its journals, *Field & Stream*. Within ten days we had settled on terms and called in lawyers. Then the president Edgar T. Rigg entered the scene. I insisted on waiting till the end of May. He insisted on knowing why. I explained. He agreed. And on June 4, 1958, the papers were signed.

III

THE LATER YEARS AND
"THE HOLTS"

It took the whole of June and July to make the transition. There were many nettlesome minor troubles to cope with besides the endless hours involved in reassigning manuscript projects and in writing letters to authors. Two weeks after my work began, Frost, in a telephone call from Vermont, "ordered" Edwards to give me his "special greetings, which he hoped to be able to do in person soon." Soon, I learned, meant autumn: at least a month after the start of my class for would-be publishers at the Graduate Institute of New York University.

By the end of July, I had finished the lengthy report that Rigg had asked me to write for his eyes only. "I want you to put down everything—the good *and* the bad—whatever we're doing that's foolish, wrong, wasteful. Spare nobody—myself included." Taking him at his word, I made no attempt to balance the good with the bad. I let myself go, never suspecting that some of my sharpest remarks were aimed at policy problems created by Rigg himself.

On the morning of my return, I was ushered into his office. "That's some report!—It's great," he began, followed by more of the same, then a series of pointed requests for specific details I'd omitted. "And now," he took a deep breath as he closed my folder, "where do we go from here? I'll give you the answer. If you're ready, starting now you've a brand-new job: my special private advisor on everything that we publish—Trade, college, juveniles, grade-school texts, *Field & Stream*—"

"Everything? But you realize I've never had anything whatever to do with children's books, grade-school texts, or the—"

"Trust me! I know what I'm doing."

"I'll be glad to try, if you keep my limitations in mind. Also . . . no managerial duties for me, and I must have time for writing."

"That's it, then? Good. *You'll* work out the time. Just remember"—he smiled—"the cleaning people come into the office at six and turn out the lights at nine. And now, let's start!" He raised some questions as he scanned each page of *The New York Times Book Review*, then set it aside. "What should we do with our General Books—Trade—department?" I shook my head. "You'd rather not say? But I *want* to hear what you think."

"Since you insist, here goes." I was taking the first steps on the path I would follow throughout my years at Holt—with Edwards also, since I promised to do whatever he thought desirable on the various visits "his poet" made to New York. I had already set aside November 12th—Frost's evening date at the New School for Social Research—and the day after. By then he would have completed his first assignment as Consultant in Poetry at the Library of Congress.

The New York Times printed a brief account of his talk with the press of October 15th, the day of his first Library speech, to an audience of high-school seniors. The week before he had traveled by train to Washington with Untermeyer, who had work of his own at the Library of Congress to arrange: the donation of the whole of his "Frost collection"—personal letters, first editions, related items. I learned of the trip some weeks later from Louis himself. Our talks at lunch for years, part of our weekly regime—were now special occasions: He was spending most of his days at home in the country, writing.

He had never seemed more ebullient as he spoke of the two full days alone with his friend. At the same time, he had never seemed so tolerant, so objective. Frost was "receiving so many honors, he couldn't count them." The spring before, he had spent a month as the State Department's "good will representative to the British Isles," from where he returned with more degrees and honors—Oxford and Cambridge and Ireland's National University. "I suppose you heard about Eliot's toast at the Books Across the Sea dinner for Robert?" I waited for Louis to tell me. " 'Mr. Frost is one of the good poets, and I might say, perhaps, *the* most eminent, the most distinguished, I must call it, Anglo-American poet.' "

I couldn't abstain from quoting what Eliot wrote in 1922 in *The*

Dial's London Letter: " 'Mr. Frost seems the nearest equivalent to an English poet, specializing in New England torpor; his verse, it is regretfully said, is uninteresting, and what is uninteresting is unreadable, and what is unreadable is not read. There, that is done.' "

"By the way," Louis broke into my thought, "have you met Larry Thompson, Robert's official biographer?" I shook my head.

"Officially official." Louis frowned. "While Robert blesses Elizabeth Sergeant's biography-in-the-making. Better not mention her book when you talk with Thompson or his strange *Times* review of *The Masque of Reason.*"

Back at my desk, I started to type some notes of what Louis had said about Frost: "Impossible to guess no. of colleges, highschs, preps, forums, instit., clubs, etc. 'Barding around'—can't get enough of it. . . . Divides readers—must mean hearers—into four groups, prob. based on remarks they make, questions, etc., at end of his talks: 25% like him and 25% hate him for the WRONG reasons; 25% hate him for the RIGHT reasons; is worried about the 'last 25%.' Didn't explain. Could he mean that—" I stopped, looked around. Rigg was watching me quietly. "Can we talk for a minute? Keep right on, but as soon as you finish—"

November 12th, about 11:00 A.M. Office of Alfred C. Edwards: "Robert just called. He's taking the train around noon. Joe Blumenthal will pick him up at the Westbury Hotel and deliver him on time for the reading. I'll meet you in the New School lobby with tickets, and I'll introduce you to Kay—Kay Morrison—then I'll leave. Robert knows why I won't be able to stay tonight. Now, you won't see Robert till after the meeting—at Joe's apartment—433 West 21st. Robert's planning to see you tomorrow at one. Call him from the Westbury lobby. The people from Sarah Lawrence will be there with a car at five, so keep your eye on the time. Any questions?"

A few: Would Thompson be there? Almost certainly no. Where would Frost have dinner? At the Blumenthals: always the same wherever he is—two raw egg yolks. And then? Always the same schedule: He remains alone for an hour, maybe longer; comes out about seven, then taxis with Joe and Ann to the lecture hall. On the way, no conversation, though he might ask Joe if he had in mind a particular poem he wanted to hear. After the reading, Joe taxis him back for his supper: sandwiches, salad, cold cuts. Then special guests, fellow poets, and

friends arrive. After a while, Robert appears. But how long the evening lasts no one can know. It depends on Robert. . . .

By cutting short my Institute class, I was able to reach the New
School lobby in time. Edwards hurriedly introduced me to Kay, apologized, and fled. Feeling neither at ease nor ill at ease, after a moment
or two, she drew herself up and announced that alas she would have to
go off—her friends in the hall were waiting. But, oh we two had so
many things to discuss! We should make a date for a talk soon—before
Florida. Mid-December? She would check her Cambridge calendar
and telephone.

Like everyone else in the hall, I expected that Frost "any second
now" would come striding down toward the podium. We were
wrong. But by failing to start on schedule, he provided me time
enough to try to order my thoughts of my new acquaintance. I had
heard almost nothing about her beyond a few parenthetical facts that
Edwards and Louis had mentioned in passing. The first: 1918—Frost
had given a reading and talk to a group of Bryn Mawr poetry students
to which she belonged. The second: 1936—on five of the six evenings
after his Harvard "Norton" lectures, she and Ted had invited Frost and
a circle of friends to their Cambridge home (for the last of the series,
Elinor held an evening event of her own). The third: 1938, six months
after Elinor's death—Frost, "in need of someone to pull his life together, pleaded with her" (Kay's words) to become his managing secretary. She consented, gave up her part-time publishing job, and went
to work for the poet. Now a woman of sixty, she was strikingly quick
in speech, clear-eyed, determined, yet, at moments, signs of an un-
dercurrent of strain broke through her prudent composure. Was it
fear? Was she striving to come to terms with the recent death of her
son?

Frost's arrival, signaled by loud applause, interrupted my reverie.
The face gleaming beneath its veil of age looked, from my distant seat,
much the same as the one I had seen up close decades before. He
moved his head and gestured more slowly, but his talk, as Louis had
said, was "as lively as ever and peppered" with anecdotes, comments,
cryptic stories, playful remarks. He seemed to take greater delight
in his prose obbligato than the poems. Most of them he read at too
fast a tempo to allow the words to spread out and ignite one another
in the listener's mind. But—how many hundreds of times had he
"said" the lines of "Reluctance," "Design," "After Apple-Picking,"
"Mowing"?

I knew from Edwards' account of the after-lecture routine that I need not hurry to the Blumenthals on West 21st Street. Once inside, I was introduced to the earlier guests, one of whom, I saw with surprise, was Marianne Moore. Our relationship went back to 1928, when as editor of *The Dial,* she had *telegraphed* her acceptance of a poem I had offered. Recently, from an intimate letter written soon after my last book of verse appeared, I learned that her passions included not only poetry-writing and baseball but also printing, book design, and typography. We were speaking about our respective troubles in French translation—hers with La Fontaine, mine with the modernist poets—when we both saw Frost quietly enter the room. "It's twenty-four years since we talked," I remarked half to myself. She looked up, waiting for more. "He motioned to me from the New School aisle—stopped on his way to the podium. I'll tell you his words some time. I could hardly believe them."

When at last I walked to where he was standing, he took my hand and enclosed it with his own. "Isn't it fine, our coming together after all those years! Let's see—how long is it since we first became friends? Was it 1924 when you were in Pittsburgh?" I was too startled to speak as he went on naming my college, the steel mill where I worked, my August visit "when Wade was putting The Gulley into condition." After some minutes, he pointed his finger at me. "Al says that you're careful to come on time. So am I. Tomorrow, then, we'll have our first long talk again, just you and I." He glanced at the guests scattered around the room. "Oh, Marianne, down there! I must talk with her. Now remember, the Westbury Hotel. We won't have time for a talk tonight with all these friends of mine waiting, but we will tomorrow."

He preferred to stand and move from person to person, group to group, asking questions but doing most of the speaking himself while appearing to analyze his listeners' faces. Of the score of people, Blumenthal was the only one I had met a number of times before, and then rather formally, as a fellow-director of the American Institute of Graphic Arts. I was eager to hear the tale of his friendship with Frost, but he thought that had better wait for another time. Meanwhile, the longer we talked, the more we seemed to have "shared," including my former production man who had been an apprentice of Joe's at the Spiral Press. Our conversation stopped the instant we saw Miss Moore beginning to say goodnight to Frost. I looked at my watch— 1:40 A.M.—and approached them.

"I must go *right now*, Robert," she said, then turned to her hosts. I told Frost I also was leaving—to see her home. Leading her down the stairs, I remarked that a cab would be easy to find on 23rd Street. "Yes, of course. That's where I'll take my subway."

"At 2:00 A.M.? Not while I can prevent you. I'll hail a taxi."

We argued as we walked the two blocks north, but at last she relented: "I'd be happy to have you accompany me on the train, but oh the thought of your waiting, then riding all the way back!"

I whistled to a roving cab. "Take us to Brooklyn, please." I smiled. He shrugged, but when I added "260 Cumberland Street," he instantly shook his head.

"Not 260! You know where that is, mister? Right near the Navy Yard."

"I think Miss Moore knows where it is. Please, let's go."

He opened the door, glowering, then tested all four locks. "260 Cumberland! Whew!" repeating the number twice. When the cab reached our destination, he braked and instantly turned off the lights, waiting for me to pay. I explained, "I'll be out in a second, then take me back to Manhattan."

I opened the iron grill door. "Oh, won't you come in?" she asked. I shook my head, raising my watch to her eyes. "Oh, of course you must leave at once. But thank you for being so generous. Good night, then."

The driver, snapping the locks, switched on his lights and raced so fast that the car careened around corners. Not till we came into well-lighted streets, did he drop his speed. "You *know* that lady, mister?"

"Know her?" I laughed. "Miss Moore's not only a famous poet but the greatest woman baseball fan in the world."

"What?" he shouted. Then more quietly, "Okay, if you say so. But why if that lady's so great does she live in *that* place? Didn't she tell you two people were shot on that street last week? It was all over *The News*. I guess you didn't know or you wouldn't have—oh well, we're out of there now, thank God!" Then: "You told me Manhattan but didn't say what street, mister."

I entered the Westbury lobby minutes before the proper time, only to catch the poet eyeing the clock. Remembering from Van Dore how Frost felt about shaking hands, I swung my arm over my head to greet him. He grinned, pointed above to the clock, and, without speaking, waved to me to follow him outside to Madison Avenue.

"A good day for a walk—a long one, if you're up to it," he said slowly. At the first corner—67th Street—we moved west toward Central Park. I caught a glimpse of his profile—with the lower lip jutting forward. And the face?—mottled with age spots, and the hollow close to the right cheek, and the pursed lips . . .

From all that Louis had said of his recent visits with Frost, I expected that, instead of a two-way exchange, our "talk together" would become a steady monologue. Hence my surprise when he started out with a series of questions. What *really* had made me surrender the freedom I had in running a press of my own? Had I any regrets? Did Rigg know the *names* of the people I'd published, and the ones I wanted to take to Holt?—I tried to be brief, also to answer all that he asked. He pressed me for specificities. Who were the others I hoped to take in addition to Lionel Trilling and "the art-man John Canaday" and "maybe Saul Bellow and Delmore Schwartz"? What were the names of some of the best books I had published? Had I set aside some "extras"? Could I spare a few? I started naming: *The Negro Caravan, White Collar Crime,* Fitts's *Greek Plays,* Van Doren's anthology, the *Botany* by Carl Wilson—"The Dartmouth man?" he asked. "I know him. I'd be glad to have it." I promised to send him a copy.

"You told Al Edwards you needed more time for writing, but then you took on this extra teaching work at your Graduate Institute." Knowing by now that a terse account would never suffice, I told the whole story, based on the Pennsylvania School of Social Work plan that my wife had followed. Our students work in publishing houses from nine to one, then take technical courses from two to five, and some evening classes. All I had to prepare were five or six lectures; the rest would be given by visiting writers: Fitts, Trilling, Barzun, Gassner, Ciardi, Van Doren, Rexroth.

"Your friend Rexroth won a thousand-dollar prize at the Poetry Society in January."

"And they gave you a gold medal for coming back to the fold after seventeen years."

"How did you know that? Were you there?"

"The *Times* had the story. It had another from Washington last month, on your opening speech as the Poetry Consultant."

" 'Poet in Waiting' it ought to be called."

"But you go there only twice a year—May and October."

"Oh no. I had to be there to free Ezra." He looked at me, wondering. "Do you know how it happened?" I waited. "Archie MacLeish

93

told me in April that I *had* to go down to see the Attorney General, Rogers. I'd met him before. A month or so after our talk, Rogers spoke to the press. That made Archie *insist* on my visiting Rogers again. He was at his desk when I called. 'What's your mood?' I asked him. He knew what I meant but, just to be sure, I added 'in the case of Ezra Pound.' 'Our mood is your mood,' he answered. 'Well, then, let's get him out right away,' I said. And that's how it ended—except for the lawyers and so on. Thurman Arnold asked me to write a statement to read in the court. It took me most of the night, and then I went home. But Arnold wanted me back. 'Do I *have* to appear in court?' I asked. No, he said, he would read what I had written. And he did. Three days after my talk with Rogers, Ezra was freed."

It had been thirteen years since the time they had indicted him and locked him in St. Elizabeths. Pound must have known what Frost had done to get him released, yet I'd heard that all he said was, "He ain't been in much of a hurry."

"Ezra's still pretty crazy. Eliot thought so too when we talked last year." He paused. "People think it was Pound who discovered me. It was Frank Flint," he shouted. "Someone I'll never forget." He was now well launched on the Pound subject, shifting about in time, unfailingly thoughtful—grave, grim, at moments; at others, earnest, humorous, generous, sharply critical, troubled, relieved. . . .

"The last time I saw him was forty-three years ago. I suppose I acted out of sentiment for a good poet in trouble with himself, the world, and the law. He wrote some fine verse, rimed and free, when he was young. But those *Cantos!* I hear there's an annotated index, 300 pages. Lengthy things, those *Cantos*. Nobody ought to like them, but some do. . . . Funny, he was sometimes a good editor—for *others*. You know he cut out half of Eliot's original *Waste Land*. . . . And oh, the flashy dresser he was when I knew him—Byron collars, dressing gowns from Japan—out to impress people—with his learning too, though he's not a scholar. . . . But we have to remember Ezra's done enough poems to earn a place in the story of American literature." He sighed. "It's a funny world. . . ." Then back to "the Pound Case," to the Bollingen Prize "awarded to him while adjudged insane," that Archie tried to justify by separating loyalty to art from loyalty to society—"odd position for Archie, considering where he stood in the thirties." Frost talked on. Archie knew that Pound despised his poems; but he went to work last January with a letter to the Attorney General signed by Eliot, Hemingway, and Frost and *he made him* promise to talk to Rogers. He had misgivings but hated to see Ezra die "ignominiously in that wretched place for a crime that couldn't have kept him all these years in prison." Frost and MacLeish called together on Rogers, who told them Pound was tied to a segregationist-poet, so-called. Archie agreed to act on that and Frost agreed to work for a monthly advance for Ezra from his publisher, James Laughlin of *New Directions*. Laughlin consented. Then Archie made Frost go again to Washington. He talked with Rogers and when he got home, thanked him. Things remained at a standstill. Then Frost "had an idea." Eisenhower sent him a telegram of greetings at the Poetry Society evening. Frost asked Sherman Adams at the White House to arrange for him to thank the President in person and expressed "the hope" that Rogers would be invited. "After that White House dinner, things moved fast—by Washington standards." At Archie's urging, Frost made his fourth and last trip on behalf of Pound, who at last was released, in his wife's custody. They sailed to Europe in June. When the ship landed at Naples, Pound gave the "Fascist salute and called the United States 'an insane asylum.' " We looked at each other. But Frost hadn't quite finished. "Archie," he repeated carefully, "deserves a lot of the credit.[3] He knew that Pound hated his poems but that didn't matter. He made up his mind after seeing him there—at the hospital. That's when he started writing letters and talking around—three years ago—and he never stopped. He did all the work he could but it wasn't enough and he knew it."

"Two summers ago in France I saw an early letter from Pound to André Spire, the poet I've told you about. They were friends. Pound was also an admirer. His letter graciously asked permission to bring a friend to a party at Spire's—'a promising Irish writer,' he called him. That was where Joyce met his future publisher: at the home of a French Zionist, introduced by the antisemite-to-be."

For the first time since our walk began, Frost kept silent. I proposed

---

[3] *The New York Times*, April 18, 1958: "The person most responsible for today's announcement of the dismissal of the indictment against Pound was Robert Frost." Quite typically, Frost's official biography states that "Anyone who was aware of the behind-the-scenes efforts of Archibald MacLeish might well have said that it was he, not Frost, who was 'most responsible' for today's announcement." (Vol. III, p. 258). Compare: MacLeish's letter to Hemingway: "I think Frost gets a large part of the credit. The old boy despises Ez for personal reasons but once he got started nothing could stop him and I think Rogers finally gave up out of sheer exhaustion." (September 30, 1958, in *Letters of Archibald MacLeish*, R. H. Winnick, ed., Houghton Mifflin, 1983)

that we now turn back. He would need some time alone before people would come to drive him to Sarah Lawrence for his speaking engagement that evening.

He waved his hand. "Time enough!" We quickened our pace slightly. "Some people tell me my readings get better; others, that I go too fast. What do *you* say?"

"Last night, you mean?" He nodded. "For me, at times, a bit too fast because I like to hear the words play on each other. But half of your audiences—maybe more, I suspect—already know the poems, so they know the words. Maybe saying them quickly doesn't matter too much."

"Then it shouldn't have mattered to you but it did. . . . It's hard, you know, to hit on the timing. I'll think of it tonight when I read. Mostly women, I guess . . . And I guess you have to be leaving now." He stopped, looked at the pavement. "Which is worse—too fast or too slow?" I threw up my hands. "Both. To be continued, then, next month." He smiled. "Al will know when I'm coming. Kay will tell him."

A note reading "What about 'You Come Too?'—ACE" lay on my desk top.

"What about 'You Come Too?' " I asked, waving the note as I walked into Edwards' office.

Assuming that Frost had told me just how he pictured the book, Edwards talked of production arrangements. Joe Blumenthal would print it. He wanted to use Nason's woodcuts, but I'd better ask to see them along with his plans for design. Hyde Cox would be writing the foreword. He handed me the folder: title, ideas, and so on. "Just make sure that Robert goes over the proofs of the dedication." He pulled out the page: *To Belle Moodie Frost who knew as a teacher that no poetry was good for children that wasn't equally good for their elders.*

"Vintage Frost!" I read it again. "To his mother—in his own writing!" When would I see the foreword? Had Robert read it? What was the publishing date? And who had chosen the poems—Holt's children's book editor? Edwards looked at me, puzzled. "All I heard about *You Come Too* from Robert," I explained, "was the book's title and that Hyde Cox—'a fine young friend of mine'—is doing the preface. 'I'm leaving it all to you, Stanley,' he said. 'Make it the way you think it should be!' And that's the whole of his speech on the subject and *all that I know*."

"Why didn't you ask him to tell you more?"

"I wanted to hear him talk on whatever entered his head. And talk, he did, asking me lots of questions." I mused for an instant. "It's strange—that it seems so natural, walking side by side and listening—as I did in Vermont when Van Dore was fixing The Gulley twenty-nine years ago. Do you—feel what I'm trying to say?" Edwards nodded. "But now, please tell me all I should know before I begin. First, who is Hyde Cox and how do I reach him?"

From what I learned, Frost and Cox had met by chance in 1940— Key West. Cox, with his Harvard degree, had been traveling all over, trying out dozens of jobs but hadn't as yet found anything "right," and he planned to keep looking. Frost was forty years older, but their family backgrounds were similar and, most important, they shared two passions: painting and poetry. They talked and talked for days and nights, and a warm friendship began that became ever closer. If I wanted to get in touch with Cox, Cecile Daly, Edwards' secretary, would give me his Manchester number. He had finally found his niche, in regional history. . . . An interesting story—I was looking forward to meeting Cox—but I still hadn't learned what qualified him for writing the foreword.

Could Blumenthal say? When he came to discuss production plans for *You Come Too,* I somehow felt it improper to ask. Besides, I was eager to know how his friendship had started with Frost, who had "one time threatened himself to become a printer" (10). All I knew was that Joe had designed the special Random House issue of Frost's *Collected Poems*. What I hadn't known was that at that time he had asked Holt's permission to use Frost's "Christmas Trees" as a holiday greeting card for himself and his wife. Out of "unpardonable diffidence" (his words), he had failed to ask Frost if he cared to have any copies. Not till the spring of the following year, did he meet with the poet. "The encounter was a wholly new experience for me. I was talking with a great man and a great poet with easy confidence and completely unself-consciously. I learned in time that the sense of elation, the enlargement of the spirit, the evocation of better than one's best, the sense of having given more than one had—all this was a common experience among those who were lucky enough to have spent some time alone with Robert. You know what I'm trying to say." I knew indeed, for I realized from our recent talk—our first after more than two decades—why most of his words would be past my power of preserving; that from all that would enter my mind, I should not be able to put on paper—if ever the need should arise—more than a minor part of all he'd been saying, nor hope to describe how it *felt* to be "talking with Frost" in his final years, hour upon endless hour.

Joe and I also discussed production plans for "Away!"—the new 1958 Christmas poem. His Spiral Press had produced nineteen of this annual keepsake series, the first of which, "Two Tramps in Mud Time," appeared in 1934. By now, Frost's greeting-booklets were an envied Holt tradition, consisting, for the most part, of initial printings of new Frost poems in unusual formats. "Away!" was typical: twelve pages and a cover, vertically bound, embellished with color woodcuts.

The poem repeated "I'm—bound—away," the folksong line from *Shenandoah,* that had also appeared in *A Masque of Mercy*—which led me to think of the *Masque of Reason* and Thompson's *New York Times* review that had angered and worried Frost. Were the closing lines of "Away!" a disguised-by-make-believe warning ("And I may return/ If dissatisfied/ With what I learn/ From having died")? Not if stanza four ("There is no one I/ Am put out with/ Or put out by") could induce unwary readers to dismiss the poem as purely innocuous play. It struck me as more than strange that no one at Holt cared to talk of the poem.

Nor did Edwards or anyone else mention the incredible challenge by Frost in the interview that had just appeared in *The New York Times Magazine.* As for "the two powers [U.S.A. and U.S.S.R.] that seemed in contention for this planet (as well as in a race to the moon)," Frost "saw their opposed systems as evidencing 'two great ideas—*who's to say they're not both valid?*' " (italics added). So much for people who praised his poems but condemned his "hopelessly blindered conservatism." So much also for readers of "Into My Own" who regarded "They would not find me changed from him they knew— Only more sure of all I thought was true" as absolute proof of the poet's invulnerability to any lapse into open-minded change. And what might the Leftwing foes of *A Further Range* make of their Rightwing conservative-now-turned-liberal? So far as Holt was concerned, Frost's words might never have been uttered. Edwards merely remarked to me that either before or after the poet's Washington visit—of December 7th to 13th—he would stop in New York, and

would I kindly arrange to be with him, which meant the entire afternoon till he'd board the train to Boston. This was his last stay in New
York till March. He would want to hear all about *You Come Too* in
particular and anything else that was on my mind. . . .

"How's our firm?" Frost chuckled, ever inquisitive about the house of
which for years he had been the most privileged member. Fixing his
tie, he led me into his Westbury suite.

"Almost very much better." He turned to eye me quizzically, waiting to hear. I offered a capsule account from the day Rigg welcomed
my notion of sounding out Random House. "Holt has virtues that
Random lacks and vice versa, and things went well till your president
lost control of his tongue. So Hiram Haydn won't be joining us as
editor."

Frost kept shaking his head. "Are you still friends with Random
House—you personally?" I nodded, adding that *You Come Too* had
provided a logical reason. I'd talked by phone with Donald Klopfer
again. Might I borrow the children's editor from Random House after
hours to choose the poems for the book by Frost in-the-making.
"Delighted," he said. "You know how we feel about Frost." My call
had been luckily timed. At the end of the month Nancy Larrick was
leaving her job for a free-lance career, and no one he knew would be
able to make a better selection.

"I'd like to see the titles and the order of poems," said Frost. They
would reach him wherever he was, I promised, as soon as she made
the choice. "So Random House is involved with us after all," he
smiled. "You know, I've always wanted to have all those Modern Library books standing together on a wall to themselves. When I heard
how much it would cost, I gave up the thought."

"Do you still have space on the wall?" I asked as we went from his
rooms through the lobby onto the street.

"I'd *make* the space." He nodded. "The thought of all those books
looking down at me!" We walked northward, now at a quickened
pace. "Too bad about Rigg," he sighed.

"I guess *I* should have suspected that Rigg would never surrender
control, though at times he can be surprising. You recall his right-
about-face when I gave him the reason why Holt ought to publish
more than one poet? I expect to send you something after the first of
the year."

"Poems by some of your friends?"

"I have few friends who are poets, and the ones that are have their own publishers. I've asked Dudley Fitts to suggest some manuscripts. He's always doing reviews for the *Times* and he knows a good many poets. Besides, I trust his judgment. Don't you?"

"Should I?" I reminded him of the brilliant review of *A Further Range*. "Never saw it," he said, but he'd like to look at it now. Could I find a copy? Probably, I explained, since Fitts and I were in constant correspondence. "Constant correspondence? Why?"

"My new project: I had no time to explain when we talked last month." He gestured to me to continue. In as few words as possible, I described how the book that became *The Poem Itself* had been born. Anxious to have my eighteen-year-old daughter really know the modern French poets, I set to work on a Mallarmé sonnet only to find that no matter how faithful an English version might be, it could never succeed in bringing her even close to the poem in French. And so, abandoning verse, I gave her two pages, one with the Mallarmé text, the other a prose discussion that offered the multiple meanings of words, the allusions, and similar aids, as well as some clues to the sound of the sense. "Fitts will co-edit the Spanish-Portuguese section. My Mallarmé is the model. I'll send it as soon as it's set in type. It should reach you in Florida."

"Why mail it? Come down to see me there and bring it along. We'll read it together."

"Tempting—and I'd like to visit your Pencil Pines." I glanced at my watch. We had plenty of time, and I wanted to ask what he thought of the *Times* report. Was it faithful? Had he said of the U.S.A. and the U.S.S.R.: their "opposed systems evidence 'two great ideas—who's to say they're not both valid'?" But I never had a chance to ask my questions. Frost had embarked on a monologue that lasted until we parted.

A week or so later I found on my desk a page from the *Washington Evening Star* of December 10, 1958, with a note marked: "Please return—ACE." Except for reporter's interpolations, "The Consultant Complains at Not Being Consulted" was largely the monologue I'd heard from the poet's lips. To be sure, there were many omissions—also a disconnected account about Frost's "first call on the White House," during which he had said that since "all his educated friends think socialism is inevitable . . . why don't we join up and hurry it along. It won't last and we'll get it over with. The White

House laughed and said he didn't agree with that policy." The report-er failed to state the identity of "he" and to name the date of the call. Worse, she made no attempt to suggest to Frost that he reconcile or even relate this position with the one he set forth in the *Times Maga-zine* ten days before. I returned the paper to Edwards, writing below his initials: "Another somersault. Back to where he had been, but maybe he's being misquoted. For *who* is the White House?—By the way, I've signed with Nancy Larrick, Random's children books edi-tor, who quits her job at the end of this month. I should have her table of contents for *You Come Too* in February."

It arrived on time. I sent a copy to Frost, who sent it to Frederick Melcher, his friend at *Publishers Weekly,* who was making a list of his own. The selections proved almost identical. All that I lacked was the brief foreword by Hyde Cox, who would bring it in person on March 26th. He was due to attend the dinner that evening for Frost's eighty-fifth birthday.

Some weeks before the date, Rigg summoned me into his office, but before I sat down, he announced, "I've been thinking about our party for Frost and the man to deliver the speech. I know you agree that we have to get someone important." I nodded. "Well, I've found the answer. I've talked with my Washington people and they're sure he'd be willing to come. Want to know his name?" Rigg beamed. "Richard M. Nixon."

"Oh no! You can't *do* this to Frost. It's impossible!" I could hear myself shouting.

"What? Impossible? He's the vice-president of the United States!"

"But what does he know about *poetry?* This is a *literature* banquet. All the guests will be writers, critics, reviewers, professors—people involved in the *arts*." I stopped for breath. "If Nixon's invited, *I* won't come and I doubt that—"

Rigg lifted his hand to stop me. Pushing a pile of papers aside, he leaned back, folding his arms. "Okay, then. Who do *you* want?"

"Someone who knows Frost's work—a critic of stature—respected—well known. If possible, a man who'd have something refreshing to say about Frost and his work."

"For example."

"Trilling." The name leaped out of my mouth on its own.

"Trilling? Who's Trilling?"

"One of the country's best critics—a professor as well—Columbia. I'm certain he's never yet published a line about Frost. It took him some years to appreciate his work, but I *know* from our talks how highly he values him now. And I'm sure that the guests would be more than eager to hear what Trilling would say. And you would too."

He sighed wearily. "Then go ahead and get him!"

I telephoned at once. Shocked at first and also pleased, Trilling asked for time to consider the offer. Whereupon I reported the Nixon danger. Impressed, he promised to let me know in an hour. I replied that I wanted to nail things down before Ed Rigg could change his mind. Ten minutes later Lionel called: He accepted. I blessed him, adding how eager I was to know what he'd say. He would not be a jot less eager, he said, to hear my reaction, and he'd send me his typewritten speech "in plenty of time."

He failed to do so. On the morning of March 26th, he phoned to say that his typist would make the final copy soon after lunch, and would give it directly to me. It would be in my hands by 4:00 P.M. at the latest. Right now he was busily polishing. As I hung up the phone, a flood of reviewers and news reporters poured by my door en route to the president's office.

The conference began as the thirty or more correspondents might have expected. "Poetry has always played a lesser role," said Frost. "When you're in college, half of all you read is poetry. When you're out, not so. Funny, isn't it? Out of all proportion." Though most of his views had been aired before to the press, one or two thoughts, he insisted, were new. He was starting to "hate the word 'peace' for the way it was being thrown around." As for people being "the same," "in the arts we want all the differences we can get . . . In society too, we really want people to be different, even if it means a risk of fighting with each other." The great surprise came after one of his listeners asked if New England was now in decay!

> People ask me that on my travels. Often they ask me in the South. And I ask, "Where did you go to school?" And they say Harvard—or Yale. And then I say the successor to Mr. Dulles [then Secretary of State] will be from Boston: Mr. Herter. And the next President of the United States will be from Boston.

Pressed for the name, Frost shrugged. "He's a Puritan named Kennedy. The only Puritans left these days are the Roman Catholics. There! I guess I wear my politics on my sleeve." So far as the press was concerned, the conference was over. Headlines appeared all over the country—"Frost Predicts Kennedy Will Be President."

News of a different sort, but equally controversial, was still to come. The birthday dinner at the Waldorf-Astoria began in the usual manner—cocktails and drinks—for a hundred fellow-poets, critics, and friends. Rigg seated himself between Frost and Trilling. My name card had been placed six settings to the left, next to Van Doren's. "Lionel speaking on *poetry!*" Auden scoffed beside me. I muttered a word about wishing to know what he'd say. Mark, overhearing me, asked why I hadn't been given the text. Trilling was still revising, I said, when he entered the hall, and I hurriedly led him to Rigg and some people he recognized, Barzun among them. After his second drink, Trilling looked much relieved.

He began his speech by confessing a certain diffidence in approaching his task at this "surely momentous occasion." After a playful sketch of how archaeologists of the future might describe this evening's ritual, he referred to the myths about Frost. "We have come to think of him as virtually a symbol of America." But "the manifest America of Robert Frost's poems is not the America that has its place in my own mind." This "manifest America . . . is rural in a highly . . . aggressively moralized way," thus representing "an ideal common to many Americans" who share "a distaste for the life of the city and for all that the city implies of excessive complexity, of uncertainty, of anxiety.

> I do not share this ideal [he went on], though I know . . . how intense can be the pleasure in the hills and the snow, in the meadows and woods and swamps that make the landscape of Mr. Frost's manifest America. . . . But these natural things . . . are not the ruling elements of my imagination of actual life. Those elements are urban—I speak here tonight incongruously as a man of the city. . . . Of course . . . I know all that can be charged against the restless, combative, abstract urban intellect . . . [yet] I also know that when it flags, something goes out of the nation's spirit, and that if it were to cease, the state of the nation would be much the worse.

He paused, then proceeded to say that "but recently" had his long "resistance to Frost's great canon of work . . . yielded to admiration." He had more to confess:

I have to say that *my* Frost . . . is not the Frost I seem to perceive existing in the minds of so many of his admirers. . . . He is not the Frost who controverts the bitter modern astonishment at the nature of human life: the opposite is so. He is not the Frost who reassures us by his affirmations of old virtues, simplicities, pieties, and ways of feeling: anything but. [At the same time] I believe that he is quite as American as everyone thinks he is, but not in the way that everyone thinks he is . . .

I conceive that Robert Frost is doing in his poems what [D. H.] Lawrence said the great writers of the classic American tradition did . . . [whose] enterprise was of an ultimate radicalism. . . . So radical a work . . . is carried out by the representation of the terrible actualities of life in a new way. I think of Robert Frost as a terrifying poet. Call him, if it makes things any easier, a tragic poet. . . . The universe he conceives is a terrifying universe. Read the poem called 'Design' and see if you sleep the better for it. Read 'Neither Out Far nor In Deep,' which often seems to me the most perfect poem of our time. . . .

But the *people,* it will be objected, the *people* who inhabit this possibly terrifying universe. . . . It may well be that ultimately they reassure us in some sense, but first they terrify us, or should. We must not be misled about them by the curious tenderness with which they are represented, a tenderness which extends to a recognition of the tenderness which they themselves can often give. But when ever have people been so isolated, so lightning-blasted, so tried down and calcined by life, so reduced, each in his own way, to some last irreducible core of being. Talk of the disintegration and sloughing off of the old consciousness! . . . [of] 'the post-Renaissance humanism of Europe,' 'the old European spontaneity,' 'the flowing easy humor of Europe.' . . . In the interests of what great other thing these people have made this rejection we cannot know for certain. But we can guess that it was in the interest of truth, of some truth of the self. This is what they affirm by their humor, by their irony, by their separateness and isolateness. They affirm *this* of themselves; that they are what they are, that this is their truth, and that if the truth be bare, as truth often is, it is far better than a lie. . . . The manifest America of Mr. Frost's poems may be pastoral; the actual America is tragic. . . .

Mr. Frost: . . . I hope you will not think it graceless of me that on your birthday I have made you out to be a poet who terrifies. When I began to speak I called your birthday Sophoclean . . . Like you, Sophocles lived to a great age, writing well; and like you, Sophocles was the poet his people loved most. Surely they loved him in some part because he praised their common country. But I think that they loved him chiefly because he made plain to them the terrible things of human life: they felt, perhaps, that only a poet who could make plain the terrible things could possibly give them comfort.

Applause followed. Before it died, I muttered to Mark, "Lionel's going to be jumped on fiercely for all that he's said."

"He was right! To hell with them!" I had never heard any such burst from the imperturbable Mark.

Frost rose from his chair. He was blocked from my line of vision, facing the people before him. Though I found it difficult to follow all that he said, there could be no doubt that the Trilling speech had upset him—not only the words but also the angered faces of some of the guests. Donald Adams kept shaking his head in fury, as Frost said something about his having "enjoyed" being looked into "more penetratingly" than ever before. When, after uttering some rambling words—among them "But *am* I terrifying?"—he began to "say" some poems, the measure of his disturbance became apparent. Lines he had spoken numberless times jumbled in his memory. "I'm nervous tonight, very nervous." The sentence came through sharply. He started another poem, which he prefaced with jittery lightness, "as having a happy ending." It was all too obvious now: He was in no state for any sustained performance. Before concluding, he assured his guests that he "usually knew" the poems, "but I'm a little nervous tonight." I was able to hear his closing words: "I'm still investigating myself . . . I'll be investigating myself for a week. . . ."

Prolonged applause at last gave way to an odd commotion, as scores of guests gathered in groups. Others stepped close to the poet, several speaking at once. Trilling, clutching his keepsake, *A Remembrance Collection* of new Frost poems, quickly excused himself and departed for home. Edwards and Rabbi Reichert, Frost's "summer Methodist minister," stood at one side as the hall started to empty. I wondered why the poet's official biographer, Lawrance Thompson, wasn't there.

At Frost's signal, the four of us walked to the elevator lobby. No one spoke as the car sped up to the Bridal Suite. Edwards, stepping out first, followed by Reichert, led us into a drawing room. Suddenly Frost turned on me: "Do I terrify *you?*" he barked.

"What do *you* think?" I nodded, holding his glance.

"Where?" he barked again, head jutting forward close to my face. "*Fiat nox.*"

"Ohhhhh" he grunted. Wheeling around, he resumed the walk. We chose our places. Frost, seating himself at the table, motioned to me to pull up a dining chair at his side. Reichert, off to my left, lighted a large cigar. Edwards gazed at us both from an armchair six feet away. At the sound of a knock, he opened the door. The waiter lost no time in arranging the large cold supper prepared in advance for the poet.

"*Fiat nox*—it was just a way"—Frost said mildly—"of putting together some of the poems I had saved for the book," as though no time had passed since his grunted "ohhhhh."

"Should I wonder why you bothered to group them under a special title: *Let there be night?* And coming right after 'Acceptance'? Could any reader have missed the point?"

"I did that only in *West-Running Brook,*" he retorted. "Not in *Collected Poems.*"

"Were there no 'Fiat Nox' poems in the earlier books? 'An Old Man's Winter Night'?—'House Fear' from 'The Hill Wife'?—'Out, Out—'? What would you have me say about 'Desert Places'?" His piercing glance carried a meaning I couldn't construe, but I owed myself the right to go on: "And some of your eclogues—'Home Burial,' 'A Servant to Servants'?"

He had started his meal. During the sudden silence, I reamed my pipe, blew out the stem, packed the bowl. "Here," said Frost, "have something!" He pointed to one of the platters. I shook my head, lighting my pipe.

"All this—that was said tonight"—his tone had an odd satisfaction—"it's *good* for me. It will take me time to get used to it, but it's *good* for me." He had started to speak as his old articulate self. Edwards said nothing. Reichert lighted a fresh cigar as Frost plied me with question on question. How long had I known Trilling? What had he written? . . . I heard myself putting together a capsule biography, from the year I had met Trilling at the old *Menorah Journal,* through his teaching troubles at Columbia, his spell at Madison, Wisconsin, then back again, and finally his *Matthew Arnold* book that won him astonishing praise from Columbia's president, Nicholas Murray Butler. "Trilling thinks of himself, not as a teacher: as a man of letters. He's published a novel and two remarkable short stories. One of them, 'Of This Time, Of That Place,' is a gem."

"I'll read it. I'd like to *read* his speech."

"So would I." All six eyes looked at me in amazement. "He had promised to get it into my hands by 4:00 P.M. He telephoned instead—needed more time. I reminded him that he'd sworn to give it to me *before* the festivities. He was still making revisions when he entered the hall."

I started to talk of Trilling's unusual role as a critic—an intermediary looking two ways at once: at literature and society, standing somewhere in between and explaining them to each other. He had dedicated his best-known book to his friend Barzun, who had been there tonight.

"What's it called?"

"*The Liberal Imagination,* but he's often very conservative. Can't abide Franz Kafka, at least not yet—maybe in time . . ." I had probably said much more than he wanted to hear. "Time to be quiet," I warned myself, hoping that any minute now, Frost would take off on a monologue—which is just what he started to do, while the three of us marveled: Was this the man who had lost command of himself? Confessed he was "feeling nervous tonight"? Stumbled on lines that he knew as well as his name? The lightning change was too much to believe. It threatened to keep us listening there till dawn.

"Yesterday Trilling, today the New Critics. No more worlds to conquer, Robert!"

"Many, oh many, many," he chided playfully, as we went to our places, guided by Robert Penn Warren and Cleanth Brooks. Frost had agreed to be interviewed on some technical aspects of prosody, the tape to be used with the new edition of *Understanding Poetry.* Though neither Warren nor Brooks had invented the term "New Criticism" or its methods for studying poems, their book had become the bible for schools all over the country.

Nothing that Frost hadn't stated before came forth in the course of the interview, though his stress on the "tune" of a poem, on the defects of "true" free verse, on the test he relied on for sound—"something my ear refused"—struck me as quite at odds with New Critical scripture. But Brooks and Warren were more than pleased, they assured him, as we made our way to the nearby Century Club. Lunch would be served in about ten minutes at most in a private room. While Frost, Warren, and Brooks were chatting, I spied a familiar figure enter the checkroom at the farthest end of the hall. Hurrying there at once, I called out, "Lionel! Lionel! What wonderful luck! Frost is here." I pointed to where he was seated. "We're lunching with Brooks and Warren. You know you created an international incident last night."

"Who, *me*?"

"Well, at least national. But come with me, come with me *now*. He's *there!*" I pointed again. "And tell him how much you love him!"

"Gladly. Of course! Gladly, gladly . . ."

The two of them greeted each other with an almost loving embrace. I tried to make out what they said, but the most I heard were phrases from Frost about joining with us at lunch and Trilling's "regret—an engagement with Edgar Johnson," followed by Frost's "we should see something more of each other. . . ."

During our leisurely lunch not a word was said of the night before. Frost was too busy recounting his earliest meetings in England—with Yeats in particular, whom he took delight in mimicking for "his talk of the agony each of his lyrics had cost him." Then, mockingly, praised him. I had never heard him speak with more ease or high animation, not since that first long afternoon on the porch of his Shingle Cottage some thirty summers before. Had the shocks of the banquet evening carried him up to some higher summit of self-acceptance? Or was it that I, grown used to the easefulness of our private talks, had only to hear him converse with others to feel anew the spell of his speaking presence?

"Then nothing new has gone on at 'the Holts,' " Frost asked as the waiter left with our order, "or you would have told me? Nothing bad, that is."

I offered a quick summary of the one item of consequence: a promising editor from Doubleday would arrive May 1st as the new head of "the trade." "He's fully forewarned: I told him all about Rigg, but he shrugged it aside. Thinks it a challenge." Frost gazed at me, waiting. "I also asked John Ciardi to join in a literary advisorship—something easy to do since he lectures from coast to coast and hears what writers are doing. John roared at my notion. Nothing could make him take on an added commitment—and neither should I, he warned. A week later he called me to say he had hit on a great idea for a brand-new book. It was on its way to me in the mails."

He was full of ideas about Ciardi, more than his most assiduous hearer could hope to remember. John was not only clever, charming but sharply perceptive. Maybe at times a bit blunt, though *his* frankness was healthy. Maybe at times too sure of his judgment or seeming to be, forgetting the danger of getting things wrong. And a poet, a good one, too. A good companion. Also a bold one. Bold enough to have risked his luck in his army days. Saved up enough out of winning at cards to be able to buy up property, houses—another gamble —successful. "So he confessed when I asked him. You know why he couldn't afford to keep on teaching? Says that it interfered with his lecture traveling."

"The birthday story he wrote about you after his Florida visit told me things I never had known. For one, the name of your next book of poems, *The Great Misgiving*. I must ask about that some time. When Ciardi quoted you, I felt I was hearing your words."

"We had a good time together. He sent me the article. It's one of the few about me that I've read." He stared at the window. "Uncannily accurate." The phrase didn't sound like Frost's. He used it again before going on with: "Didn't you say he's printing your piece from the foreign-poetry book?"

I nodded. "He's also named it *The Poem Itself*. I don't suppose you looked at the—"

"Why don't we wait till we see what comes out of it all as a book? You're depending on others to follow your lead. Is that hoping too much? Maybe not, since you picked your helpers." He gazed at the plate of cakes he had ordered. "Some other dessert?" I shook my head. "Then we ought to begin our walk."

"Funny, your living in France and reading their poets didn't affect your work as it did some others'—Eliot, Pound, MacLeish."

We were off on discussions of influence, living abroad surrounded by foreign sounds, and the loss to a writer's ear. In defense of Archie, I said that a kind of international traveler's aura marked a few of the best of his poems, though his famous "A poem should not mean but be" was unfortunate nonsense. As for his latest work, *JB*, I hadn't read it. I'd *heard* it. That was enough. Heard God's voice coming over the loudspeaker.

"Heard it? Where?" Frost wanted to know. I described the evening at Yale when my wife and I had been asked by our friend John Gassner of the Drama School to attend the gala premiere. "Your former Amherst colleague Canfield did the directing, and he spared nothing. A lavishly staged spectacle! Just a year ago this month—but you know the rest."

"No, I don't," he said in an unconvincing tone. Nonetheless I obliged by stating facts that were public knowledge, after a word on the party honoring Archie at the president's house. " 'Not quite the same as it was twenty-three years ago,' I said to Archie when we were alone, 'or don't you recall the post-performance symposium that we held for *Panic* (57)?' He smiled. 'Do you think I could ever forget it?' I wasn't sure what he meant but it didn't matter. In any case, it wasn't till last December that *JB* came to New York—at a terrible time: the middle of the newspaper strike. No one could read the advertisements or the critics' reviews. Nobody thought the play could survive till lo and behold! radio and television came to the rescue with broadcasts of rave reviews from the *Times* and *Herald Tribune*. They made *JB* a major success."

Jealousy flashed from his face. "Archie has power, hasn't he? Power." My nod was the obvious answer. Elia Kazan, erstwhile Leftwing theater thunderbolt, had staged *JB* with the best available actors, setting, costumes, music aimed to achieve, as the *Times* declared, "theatre at its highest level." The jealousy went back to his "days of badness," months after Elinor's death, to the night of Archie's much applauded Bread Loaf reading when Frost, unable to bear it, downed a tumbler of whiskey and embarrassed the audience (73). And now, twenty years later, *JB* was "the only" poetic drama on Job: For serious playgoers, critics included, no such work as *A Masque of Reason* existed.

"You and I know," Frost pondered, "Archie has always been a derivative writer." Had he read one negative critic's remark that the play not only made use of masks but itself was a mask? Or had he been thinking of Archie's echoes of other poets? Neither, as his next remark explained: "Did you catch the end of *JB*—the resolution through love? People think that everything is solved by love, but maybe just as many things are solved by hate." He pondered for a moment. "Part of Archie's thought may be traced to his inheritance. Think of his folks—big merchants in Chicago. Always had money. Lots of it. Also a place in the West Indies to run off to when he needed."

"Antigua? Beautiful island. Some time ago I learned from one of my friends who's known him for years that when Archie lived in Paris trying to write, in the twenties, his wife helped to support them by her singing."

"My!" he shouted. "Never heard about *that*. I'm glad you thought of telling me." I assumed by now that Archie-as-subject was done with, but he couldn't leave it alone. "You heard, I guess, what happened with Archie's book and yours and the Pulitzer people?" I had heard a tale some time before from a Southern professor whose friend had been close to the jury. "Yours had the votes," Frost glowered, "but the judges were overruled." Though columnists were saying such things often happened with Pulitzer prizes, all that I'd heard was a second-hand story. So, I also assumed, was Frost's. I remarked that it might have been just a case of a small new book competing against an established writer's *Collected Poems*. "Oh no," he insisted. "It should have been yours, not Archie's. Things seem to come his way—always have." He spied me taking a hurried glance at my watch. "Time to travel? Did you say you'll leave me at Joe's on your way to teaching?"

"Yes. I'll look out for a cab. Wish I could hear you read, but I too have to speak tonight."

As it happened, there were too many guests surrounding Frost to enable us to continue. While I talked with Joe of my coming Midwest trip with my daughter, Frost came over to join us. What kind of college was right for a girl who had always been a painter *and* an avid reader? Frost stood quietly listening. Maybe, I sighed, it's only a matter of luck and the student can make the difference? "Don't ask me," said Joe. "Ask Robert! He's the expert on colleges." "And I'm still learning." He chuckled. "Last month I heard that the girls at Radcliffe read more books in a week than I do in a year. Does that help?" Before the evening ended, he led me into a corner. "Make sure you're back in time for my Washington party. Al will tell you the day. I'm counting on you to be there."

Why should Frost insist that I come down to his "farewell Library party in May," especially since no one I knew would be present? Before flying to Washington, I sought in vain for some answer at Holt, and when the reception closed it was still missing. I arrived at about the time that Frost had expected me. Twenty, thirty people, possibly more, filled part of the large reception hall, standing in busy clusters. Here and there a face, vaguely familiar, called to mind some photographs I had seen in the press. My first act was to greet the host, which called for standing off to one side while the conversation in which he took part continued. Catching a sudden glimpse of me, he started to make his excuses: "Friend of mine, down from New York. But wait here! I'll be back." And back he went after our brief exchange. "Two things to report," I said. "One, Hyde Cox's proofs will be waiting in Cambridge. Two, my Nancy Larrick and your Fred Melcher agree ninety percent on the contents for *You Come Too* (101)." I added that Trilling's speech would appear in the *Partisan Review* with a note on the letters the *Times* had printed. "Your *Atlantic* friend Ted Weeks was the only one who had heard the speech; the other attackers knew only Adams' report. But I mustn't keep you away from your guests. . . ."

He reeled off name after name, then stopped to remark, "The Supreme Court is the most interesting body in government. And three of the judges are among my best of friends. They're here." He pointed to Warren—"I see him only occasionally now"—then Douglas, who was retiring, and Frankfurter. "Oh, here come two of the people I want you to meet: Quincy Mumford, Librarian of Congress, and Senator Kennedy. I think you three should get to know each other," he said carefully; then left to rejoin the group he had met with before. Our conversation touched on Frost's political bombshell set off on the morning of March 26th, the Library title Frost had given himself as "Poet-in-Waiting," and inevitably the Adams attack on Trilling. Mumford made no comment. Kennedy listened and beamed. At an awkward pause, I dropped a remark that made him beam even more: "My older daughter thinks she's a bit in love with you. Do you mind?" Later that evening, the Boston Senator, just before taking his leave, rushed back with a message: "Give your daughter my very best wishes, please!"

My eyes meanwhile were drawn to the curious sight to the left where Frost and his old friend Frankfurter both kept talking at once into each other's faces. What they were arguing about, nobody even in earshot could have been sure. Wagging fingers and pointing to prove the truths that they uttered, each was too happily busy declaiming to pause for a second to hear what the other would say. The debate that must have started minutes before the Kennedy parting held me fixed till Mumford appeared with questions about translation. Then we both turned to gaze for another few minutes. I recalled the curious way that the lawyer-liberal and poet-conservative by chance encountered each other at the Dunster House Bookshop in Cambridge. Though not introduced, each of them talked at the other without any thought of stopping. In fact they kept on and on till the weary manager, seeing no way to resolve the problem, gave them the key and went home. Was Mumford thinking of doing the same? Luckily three of the guests timidly made their way toward Frost and said goodbye. Frankfurter instantly threw up his hands and did the same. Minutes later, I followed. I was still unclear as to why the poet insisted I come to this party. Surely he had had some specific reason. Perhaps I should ask him now, while saying goodbye. He may have foreseen my plan. Before I could raise the question, he took the lead: "I know you sail in July. You've plenty of time for your visit to 'Brewster Village.' I've a fine French place for dining. If we try it together, you can tell me after you're back if you find one better in France."

I had more than enough outside my duties at Holt to keep me busy in the weeks that remained before my trip—correspondence with nineteen men and women at work on *The Poem Itself;* lecture notes to prepare, and guests to invite for my Institute classes. Meanwhile Trilling had called: He'd received a letter from Frost; he would send it at once. I showed it to Rigg and Edwards: "Read the final word from Frost on the Trilling affair. I wish it could get to the eyes of the people who read the Adams attack and the scurrilous letters. I suppose instead it will have to wait for posterity—or till Doubleday sends out a press release with their Trilling anthology."

Ripton, Vermont
June 18, 1959

Dear Trilling:

    Not distressed at all. Just a little taken aback or thrown back on myself by being so closely examined so close by. It took me more than a few minutes to change from thoughts of myself to thoughts of the difficulty you had had with me. You made my birthday party a surprise party. I should like nothing better than to do a thing like that myself—to depart from the Rotarian norm in a Rotarian situation. You weren't there to sing "Happy Birthday, dear Robert," and I don't mind being made controversial. No sweeter music can come to my ears than the clash of arms over my dead body when I am down. We should see something more of each other. I wish the Holts hadn't let your trade book get away from them.

Sincerely yours
Robert Frost

A few days later Frost called Edwards to say that Quincy Mumford had "made" him Honorary Consultant in the Humanities for a three-year term. Two weeks passed before he accepted the offer. By then he had surely received the three verse manuscripts we agreed to review as part of our scheme for expanding Holt's poetry list. Dudley Fitts, who had led me to all three writers, "almost had chosen" the book by Maxine Kumin for his Yale Series of Younger Poets. I passed this intelligence on to Frost. Though my letter offered qualified views of my own on all three manuscripts, we agreed that to publish or not to publish would be his decision. He had made his choice before I returned from Europe in mid-September.

Finished copies of *You Come Too* had already been mailed to reviewers. Would the title lead them to *North of Boston* in which "The Pasture" had first appeared? I hoped that *Robert Frost: The Trial by Existence,* the soon-to-be-issued biography by Elizabeth Shepley Sergeant, a longtime friend of the poet, would remind readers that Frost had made this lovesong for Elinor the introductory poem in all his collections. The announcement of the Sergeant book led me to wonder about the poet's endorsement of Thompson, who had been his official biographer for twenty years. I asked a few innocent questions. I could learn nothing beyond the fact that Thompson had been disgruntled enough to evoke from Frost a reassuring response.

A note on my desk at the end of September read: "Robert anxious to see you today. Important!!! Hasn't much time, so be there by three. If you can't, let me know at once.—ACE"

I explained to myself: He wants to talk about Kumin's book since he's probably had his fill of "The Future of Man" symposium. Possibly not, since surely three of the speakers would be worth hearing—Bertrand Russell, Julian Huxley, Hermann Muller.

"I started off with a statement," said Frost as we seated ourselves, "so they'd have an idea of how I was taking the future—give them a hint of my thought about science and Darwin, eugenics, even Karl Marx. They were startled a bit when I said at the end that people perhaps were just superstitious enough to leave their directions to what I like to call passionate preference—passionate preference for something we can't help wishing were true."

"I always thought that a wonderful phrase, though—"

"Always?" His questioning face jutted forward.

"Well—years ago I copied it out of a book by a man you dislike: George Santayana, *The Sense of Beauty*. He's discussing Whitman, democracy's beauties, and 'the charm of uniformity in multiplicity'—without quotation marks. Everywhere in Whitman, he says, 'it greets us with a passionate preference.' And then he starts to demean democracy as a 'terrible leveling.' The paragraph ends in confusion."

"I'm not surprised. I would puzzle over his meaning when I sat in his class at Harvard." But the man, he added carefully, was a "beautiful speaker" and he also wrote "good poems."

"Good sentences, too, that refute his official philosophy. 'It is not wisdom to be only wise . . . But it is wisdom to believe the heart.' Can't recall where he said it. Or where he declares that it's *probable* that the supernatural exists—decidedly probable!"

Frost shrugged. "I went back to Harvard a second year hoping to study with James. He was away—sickness." Frost enrolled under one of his pupils instead: Santayana, who not only had taken "a different turn" but was sometimes scornful of James's ideas. "I could tell—I had read his *Psychology* in another class." Santayana would talk about history, saying the way that people behaved proved they were not believers, because when confronted with danger, they dealt with it *practically*, for all their praying! "It seems to me"—Frost quoted the words slowly—" 'those who are not materialists cannot be good observers of themselves.' He leaves out the *other* part of ourselves, and the other part is *there*. James knew it. So do we all."

"And so did Santayana," I said, "for all his words on illusion. He talks down mind or spirit so much—art, morality, religion—yet the worst he can do is to say they entice us away from material truth—for him the only reality. Reconcile that with the poet he was! 'And some are born to stand perplexed aside/ From so much sorrow' . . . note where he places 'aside' after 'perplexed.' "

"You know a lot more about him than I thought you would. Why?"

"I was carried off by his way with words, verse, prose, cleverness: 'There is no God and Mary is his mother,' and so on. When I first came across his term 'animal faith,' I said 'a kindred spirit.' Then I read more. Something similar happened to me with Emerson, till I learned to ignore what I couldn't accept while holding onto the best."

"You've heard what I think of 'Uriel'—the greatest Western poem yet, I call it. And so much else in Emerson but not all. He could see, as he says, 'the good of evil born,' but there he stopped. He couldn't bring himself to say the 'evil of good born.' You know from my *Masque of Reason* that evil is real. It's in your part of the Bible."

"Yours too, if you really are an 'Old Testament Christian.' "

"I'm just as strong on badness as on goodness."

The *Masque* led me again to think of Thompson's review. I asked if he "had been in" on the Future of Man? "No," Frost grunted, adding casually, "How do you feel about Larry?"

"I haven't seen enough of the man to say. Obviously he has charm and wit and apparent brightness. I never thought much of his *Fire and Ice,* but it's almost twenty years old. Your *Masque of Reason,* I felt after reading his comment, seemed to be out of his reach as a critic. I'm eager to see the pamphlet he's just published. One thing I liked—the tone of his birthday piece in the *Saturday Review.* It helped me understand why you chose him to be your biographer."

"That's *all* of it?"

I thought a moment before confessing my shock at Thompson's rushing away the night of the Trilling affair. "How could he let himself stay away after what happened?" Frost looked at me quietly. "There must have been some emergency to make him run off, and he must have told you the reason." Frost looked to one side. "By the way, have you ever read Randall Jarrell's essays on you? I'll send the book if you'll read it."

My words were lost or he wilfully shut his ears. After his long silence, he raised his head and gazed in my eyes. "I'm counting on you to protect me from Larry."

I lurched at him in amazement. He nodded steadily. "But he's your official biographer! *You* picked him."

"I'm *counting* on you," he repeated gravely. "You will be here. I won't."

"If you need protection, simply undo what you did."

"Too late now."

"*Anyone* has the right to retract for a valid reason."

"I gave him my word."

"You gave him your word how many years ago? Twenty? You gave yourself up to a person you thought you could trust. How could you *know* he would change? He *must* have changed or you wouldn't be asking for protection."

"I want the truth. I need protection from lies, all sorts of lies."

"Edwards ought to hear about this. Have you told him?" He shook his head. "Edwards should know."

"Maybe—in time. But now: you and I only." He grasped my hand. Moments later he rose to his feet. I followed him to the door. "And to think"—he wrinkled his forehead—"I haven't even asked you about your daughter! How rude of me, all this talk of myself! Where is she now?"

"Carnegie School of the Arts," I said uneasily, "at least from my last account. Six girl-strangers sharing whatever the rooming-place calls it—having to like one another. From her voice on the phone, she's not too pleased."

"Why don't you go there to see her? Sometimes a talk can help a child—sometimes, at least." The words led me to Carol, to the night of talk between father and son, to the tragedy three days later. "Be sure to tell me about her when I come next month." He turned around to explain. "The poets' big Academy dinner. Don't you know of it? Their twenty-fifth something . . ."

The something was the twenty-fifth anniversary of the Academy of American Poets, on November 4, 1959, at the Waldorf-Astoria. Frost appeared, after his train arrived, for a short visit at Holt, following which I drove him to his hotel. "You won't rush back, I hope," he said, closing the door. "We probably won't have time to talk after that party, with all the poets crowding about."

In case Ciardi were to ask what he thought of his plan, I'd better tell him now: an anthology of thirty poets born since 1900 to be made, he said, "objectively" by the *vote* of a large group of critics, reviewers, poets, and what he calls experts. Each of the thirty winners will have 300 lines of his own and will write an essay on what he considers himself to be doing as a poet. The book was to be the successor to John's *American Poets at Midcentury*.

"Objective, is it?" Frost glowered. "Choose the best of the poets by *vote*? Count me out of it! Count yourself out of it too!"

John was excited by the project—"for once an anthology free from an editor's prejudice." I had liked it too, for a while, but its very virtue made it inhuman. I took a long breath. "John may not be there to-night, but Maxine Kumin, the poet we agreed to publish, will sit at my table. If your crowd thins out at the end, I'll lead her over to meet you."

"Where's your daughter now?"—my words on Maxine may have led him to ask. I summarized quickly: Before I could "go to see her," a bad hepatitis had literally sent her flying home.

"She wants to look at the Boston Museum School. I'll drive her there in May, which should give me a chance to come to Brewster Village, then on to visit with Fitts—who, by the way, asked if I thought he might lure you to Andover to speak to his charges. I hope you'll agree. You'd be taken there by car. Fitts is the Emerson of that Concord."

"He should telephone Kay. Tomorrow I go to Wellesley; Friday to Bread Loaf to meet with some Middlebury alumnae. Will you visit me there next summer?"

"I won't have time to leave my Poundridge place. I've all I can do to keep up, and I can't find help on weekends. But it's all worth doing even when I'm not sure. It was last July, for example, while walking around, admiring our handsomest apple tree, that I noticed half the trunk at the base was rotting away. I dug out three full buckets, then filled the hollow with Sakrete cement. You should look at it now! I'm waiting to see it break into blossom in May. When I worked on the wound, I thought it was probably hopeless."

"Hopeless? One time at my farm in New Hampshire—can't re-member which one—I came on a little birch that had fallen across the road where a wagon wheel had run over it. When I saw how crushed it was—half broken, lying there—I wasn't sure there was anything I might do that would save it. But I lifted it up, slowly, as high as I could without breaking it off, then bound it with splints, drove in stubs, and tied it up. Later—I forget how much later it was but it couldn't have been very long—I found that nature had helped me out. The tree was taking on life, new life: The sap was running; leaves coming out. . . . The birch never quite straightened up, but it *grew*—grew tall, sturdy, and strong. . . . More than once I've seen how nature reasserted it-self." He paused. "You've heard me say this before and I'll keep saying it: Nothing is irredeemable." Noting my quizzical glance, he went a step further: "Least of all the human race."

★   ★   ★

After introducing my out-of-town guests (Maxine Kumin, Cleanth Brooks) to my friends from Holt, I mentioned my earlier visit with Frost, and his birch-tree story. "I half-suggested he tell it tonight, but then I had no idea how huge this party would be. Six hundred? More? Plus those on the three daises?" At the scheduled time, Mrs. Hugh Bullock, the president, awarded two prizes to poets Léonie Adams and Donald Justice, with a trio of speakers to follow. Hindsight shows me I ought to have known that Detlev Bronk, the scientist; Sir Pierson Dixon, United Nations Ambassador; and Arthur Flemming, Secretary of Health, Education, and Welfare and former political science advisor at Dryden, would outdo one another in lauding the virtues, the glories, the numberless marvels of poetry. Mrs. Bullock was doing her gracious best, yet I couldn't suppress my dismay. This twenty-fifth banquet, despite the finest intentions, was becoming too grand, too sumptuous, too magniloquent—something was needed at once to tumble it down to realities. It was up to the closing speaker, Frost, who began not an instant too soon: "Poetry has always been a beggar. Homer was a beggar. He begged through seven cities. He ate at the table of the patrons—I suppose in those days he sat at the foot of the table instead of up where I have been sitting tonight. He sat probably under the table." Mixing jokes with barbs and ambiguous side-remarks, he proceeded to add: "My own idea of poetry isn't of its climbing on top of the earth, nor of its standing on top of the earth, but of its reclining on top of the earth and giving way to its moods. Like a spoiled actress, you know, the day after she has been on the stage, reclining on top of the world and giving way to her moods. . . ." Having blown the hall clean of the early orators' pieties, he ended with four of his poems, including the prayer that was now his signature: "Forgive, O Lord, my little jokes on Thee,/ And I'll forgive Thy great big one on me."

December brought an elating response to *The Poem Itself* from Louis. Burdened with writing commitments, he rarely indulged in a pleasure trip to New York. Yet we kept in touch, "seeing" each other by mail; and I used the occasion for thanking him for his words on my Mallarmé model to ask about the new Frost poem we received for our Christmas keepsake. Was "Enormous Caf" in line forty-two of "A-Wishing Well" an echo of Milton or Keats? Did it call up the Muslim myth of the mountain in which the earth was sunk or some other allusion?

Whoever typed the manuscript had made one obvious error. I showed it to Edwards. "Shall I telephone Kay for the missing foot or will you?" He studied the page for minutes. I read the final lines aloud, thumping his desk on the stresses:

> There's always been an Ararat
> Where someone else begat
> To start the world all over at.

"Every line has four unmistakable beats except the next-to-the-last, which has three. Besides, as it stands it makes no sense—'Where someone else begat.' Either the typist miscopied or she couldn't believe that the missing foot was a second 'someone.' Listen! This is how it should read: 'Where someone someone else begat.' "

Nothing I said that day or the next or the one that followed had any effect. "Do me one last favor?" I asked Edwards. "Call up Louis or Sergeant or Melcher or even Larry, if you think I'm wrong. Robert will never forgive us," I scrawled on the galley I placed on his desk. "He'll forgive *you!*" he scrawled below, before he returned it to me.

"If you've never met Robert Graves, you will in a couple of weeks," Edwards announced. He was flying from Spain—Poetry Society business. Robert had invited us for dinner—the 20th. Just the four of us. (By now the missing "someone" had made of the Holt Christmas card an embarrassed collector's item, for which a repentant Edwards had offered apologies: Nothing like it would happen again and so on.)

"Robert Graves?" I moaned as I wrote the date down on my 1960 calendar. I couldn't believe Frost thought very much of his poems or of Laura Riding's, the writer he worked with, or his stinging attacks on Milton, Pope, Wordsworth, Keats, Yeats, Eliot. His plane arrived and the "four of us" became five. After the dinner, while Frost and Graves reminisced about London and World War I, Edwards made his excuses. I spent the remaining hours with Gordon Wasson, Graves's banker-mycologist friend, who told me immensely more than I cared to hear of the "crucial" mushroom world and the "crucial" part some people knew it has played throughout human history.

Frost neither mentioned Graves nor spoke of "A-Wishing Well" when we met next day. He was brimming with other questions. Had I seen "anything of Trilling?" Would his speech make a "lasting difference"? I ventured it would, though the views of Randall Jarrell, which were close to Trilling's, hadn't shifted the critical stream. But the *Times* and Adams, of course, had made it an *issue* for everyone. "Everyone?" he chuckled . . .

And how was my daughter feeling now? Discharged by the doctors "for good, I hope?" "And that Minnesota pamphlet by Larry?" I hadn't seen it. "Kay read it to me—enough of it. *You* can live without it. *I* can." And oh, had I heard he had taken part in a Hanukah service at Christmas? "Newport. Visited the Touro synagogue there and the graveyard Longfellow wrote about in a poem." No, I hadn't been told, though I knew it was made an official historical site, like one I'd seen in the south of France: Louis XIV design, with a minuscule chair high up on the wall, awaiting Elijah—which led us to talk of Elizabeth Shepley Sergeant: her years in France.

No, he had never read her *Shadow-Shapes: The Journal of a Wounded Woman: October 1918–May 1919.* It had introduced me to Spire, the old French poet I later wrote about. They were intimate friends. She even quoted one of his poems on the war. I would read her *Trial by Existence* as soon as the book arrived. I was hoping she'd tell me things I had never known. "You'll look for surprises?" he laughed. Then he spoke of her "odd affection for France." I hoped she hadn't followed the current reviews—*Europe* and its issue devoted to living American poets which completely ignored Frost.

"Her odd affection for France?" I began. "The French oddity for me is their way of mishearing English. Some of the best of their poets—Baudelaire, Mallarmé, Valéry—couldn't find words to express their delight in the jingle-jangles of Poe. The Poe they adore—the writer and 'insidiously learned' critic—is their own invention. But it's no one's fault. The language a person speaks accounts—among other things—for his ear, and to carry some of *your* lines into French just cannot be done. What to do in 'Acquainted with the Night' with 'unearthly'? 'Unearthly height' becomes 'unthinkable height'—*incroyable.* And 'For Once, Then, Something: water came to rebuke the too clear water.' 'Rebuke' in French is to reprimand, or blame, so the translator writes that the water violently or passionately—*rageusement*—comes scrambling, confusing, or mixing up the too clear water—*vint brouiller.* All those words for your single, crucial 'rebuke.' But the worst is 'The Secret sits in the middle and knows.' It becomes 'But the Secret, in the middle, knows that he is right'—*qu'il a raison.* Are you bored by all-this-now-too-much-for-them?"

"I'm sympathetic. I worked too long at translation to be perfectly happy about anything that ever comes of it."

"*You* wrote translations? This is the first I hear of it!"

"Years ago I said so in a letter to Louis, after I read his Heine poems in English. I said I could never be perfectly happy with anything that ever comes of it, and—"

"Because what hadn't come through was the poetry—it was lost?"

Ignoring my interruption, he continued. "And I told Louis to pay no attention to me, to what I was saying; that I had congenital limitations. He was understanding. He has always been." He paused. "We used to see more of each other. Now we depend on 'arrangements.' We meet halfway—Sturbridge. We met there two weeks ago. Kay and I drove down; Louis and Bryna drove up. We had a long lunch and a talk . . ."

He went on to speak of *The Letters of Robert Frost to Louis Untermeyer,* which I planned to edit. Teeming with questions, I could ask but few. The clock had already caught up with us.

Marianne Moore, Frost, and Graves received an ovation at the speakers' table, and after the usual Waldorf dinner, the rites began; congratulatory messages on the fiftieth anniversary, short speeches, and a series of prizes—Louis accepting the first for his *Lives of the Poets* and Graves the last. More honors and honorariums followed the Britisher's setting the stage for the last event: the Robert Frost Annual Poetry Award to Thomas Hornsby Ferril. The winning narrative was read by the author, after which Frost made fitting remarks, and then, at his hearers' insistence, "said" a few poems.

All through the evening's festivities my thoughts kept flittering back to the revelation I'd stumbled upon not many hours before—the genesis of Frost's most quoted definition of poetry: what "gets lost from verse or prose in translation." I rehearsed part of my introduction for *The Poem Itself:*

A verse translation offers an experience in *English* poetry. It takes the reader away from the foreign literature and into his own, away from the original and into something different. The instant he departs from the words of the original, he departs from *its* poetry. For the words are the poem. Ideas can often be carried across, but poems are not made of ideas (as Degas was informed): they are made of words. Regardless of how close it may seem to the foreign poem that "it came from," an English translation is always a different thing: it is always an *English* poem. . . .

This is all that Frost could have meant, but his phrase had led to false implications. His well-known statement should read: "*The poetry of the original* is the poetry that gets lost from verse or prose in translation." This is what he concluded after years of trying; he never denies that poetry *different from the poetry of the foreign original* can be found in a work of translation (155). Obviously, if poetry can exist in an English poem (as of course it can) and if verse translations in English are, in reality, English poems (as most surely they are), how can one doubt that a fine translation may contain *its own* poetry? Frost's definition considers one factor only: what "gets lost" the instant *the original words in which the original's poetry lies* are rejected for words in another language. That and no more. He singled out only one of the places where poetry lies and can be experienced (*i.e.,* in poems of another tongue) and how that particular poetry gets lost.

"Just started to read Elizabeth Sergeant's book," said the hasty postscript in my letter to Fitts with which I enclosed my fourth rewriting for *The Poem Itself* of Florit's essays on César Vallejo's poems. My deadline, though less than a month away, would be met on time. "But don't print more than 2500 copies. It's poetry—worse: translation—and not even that!" Walter Bradbury, now head of Holt's Trade department, doubled my figure. I diverted myself by picking up the jacket and galleys of *Robert Frost: The Trial by Existence*.

As the introduction explained, Sergeant enjoyed *carte blanche* to quote from the verse, prose, published and unpublished letters to friends, family members, and so on. This "selective record" (her term) had begun when *The New Republic* had urged her to write a portrait based on their visits at Amherst: "Robert Frost—A Good Greek out of New England" (1925) and *Fire Under the Andes* (1927). Nine years later she asked the poet about a full-length biography. He agreed at once. In the summer of 1949 they started working together.

Though I knew enough of his life from hearing him talk in public and private, from reading what many had written, and from listening to Louis, Van Dore, and other close friends, I hoped for surprises. And I found more than a few—poems from Marjorie's *Franconia*, facts about Frost's one-act play *The Way Out*, the almost mystical incident that Sergeant thought might have been the seed of "The Road Not Taken." Most welcome to me was her recreation of the one person in Frost's life, Elinor, whom no one had pictured clearly. Drawing from all the hours she had spent in their household over many years, Sergeant conveyed a living sense of Elinor's presence. The other "new" parts of the book consisted of vivid enlargements on matters of which I had known but the essence—Frost's relationship with Edward Thomas, his stay at Little Iddens (1914), where he said "To Earthward" was written, the childhood California years, the start of his "barding around" (1916). Though certain remarks on the poems struck me as too biographical, arbitrary, or wrong, a few did better than others in hinting at covered-up meanings. All through the work I sensed a feeling of ease between "Robert and Elsie," of the kind that had marked her friendship with Spire toward the end of World War I.

Only a sixth of her book dealt with the life after Elinor's death (1938), decades she saw as a "diastolic-systolic motion": his lecture tours and speaking his mind on politics, then back to his base in Vermont. After the deaths of Marjorie, Elinor, and Carol, he had come, as she said, "into safety out of the chaos"—merely by changing his pattern: summers in Ripton; winters in Boston-Florida-Cambridge; teaching: Harvard, Dartmouth, finally Amherst.

A copy placed on my desk of a letter from Edwards to Dag Hammarskjöld was the first news I had of the March 17, 1960, United Nations luncheon arranged so that Frost could "exchange greetings" with a group of Soviet writers. A State Department official, two interpreters, Edwards, and I would attend. My request for information on each of the delegates yielded nothing more than the names of the leader and his cohorts. Thanks to my wife's coaching, I was ready to help the poet pronounce the names, but as soon as we'd started, he shook his head; he would never be able to speak them decently anyway, and besides, the interpreters could do whatever was needed. Then, nodding to me, he "thought we might try out one of the names, maybe the leader's." *Shéviakoff,* I repeated over and over, mimicking the Russian my wife had spoken last at the age of four. Ten pained minutes of repetition were enough. *Krushchev* remained *Kerchief.* Frost walked to the window. Rain dimmed the facing buildings. "Why are we going there anyway? They don't care about us, and besides . . ."

The trim United Nations official who greeted us sped us at once to the topmost floor, then led the way through a room-wide corridor hung with enormous paintings, some of which I'd viewed at loan exhibitions. "Our guests will be here presently." He bowed as we entered the empty hall. Standing in front of a window, we stared at the rain graying the streets below. Frost's face seemed gloomier than ever. All at once a band of chattering people strode through the open door. Shéviakoff, trailed by his three underlings, quickened his steps toward Frost and, in what was intended as English, spoke about feeling greatly honored to meet with "Mjeester Frustum." Frost, beaming, grasped his hand. "And to think"—he nodded, gazing into his visitor's eyes—"to think that you came all the way from Russia to see *me!*" Gloom had turned into brightness. What if the puzzled interpreter hesitated before attempting to speak? Much relieved, Andrew Cordier, Hammarskjöld's assistant, urged us all to be seated. With the help of six interpreters, he set out at once making introductions and placing guests at the U-shaped table. Frost sat in the center; Cordier at his left; Shéviakoff at his right. My place, to the right of the latter, faced the Soviet's chief United Nations interpreter.

Just as the waiters entered bearing the main course of the banquet, Shéviakoff snapped to his feet. He was moved to recite a poem right now, said his own pretty, dark-eyed interpreter. The poem, in its English version at least, was a typical propaganda piece that stirred none of his hearers. At once he recited another poem. Apparently better, it was given long, sympathetic applause; whereupon he called upon Mjeester Frustum to read a poem of his own. Frost smiled and, shaking his head, announced that he much preferred to "put" a few questions and to do some talking instead. After polite applause, he eyed in turn each of the Soviet writers. "Do you sleep at night?" The interpreter, nonplussed, gave me an icy glance before undertaking his duty, following which the four writers answered, one by one, with bewildered *Yes, yes, of course.* Frost snapped, "I thought so. We do too, and that is because *our* revolution was over a long time ago. Yours is over now too. People can't sleep when there's a revolution going on." Uneasy silence ensued as the chief United Nations interpreter strove with the poet's thought. Frost quickly entered the breach, stating that he profoundly and unalterably opposed the current idea that "all the peoples of the world ought to be alike. We are ourselves and you are yourselves," he added, pointing his finger. "We're each different. That's the way it should be. And I *love* you for your difference."

This was the second shock, and before the visitors absorbed it, Frost had begun "some thoughts on religion," in the middle of which he recited his well-known prayer "Forgive, O Lord, my little jokes on Thee/ And I'll forgive Thy great big one on me." From the tone of their whispers, it was clear that they hadn't expected anything even approaching such irreverent utterance from the quasi-official American poet. But before they had time to regain their balance, Frost had returned to his views on the difference among the world's peoples.

Then came another couplet, written, he explained, about a huge lump of iron sent by the King of Sweden, a meteor fragment fallen from the sky, which everyone could gaze at later: It was on exhibition in "a Meditation Room" below. "A symbol. It stands for unity. But even as you look at it, it seems to split. You think of the tools that can be made of it, and the weapons: 'Nature within her inmost self divides/ To trouble men with having to take sides.' " From the look on his listeners' faces, he could tell that the point he was trying to make had escaped them. He recited "The Objection to Being Stepped On"—an "innocent pastoral poem, which should be familiar to Russians, who have always been a great agricultural people:

> At the end of the row
> I stepped on the toe
> Of an unemployed hoe.
> It rose in offense
> And struck me a blow
> In the seat of my sense.
> It wasn't to blame
> But I called it a name.
> And I must say it dealt
> Me a blow that I felt
> Like malice prepense.
> You may call me a fool,
> But, *was* there a rule
> The weapon should be
> Turned into a tool?
> And what do we see?
> The first tool I step on
> Turned into a weapon.

The interpreter facing me threw up his hands. "Hoe? hoe? Did he say 'hoe'?" Frost turned on me suddenly—I was now his authority on the

U.S.S.R. "Is there *no* word in Russian for hoe? I thought you told me the Soviets have millions of farmers!"

On the back of the menu I made a sketch which looked enough like a hoe to show the interpreter what was meant. He studied it quickly, then handing it back to me, cried out, annoyed—"I'm an intellectual. *Why* should I know about farm tools?"—whereupon he broke into Russian. I had no idea what he said, yet he must have explained the point of the poem, for the visitors applauded heartily. Before we left, Frost took care to bid a warm goodbye and thanks to everyone present, and especially to congratulate the United Nations interpreter on having enlarged his command of our tongue with "one of my favorite non-intellectual words."

Minutes after the first bound copies of *The Poem Itself* arrived, I autographed one for Edwards. I handed him the very first book with the new firm name [Holt, Rinehart and Winston] on the title page, and said, "Now that you're really President, I expect you to say what you really think of my handiwork." He swore he would read it that night; but I'd better also inscribe one for Frost, who was coming for National Library Week, probably by train a day before, April 3rd, provided his knee didn't worsen and keep him at home.

I stood prepared with a wheelchair while his train at the Pennsylvania station slowed to a stop. Though it took him some time to hobble out to the platform, cane in hand, the instant he spied the chair, he waved it away with a growl. "No, no!" I assured him we wouldn't be noticed and, besides, did he relish climbing the two steep staircases to the street-floor level? He scanned the platform—no one in sight—then settled into the chair, only to lift himself to his feet when we neared the lobby. "There's something I have to do—not very serious. Do you know this place?"

I led the way to the men's room. While doing the not-very-serious acts, I recalled that Frost at times had failed to button his trousers. "These days," I said, "I remind myself to zip up my pants. I sometimes forget."

"I do too, and when somebody comes to remind me, I tell him the reason. It's because I'm not so dangerous as I used to be."

At the Westbury the *maître d'hôtel* led us at once to the table reserved for Frost. He asked about Trilling while easing himself slowly into his chair.

"Writing reviews when he ought to be writing stories. I sent you one."

"Haven't got round to it yet but I must."

"I'm told that you seldom praise a work to the writer himself, but in Trilling's case, if you find the story as good as I think, you might make an exception. It could wean him away from reviewer-chores and save him for—what shall I christen it—'literature'?"

"That night he spoke, I was a little bothered by him, but chiefly I didn't hear very well."

"He was simply stressing what *he* considered the most significant part of your writing—most significant for him. A personal statement—which is all that a critic has to depend on at last. When I strip their coverings off, what I find, if you'll let me borrow the word, is passionate preference. In Trilling's case, for the tragic."

"Eliot's boys found something else in 'Directive.' They call it great and they call most of the rest of my work trivia." He turned to ask the waiter about the desserts—"the best part of a meal"—before going on. "I've said it before, that I don't read criticism about my work but I know all about it from friends. Yet I wonder at times how much of my poetry is understood."

What did he mean by "understood"? And how could anyone know? A poet like Mallarmé, I remarked, professed not to care—and he may have been quite sincere. His disciple Valéry wondered about something else: How could a poet *know* when he'd finished a poem? And since he had no sure way of knowing which of a number of endings was best, he argued for keeping them all. "Sometimes he wasn't quite sure about stanza order, as in his 'Graveyard by the Sea.' It's in *The Poem Itself*, which is waiting for you at home."

Frost asked about Fitts and my "other helpers." I thought at once of John Nims and "Directive's" opening: "Back out of all this now too much for us." When I asked if he knew Nims, he remembered meeting him. "Nims," I remarked, "once told me he wondered if Latin syntax, especially Horace's, had something to do with it. It seemed to me more like something you wrote at a single stroke and never considered revising. Not like a few of your other poems." He glanced at me in surprise. "Not like the opening line of the Keats nightingale ode," I went on, "or Whitman's 'Out of the rock'd cradle.'" We were launched on the subject that William Cullen Bryant "had rightly called *re*-vision." And was it a fact that eleven years passed before the last three lines of "Nothing Gold Can Stay" were written? Where had I heard about *that?* he asked. "From my Michigan friend who was close to Wade." There was more to it, a good deal more. He nodded. I waited, hoping to hear, but he didn't pursue it.

"I've always wanted to know when it was that you changed the end of 'A Minor Bird.' " It had *never* been changed, he replied; it was always "And of course there must be something wrong/ In wanting to silence any song." My same Michigan friend, I countered, had sent me *The Inlander* for 1926, "and your title then was '*The* Minor Bird.' " Frost peered at me sternly. "I have the tearsheet at home—it's not even yellowed in all these years. I'll bring it next time we meet. It reads 'And I own there must be something wrong/ In ever wanting to silence song.' "

Frost shook his head. He could "willingly forget other revisions. 'Birches' was two fragments soldered together so long ago I have forgotten where the joint is." He was clearly disturbed. To me the change revealed a shift in belief, which was why I had questioned "when?" He reached for his cane. "Why don't we go upstairs and talk?"

The elevator let us out at his floor. "There! Read it!" He pointed to the stairway sign on the wall EXIT. "That's for me."

"You and everyone else on earth."

"Damn this cane!" he snarled, limping to the door.

Once inside, I stepped to the bathroom, "May I?" He was much too busy to listen, struggling onto his bed; but when I came out, he appeared almost benign. "That's where you ought to have been instead of downstairs. Luncheon in bed."

"No, no," he growled, lying flat on his back, his hands clasped under his chin on a pillow. "I've been thinking of Al Edwards and all that Wall Street business with Holt. I hope that's over now." I assured him it was. "I guess he never said where his father came from? Did you know the man was Welsh, like Edward Thomas. And does Al ever talk of his college career? Played lacrosse—one of the best.

"Did you ever hear of 'Parson' Lewis—Edwin Morgan Lewis, called 'Parson' because he would never play on Sunday? Great friend of mine. He pitched for the Boston teams, both leagues, at different times. He won two pennants, twenty-five games all in one season. But then he gave it up to become a teacher—Columbia, later at Williams College. He specialized in the Victorian poets. At the time he died he was president of New Hampshire at Durham. There were many things that he and I loved in common. . . ."

"Poetry and baseball! I know about Frost the Poet, but nothing at all about Frost the Baseball Pitcher."

"And Batter and Runner," he added quickly. "I still play—at playing, you know. Are you sure you want the story?" I nodded. "Where should I start? At the start?" I nodded again pulling my chair toward his bed. "I guess it was Salem Depot where it began—in Salem township. The year after my father's death. My mother moved us in September. I was twelve years old. In no time at all I knew what I wanted to be: a great pitcher. And so . . ." He stopped. "You *really* want to hear?" For the third time I nodded. "All right, then. Prepare yourself! As I said, it began in Salem Depot. One afternoon . . ."

By the 21st, 1960, when he came to read at the Poetry Center,** his recent "incapacitating knee" was no more than a quirk of the past. In fact, as I learned at Holt, Frost would be much too busy going around town on his own even to let us know where to reach him by phone. My evening class forced me to miss his performance, but, as always after a New York reading, he spent the after-hours at the Blumenthal home. Shifting groups of guests hemmed him in for the first few hours. I wondered if we'd have a moment alone. Toward midnight, after most of the people were saying goodbye, I caught him looking toward me. Glancing back, I waved a sheet of paper over my head. We started toward each other. "Summons?" he asked mock-seriously. "What's the crime?"

"Printing a poem thirty-four years ago called 'phon *The* Minor Bird' in a Michigan campus journal. I promised to bring you proof. Here!" I gave him the tearsheet. He stared hard, then handed it back to me. As we stepped toward a vacant couch, he repeated the words he had used when I'd first mentioned the poem. "When did I change the ending? You wanted to know, and I said 'Never.' You've kept that page a long time"—he smiled—"just to surprise me?" Hoping he might finally speak about "Nothing Gold Can Stay," I kept repeating my view on revising. He hadn't seemed to be listening till I mentioned "my gripe against Trilling's great admiration for what he calls 'conscious artistry.' A great misnomer, I think. Half-conscious at best and surely the meagerest part when the words one reaches for suddenly come."

Frost smiled unhappily. "I'd like to know what he would have thought if I were to let him know how 'For Once, Then, Something' happened." The poem, he said very briefly, came into being years ago when Lesley was still in her teens. One afternoon, after explaining some of the metrical patterns in Latin, he proposed a competition: Each would write a poem made up of lines of eleven syllables. Within an hour, maybe more, "The Well" was written, and that was all there was to it, "for a while." He kept the poem around, changed the title— had called it "Wrong to the Light"—till a year before it appeared.

He spoke of his coming plans—some speeches, then back to Boston. "You're still coming to see me there, aren't you?" I nodded. "Waller Barrett's book donation at Charlottesville, Jefferson's University. Then Washington—starting my Humanities Consultant job at the Library, with a speech at night, May 4th. Quincy says 'it should draw many members of Congress.' I hope that I'll draw even more on the morning after." The Senate had scheduled hearings for the committee on Labor and Public Welfare—the bill for a National Academy of Culture. "I want to get an *assurance* that our government's aware of the arts—aware of us as artists, writers, sculptors, painters, and all. I'm after creating a 'center of general favor' to the arts—poetry's equality, for one thing. . . ."

Louis laughed when we talked by phone a few days after the hearings. "Yes, I know," I said, "that we have a National Institute of Arts and Letters here, but he wants an official academy bearing the government's seal of approval, not just a houseful of self-elected immortals." I had called Louis to thank him for his note on *The Poem Itself* and to ask how soon I might see some part of his Frost Letters volume. We would talk about that, he said, at Elizabeth Sergeant's party in June.

May 8th found me at 35 Brewster Street, Frost's Cambridge home since 1941. The furnishings made me think of Vermont: the Shingle Cottage. Eager to prove the excellence of New England's French cuisine, he proposed that we go at once to "his" small Hotel Vendôme. "How did you manage those stairs when your knee was bad?" I asked, taking a last long glance at the steepest flight of steps I had ever seen.

"Stairs?" He chuckled. "They're just what I need. When the streets are icy, I don't go out for my midnight walk. I go instead to the second floor with a dish of pennies. Then I climb the stairs fifteen times, and every time I get to the top I reward myself with one of them. . . . Ready to go now?"

From the small table reserved for us, I was able to see each face in the room. None looked familiar; none of them showed any sign of recognizing Frost. At the far corner, a man seated alone kept looking at us from behind his morning paper. I ignored him at first, but the frequency of his glances led me to think he was keeping watch on us. Halfway through our elaborate lunch, I mumbled to Frost, "Don't look at him now, but unless I'm imagining, someone's sent you a bodyguard."

"I never saw that man before. Did you?"

"No, but the type's familiar." Years after my *Masses* days, the FBI had kept track of me. About once a month one of them came to my office, loaded with questions—on the surface, not about me but the people I'd known on the Left. I had nothing to hide. I never had joined the Party, but that didn't matter. What was I *really* doing, publishing every so often books like Sutherland's *White Collar Crime,* Sterling Brown's *Negro Caravan,* Winspear's radical work on Plato, Blake's *An American Looks at Karl Marx,* the sociological book on *Industrial Conflict.* "Maybe our friend down there called on me once. Later they gave me an agent all my own."

"Oh, you're too respectable now—and after that *Fortune* article on Holt—the picture of you with Rigg and the rest? And all that you went through fighting that union leader when you came to Holt— part of the Teamsters' crowd?—How much did it cost your firm to pay him off?" His question led me back to our *Who's Who in Labor* book and the time I argued the Dryden staff into joining a union. "Rigg hasn't yet got over the joke. He still tells Al it was Stanley's fault and he learned his lesson."

"He's right that it *was* my fault, for after a while they had nothing more to demand, so they asked time off for their birthdays. As for learning my lesson—did you hear that Holt will be issuing *The Partisan Review Reader?*"

"The magazine Trilling 'most enjoys writing for,' as he said in his speech? They tell me Eliot praised it but doesn't write for it now." Had I seen him in London?

"He was out when I called, though I doubt he'd have taken the time to read my *Poem Itself* model. Herbert Read told me last summer that Eliot talks about nothing else but the theater—brushes you off when you mention poetry."

Frost mused. No, they had never really *discussed* any poet or poem when they met in England, nor the theater. It was all easy, friendly, *polite*. He seemed to like to listen more than to speak. And "of course those fine words he said that night in his toast at the special dinner for me." I waited for him to go on. "Did I ever tell you about the day he called at Brewster Street—1947, the month *Steeple Bush* came out? Without a warning, he knocked at my door. He had come from London to see his brother, sick at the time. He was making the travel money he needed by lectures and readings. That's what brought him to Boston. When I opened the door, I couldn't believe what I saw. What do you think he said? That he couldn't leave town without coming 'to pay his respects.' I welcomed him in, still amazed. And there we sat—in my front room—soon at ease with each other, talking about everything in the world: his own writing, mine, the War." He sighed. "I hadn't liked him at all when we'd met before, twice. The first time in London, about twenty years ago; then here at St. Botolph's Club a few years later (269f.). Nothing between that time and the knock at my door. Everything changed."

"Everything?" I ventured. "Mostly Eliot, if my dates are right." It was twelve years since he'd published *After Strange Gods,* with its hard attack on Jews at the time of Hitler's massacres. I knew that at least one of his friends urged him not to reprint it. And he'd changed in other ways too—turned against the critical school he helped create: New Criticism. Speaks of it now as "lemon-grinding"—that is, at its worst. I stopped, seeing the waiter approach.

Were we ready to order dessert? "Name your choice," Frost announced. "I'll follow." His eye accidentally saw the "bodyguard" far in the corner. "He's still watching. I wonder why." He turned on me, "Are you *that* dangerous?" I nodded.

"Ready?" His conversation veered to a brand-new topic—an enlarged and special edition of *North of Boston.*

"I've been ready since 1949 when I wrote to the Holts. Bill Sloane had gone off on his own, Denver Lindley lasted a year or so, then Glenn Gosling took over. I sent him a long letter. What I dreamed of, I said, was a new *North of Boston,* with a few pictures and eight more poems that belonged—"West-Running Brook," "The Witch of Coös," "Two Look at Two," and the rest. Gosling liked the idea, but my next book, he said, ought to be a collection of poems for children. Nothing happened. A few years later I asked Hyde Cox if Andrew Wyeth, one of his friends, might be willing to join in the book. Wyeth knew exactly what should be done. I thanked him and told the Holts we were ready to start. There were lots of discussions. Time went by, then the whole idea was forgotten—but not by me." He seized my arm. "Don't try to answer now! I want you to think of the whole idea—think of it hard! I've been waiting long, I can wait longer still."

"The question's tabled, then?" I managed to say. "I'll think of it hard—you have my word—though people are waiting to hear when your *new* book of poems will appear. I am too. Have you any idea?"

"I've been dropping bits and pieces of it all over the country in readings and talks. I'll do the same tomorrow with the Andover boys."

"And the Abbot girls. They'll also be there. Brother-and-sister academies. I hope you'll save one private dinner with Fitts and his wife Cornelia. You know, I suppose, of his terrible trouble in walking—iron braces, cane, and the rest."

"No," he shouted. "Iron braces? When did this happen? Tell me about it, please! . . ."

On the long drive home I thanked fate that question three had been tabled. I recalled Robinson Jeffers spoke of Frost as "a regional poet who is universal also." And Frost's own declaration: that every "real reader knows good poetry doesn't depend on geography." What if he happened to ask for Fitts's reaction? Fitts would, as always, have been polite while deploring the book as sure to diminish Frost. On arriving home I found a letter: "Frost will be here for three days—May 9-10-11—barring calamity. The boys are all of a twitter; the Abbot girls, of a twitch. I hope we shan't bore him too much." A week later he wrote an account of the visit:

> Frost was here indeed. If he had slowed down, it was not percep-
> tible. I can testify that he wore me out, and my junior colleagues,
> just as a spectacle. He came with strict warning from Mrs.
> Morrison that he must not over-do, that he must take his after-
> noon nap, that he must not be subjected to lots of sudden people,
> and that he must get to bed early. Perhaps he did not over-do; I
> have no way of judging; but he refused naps in favour of long
> walks; he refused to go to bed before 2 am; he went out of his way
> to collect hordes of undergraduates around him (on his feet with a
> rest for three hours tuesday morning and three hours on wednes-

day; luncheons; dinners; constant book-signing . . .) My own case was typical. He asked me to luncheon on tuesday, and I went warned that I must not stay more than an hour—must leave him to his nap at two. The lunch went on until 4:30; and even then Cornelia and I should not have managed to tear ourselves away unless I had had a class that I simply had to meet at five. He wowed the boys; he wowed the faculty; he wowed the waitresses; Cornelia fell in love with him ('he's a lamb, he's a doll'); and so, of course, did I; all over again. I think he did not repeat himself once—certainly not in my hearing, and I was around a great deal of the time. You came in for a great deal of exposition, too: how the Holts had . . . acquired you to give a literate respectability to the firm; and he described (this happened to be in the big speech, before the school) the three offices at 'the Holts', and how yours was clearly The Shrine; and filled, moreover, with adoring and decorative young secretaries, 'like Lorenzo the Magnificent, you know, or Haroun el Rhaschid'; and oh god, it was fun.

His visit had one odd moment: the night of the farewell dinner when, at somebody's signal, all the assembled students started to shout to the beat of "*Hernando's Hideway*" from the play *Pajama Game*: "Whose woods/ these are/ IthinkIknow—His house/ is in/ thevillage-though. . . ." Whatever he felt and thought as he sat through the loud performance, Frost concealed with a glassy smile till the last of the sounds died down.

"I gave my wife your breakfast menu," I said as we settled back in the cab. "She couldn't believe it, but that's what she's going to serve." We were riding from the Westbury to my home on Central Park. Glancing up at the clouded sky broken by May sunlight, he pointed north. "You were born up there, and I might have been reborn not far from where we are this minute." It was March 1903. The Frosts had come by boat from Boston; arrived in the early morning; rented a small apartment. He had planned the visit partly as a holiday for Elinor, who expected her fourth child some time in June. Now he lurched to the left, "Where's the zoo? Down there?" I nodded. "Can we pass it when we go back?" I nodded again. "Lesley was four years old—the right age for all the surprises. How she stared at the elephants, giraffes, the badgers especially—and those trained cats and dogs at the great Hippodrome right near us—right near us—and that fine aquarium!

"Elinor knew I had another idea. I called on the editor of *The New York Sun* and of other periodicals in the hope of finding a market for my poems. What if some had said yes instead of no? Then we'd have been neighbors." He mused for a moment. "I never told you but not long after Elinor's death, I thought I would make New York my home. I said so to Ted and Kay. They made me decide not to. I still think of it. . . ."

I lost count of the number of trips my wife, Leda, made from the kitchen to the dining room, each time bearing a tall glass of heated water with milk, to which he added spoonfuls of sugar. After a pleasant beginning, in which we all took part—including my daughter, who said how pleased her younger sister would be if he wrote her name above his own in her copy of *You Come Too*—the conversation changed to a Frost monologue. It might have gone on for hours. At 3:00 P.M. I was due at the Cosmopolitan Club, one of three or four males permitted to pass through the entrance to hear Elizabeth Sergeant reveal to her fellow-members "some remarkable things" she had learned in writing her forthcoming book.

"Five o'clock, May 18, 1960: Hotel Waldorf-Astoria" read the invitations sent out to critics, reviewers, editors, special authors, friends, *et al.*, to launch *The Poem Itself.* I arrived ten minutes late, with a score of early-comers who were eager (some of them, anxious) to see with their eyes "what this novel way of dealing with foreign poems is all about." Only six of the men and women contributors lived in the New York area, but friends of a few of the others came in their stead. As at many publishing parties, most of the guests chatted with people they knew on any subject except the present occasion, yet the Holt hostess saw to it that everyone spent at least some minutes with the book and three or four with the author. I apologized in advance to Germaine Brée, who hoped she might meet Frost: Because he was giving a reading tonight, I *couldn't* expect him to come. Just as I finished explaining, Edwards tapped my shoulder: "Robert's there, at the door." I excused myself and hurried to him.

"Oh, you knew I would come." He smiled.

"I admit that I hoped."

"I wouldn't have missed it. And I'll give you a line," he said, raising his hand. "You agree with me. You don't believe you can carry a foreign poem into English and keep its poetry. So you don't try to translate poems—you *discuss them into English.*"

No one but Frost could have summed up the book in a phrase. "It's exact!"

"Use it—it's yours! That's a very good work, you know. And now go back to your party and I'll go back to prepare for mine. You know where I'm reading tonight—oh!, good! Al—" Edwards approached. "I've been waiting for you." I tried to keep track of his movements, but after staying about ten minutes, he disappeared.

When I saw him again, at night at the Blumenthal home, he was much too busy talking with guests for me to intrude, yet I hoped I could find a way of expressing my thanks. Joe's eyes gleamed as I told him about the "line"; then Frost suddenly joined us. I waited for him to speak, most likely of some of his friends at the Y. His thought was elsewhere. "I haven't told you about my Andover visit." It was not what he had expected. And the way the boys insisted on asking their questions—"good ones too; better than most I'm asked—and they wouldn't stop. They kept me standing for hours when I ought to have taken the nap that Kay told me I should." And the banquet!—singing one of his poems "to a beat of their own! But your friend Dudley"— his face darkened—"dragging himself on those irons and cane! What's wrong with these people at Andover? What do they mean by making him work sixteen hours a week? We ought to do something about it." I countered: Fitts must be happy in spite of those hours, since he regularly turns down tempting offers from Harvard and others. Though my reassurance relieved him, he was still concerned. "We plan to see more of each other." He paused, his eyes twinkling. "Did you know that Laughlin depends on him to correct the mistakes that Ezra doesn't know are mistakes? And the critics call Ezra a *scholar!* . . ."

All Holt's efforts were focused now on Elizabeth Sergeant's *Robert Frost: The Trial by Existence.* A large reception to honor both the poet and the author had been arranged for June 1st at the Grolier Club. Friends, writers, bibliophiles joined the usual contingent from the book-review world. Although there was no receiving line, Frost and "Elsie" Sergeant did what they could to acquaint Rigg with people he never had met, some of whom were to be his guests at dinner. The large hall buzzed with excited talk, friends standing with friends in a score of clusters served by a host of waiters. Because the special guest I awaited hadn't arrived, I sought a clear view of the entrance door by standing close to a row of tall glass cases which housed the Society's gems of the bookmakers' art. Unexpectedly I caught a glimpse of Rigg nearby, gazing at one of the displays. A man unknown to me walked to his side, hailing him heartily: "I can see, sir, you're one who really belongs here. You're a true bibliophile."

"Who me?" Rigg laughed, shaking his head. "I'm a biblio*phobe.*" I moved away only to hear him call to me: "There's your Howard University friend, Professor Brown."

I rushed toward the entrance. "Sterling. So glad you decided to make it. Come, come!" We found a place to sit down and talk. "Frost knows all about you—*The Negro Caravan, Southern Road,* and your poems. He was happy to hear you were coming. Look!"— I pointed—"Frost surrounded again. We'll wait for an opening. Meanwhile, if you're willing, let me do some introducing—not to the writers you've met before but Mark Van Doren and Untermeyer. Maybe we ought to start with the guest of honor, Elizabeth Sergeant. . . ."

It took more time than I'd anticipated for Frost to be free. After I brought them together, the two poets walked toward the rear of the hall, each speaking, it seemed, with peculiar intensity. I turned to join Miss Sergeant, who asked for news "of our dear friend André Spire." In the midst of our words, my wife appeared at the door. Busy with new introductions, I mentioned that Sterling, in spite of our doubts, had in fact arrived. She was eager to see him again. I promised to find him, when Mark Van Doren came over to greet her, followed by Louis. While they were talking, I searched the hall for Frost. He and Sterling seemed to be saying goodbye. Minutes later they parted. Sterling, joining us quickly, kissed Leda and tendered his wife's greetings.

"Tell me," I grabbed his arm, "what were you and Frost speaking about so tensely?"

"Six great lines from *A Further Range.* Nobody mentions them. He says I'm the only one he knows who knows that poem. I'll tell you about it the next time we talk, or I'll write you a letter. But now— thanks. . . ." He was gone before I could stop him.

By now most of the guests had either left the hall or were leaving. Edwards was calmly assuring Frost that despite the mixup in plans, he would make sure that Louis would have a place at the dinner. Frost nodded, beckoning me: "I haven't seen you at all after you came to me with your poet-friend Brown. Do you know a Negro song about Dives, rich man Dives?" I shook my head. "If you find it, send it to me." We chatted of various things—the article in *The New York Times Magazine* on his national arts academy and its worried effect on Institute people uptown; Thompson's response to the Sergeant book—"He hates Elsie and can't forgive me for letting her write it"—the USIA movie—"You're planning to see me this summer, you said. Why don't you come while they're making it?" . . .

With dinner about to be served, the invited guests made their way to the Council Room above. Name-cards saved us the trouble of choosing places, and once the host had offered a word of welcome, the dinner began. After the hours of talk in the hall, even one formal speech would have been out of place; besides a much more pleasant event had been planned. Copies of *The Trial by Existence* were passed around the table so that each of the twenty-four guests would take away, as the evening's memento, a volume signed by everyone at the table. Rigg, speaking for Holt at the dinner's conclusion, offered congratulations to Miss Sergeant and to Frost, followed by thanks to all the guests for their "gracious presence."

Where? I asked myself on arriving home, where was the six-line poem Sterling had mentioned? I found but two in *A Further Range*—"Waspish," "In Divés Den"—neither of which I remembered. Nor did Sterling send me his promised letter. Not until 1983 did I learn the answer, and then only by chance: reading the speech Brown had given a decade before at Williams College, his alma mater. Quoting "In Divés Den," and also the Negro spiritual "Rich man Dives . . .", he "explicated" the poem in his tragi-comic way that made it suddenly memorable. How could I and everyone else but Sterling have missed the meaning, its "autobiographical 'sounding off ' "? Probably because in 1936 when the book appeared I was so concerned with Frost's overtly political statements that I missed the subtle assertions, that I couldn't see what Sterling showed it to be: "a strong statement of a man's belief in America and in himself."

> It is late at night and still I am losing,
> But still I am steady and unaccusing.
>
> As long as the Declaration guards
> My right to be equal in number of cards,

It is nothing to me who runs the Dive.
Let's have a look at another five.

Half of June and most of July were taken up with making ready our
summer retreat in Connecticut, but nevertheless there seemed nothing to lose by making a trip to Ripton. The foreman vetoed the
thought—once we were gone, his men might also take a vacation, and
then how could he *possibly* finish? And so on.

The trip would have offered the chance I wanted to be with Frost in
his summer habitat, visit his cabin above the slope, the Morrisons'
place below, and the made-over schoolhouse home of Victor Reichert, Frost's summer minister friend. Had the rabbi been to Israel? Had
he heard about *The Encyclopedia Judaica?* I had told Frost of the project
and all about my talks with the man representing the sponsor, Nahum
Goldmann, President of The World Zionist Congress. The undertaking was large: twelve volumes directed by Israel's leading editor.
Holt, the spokesman insisted, was "the ideal firm to bring this work
to America. There was no monetary risk. Finished books, subject to
Holt's approval, would be manufactured in Israel. I'm sure you've
lots of questions, but once you speak with the editor, I know you'll be
convinced."

I was more than convinced: Benzion Netanyahu was all he'd been
painted to be. In fact, I had never hoped to meet a more learned scholar
who could understand all that this project involved. Within a week we
were friendly enough for him to advise that before commending the
work to Holt, I fly to Israel, meet with the sponsor, test the printer's
facilities. And then one evening, without forewarning, he knocked at
my door, clutching *The Poem Itself.* Before I could usher him in, he
began: "If you think your method is needed for Europe's writers, it's
simply essential for Israel's."

I sighed, doubtful. "All the translations from Hebrew I've read
seemed—how shall I put it?—worthless."

"They *had* to be, and that's why I came so suddenly. Will you listen
while I explain?" Illustrating his argument with "characteristically
resonant" lines from Israeli poets, he opened my mind to a world I had
never imagined. And his logic was so compelling that I half-agreed
when he said: "You must go to Israel *soon.* I'll give you the names of
people. See what they have to show you. I know what your answer
will be." Before he left, he "hoped" I would bear in mind that *Judaica's*
sponsor had urged me to visit Jerusalem as their guest. "Now you

have a second reason to go, although, as I said before, you can't afford *not* to examine the whole 'operation' in Israel before you commit your firm."

Edwards favored the plan, and the more I thought of my friend's insistence, the sounder it seemed. *Judaica's* New York agent, anxious to act before I could change my mind, urged that I leave in January. I sent Edwards a memo: *Leave: Jan. 12; return: Feb. 10.* He replied: *Fine, if you're here by Feb 10.* Why the "if"? The date meant nothing until I learned that Frost had also been offered a trip to Israel. If he were to go, the date would be early March 1961. It was not until many years later that I learned of Frost's conversation the year before with his friend Charles Feinberg, who invited him to the Hebrew University. Neither man knew that Bernard Cherrick, of the same institution, had been planning to ask Frost to serve as its first Samuel Paley Foundation Lecturer. Cherrick visited Ripton in June. By the end of their talk it was understood that archaeological trips would be scheduled well in advance and that Thompson would travel with Frost and hold a few classes.

On a cold morning in mid-November my telephone woke me. Who could be calling at 7:00 A.M.? A gravelly voice asked slowly, "What do you eat for breakfast? Name it, and you'll find it here as soon as you come."

"Here" was of course the Westbury. "I changed plans," he said as he opened his door, "came last night." I seated myself at the table. "Help yourself! If it's not enough, we'll send for more." Noting my curious glance, he said, "Oh this? Nothing mysterious: orange juice with a raw egg in it. And that"—pointing to two large pitchers—"you've seen before: coffee and boiled water." He poured a dash of the first in a cup of the second. "I kept expecting you'd find a way to visit Ripton." The summer months, he remarked, "seemed busier than ever," with callers, family, friends of friends, professors, writers, all in addition to those who were always there—and the people making the film," and then Dr. Cherrick coming to lure me to Israel and inviting me." Instead of talking around "the whole idea of going there," which, he said, was much on his mind, he centered on me: "I don't understand why all at once you decide to go to Jerusalem. You've told me about that encyclopedia, but that's been going on for more than a year. There must be *something*—or shouldn't I know?"

"If anyone should, it's you; and you would have heard if I'd had the chance." After a quick account of all that had happened, I explained: Blame the *Judaica* editor, blame Hebrew poetry. Netanyahu opened my eyes.

He mentioned *Poetry*'s special number on poets writing in Israel. "I thought so well of it I wrote to the editor Henry Rago—that I thought it achieved 'a dominant idea without excogitation'—the whole issue, 'with all those young poets intent on themselves'—very striking, very moving. Did your friend ever see it?"

"Poem by poem. He used a short one, 'Isaac,' to show why the special resonance in Hebrew can't be kept in translation."

"Special resonance?"

"I can try to explain. The best English translation starts by saying that Isaac took a walk in the woods with his father. Two things missing: It's not the formal 'my father' but 'daddy,' and the Hebrew says that the *sun* was taking a walk. But these are minor—and, in any case, beside the crucial point that occurs when Isaac adds: 'My right hand in his left.' This, says my friend, is a pure evocation of *The Song of Songs:* 'His left hand is beneath my head, and his right hand doth embrace me.' " Frost nodded, somewhat surprised when I added: "One additional resonance—of a recent event. It comes after Isaac cries to his father to save him and Abraham answers: 'It is I who am being slaughtered,' evoking the Nazi massacres as he says, 'my blood is already on the leaves.' "

"Make sure when you're there to talk with Simon Halkin. That was a fine essay he wrote for the *Poetry* number. Tell him I said that to Rago." Rising out of his chair, he walked to the sunlit window, peered up and down the street. "Will they fire you if we take time off for a walk? We haven't talked since Elsie's dinner party."

We started out on the eastern side of the avenue facing the park. Few people passed us, though the windless sunny November day should have crowded the street with walkers. He rambled on about various small events of his summer and fall, stopping himself to ask me questions. Was my Cornell talk on *The Poem Itself* better or worse than the ones I'd made at the Y? Was it worth the trouble, flashing slides on the screen for the audience to read? Rounding up native reciters? Were the poems in Spanish spoken slowly enough for people to follow? And what about Sterling Brown? Had I heard? "He seems to have read every line I've published. Victor told me he came last year to your daughter's wedding. He wasn't sure if his wife was white."

"You know the rule, if ten percent of your blood is black, you're a Negro. According to some of their cracker neighbors, Daisy Brown is so lily-white that they yell at her 'Nigger-lover.' Not that they *have* to stay where they live."

"I know. Vassar wants him, also some other places, but he'll live and die, he says, where he is, at Howard." He paused. "He *has* to be with his people! I wonder why." From the dozen comments that followed, there was little doubt that whatever Sterling had told him stayed in his mind—from the use of "living dialect" speech in most of his verse to the need for using hawkers to sell *The Negro Caravan* in Harlem and all through the South. Could I send him a copy of *Southern Road* through my "Negro connections"? And what about all the stories Sterling "had gathered over the years for a book that 'might never be written?' We had a good talk at the party. I said we should have another in Brewster Village. He knows Cambridge from his Harvard year . . ." Which led him to ask if my daughter was still at the Boston Museum.

"Still at its School of Art, and I'm coming up in January to say goodbye before I take off for Israel."

"If you make it early enough, we could meet at the same hotel for a goodbye lunch. Just be sure that you let Kay know the date."

For the first time in all our walks, he was silent. I wondered if he'd say, if I asked, when his latest Christmas poem "Accidentally on Purpose" had been written. From its last line, with the Santayana phrase we had talked of before, I had guessed it was recent: Last year in "The Future of Man" symposium, he had used "passionate preference" more than once. Here he was taking a further step:

> And yet for all this help of head and brain
> How happily instinctive we remain,
> Our best guide upward further to the light,
> Passionate preference such as love at sight.

While debating whether or not to ask, I heard him sigh. "It's a funny world," but not in the usual way. This time he sighed to himself in what seemed to be self-communion. "Kay's had so many things to do this summer"—he remarked suddenly—"but she always has." Silence again. Then turning slowly to me, "You must have known about Kay . . . You and Louis talked often, I know." Taking my arm, he drew me close. "Between us now . . . as friends"—he whispered, pausing after each phrase—"We wanted to marry . . . It was all decided . . . But you know how matters seem . . . at times . . . Others to think of. . . ." He stopped, took a long breath. "And so . . . It was thought best . . . It was thought best . . ."

While I was busily planning my coming trip, Edwards dropped by my office: "Exciting news"—at the invitation of the President-elect, Frost would recite "The Gift Outright" at the coming inauguration. "Fine!" I replied. "Short enough and perfect for the occasion. Best of all, it's not an occasional poem. Lucky for Robert he hadn't been asked to write to order. It's the 20th, isn't it? I'll try to make sure to see the tee vee broadcast in Israel."

On Christmas morning I learned that there weren't any TV sets in Israel. I mentioned the fact to Edwards while waving a letter received the following morning from Fitts. "Here's the relevant passage:

C. [Cornelia] and I went to call on Frost last Thursday, and had a fine relaxt hour and a half; although C. was much concerned about his being alone (as he sure-God is) in that steepstair house. F. was dimly apprehensive about this Israel trip; seems to feel that he's being dragoon'd into it for 'political' purposes; and promises to 'give them the slip' if they try to use him versus Arabs, or versus anybody else. Or pro anybody else. The day after we saw him, the news broke about Israel's getting into the atomic club. I wish I could have heard what F. said when he read that item; but I suspect that he may decide to call the whole trip off and retire to dudgeon in Ripton. The quality that fascinates me in F. is the radiance of the young face that keeps breaking through the wrinkles: at intervals, and disconcertingly.

He worried needlessly, I thought. The Paley lectureship was a strictly cultural, literary, academic affair—not a whiff of politics about it. I would strongly assure him of that when we met in Boston.

"Where's your spy?" he asked, scanning the length and breadth of the restaurant. "I made them promise to keep him out if he comes. You're safe. So am I." Not once in all the hours of talk did I hear a hint of any concern about Israel. "Kennedy" and "the great event" were his opening words. When had I learned of the invitation and the name of the poem? Did I know how it came about? First time in our history—asking a poet to play a part in a President's inauguration. "When I heard who'd won the election, I called it a 'triumph of Protestantism over itself.' Nobody seemed to know what I meant, I could see; but I didn't explain . . . Now, when do you go? And only to Israel?"

"After Jerusalem: Istanbul, Ephesus, Pergamum—my step-daughter's surgeon-husband runs the Air Force Hospital in what we used to call Smyrna. Athens next, and Delphi, then London for a day or two. All but the last are new to my eyes, not to my head. Countries of the imagination."

"And maybe that's what we ought to let them remain. But we don't allow it. We can't." Not in this age when it's much too easy to circle the planet. "All we will ever see are the leavings of what used to be Jerusalem or the Parthenon. Not the same thing at all, but once in a while"—his eyes brightened—"somebody—no tourist-traveler—stumbles against a treasure. Do you know of the archaeologist Sukenik? I met him accidentally ten years ago when I called on Freddy Adams. He had taken four of the Dead Sea Scrolls from Israel to the Morgan Library to have them make some infrared photographs. What a sight they made! Think of it—they were written by scribes in the first century. They're a thousand years older than any biblical manuscript known—and in almost perfect condition! Sukenik and I became friends quickly; we understood each other. He wanted me to come to Israel; he'd take me to special places. Now that I'm finally going, he won't be there. His son is an archaeologist.** I plan to see him."

The Scrolls may have made him remember that I broke away from our last visit to call for Mary Ellen Chase, who would speak to my class on the Bible. "Did you learn any thing that you hadn't known?" he asked rather sharply. She had come, I explained, not to enlighten me but the students, yet I learned enough that was new to be able to answer yes and to give him examples. First, about "feet"—their un-suspected importance. And to judge from some of the lines she quot-ed, "feet" were exalted. Second, the crucially different "function" of each of the Testaments.

Frost thought for a moment. "Victor says that everything found in the New was there before in the Old. Victor, of course, is religious. What about Mary Chase?" I admitted the question hadn't entered my mind. "What would you say if someone asked about me?" Nonplussed, all I could do was stare. "Oh come, it's easy." He chuckled. "All you need do, if your questioner's up to it, is to make him compare me with Eliot. He's a pessimistic Christian. I'm an optimistic pagan. That's what I always say when they try to corner me."

Who, I wondered, had tried? Surely not Reichert. Thompson, perhaps? In fact quite probably, considering his *Times* review of *A Masque of Reason* and Frost's enraged response (212). "Larry," he mused—was he reading my mind?—"didn't seem as much surprised as I thought he'd be when I talked of going to Israel." Pause. "He'll have a class at the university—important business—of his own."

"I've been thinking"—I tried not to stammer—"with a bit of hope—of your trip together. Not knowing the language, both of you may be forced to depend on each other more than you'd like. It will offer the chance for—dare I come out with it?" Frost gazed at me steadily. "Mending fences, frank talk of the way things changed— why and how to go back to what they had been at the start."

"Too late. Couldn't go back if we wanted." He stared at the table-cloth, unaware of the waiter beside him. "You are the only one I can count on now and I know you haven't forgotten." I nodded, pointing a thumb toward the waiter. Frost looked up. "Time for desserts?" The "young face breaking through the wrinkles" that had so disconcerted Fitts was visible now in its "radiance."

We had time enough to parry a dozen subjects and to lay them neatly at rest. In fact, he had never seemed better, though one of the questioned words—"play" in "Two Tramps in Mud Time"—had to be left unsettled. "Only where love and need are one,/ And work is play for mortal stakes"—what he wanted of "work is play" was the gambler's word. "A punctuation mark isn't the answer. Something we'll have to return to after we both come back."

"I plan to be your advance scout when I get to Israel. Any instructions?"

"One—and very important." His hand covered a smile. "Tell them how bad I can be if they're not careful!"

Few events in my twenty-four days in Israel involved Frost. I had other concerns: the encyclopedia and a possible *Modern Hebrew Poem Itself.* That the brief visit would add a world to my life, nobody could have made me imagine, or that all I heard and saw and dreamed as I traveled this "Old-New Country" would alter my years ahead. As

Frost's advance scout, I briefed a number of writers, professors, public relations people, and others eager to learn whatever might make Frost's visit "all it should be." They asked about food and drink ("his favorite is ginger ale, with rum if possible"), his hearing ("slightly deaf, but unpredictably"), his physical endurance ("seemingly limitless, but needs to be held in check"), his attitude toward well-intentioned praisers ("he hates apple-polishing"). Other questions, about his likes and dislikes and "things to watch for," demanded care. I spoke of his playfulness—light, and serious, often baffling—of his special interest in Israel's archaeology. As for religion, they knew, I supposed, Cook's discussion, ** also the *Masques*. His dislikes? I advised against praising other living poets. And I urged them to choose a first-rate guide to show him the country: "Someone who knows the names of all your trees and flowers." Frost might even decide to "go off botanizing" on his own . . .

Welcomed home three weeks later by Edwards, Rigg, and their aides, Cecile Daly and Frances Keegan, I rolled up my sleeves and attacked the mail hiding my desk top. A swift hour passed, then Edwards called for "a short talk" that was long enough for him to say how happy he was at my having arranged for a book by the Prime Minister. And what sort of person was Ben Gurion? How could he find the time for writing? Robert, I said, ought to meet him. They'd understand each other. Besides, the Jerusalem hosts would stand on their heads to please him. "Robert," Edwards reported, "phoned from the Coast while you were away. No message, no question. All he said was: 'I want to hear myself praised.' "

I wondered how much praise he could take after the recent event, with the "eyes of the nation" watching him. The night before, my wife had described the Inauguration. Frost, I realized, in spite of himself, had written a poem-to-order as a prelude to "The Gift Outright." The rites began at 10:00 A.M., with Cardinal Cushing's benediction; Marian Anderson next, with the national anthem; another prayer; Vice-president's oath of office taken by Lyndon Johnson; then another prayer. Frost, next on the program, walked through the bitter-cold air to the lectern. "First, the dedication," he announced, holding wind-blown pages. Brilliant sunlight glared on his head. He stumbled over the opening word, but after five or six lines, he stopped: "Not having a good light here at—" Not all the words came through on the small television but the picture was clear. Frost struggled on, then stopped: "Can't see in the sun." When Lyndon Johnson tried to cut off the glare with his hat, Frost pushed it aside, uttering something that made the audience roar and applaud. Then he set the typescript aside. "This was to be the preface to the poem I can say without reading. It goes like this." Another round of applause and then, without hesitation, he recited "The Gift Outright" in a clear, full voice. At the last line, after mentioning a change for the present occasion, he finished the verse and added at once: "What I was leading up to was a dedication of the poem to the President-elect—" He was still speaking but the words were lost to my wife. They were not lost to the people at Holt. In his nervous state, Frost had said "to the President-elect John Finley," substituting a Harvard professor's name for Kennedy's. The blunder—he had dropped his voice—must have been missed by most listeners, who rounded out their tribute to him with long applause.

First on my list of tasks after jousts with my mail was a detailed letter to Frost provoked by the plans prepared by his hosts. Three packed typewritten pages were needed to show why the places they failed to include *had* to be visited—Megiddo (*i.e.,* Armageddon), above the caravan route to Damascus; King Solomon's copper mines in the desert; the mad-looking Arab townlet Jaffa (Joppa of Jonah's memory); the farm kibbutz on the Galilee. I mailed a copy to Thompson, adding a note on the archaeological remains of the Nabateans and the Dead Sea "sculptures" of Sodom above "Chez Mme Lot."

Larry, who had come to New York for a business talk with Edwards, called at my office afterward. He had read each word of my letter; he wanted to see every last place I had mentioned. But, alas, I was much too hopeful: Frost would never agree—if it smacks of rubber-necking. "Curious word to apply to the Galilee, Joppa, Megiddo," I said. "Besides, he told me quite firmly that he's planning to talk with Sukenik's son . . . Nothing in Israel means more to Frost than its archaeology." Larry smiled, shaking his head for moments. Was he mocking my innocence?

"What a time you had!" he mused. "At least I can try to match it."

"You'll probably go me one better. After all, I missed the Inauguration while you and Kay had a perfect view of it." His forehead furrowed. "What a terrible time for Robert," I said. "Bungling his lines—blind in the sun—unable to see what he'd written—forced to give up in front of the crowd—to throw himself on their mercies. Lucky he did so well with 'The Gift Outright.' "

"You really *believe* that story!" He nodded, half-smiling.

"Story?"

"Frost had it planned from the start. Everything—down to the oversize typewritten pages Stewart Udall had made when he said that the regular ones would be hard to read in the sun."

"Are you saying he really *could* read them?"

"He never intended to—not with the wonderful chance he had, with the eyes of the crowd on *him*—Frost, not Kennedy—watching for what he'd do next. So he tricked them all, pushing the papers aside with a canny apology, then with the limelight all to himself, he recited at the top of his form 'The Gift Outright,' which he'd spoken hundreds of times."

I stared at him. "Are you going to say *that* when you write the biography?" I asked quietly.

"Maybe"—lifting an eyebrow.

"I shouldn't if I were you. Readers will think you're mad." He laughed in scorn, shaking his head. He waved goodbye from the doorway.

More than once I had wondered about Frost's fears: He had never offered proof of his need for "protection from Larry." Now I could stop wondering. Thompson hadn't bothered to try to reconcile his claim (that Frost had planned each move "from the start") with the blundering of "Finley" at the close. Would a person in full control of "everything" ruin his crowning moment? Too unlikely even for Thompson, who had long before arrived at the stage at which he found it impossible not to *believe* the worst. The distorting lens through which he saw the poet by now had become his eyes. How protect anyone from the havoc of warped vision? By resolute efforts to question, modify, temper? Offer interpretations that Thompson would wave aside as foolishly wrong?

What of the etiology of this deep and grave distrust? Hints were all I had heard, and not of the still redeemable sort that suggested answers. In the eyes of the public the two were friends, while the truth! . . . I should probably learn the reasons in time. Meanwhile what mattered most was the course to choose.

What if Frost were to break the relationship? Thompson would then be free to write whatever he pleased, to paint the alarming picture he considered true. Frost would surrender all constraints that his publishers and his friends might conceivably force on the man he no longer dared trust. Yet Thompson, once deprived of the seal of official biographer, could not venture too far in his vilifications for fear of portraying himself as the spiteful avenger. Frost would have to choose between two risks, and to me the decision was clear, since no amount of constraining could cleanse the official biography of its author's bias. This is what I should have to propose, now that Thompson had forced me to see his vision of Frost.

My next meeting with Frost—March 8th, the day before his departure—proved too hurried to talk of anything other than Israel. He had heard all about my trip, but if I had kept some special advice to give him, now was the time to speak. Nothing, I said, that he probably hadn't already been told, though two different reading groups had been studying all his poems, for which he could blame Charles Feinberg, whose speech in October had started "the Frost ball rolling. And, of course, as you ordered, Robert, I warned them about your badness. Everything else seems too subjective to call 'advice.' " For example? he asked. "The sense of aliveness there, curiosity, questions, excited talk talk talk as though they had lowered me into a pressure cooker. Unbelievably different from what I'd expected, for the minute I stepped from the plane it was as though I had known the country before—another homecoming, mad though it sounds."

"I know." He nodded. "Like the feeling I had when we took the boat to Glasgow and I looked at the Hebrides and the shore of Scotland. Same kind of thing. Generations removed, but not the language." He chuckled. "In your case too, since they all speak English, don't they?" He thought for an instant. "But you must have learned *something* from all those people you talked with on the book. You learned no Hebrew at all?"

"Not much. But enough to make me wonder if Whorf and Sapir were right—that the language a person speaks conditions his thinking. What would you make of the fact that because Hebrew has no word for 'dawn,' they call it 'the morning of the morning'? Or the moon: When they want to describe what it *does* in the sky, they can't say it rises or shines or sets or anything else that's limiting; they say the 'the moon moons.' " We were plunging into one of our favorite subjects, the last word calling to mind the difference between the Greek and Latin for "moon," one concerned with measuring time, the other with giving light. From there we moved to a grander view of the skies—Einstein's relativity, which a Hopi Indian had much less trouble conceiving than a Spaniard or ourselves. We were skipping about to the different uses of "you" in German and French—*tu-vous, du-Sie*—when the telephone rang. I raised the receiver. "It's the operator. Asks if you'll accept the call. It's personal and important." Shaking his head in annoyance, he grasped the instrument. The call might go on for an hour. I raised my wristwatch. "See you tomorrow." He nodded, looking up from the phone, "Here at eleven!"

The day's plan called for a farewell luncheon at the American Friends of the Hebrew University, two blocks away. Entering Frost's hotel at the hour expected, I went directly to his suite. Kay answered my knock. "Please follow me, please!" she whispered, then opened the door. What I saw made me gasp: Frost seated alone at the end of the room, close to a window, his gaze fixed on a wall. I was barely able to say hello and to wave my hand.

Turning around, he shouted at me, "Desert me! Desert me!"

Kay, standing silent in the passageway to the smaller room, beckoned to me. I stepped to her side, his haggard image clouding my eyes. "What"—I stammered—"what can we . . . do? Wait and . . . hope?" She shrugged, uncertain. There was no need for either of us to speak. Wild thoughts clashed through my head, with "Desert me! Desert me!" still in my ears. Kay finally rose from her chair, glimpsed at the street below, then stepped toward the passageway close to the other room. "Has this ever happened before?" I asked quietly. She glared at me, then averted her eyes. I thought out loud: "The farthest distance he would travel from home!" We remained standing for moments, then made our way back to the smaller room.

How long we waited there, I can't even guess—ten, twenty, thirty minutes?—when a strong call from the other room shook us awake: "Maybe we ought to go now." Frost, walking calmly into the passageway, turned to me, "What does your watch say?"

"Twelve, nearly."

"Then they won't have to wait. You said the place is around the corner."

We reached the building sooner than they expected. "Welcome! And right on the hour, Mr. Frost," said the man who greeted us.

"I haven't yet learned to be late, but give me time and I may."

Warm waves of friendliness spread through the hall from the long dais to the score of tables below, each with its cluster of guests. "The Friends" made no effort to hide their delight that "America's poet, now in his ninth decade," had "consented to brave the longest journey yet to a land that his presence will honor." While listening to the men at the speakers' table, I remembered Frost's telephone call to Edwards: "I want to hear myself praised." Was he now having more than his fill? When at last he rose to make a reply, he was graciousness itself. Facing a worshipful audience, he was completely in command. "How hard it is to keep from being king," I heard myself quoting, "When it's in you and in the situation."

The words applied as well to the conference that followed. "Go ahead and ask them hard," he charged the reporters. For sixty minutes or more, he and his challengers joined in a potpourri of questions; answers (straight or elusive); rimed couplets; explications of earlier *mots,* epigrams, jokes; comments on Kennedy, San Francisco, the New School, science, our monkey ancestors, the Russians, and war. He was going to Israel not to see the sights but "to give two lectures and sit around with the students. I'll simply rumple their brains, *fondly.*" Why was he going to Israel? Because he looked on the young nation "as a sort of American colony" with "so much of the American people's spirit. They have many, many things in common with us— more than anyone else." What troubled him, however, was the "boundary right in the middle" of Jerusalem. Throughout history "fences are always being set up . . . and falling down." As for his line—"Good fences make good neighbors": "It's the other fellow in the poem who says that . . . I don't know. Maybe I was both fellows in the poem. . . ."

After an hour or so of supposed relaxation at the Westbury, he was ready to leave for his next event: a small dinner with Kay, Lesley, Edwards, and Thompson. I offered to take him by cab to the Holt building en route to my early class. The driver, who had opened the two door-windows as well as his glass partition, seemed to enjoy Frost's jokingly spiced monologue. As we drove past 55th Street, I drew from my pocket a three-inch box with a bottle inside. "Robert, for you: my going-away present. It's just the thing in case you should feel a hurried call coming on. Paregoric—twenty drops in some water."

"Water? You told me the water was bad."

"Trust me! This works. I know. Take it along with you! Don't be afraid; you won't be addicted."

At the Holt building both of us stepped to the street. "Goodbye." I smiled. "Sorry I won't be with you, but I'll pray for you."

"That's too easy." He shook his head. Gazing into my eyes and wagging his finger, he intoned slowly, "I want you to think of me every day." I nodded. He shook my hand, then entered the building.

"Madison to 32nd," I said, settling back in the cab.

"What a wonderful man! What a *talker!*" The driver repeated "wonderful" twice, then "talker." "Wouldn't know he comes from the city from how he sounds."

"I suppose you know who he is, don't you?"

"Sure, I know, sure, sure. I seen him on TV too. He's that famous rabbi from Brooklyn. . . ."

Ten days in Israel, then Athens, where the wife of Ambassador Briggs cured his intestinal trouble with tea and custard. A press conference, a formal reception, three full lectures, one per day, and a climb with Amherst friends to walk the Acropolis—then England. More events, but the cure had lost its effect. Sick enough to agree to shorten his stay, he returned the night of March 31st. I called on him next morning. When I asked about Israel, he picked up the phone and pointed to Larry—"he must have made notes on it all." Larry's interpretations were not what I'd come to hear. I asked him questions of fact; he answered in kind; and before long I was bidding *bon voyage* to Frost on his trip to Boston. We would meet on the 7th at Joe Blumenthal's after the New School reading.

We had little time to talk. The guests kept circling him in. Twice he was able to break away to speak with Joe. He turned to me en route, "supposing" Larry had told me all I had wanted to know. Facts, I said, were all I asked; I wasn't interested in his views. He paused, peering at me. Tonight, I said, at the New School; Monday, April 10th, the Y. Two readings in four days! Hard going? "Not hard at all," but lots of people to see—*"friends:* Wescott, Cousins, you. . . ." We would have the afternoon together after the Y reading.

From the moment we started speaking, I thought, from watching his face, he was tired of "talking Israel." Yet he wouldn't "pass" my questions, and once he was "into recollecting," his tone regained the ardor I was used to hearing. True, he had taken "one last look" at the

Dead Sea Scrolls, thanks to Cherrick; true also, he had written "special words" in Edward Thomas' copy of *North of Boston* that Feinberg had sent as a gift to their National and University Library. "And I saw something they wouldn't allow *you* to see. On the Jordan side: the Old City, the Stations of the Cross—not that you ever had asked." On the other hand, they "hadn't arranged time enough for Jonah's Joppa, Solomon's mines, or your other suggestions; but one of the poets for your book, an American, showed me the wall—and the barbed wires" dividing Jerusalem. The more he talked, the more I felt that for him the visit had larger meaning now than when he was there. He had come to be "fond of each of the men and women" who had been his guides. Also the President, "who's said to know all about all the Hebrew poets. I wanted to meet one of his older favorites, but she can't speak English."

"Larry told me the great event was your evening lecture to inaugurate the Paley series—it went extremely well—with a fine audience."

"And a keener introduction. Do you know Daniel Fineman?" I shook my head. "He began in Hebrew, then changed to English and turned toward me. Most of the time, you know, I try to ignore introductions but *this* one I listened to, all of it—and the ending. He said: 'It is well that before our lectures, we should now begin, not with something *about* American civilization, but with what Mr. Frost *is*— the thing itself.' That was too good a joke to be left alone, so I used it; and they all knew how to take it. I began: 'I *am* American civilization.' The rest of my talk you pretty well know."

I wondered if someone had sent a copy to the *Times Book Review*.**

"I should have asked Fineman. I wrote him saying some things I ought to have said when I was there:

> The way you turned on me on the platform to make your introduction personal is one of my chief memories. I got a lot more out of Israel than you might have thought from my ornery resistance. It was much that I saw why you were there—and your wife. . . . You are only more an Israelite than you are American. I am more an American than I am an Israelite. I am all for nationalities. Keep thinking of me as I will keep thinking of you.

"If you go there again, be sure to see him. I spoke about you and your book. I would have asked if he knew the writer you're working with. I forgot his name."

"Carmi—means 'my vineyard.' He knew all about your coming."

"Maybe he was there at the talking sessions. And maybe he didn't like to hear that all of us will go down the drain except Homer and Shakespeare. Ask him, when you write!" He looked at me. "You don't agree? Neither can I, much of the time." Homer led him to Greece, and "the kind of homecoming you said you felt about Israel."

"And also like the feeling I had when I went from outside London to Brighton by footpaths through the back-country—three days' walking through Shakespeare's England. Bob Fitzgerald said when he met you in London, you were bleary-eyed from spending the whole night reading his *Odyssey*. Homer's, that is, whoever he was. Homer, Shakespeare, the two greats, and each without a biography!" Biography drew us forward to Eliot and back to Henry James. Had he read, I asked, Leon Edel?—two volumes already and more to come. No, he hadn't, but he'd gladly wear out his eyes with five on William.

He was apt to bring him into our talks when a question touched some passage of relevance stored in his mind. Nothing he said connected the thought of James to the wall dividing Jerusalem. "William James"—he nodded suddenly—"*believed:* 'Believe that life *is* worth living, and your belief will help create the fact.' I quote it because of that wall, that wall in the city. A bad thing. I hadn't come to advise and they wouldn't have listened, but they know that peace is what they need more than anything else. And peace can be had. Not by waiting for evidence. We live by believing ahead of the evidence. They have to believe peace *into* existence; they have to believe it *in* and do what is needed. . . ."

It was getting late—time for an hour or two alone, before his dinner with Wescott at the National Institute. He wouldn't return till June, and then for a day, our last talk until fall, unless I should "properly follow orders and come to Ripton." Before leaving, he urged me not to forget May 1st, the "Evening with Robert Frost" at the State Department. Wouldn't I like to come and watch it all?—James once more, I thought to myself: our "innate propensity to get ourselves noticed, and noticed favorably, by our kind. . . ."

Three mid-April readings: one each at Amherst, Smith, and New York, at the Asia Society. More engagements: Amherst, Cambridge, the University of Vermont. . . . Finally (April 26th) a day's vacation before going for Washington, then the University of Virginia and back, to prepare for the May 1st talk, sponsored by the State Department. "Heavy going?" one of his friends remarked, "for a man in his eighty-seventh year, ordered back home by a London doctor a fortnight before." Except for President Kennedy and Secretary Rusk, everyone—from Supreme Court justices to generals, cabinet members to ambassadors, senators to unofficial notables—crowded the new auditorium. They seemed to treasure his words as he spoke his mind about science "opposed" to poetry, complementing his views with readings of well-known poems. He had been on stage for more than an hour, but the audience wouldn't allow him to leave—standing ovations and calls for encores. The long reception that followed fittingly closed "An Evening of Triumph"—all the more precious for being won in a place whose tribute affirmed his faith in the arts as an unsuspected, still-to-be tapped source of public power.

But why, some asked, was "Liberal Washington" honoring "Conservative Frost"? One reporter, Leonard Lyons of the *New York Post,* during a cordial exchange on the El Al flight to Israel, had confessed his confusion. Frost explained quickly: "A liberal is someone who can't take his own side in an argument." Liberals, moreover, are agnostic, but no Catholic can be agnostic. And, hating "stalemates," he wanted "someone to cut the Gordian knots"—which Kennedy surely would do. The conversation closed on a promise to meet for lunch at the poet's convenience. Two months later he set the date; Lyons proposed the place. Frost would be coming down for a granddaughter's wedding, and June 14th looked free.

We began as four but halfway through the second course, Mrs. Lyons made her excuses. The three of us—for the most part, Frost—continued to talk. A few days later "The Lyons Den" printed a brief account:

> POET: Gene Tunney, lunching at the Four Seasons the other day, crossed the room to our table and embraced silver-haired poet Robert Frost. The former champ mentioned Frost's travels, and the poet said: "The only place I want to go now is nowhere." When he travels, he added, he doesn't look for the sights but for the insights.

Obviously, he was back on stage for the press, having often made the quip before; and despite the setting and Lyons' attempts to control the discussion, Frost rambled about as he pleased. He had stayed with Holt forty-five years, "longer than any author has ever been with one firm." More talk about publishing—of the house of which he had just discovered that he owned Stock Certificate No. 1. As for his friend from Cambridge, Justice Frankfurter, "He says something first, and *then* believes it"; and even when he quite agrees with the Court, "he feels he has to write an extra opinion."

Frost suddenly asked if he might walk the aisle to inspect the potted birch trees. Lyons and I followed. Gene Tunney, about to leave, mentioned something about the price of a poem. "One thousand dollars a line," Frost snapped. "Four thousand for a quatrain, but for a sonnet, $12,000. The last two lines of a sonnet don't mean anything anyway." Tunney's face looked troubled. I wondered if Tunney knew how to take Frost's quip. Ought I tell him to look at "Putting in the Seed" or "The Silken Tent," which is actually one long sentence.

The waiter moved aside as we took our seats again. It was nearing time to leave, but not till the book I had brought along had been duly inscribed. "Not much," said Frost, riffling the pages. "Not much when you add them up—six hundred pages besides the *Masques*— about ten a year." He had said this once before to me, in a half-despondent voice; now it was more like a challenge. Lyons made no reply. "The title is wrong, you know. It ought to be 'The Complete Poems So Far.' I'll have another book next spring—that is, if my publisher likes it."

"Any day now," I said as we started our walk, "Lyons will break the news." Usually we avoided Park but today the avenue looked deserted and, except for the rush of cars, pleasantly quiet. "Have you found your final title?" I asked. His instant glance bade me explain: "Ciardi said it would be 'The Great Misgiving,' but that was 1959, after his Florida visit, and I haven't heard of it since." The silence goaded me on. "Of course it made me think of your own adjective-less 'Misgiving' in *New Hampshire*. And Melville's in his *Battle Pieces*. I suppose 'The Great' before 'Misgiving' changes it all. There's no hurry, I know. You've plenty of time."

He mused. "Time, time. I've always felt I had all the time in the world, all the time in the world." He shook his head, "I still feel that way." I remarked how lucky he was, since I'd never found time enough for half the things I felt driven to do. "Driven?" he wondered. By whom? Who was it made me so concerned with training people for publishing? "But all that's over soon, after the spring. Or aren't you going to let the poor thing die?"

"N.Y.U. wants us to keep it alive, and they're even willing to carve the name of the angel on a plaque or something, *if* we find one."

"Rigg must have lots of money."

"Is that a suggestion? Just last month I mentioned N.Y.U., which he's called 'a boon for publishers.' But as for becoming an angel, he hates all charity gifts, all grants, all foundations, especially when the donor is named. I've given up angel-hunting."

"There's always money for colleges, but I want it where it belongs. I want it for the high schools"—permanent chairs endowed for teachers of literature, deserving ones. "Barzun wouldn't agree. He wants to make our system like the French. And it's good, it's brilliant, you know. He wants to speed up the system and harden it up but I want to *tone* it up. I'd tone it up by elevating the high school in some way. I made a plan to do something. We'll see what comes of it. Nothing, probably. Do you know Barzun well?"

"I've just received his essay for my *Varieties* book. One of the best-and-worst is on *Moby-Dick*. In some places it's mad, in others excellent. I hope you'll look at it some time."

"Did you ever read *Melville's Quarrel with God?*"

"No. Should I?"

"One reviewer said it should have been called *Thompson's Quarrel with Melville*. Tell me what you think of it—if you read it." I asked if he'd ever taught Melville. "*Typee* once—at Amherst—to give them a taste of the rebel. But the best way is through Bartleby." We'd been walking up and down 67th Street, near the Westbury. "You know," he remarked, "we ought to talk about Larry's *Quarrel* book—if you get to read it. You should."

"I'll try to get to it sometime in August."

"Good. And then you must come to Ripton. Remember!" I nodded. "I'm also working on a book this summer, but I'll take time off for baseball."

With my Ridgefield house a half-hour's drive from the Untermeyers' in Newtown, we indulged ourselves in more than a few visits. High on our list of current concerns was the book that Frost had told me about eighteen months before: *The Letters of Robert Frost to Louis Un-*

termeyer. The manuscript was ready for editing and plans had been made for issuing it in the current year. Frost, however, had interposed delays. Finally, on July 11th, he confessed his concerns. "Come up and see us," he wrote to his oldest friend and critic, "and I will go to work arranging the manuscript for my next book that, until I get it out, stands in the way I feel of your publishing my letters." It was clear from reading between the lines that the *Letters* would not appear within Frost's lifetime. Setting the work aside, Louis at once redirected his time to immediate projects, among them new tasks required by his recent appointment as Poetry Consultant at the Library of Congress.

By late September I presented Frost with the small surprise:

Remember my telling you that your old friend Wallace Stevens had once written a poem about me, called "Mr. Burnshaw and the Statue"? Well, an English critic, Frank Kermode, published a book on Stevens and a young writer came to me in May and showed me some of the things that were being said about the origin of that poem: my review of *Ideas of Order* in the *New Masses.* He asked: "Well, aren't you going to do something about it?"

I did—I wrote an essay and sent it on to the *Sewanee Review,* and they took it at once for the Summer issue. I've sent a copy to you in care of Kay. I think you may be interested in the article.

Al Edwards says that the manuscript of your new book of poems will be here in a month or so. Joe Blumenthal is already thinking of the format, but he ought to know the title, so that he can think of that too. . . .

Would it be *The Great Misgiving* after all? I was not the only one who questioned its rightness. Louis had urged him to settle on "One More Brevity," the title of the 1953 Christmas poem. And even after the choice had been made, at least one steadfast admirer argued against it. In any case, the book would be named for one of its poems. Of the few possibilities, *In the Clearing* seemed to Frost an acceptable title for what he knew would be his final collection.

Weeks passed—not a word from Frost. "Why the great hurry?" my secretary Frances Keegan said each time I asked if "the package from

Cambridge" had come. When at last it arrived and she planted it on my desk, my anxiety may have been evident. "We'll open it together," she smiled, slowly undoing the wrappers. "And I'll see that you won't be distracted by telephone calls. Please sit back and enjoy it."

The instant she left, I reached for the table of contents. Forty titles—only a third with an unfamiliar ring! Much relief—yet why? After all, I had probably heard every poem he had published since *Steeple Bush*—in the Christmas keepsakes, magazines, *A Remembrance Collection,* the readings. But what of those he'd held back? The epigraph from "Kitty Hawk" and the second and fourth titled sections made it essential to read the entire book. This was no random assemblage.

The first eight poems, each well known, were followed by five grouped under "Cluster of Faith." "Kitty Hawk" led off the lengthiest section: fifteen poems, 1,140 lines out of 1,707. "Quandary," the title piece of the fourth unit, "stopped" the book—willingly, perhaps wilfully, on an open-ended note. Among these nine short pieces were two that I hoped could be "lost." How convey this to Frost? He often referred to the book as his "last go-down" and, viewed as a work brought forth in the eighty-ninth year of a poet, it was surely (so far as I knew) without compare. To my own surprise, without even noting the score of remarkable lines in otherwise unremarkable poems, I counted eight or nine that would have to form part of any book representative of Frost—"The Draft Horse" included, a lyric as dark as any his readers had known.

The moment I gave my report to Edwards, his face broke into smiles, and the longer I talked, the happier he seemed. Because I knew he'd repeat my words to Frost, I said nothing about the poems I hoped would be dropped or the odd way in which the manuscript ended. And because I had never liked "Kitty Hawk" and Edwards knew it, I made my case by speaking of Huntington Cairns, to whom it was dedicated. Cairns, whom I knew through *The Limits of Art* anthology, was "the ideal person," I said, "to savor the 'skylark mixture'— pardon the phrase!—of autobiography, myth, metaphysics, faith, religion, and doggerel. Besides, Robert quotes from 'Kitty' whenever he can. The poem's not to my taste but I can't doubt its importance. Do you really *like* it?"

Edwards rose as I started to leave. "Robert's adding one more poem to the book. It will be here before you see him."

Frost was due to arrive for the Poetry Society dinner on January 18th, with the morning after reserved for *Life's* photographers. Several days before we met, the promised poem arrived, with "Jan 12 62" written in the poet's hand: "In winter in the woods" the twelve-line lyric (untitled) began. Placed as the final poem, it changed the tenor of "Quandary" as the name for the closing section, sending one back to the centerpiece "Kitty Hawk" and the second poem, "Away!" For these and related reasons, it could hardly fail to suggest various special meanings.**

As I made my way to the Westbury, I felt we had both been wrong in alloting so little time to a matter so large as the book he had finally made up his mind to publish. Yet there were no questions apart from spelling and, possibly, punctuation; nor could he need any proof of the care with which I had read each phrase and line. He'd already heard how moved and pleased and startled I'd been, as I realized how the work would stand as a whole. "It's all right, then?" he asked as I entered his room. "Nothing to argue about?"

"I've queried some commas and spellings. You can handle them quickly—unless *you* have some changes."

"None at the moment."

"Why don't we run through the pages. One or two points you will want to consider. Indulge the editor-part of me which takes for granted all the manuscript's virtues."

"That's a relief."

Glancing slowly at every page, we came on nothing to question till we reached the first of the poems I wanted to lose. I looked at him without speaking. "You want me to take it out?" he asked.

"Not if you're really sure it strengthens the book."

"Any others?" I flipped the page to the second poem and waited. "This doesn't help either?" I said nothing. "Let's go on to the end."

We gazed for minutes at the new closing poem. "Joe will enclose the opening line," I said, "within square brackets, unless you've discovered a title." He shook his head. "But you still want it to stand alone as the last page of the book?" He nodded. "What of the date you've written below at the left. Should it stay?"

"Not if you think it shouldn't."

"Shall I take the manuscript when I call in the morning?"

"Take it away after we've had our walk, unless you have to be going now—though I may decide to look at it after the dinner."

It was cool outside but the sun still glowed on the street we took toward the park. "We have time enough," he said, "till the dinner to-night. Starts at seven."

Ends by eleven, I feared. But with all that the Poetry Society is planning to do it may take that long: the sculpture of Frost by Leo Cherne and the money prizes. "I suppose you know who's getting the one given by Holt in your name. Richard Wilbur's receiving the Melville Cane, Theodore Roethke the Shelley award." I asked if he'd seen Roethke's newest book, *Words for the Wind*.

"I have it at home." He nodded. "Did I ever tell you what happened after we'd talked one afternoon?" He went on to describe how Roethke, after driving to a "special, secret, open field," had taken each sheet from his typewritten manuscript and set it down on the grass—each one separately, maybe sixty or eighty, side by side in rows in a kind of square. Then walking back to where Frost stood, shouted, "Just look at them there! *Please* look; look at them! Look at my *poems!*" "Yes, yes," Frost had replied, "I see them all." Then Roethke carefully lifted each sheet from the grass, gathered them up, and led Frost back to the car. I waited to hear if Roethke had made any explanation, but Frost started to talk of Roethke and Robert Lowell. He was not quite sure of the year—1947 perhaps—but it happened in August at Ripton. "I came on them unaware. They kept addressing each other: 'Come on, you manic! Come on, you manic.' How these manics talk about *their* misery!" Frost stared at the pavement. Minutes went by in silence; then he stopped, pointing east. We started back. "I've never listened to Roethke. I'm told he's a 'great performer.' "

"Two parts poet, one part vaudeville actor—at least the night I was there. He might have had one drink too much. In any case, I'd rather read him than hear him and skip his echoes of Yeats. But his *own* poems! his own voice!" I added with warm approval, "He'll be reading something tonight—he'll have to, in return for the Shelley prize."

I left Frost at the Westbury door. "That story of the poems on the grass"—he called me back—"it's not for the world to know." He waved and entered the lobby.

The next morning at ten, when he opened the door, he appeared little the worse for the night before. Tedious formalities had taken up more than an hour before the food was served. Then the president, Cecil Hemley, announced a host of minor prizes, clearing the way for the major ones ahead. Wilbur, accepting the first for *Advice to a Prophet & Other Poems,* read a Villon translation. Roethke, next on the list, for the largest award, said he would read, instead of a poem of his own, a quatrain "inspired by that old woodchuck at my right":

I like New England men,
Their women now and then.
Of poets they're the most—
But mostly Robert Frōst.

After amused applause, Hemley announced the winner of Holt's prize in honor of Frost. A young poet and post-office worker from Texas, William Barney, rose to receive the check and a friendly embrace from Frost.

Hemley's predecessor introduced "Mr. Leo Cherne, economist and Sunday sculptor." After the portrait bust of Frost was unveiled, the poet-subject made a surprisingly brief speech on behalf of the Poetry Society. Trying hard to hide his dislike of the sculpture, he succeeded enough to rouse the hall to cheer and urge him to "say" some poems. He complied with one by Browning, a second by John Davies, then a line from "Faith without Words." Though some in the audience recognized Browning and Davies, nobody rose to name them. Anxious to end the evening, Frost recited "Fire and Ice," then "Lines Written in Dejection on the Eve of Great Success," stressing the title. Amid loud cheering, Hemley adjourned the meeting.

The doorman found us a cab. "Will you take us west, 54th Street; it's 237?" I said as we settled ourselves. I mentioned that Roethke had left a message for me at Holt. Frost hadn't bothered to listen. "Maybe I should have said my poem on the King—tested it out." He mentioned the source: the Arabian Nights—"one of those seldom noted tales that has no sex in it." I waited for more, but the cab had reached our destination.

A man from *Life* welcomed us at the entrance. Dmitri Kessel would be making a cover portrait of Frost in color for its March 30th issue on *In the Clearing*. Movable platforms cluttered the bare gray room. We were shown to some chairs. The shooting would soon begin.

Having been pictured in *Life* many times, Frost followed orders as well as he could, but Kessel, fearing to strain the poet, ordered a number of "breaks." Halfway through a rather long session, Frost fixed his eyes squarely on me while his fingers counted out 1-2-3-4-5. Kessel called for a recess. Frost stepped down and walked toward me, his head shaking: "That title line near the end"—I assumed he meant the poem on the King—"it bothers me. 'How hard it is to keep from being King.' I want to change it: 'It is so hard to keep from being King.' " My face must have shown my dismay. "You don't agree," he muttered, stared at the floor, pondered. Suddenly—"Leave the line as it is." I sighed, relieved. Seconds later he shouted, "What's wrong with the change?"

"The closing needs the power of an exclamation: 'How *hard* it is to keep from being King.' Besides, if you made the change, what could you do with the title? Change that too?" His eyes kept gazing intently. "Also, in the very first use—line thirty or so—you write 'For hard it is . . .' with your same stressing of 'hard.' "

A Kessel assistant called, "Mr. Frost, if you're ready . . ."

"Leave it as it stands," he said, walking back to the platform.

More shooting, thank yous, goodbyes—then we taxied off, eastward on 54th Street. As we drove toward number 31, I pointed— "That was the Dryden building, opposite the Whitney Museum—you probably knew it long ago on Eighth Street."

At lunch in the Westbury dining room, I mentioned his recent Christmas card "The Wood-Pile." It was still one of his favorites. "Mark said it was untranslatable—that phrase, the 'smokeless burning of decay.' One of my lucky snatches from an advertising page in the *Literary Digest,* before you were born"—a firearms firm advertisement which described an 'Infallible Smokeless' powder—one of those things a writer picks up by chance and steals them to new uses." By chance, I wondered? Where draw the line between Eliot's quoting other men's words in *The Waste Land* and *Little Gidding* and his shocked surprise when he learned that Washington Allston had used "his" objective correlative decades before? Thinking twice, I postponed mentioning the quatrain-draft by Keats that began "Keen fitful gusts" and closed with "And I have many miles on foot to fare."* *

"When did you say you leave for Greece?" he suddenly asked. On April 6th, I said, about a month after we'll have finished "your job" in Florida. "And how many times will I have to sign my name?" Sixteen hundred, I guessed, since each of the sheets I promised to bring would be bound into one of the 1,500 numbered autographed copies of the special edition of *In the Clearing.* "Oh, that sounds like a lot of writing time. Better plan to stay a week. You can tell Al I said so." Instead of adding the usual goodbye wave of his hand, he pointed his finger slowly with every word: "We need time to talk, both of us. Don't let anything keep you away *this* time!"

Dinner at night in his honor at Lesley's apartment. The next day— south for Miami, with stops en route at the University of Georgia and Agnes Scott College. Two or three days after arriving in Florida, he was sick enough to telephone Kay Morrison, who in turn persuaded a woman neighbor to "look in on" the poet. She called a physician at once. Frost was ordered to bed and a nurse engaged to attend him, and within a few days he felt well enough to go out for a walk. The wet grass brought on a chill. The nurse, distraught by her patient's behavior, summoned the doctor. Frost had contracted pneumonia. He had no choice but to follow orders: enter a hospital. Ten days later, back in his winter retreat, he began the month of convalescence prescribed by the doctor, but before two weeks had elapsed, he was facing the labor of signing those 1,600 sheets for his forthcoming book.

I arrived at 5240 Southwest 80th Street and drove down the half-block lane to the rear of the property. Frost, busily pruning a tall palmetto, his arms rivered with sweat, stopped quickly to greet me. Then leading me straight to his small white cottage, he showed me where to unload my bundles of sheets. Meanwhile Kay emerged from the larger cottage across the court to invite us in for a snack. We talked about all that came into our heads—Frost's illness, "the antibiotics that saved my life," the nurse, the doctor, Holt, Edwards, Florida weather—till Frost interrupted to ask if I'd like a look at his garden. I followed him over the grassy court between the two New England houses and under the latticed arch overgrown with "morning glories" of blue, his favorite color. Then we started his farmer's tour of the two-acre grove of kumquats, loquats, avocadoes, limes, oranges, mangoes, grapefruit, pines, palms of various sorts, and other trees new to my eyes. He had planted them all, cared for them all, and now after twenty-two years, he beheld the reward: his own subtropical paradise spread out below his towering "pencil pines." He was eager to have me taste the loquats and egg-fruit. Most of the "crops" were in varying stages of ripeness, some of them ready now. He displayed a special content when walking his garden. He would move up close to a tree, study its bark, test the leaves, finger the soil below. Once a day, sometimes twice, he would make the tour—alone.

At dinner we planned our program. Tomorrow was March 1st; I

would take the late plane back on Sunday, the 4th. How much time would the signing take? I had reckoned one hundred sheets an hour, allowing for cramped fingers and backache from sitting too long. Kay would not need to assist us. We would work in his house on a make-shift assembly-line. Thirty seconds per sheet meant 120 an hour at our highest speed; hence fourteen hours might finish the job. Three days plus, of four hours each. We should start around 10:00, break for lunch, then another session of signing, with Sunday for whatever pages remained.

Frost suggested a walk—"not a long one, since you ought to rest up for the morning." We took the lane to the street. "That's Lesley's house"—he pointed to 5240. "She owns a third of my five acres. I gave it to her as a wedding present." Despite the dark, her house looked much the same as the others I'd passed en route from the airport, some barely half-finished: stone mat, concrete blocks covered with painted stucco and roofed with tiles. What made Frost prefer the Hodgson pre-cut wooden houses? I would ask at another time; he was too engrossed, at the moment, with Stevens and *The Sewanee Review*.

"There's a sequel. Frank Kermode, whose Stevens book started it all, was teaching a Harvard summer class when my piece appeared. He was much distressed, said a note from Harry Levin. Then to my great surprise, he sent an apology. True, he had never read what I'd written on Stevens. How could he make amends? He enclosed a letter to *Sewanee:* Readers must now be grateful, and so on. If it wasn't right, I should make the needed changes. I replied with thanks, approving his *Sewanee* note for setting things straight at last. I've no idea if they'll print it. Probably not."

"Did you ever meet Stevens?" I shook my head. "Kreymborg should have arranged it. You might even have liked him. I did—at times."

"I can't say why but I never had the smallest desire to know him. I admire many of his poems, but—"

"I'll have to add to the talk we had the first time we met. As you know, we were at Key West together—Stevens, I, and his friend, a judge. 'The trouble with you, Frost,' he said, 'is that you write about subjects.' 'The trouble with you Stevens,' I said, 'is that you write *bric à brac*.' Later he wrote in a book he sent: 'Some more *bric à brac*.' "

We had already turned from the street toward his private lane. "They call this 53rd Avenue." He chortled. It was time for "good-night." He waved to me as I headed for my Coconut Grove motel.

I arrived next morning at 10:00. "I'm ready if you're ready," he greeted me. In a moment he seated himself at his desk, lifted the cap from his fountain pen, and signed the first of the autograph sheets. Nothing was said for the first five minutes, but then began the talk that would "never" stop through the next three days, though "never" requires quotation marks: The talk was not a continuous stream but bursts breaking the silence—comments, questions, sudden exchanges, brief or long conversations. There were also interruptions: the mailman, telephone calls, Kay's running off to a nearby beach for a swim, Frost's sudden decisions to "lounge for a while and talk." To remember all that we spoke about twenty-three winters ago would be asking more than my memory can provide. Yet enough comes back of its own to fill many pages. Our "subjects" ranged from intimate gossip and joking remarks about friends and "foes," to no-holds-barred discussions of books, writers, and deep recollections of long-past family moments. One morning, quite without warning, he stopped, moved to an easy chair, swung his right leg over its arm, and "remembered" his father:

It was admiration and longing for his San Francisco childhood, roaming the streets, trailing after his father from bar to bar, taking in all that he could of political talk. "And it wasn't only once or twice" that his father and other newspapermen "would take out their guns and fire right into the water, for the sport of it." One of his father's "very serious thoughts" he had "never forgotten. The United States was just too big for one country." One night he took out a map and marked "the six independent nations he knew it should be. He never did much about it, or some other ideas." But no one could throw him a challenge too hard to refuse, even a "great long-distance champion walker." Their contest lasted six whole days and his father won. "Swimming and stiff-knee racing—no one was bolder." But his body weakened with drinking. "When he died, I didn't know what to do. I never spoke about him for years." He thought in silence. "Everyone knew he drank and gambled at Harvard. It was only student gambling. He had never been a professional. Larry was wrong in his article. He gambled with *fate*. He took risks." Another silence. "I suppose today they would call me a juvenile delinquent. I even walked through whore-town, though I didn't know what a prostitute was." Not a word of blame for the beatings his father gave him—punishments that were "undeservedly cruel." And no complaint about rootlessness— "we were always moving from house to hotel and back to apartment house," at his father's whim. Today, instead of judgment: homage, praise, envy, possibly a touch of perverse pride. "Eisenhower told me once he considered himself a Jeffersonian Democrat. I was a Democrat too, I said: by training, with a capital D; by birth, with a small one. But I didn't tell him that when I was ten, I helped the San Francisco machine corrupt the politics of the most corrupt city in America of its time. My father's bidding, of course. He was a rebel, a wild one, a pagan of sorts—unpredictable, passionate—above all, *daring*. And"—he laughed—"he graduated from Harvard *cum laude* with a Phi Beta Kappa key."

Father and schools were still in his mind when we went to work after our lunch with Kay. How wise his father had been to have learned his Caesar by heart! That was an option at Harvard: memorize two books and be free of classes. "What would Progressive Education make of *that?*" he snorted. "I've taught every grade. Some of my students—some; they were never many—learned *something,* but I always seemed to learn more. Teachers often can, you know, the real ones: those who care enough not to care what their enemies say against them. I call that the First Rule."

"I'd add a second, or rather another First." He stopped to look up. "I learned it from the ethologists. Every creature is born with a will to learn; it's in the genes: the exploratory instinct. But it has to be nurtured. And the terrible fact is that too many teachers and schools do the opposite: get in the way. I know two colleges now that are harming instead of helping. One of my friends says that the only solution is to light a match to those places."

"If he goes ahead, I'll help him."

I glanced at the sheet he gave me. "Robert"—I handed it back—"have you changed your name?" He had signed *Robert Forst.*

Tossing the page away, he frowned. "Maybe we shouldn't be talking." I agreed, though I knew he wouldn't obey the rule. For the rest of the afternoon, I did my part and so did he except for a brief—"When we have our walk, tell me where you are taking your wife on the trip abroad. All those sites you told me to see I never saw. Next time we should go together. I might even arrange through our State Department permission to climb Mt. Sinai. It's not too high for either of us, I'm told. . . ."

The pure morning sun gave perfect light for a second try with my camera. While Frost stood close to the lattice, posing, a cool breeze led me to mention Thompson's report that Israel had been hotter than

Florida. Frost, disdaining to answer, spoke of the days at Key West. Hemingway also was there that year, but nobody brought them together, though they both had decried the government's guilt for the hurricane deaths. Our talk meandered north to the night of Hemingway's speech on Spain at the Writers' Congress, from there to Horace Gregory's snubbing of Humphries. I wanted to tell him of Gregory's plight, struggling to live on his Sarah Lawrence pittance, when Kay strode up to "wonder just how long" we intended "to work" outside by talking.

During the first few days some of her acts and words had surprised me. Though not over-cordial, she had been calmly polite with me, even, at times, gracious. Her behavior with Frost—distant, cool—I attributed to a reticence staged for my benefit possibly, and till now I had shut my eyes to her small displays of impatience. But the tone of this last remark signaled a change: She no longer felt the need to conceal irritations. Yet what could she think such acts would evoke from me, who looked upon such discordances as one of the doleful inevitables after years of being together. Were they other than that to Frost? He had given them no attention at all, at least in my presence, pretending perhaps that they hadn't occurred; yet he knew what he'd told me of their relationship. And he acted not merely unperturbed when we went inside to work, but within the first half-hour he insisted that we talk.

Why should anyone think it important for any reader to know the date of a poem's composition? And what was the meaning of "date"?—when the writing had first begun—In the mind? On paper? Or the time of completion, if it hadn't been done at a stroke? It was wrong to try to trace any "upward Darwinian line" in a writer's attitude or faith or thought. And what if someone were able to make a "case"? What "would that prove? How could it help?" I mentioned Yeats and the crucial change supposedly caused by Pound—which I found too simple: Yeats had wanted to change—and then the continual drive of Yeats to revise, to "remake himself," as he said till the end of his life; the same Yeats who'd declared that "a poem comes right with a click like a closing box." But not only Yeats, I went on. Your good friend Ransom said he had done some "trimming" and such for his book of *Selected Poems*. "No dates there," Frost retorted. "No need. And no critics to tell him that he was 'developing—getting better.' " After which he went back to signing. Minutes passed, then he put down his pen: "When did a certain poem begin? I remember the street

I was walking on when I had that idea about our not remembering that our life was nothing but what we had somehow chosen—our life was our own willing. You know the one I mean. I've told that to others who asked."

Questions were still on his mind when, after a shorter-than-usual lunch, we returned for a signing session. "Sometimes, you know, in a public talk, I name the place behind a poem. You've heard me—'Once by the Pacific' and the Cliff House in California." He failed to add "The Road Not Taken," that he often had said was about himself together with Edward Thomas. "Of course that kind of thing has nothing to do with what critics mean by 'development,' but it does do something to satisfy the curious." Pause. "Do *you* think it helps?" He guessed my thought when I started to shrug. "Maybe but *not* for you?"

"Not when it stands in *my* way of encountering poems as I want to: directly, as things-in-themselves. You've put it in different words: that once a poem is published it's out of your hands. But," I hurried to add, "not necessarily." He stopped to look up. "Take revision, for instance, especially when the meaning's changed: the end of 'A Minor Bird' and that pivotal line in 'Neither Far Out. . . .' " He resumed signing. " 'Some say the land has more' which became 'The land may vary more.' That word 'vary.' "

Kay suddenly appeared. "Telephone call from Holt."

He left and returned quickly. "Al sends you regards. He asked how our work was going. I said if he wanted to know, he'd better come down and see how efficient we are." He wasn't inventing. In spite of our talk-interruptions, we had raised the production rate, and he hadn't written a second *Forst*. "Kay says I may have too many engagements unless I learn to get better at saying no. They're asking now for October, and promising 'greater numbers.' "

"Do you still divide your audience into halves, as you told Louis?"—he looked a bit puzzled—"half likers, half haters (89); then cut each half into quarters—one for the wrong, one for the right reasons?"

"I suppose so, though I stopped worrying about that last quarter. They may love me, if they want, for the wrong reasons."

"Eliot flatters the Y audience, calling them 'trained,' and trying his best. Auden once did the opposite: His reading, he said, would consist exclusively of notes for a poem he would never write. Poets sometimes get themselves trapped into doing things that they think their listeners demand. Dylan Thomas, I guess, is the sorriest case."

"There must be people, I'm sure—who say things just as bad as that about me." Kay entered again. "Kay, let that telephone wait!" Following her through the door, he added, "And those who do aren't entirely wrong."

I stepped outdoors for a stroll in the sun. It didn't last: Within five minutes he found me and led the way inside. Audience-talk again—this time, the quiz at the Poetry Society. I asked if he still fooled people with Sill's "Opportunity," or was Davies his standby now? "It's good to surprise them, you see. They know all about my 'position' against free verse, so I tell them I'll say 'The Lovely Shall Be Choosers'—my only free verse poem, with a few iambics thrown in. And before I start, I reveal where the poem was written—not all of it at the same time—in Franconia, on a high chair perched on a platform I built to keep the winter draughts from my feet. I also confess it's a poem about my mother." By now it was taking much less time for the signing. "Let's finish the pile you have there, then we can have an hour for a walk before you leave." He and Kay had been asked to dinner by a friend. Though welcomed to join them, I had already made a date at the university.

"While you're here"—we started our walk—"you must see the Fairchild Tropical Gardens. Not much chance for more than a glance right now, but we'll take our time on Sunday." En route he pointed to empty lots growing wild. " 'Hammocks' they call them; Florida speech for 'hummocks.' Nobody knows the word's origin." He repeated, "Origin, origin, origin," till all at once he turned on me, "What about yours? In all our years I've never asked once. I should be ashamed. Look at me!—talking all through the other morning about my father, today about my mother. Now tell me about your people."

I gave him a hasty account: that my father taught Latin and Greek in the New York schools till he changed vocations. That my mother had the greenest thumb in the world. "If you wait a few years, you'll be able to read it all in a book that I hope to write."

"Then you've hidden from me an important story!"

"I think of my father's career as a paradigm of the modern idealist who starts as the son of the Great Enlightenment, a believer in its Universal Religion, in the power of Education, in the irreversible Progress of Man toward a shining future ruled by Reason and

Brotherhood—only to witness later in life the coming of Nazi savagery and its near triumph, but living long enough to see the glimmerings of a world self-rescued." I was quoting from notes that I'd already written.

"When was he born? And where? Tell me about him! . . . Everything . . ."

The next morning, as I drove around his lane from 80th Street, he was waiting for me. "How many *more* times must I sign my name?" he asked with a poker-faced smile. I'll make the count right away, I replied. "No need to. I made it already—roughly." Though we couldn't complete it today, he wouldn't have many to sign on Sunday. "Let's get a speedy start," he said, "since we're going to dinner tonight. Caesar's Steak House, you said?"

For an hour or more we did our teamwork in silence. Then out of nowhere: "How could your father allow you to grow up 'educated' without any Greek at all—though he *loved* it, you said?" In the circumstance, it was simpler to shrug than attempt an involved explanation, especially if Frost were about to offer a paean on the classics. He had no such plan. "And to think"—he frowned—"that almost none of the poets I meet ever heard the sound of the lines!"

"Tate's one striking exception. What a day I had when I came on his *Vigil of Venus!*—which you've probably never bothered to look at, knowing the Latin." We went on for some time, agreeing and disagreeing on Tate as a critic and poet. I didn't ask if he knew about Tate's tribute to him in *Sixty American Poets;* surely someone at the Library of Congress had shown it to him. It was their publication. But what did he think of Tate's essays—on Dickinson, on Dostoevsky's "Fly"—or his definition of poetry as "communion"?

"It's better than most, but still not right. Poetry is correspondence: Its images bring forth a response from the feelings and thoughts of the reader because the reader has similar feelings and thoughts. It goes back to the reader's performing his part in a serious engagement. It's *not* the correspondence that Swedenborg meant, or Emerson, Melville, or anyone else." I almost added, "Or Baudelaire," but instead I asked if he read Tate's poems. "With effort," he groaned. "Surely not all," I retorted; "not 'The Mediterranean' or the sonnet that starts with 'The idiot greens the meadow with his eyes'—that sums up *The Sound and the Fury*." "No, not *all* his poems with effort, but many, *too* many." It was probably what he might say of some of my own if asked, though nothing of mine was so "telescoped" as Allen's "We are the eyelids of defeated caves," which I cited as one that called for more effort than I could make, till I stumbled on Cleanth Brooks's short explanation. Which led us into talking of Tate's fascination with logic and my own with a different "reasoning." "Poems," I said, "don't follow commonsense-logical rules but different *types,* of their own." "If you've written something on that, I'd like to read it." "Nothing to show," I replied, "but hundreds of pages that still aren't right, though they point the way that I'll follow. You could call it an 'organismic' approach, even if Fitts condemns that word as a hybrid of Latin and Greek. In my ignorance . . ."

Kay strode into the room to insist that we "call a stop right now. Robert, you're still convalescing. You *have* to rest, one hour at the very least. Stanley will wait, I'm sure. If you have a restful sleep, you can put in another hour after you wake." Frost, averting his eyes, capped his pen, strode toward his bedroom, and closed the door.

I stepped outside and walked through the orchard. Kay quickly caught up with me. Anger reddened her cheeks as she reeled off a dozen accounts of "the most horrible things he's been doing, and he's even confessed to another flare-up." Of what, I asked. "Cystitis—it comes and goes and worsens when he does too much." I couldn't tell what she wished me to say. "That's nothing, really," she scoffed. But from what I gleaned from her run of complaints—none of which made sense—the stings of whatever it was he had said and done had enraged her. I hoped by now she had talked them out of her system, but no. They were only the prelude. Suddenly halting to stare in my face, she cried, "Do you *know* what that man had the nerve to say?" I tried to follow her words but she sputtered so fast and frantically that I held up my hands in confusion. "All right! I'll explain slowly." Ted, her husband, had published a new novel, *The Whole Creation*. Frost, after reading the *Times* review, rushed to her side with, "Just what I said to you years ago. The man has *no feeling*—never had. Read it yourself! Even a person who's never set eyes on him sees what's missing." She pulled out the clipping. Two sentences underscored—by Frost, I assumed—"The trouble is that the interest of Mr. Morrison's novel is intellectual only. . . . One *thinks* while reading *The Whole Creation,* but *one does not feel.*"

"Is the whole review so negative?"

"Of course not! 'It's a *good* novel,' it says. Here, read it—the sentence I've underlined: 'One cannot read *The Whole Creation* without admiring its author and respecting his work.' " And then the devastating judgment: "One thinks . . . but one does not feel."

I shook my head in wonder. What she needed now, I sensed, was a listening ear; she had found one at last—in me. "Please don't think I expect you to offer your sympathy. I know how you feel about Robert. But you *can't* have known"—her voice choking—"how cruel he can be—at times." Rather than see her face, I glanced at the ground. She started to walk; I followed. "I've victimized you—I apologize, but—" A few minutes later: "Excuse me now. I need some moments alone, and Robert may come out soon."

I had lost my sense of time. Frost, I supposed, was still asleep. The hands on my watch passed four. Time to go back to my room.

All I thought of while driving to Coconut Grove was the evening to come. Had she purged herself enough to be able to play her usual public role of the well-bred, remote companion? The pained cause of her counterattack on the poet couldn't have been, by any twist of imagining, unique in their recent years. Would he ever *wholly* forgive her? He had craved marriage, but as he "explained" to me recently, "it was thought best" not to—though he might have persisted and won despite the "complexities." But now—who could fathom the heart of this woman in her sixty-fifth year, of the poet nearing his ninetieth? Everyone held that "Frost as a man could be difficult"; yet who, after spending uncountable hours in his presence, had greater knowledge of Frost as a fallible mortal? Knowledge, yes; but understanding? Forebearance? Some of the ways in which she "managed" his life showed a reversal of roles—but at what expense? Each of these two wilfully separate selves, in the course of years, had kept some parts of its difference while giving up others. If the stronger showed less loss, the weaker solaced her hurts with resentments. So they had fated their lives; the tie unbreakable. Discord would arise more often, but met with diminished efforts by each to hide them from others, though at times the engulfing air might feel tense enough to explode. Oh, well—I sighed to myself, calmer—now it was all wrapped up and explained. Yet what did I *really* know?

When I returned, Frost once again stood waiting for me. "We'll work much longer tomorrow. When do we have to leave?" Kay crossed into the court to call out the time. "Shouldn't we be at the Steak House early. You know—the crowds on Saturday nights?"

"Why don't you join us here, Kay?" he answered. She stepped

through the lattice arch to where we were standing. Could this be the sorry creature I'd gazed on hours before? To prepare for the evening rites, she had made herself radiant. "All dressed up in blue." Frost smiled, gleaming. "If you want to go, I'm ready."

Long before we were shown to our table, Frost appeared to be bursting with affable energy. Could a nap have produced this change? Even Kay glanced at him with surprise. From the moment at Pencil Pines when we entered the car till his late reluctant "goodnight," he had talked, talked, talked, and talked "as never before"; though I knew from what others had said that tonight couldn't have been the only time that "one of the master conversationalists of our age" had reached to the heights. We were overstaying our time, but the poet refused to be hurried. Kay insisted that we leave at this "quite unreasonable hour." On the homeward drive, she remarked how much they both would miss seeing me every day. I probably made some trite reply, not yet able to reconcile all I had heard from her hours before with her present tones of concern, her relaxed patience.

Sunday: More to accomplish than planned. Two full hours for the morning—more after the lunch-hour break! Work-without-talk interruptions till Kay would call us! The last bundle of sheets to be signed seemed steadily smaller, and by three, it was over. At five-thirty or so, we would drive to the airport. Packing the precious bundles with care, I loaded them into Kay's car. "Time enough for a walk," said Frost, eager to start. We would head for Fairchild Gardens, though there might be "the weekend crowd." As we walked toward Lesley's house, he stopped. "Remember the night in New York—when she gave a dinner for me? Before it was over, she took me aside to say she had made up her mind to sell this place—her wedding present. Was she trying to hurt me? I brooded about it all the way to Florida. Kay thinks it was one of the reasons I felt so ill when I came here." He sighed. "You heard all about the doctor and nurse, I suppose. Lesley came to the hospital—the first thing she did. Knocked at my door. When she leaned down over me close, I looked at her face . . . breaking with pain . . . scars of her suffering bearing down on my eyes. Not a word spoken between us. Then she stood up again, asked for the doctor or nurse—can't recall. I closed my eyes. But the ravaged look on her face! It stays with me even now."

The Fairchild crowds were not too large to keep him from making a tour. Halfway through he blurted out, "When you're sending that Stevens poem, also add the piece you wrote on *New Hampshire*." I promised, if the Library still had copies of the 1924 *Forum*. "Oh," he shouted, "look down there! Alligators! People sometimes move too close—think they're asleep." We walked through a dense hummock marked "Rain Forest," then onto a spreading meadow broken with formal flowerbeds. "Those don't belong here at all. Come!" We walked to a bench in a grove of Australian pines. "Let's stop a moment. All that signing we did!—I hope it was worth it." The edition, I said, was sure to be oversubscribed. He made no response, staring ahead. "Why don't *you* write a book about me?"

I was too surprised to speak.

"You know my work and you have my permission to say whatever you want to and quote whatever you please. Tell Al I said so." He kept looking into my eyes.

"I never imagined I'd hear such a thing—from you."

"Did you ever *think* about writing one?" he asked quietly.

I shook my head. "No, never."

"I want you to think of it *now*." Several times on our slow walk back to his cottage, he stopped to refer to "the book"—hadn't thought "you'd be taken and shaken so by surprise." And now I must promise him to "hold" the idea "high" in my mind. We would speak of it soon—on his first stop in New York, April. That's when I'd be abroad? Well, then May, for sure.

Kay looked extremely anxious the minute we saw her. Had we watched the time? If by chance the plane were to leave a few minutes early? Almost at once we climbed in her car for the airport. "Taxis will take you there faster," she advised. I scrambled out, said my goodbyes in such haste that we never shook hands. "Call us at once if you miss it," she shouted. Frost kept waving. I sank back into the cab, guarding my bundles.

Relieved that both the Trade and special editions of *In the Clearing* would be ready in time for his birthday, March 26th, I focused on ways for untangling problems I still had to face, with the burial of the much-mourned Graduate Institute and the final sessions: Trilling's on the anti-hero in literature and my own quasi-impossible "proofs" of the adversary side of the publisher-author relationship. In the light of the forthcoming Frost celebration, it seemed perverse as a subject, and yet this enormous exception promised to prove in certain respects what I knew to be true.

Robert Frost as the
senior class poet of
Lawrence High School,
1892. *(The Jones Library,
Inc., Amherst, Mass.)*

Elinor White, a portrait
taken around 1894.
*(The Jones Library, Inc.,
Amherst, Mass.)*

Frost in England on June 30, 1913. *(Photograph by Edward Sweetland, The Jones Library, Inc., Amherst, Mass.)*

The poet at his writing desk in Franconia, New Hampshire, 1915. *(The Jones Library, Inc., Amherst, Mass.)*

The Frost family in Bridgewater, New Hampshire, 1915. Marjorie and Carol in front; Leslie and Irma behind. *(Plymouth State College Library)*

Bread Loaf Writers Conference. (Bread Loaf Writers Conference)

Frost playing baseball *(Middlebury College News Bureau)*

Frost posing with his dog Gillie in 1944. *(Dartmouth College Library)*

The poet with Kathleen and Theodore Morrison, 1950. *(The Jones Library, Inc., Amherst, Mass.)*

Frost at his 80th
birthday party at the
Lord Jeffrey Amherst
Inn., March 26, 1954.
*(The Jones Library, Inc.,
Amherst, Mass.)*

At John F. Kennedy's
inaugural, with the
President and Dwight D.
Eisenhower. *(Photograph
by George Silk, Life
Magazine* © 1961 Time
Inc.)

Frost resting in a field with his dog. *(Photograph by Alfred Eisenstaedt, Life Magazine c, Time, Inc.)*

★   ★   ★

Sponsored jointly by Edwards of Holt and Interior Secretary Stewart Udall, the Birthday Dinner was aimed to crown a day of festivities such as no other American writer had known. It began with another joint sponsorship, by the libraries of the Congress and the University of Virginia; a Frost exhibition of manuscripts, first editions, and photographs. The reporters adjudged the poet to be in "remarkable form," and after some forty-five minutes of give-and-take, he was driven to the White House to accept a Congressional medal. In return for President Kennedy's brief: "We are proud of you, Mr. Frost," the poet gave him a warmly inscribed *In the Clearing*. Following his afternoon rest, he felt "more than ready to take on" the big event in the "Hall of the Americas" in the Pan American building.

Some 200 guests were making an early entrance—friends, writers, Congressmen, Cabinet members, Supreme Court justices, foreign diplomats, a handful of critics, and so on. On arrival, Frost was led to his welcoming post at the end of the dais. The receiving line looked endless. By the time my turn drew near, I expected at most a wave of the hand or a hasty smile. To my great surprise, when he saw me coming, he leaned forward, grasping my arm: "Oh, I read that review. Al gave it to me."

"Was I wrong?"

"Wrong? Oh no, no." Pointing into the crowd, he laughed. "Wrong? Look around! You were right."

"Let's say two-thirds right. Seems more than a local holiday." [4]

Shortly after the waiters served the first course, he retired from the speakers' dais to rest, resuming his place on time for the tributes. The well-meant words of Earl Warren, Adlai Stevenson, Felix Frankfurter, and Robert Penn Warren offered nothing that hadn't been said better before. The fine exception was Mark Van Doren, whose speech was a choice of single lines from the poems of Frost. It was now past midnight—time for the guest of honor. For a quick half-hour he "talked" in ways people had learned to expect—saying his poems, making remarks, offering gracious thanks (serious, playful), then a closing sonnet: "Never Would Birds' Song Be the Same," a poem which few of his listeners thought of in terms of his lifelong love

---

[4] *The Forum* (May 1924) review of *New Hampshire*: ". . . a milestone in the field of *American* letters" is at least "worthy of a local holiday."

of "the tone of meaning" in sounds. The party, technically over, continued till 1:00 A.M., as the poet kept shaking hands with the last of his guests. What did it mean to him now? I asked as I wandered off—all this sweetness and light compared with the day three years before, with his bombshell Kennedy prophecy? Today: nothing but honor, praise, glory. Never a challenge. No one to charge that like Sophocles he confronted the terrors of life for his countrymen. Nothing to urge him to come to terms with Trilling's oblation (105).

Two weeks more, then my wife and I would be flying to the lands where the experts told us "it all began." April mostly in Israel; May days roaming through Greece and the Islands; London with Bill Blake and Christina Stead. Frost meanwhile would be feted wherever he went: Michigan, Harvard, the Y Poetry Center, Sarah Lawrence, Dartmouth, Amherst, the White House, Choate, Washington, Dartmouth again, Ohio . . . And his new volume, of which he was sometimes unsure, had astounded everyone: 35,000 copies sold in the first four days. Frost and the book made the covers of the *Saturday Review* and *Life;* also the front-page review in *The New York Times, Chicago Tribune, San Francisco Chronicle.* Critics praised not only this work but his total achievement—"High-spirited, high-minded"; "Age has not narrowed his range but enlarged it." . . .

May 24th: My first day home from abroad. Frost was busy with standing engagements. We met the next afternoon long before his five o'clock train to Boston. "Rigg asked if I'd talked to his world traveler," he pointed at me. "Just between us: Did Israel disappoint you the second time round?"

"It was even better, showing my wife the sights, like a tourist guide. Besides, we've begun the book, picked the poems and contributors; but you, Robert—I hear you've been having one long birthday party."

"It's all over now—back to the farm on Sunday! You're coming to see me, I know, but Kay must set up the time"—because he'd agreed to help the filmmakers finish *A Lover's Quarrel.* "Do I know your London friends?"

"Did you ever hear of Christina Stead's *The Man Who Loved Children?* If not, you will. I may even ask for your help—help with 'the Holts,' who I'm hoping to rouse to reissue the work. It's a *rare* novel—published in 1940, quickly hailed, then quickly ignored because of the War, and except for a writers' underground—Robert

Lowell and especially Randall Jarrell—wholly forgotten. She and her husband barely manage to survive. We can rescue the book and resuscitate a truly remarkable writer. But we'll have to move carefully, slowly . . ."

"Why did you say 'especially Jarrell'?"

"He calls it one of the greatest of family novels. If he writes the introduction, the book will be sure of reviews."

"You ought to know that I don't read novels these days—not many, that is; but send me the book. Stead? Where does she come from? What part of England?"

"Sydney, Australia. The novel is based on her life, but it's set near the Chesapeake. Her father was a scientist of sorts."

"Of sorts!" His smile became a frown. "I'd call John Holmes a critic of sorts. Did you read his words about me in the *Monitor?* That 'at last he has made his peace with science, which he has so long thought the enemy of poetry.' Hard to believe when he knew what I said at the Future of Man symposium: 'I'm lost in my admiration for science.' And all I said about Keats and the rainbow before. And he'd known about Niels Bohr and the talk we had all about atoms and freedom." He looked at me, puzzled.

"There's one thing to be grateful for: Out of all the reviews, not one by an out-of-control New Critic—which doesn't mean that they're not all over the place."

"Some of them are now going in for Stevens, I'm told."

"Did you know that Stevens once wrote a letter stating that he was 'personally pro-Mussolini,' at the same time professing his 'profound belief in Leftism in every direction' and hoping he was 'headed Left'? This, from the man who declared that *everything outside himself* was chaos. Fitts calls him one of the Great Unreadables. I don't agree; but I somehow sense, from the poems, that he never cared to come close to a 'feeling mortal.' "

"That's what *we* say." Frost laughed. "But before they're done, they'll make him a Great Philosopher. Too bad for Wallace. He really didn't deserve *that*."

"Kreymborg said that he had a weakness for visiting churches, especially St. Patrick's in New York. Santayana, 'his atheist mentor of sorts,' entered some kind of retreat. Food for wonder, or not?"

"Why don't you put together a talk on Stevens? Maybe it could be arranged this summer at Bread Loaf."

"I've other things I'd rather do—one is to urge you to issue a book of prose. It wouldn't be hard. Merely choosing from all you've already written. No need for a preface, even."

"*I've* just published a book—it's *your* turn now: the one I spoke of in March when I signed those sheets." I avoided his eyes. "I made only one writing mistake down there in Florida. Remember? I made a worse one in Washington. It was all thought out—what I wanted to write. I picked up the copy numbered one of the special edition and started to write my inscription for the President. That's when it happened. I spoiled it—couldn't save it. I gave him the bookstore edition."

"You had to do something wrong that day to be human—with that big exhibition, the interviews, those unendurable speeches. What will you do next March?"

"We'll let Al Edwards think about that. Plenty of time! And now"—I had seated myself beside him; the train wouldn't pull out for about ten minutes—"what did I miss by staying so close to Athens? I wanted to see Epidaurus. Did you climb to the top? Could you hear the voices from the stage so far below? I want you to tell me—all! . . ."

A few weeks later my wife and I moved from our Ridgefield summer place to an old sprawling year-round house on Martha's Vineyard. It took some time to clear the tumbled-down acres and condition the dwelling, but by mid-July "The Jungle" was under control—gardens of herbs and flowers, fields of perennial rye. Our old canoe, tied to a tree by the pond, brought us in touch with shore birds and the teeming, shadowy wetlands. We were new city immigrants—workmen were the only people we'd met—until unexpected friends from earlier years drew us into the summer life of the island. One of them, Roger Baldwin, in a mischievous moment committed me to deliver a speech on, of all subjects, Frost.

It was scheduled for July 25th, two days after President Kennedy had asked the poet to visit the U.S.S.R. as part of a cultural exchange. Frost had gladly accepted. But this time, according to Edwards, Thompson would not go along. Instead, Frost had invited "Freddie" Adams of the Morgan Library and a young professor of Russian, Franklin Reeve, who was also a writer. Could this sudden rejection of Thompson presage the move I had hoped the poet would make: Cancel, for reasons known to them both, Thompson's prized position as official biographer.**

While making notes for my talk ("The Unknowable Robert Frost"), I wrote to ask when "Directive" had been written. The date had come up while discussing some johnny-come-latelies who had "used" this poem to show how Frost had improved with time.

> Oh dear Stanley [Frost wrote on my letter], how did I give you such an impossible date for "Directive" [c. 1891]. I wonder what I could have said to mislead. It sounds as if I might have been talking about "Trial by Existence." I'm trying to think if I ascribed any line or phrase in "Directive" to early thoughts but I fear not. The Minnesota boys have it for once—K. reminds me that the idea of not saving the wrong ones [lines 58–59] might have been way back in High School like the main idea in "Trial by Existence." I remember the street I was walking on when I had that idea about our not remembering that our life was nothing but what we had somehow chosen—our life was of our own willing.

I had planned to visit Ripton close to the date of his flight to the U.S.S.R. Now I would have to wait till his trip was over, after September 9th. But the moment his plane touched down at Idlewild Airport, Frost's words to reporters struck up a storm. Edwards, stopped by the Secret Service, failed to reach his side to head off the press. Though Frost hadn't slept for eighteen hours and was obviously (in Udall's words) "bone tired," he insisted on answering questions, suddenly blurting out, "Krushchev thought that we're too liberal to fight—he thinks we will sit on one hand and then the other." Banner headlines followed. With one stroke, as Udall remarked, Frost had broken the rules he himself had proposed for "magnanimous conduct," had misrepresented Krushchev and embarrassed the President, who was caught in a tense situation with Russia and Cuba.

Ignored by the White House, Frost began but didn't finish a letter-report to the President. Nor did he voice his doubts on the darkening missile crisis during the Washington festival that the new Poetry Consultant, Untermeyer, staged in October. Frost delivered the evening speech on the 23rd, and inevitably, when we met in New York soon after, the good *and* the bad of the three-day fete still troubled his thought. I confessed my distaste for "shows" of that kind, the unfairness, the futility apart from personal clashes and outbreaks of hidden jealousies. "Unless," I went on, "you still want to talk about poetry, hear me on prose instead!" He was willing. "For it's *necessary* to complement your hundreds of pages of verse. I asked you about this in May; now I'll *argue* the case. Hyde Cox must have saved up everything carefully, and he'd make an excellent editor, though editing isn't needed; nor a foreword, though it might be helpful to readers who've never thought of the *Prose of Robert Frost*. You might even add to your published prefaces parts of some interviews; for example, "The Future of Man" symposium. I'd urge some monologues and dialogues, and maybe a speech or two from Bread Loaf or elsewhere. And that's the *total* amount of labor you'd have to expend." He looked unconvinced. Had I left out something? "You'll have to call it *Selected Prose,* since it couldn't include any letters. But Louis' book will provide an important part of that kind of prose, to say nothing of its worth as autobiography. Case rests."

He laughed. "How long ago were you thinking of leaving Holt? And now you come up with a project that will cost you a lot of work—*work!*"

"Work? Not by my definition. Work is something I don't *want* to do; and there's nothing now I'd rather be doing than those two books—your letters to Louis, which is just about ready, and this book of prose."

"We should talk again about *North of Boston* and a new *Selected Poems.*"

"And somebody—I can't think now of the person—should put together all that you've said about poetry. A gathering between two covers of phrases, sentences, and longer passages—each complete and able to stand by itself; each printed separately with space above and below; aphorisms defiantly non-systematic. It would make a new kind of critical book—small, thirty-two pages, invaluable." His eyes kept watching. "Smile, if you will, but I think the book would be welcomed by the New Critics—the sensible ones of course."

We had talked before of the New Critics, for the most part of the ludicrous things we'd heard. Yet Frost knew quite well that his own dictum—"Read a poem carefully but not too carefully"—would have been affirmed by Tate, Ransom, Warren, and others responsible for the reigning school. They too were aware of the dangers, the stupidities, the over-interpretations that end in "analyzing itself and the poem to death," as he liked to remark. Had he heard, I asked, of the howler by Matthiessen (70), his erstwhile enemy? From the long chuckle that followed, I knew he had.[5]

But his evening dinner engagement limited our conversation. There was much to say and not enough time for the easefulness with which we had always talked. And yet, as I think back now, he spoke about dozens of subjects, from the filming of *A Lover's Quarrel* at Ripton to the "hopelessness" of biography; from the terrible "rage for privacy" of Henry James to William's hatred of system-making and on to the latter's defense of the will to believe and his troubled words on democracy:

> Democracy is on trial and no one knows how it will stand the ordeal. . . . What its critics now affirm is that its preferences are inveterately for the inferior. . . . Vulgarity enthroned and institutionalized, elbowing everything superior from the highway; this, they tell us, is our irremedial destiny.

And how, he asked, was I getting along with Larry? Hadn't he mentioned the letter explaining the trip to the Russians? Did I know their poets? I spoke of Anna Ahkmatova and two translations I made from French translations—"third-hand poems, but I'm told they're close to the Russian." John Nims had printed them in *Poetry's* special issue. Had he read it? No, but he hoped to talk with Nims, who seemed to know poems of a dozen languages. "Including," I added, "some fifteenth-century Catalan verse that might have been written by Donne." He would have to read it—would be in Chicago next month for *Poetry's* fiftieth birthday. Back in New York, however,

---

[5] The distinguished author of *American Renaissance* quoted a Melville sentence from a reprint of *White Jacket:* "But of a sudden some fashionless form brushed my side—some inert, soiled fish of the sea; the thrill of being alive again tingled in my nerves, and the strong shunning of death shocked me through." Matthiessen's comment: ". . . hardly anyone but Melville could have created the shudder that results from calling this frightening vagueness some 'soiled fish of the sea.' The unexpected linking of the medium of cleanliness with filth could only have sprung from an imagination that had apprehended the terrors of the deep." Fredson Bowers (*Textual and Literary Criticism,* Cambridge University Press, 1959) remarks: "The only difficulty with this critical *frisson* about Melville's imagination . . . is the cruel fact that . . . what Melville wrote . . . was *coiled* fish of the sea."

November 8th, to pick up a special award. We must save that afternoon for a special talk. . . .

The special award was no doubt the MacDowell Colony Medal for which he would come to New York, but the special talk—perhaps the as yet unpublicized "secret" prize and reception in England in the coming spring. Or was it involved with his private correspondence? When, early in 1959, he had given permission to Louis, Frost had "been looking forward" to what the *Letters* "might do." It would offer a faithful view of what he had thought and what he had been in the course of forty-five years: a picture not only unretouched but unguarded—an antidote to the much-too-popular image of the kindly white-haired presence. Yet the scheduled publishing date had long since passed. Frost had been causing various sorts of delays, and I'd not been shown the manuscript.

In the meantime I had hit on a plan that I hoped to proceed with at once: a book of essays on Frost's achievements from writers all over the world to confute the capricious neglect by the Nobel literature judges. Thanks to a friend, Luciano Rebay,** about to go off for a year in Paris, I would work with the aid of a leading poetry scholar at the culture center of Europe. I was straining to spring the idea on Frost when he greeted me, not with his usual smile but a studied gaze.

"Have you talked with Louis this week?" I shook my head. "I was sure he would call you, knowing how eager you've been." He frowned. "Four days ago I sent a letter by airmail special delivery, thanking him—for having mercy on my irresponsibility. I hated to keep him from printing my letters, but I lay awake nights. I reached a decision that if they came out now, I would turn my back on the world and not utter another book. You know that publicality was the last thing I was thinking of when I wrote those letters. Blame me but forgive me, I wrote to Louis, and give me time to get good *and* dead." It didn't occur to me then he was quoting his letter. "I had also given my word."

"And you hated to take it back but you *knew* you had to . . . You 'prophesied,' as you say in your Christmas poem. That was 1959. Prophecies, when they turn out wrong, *ask* to be set aside whether they deal with a book or a person—as I've urged before."

Reading my thoughts—of Thompson—he remarked at once, "By now, Larry surely has told you about my letter on Russia—how I got into the whole affair by accident: an evening with their ambassador." I shook my head. "I told him I wanted to go with people who wouldn't be too critically intent on who I am and what I am. I was breaking my word; both of us knew it. I had once promised to take him with me on every important trip."

"Progress!" I mumbled. Frost said nothing, watching me try to decide what his silence meant. I changed the subject. "Dudley wrote me about the dinner you had last Sunday, the three of you, with Cornelia. 'In high shape he,' he said of you, and wasn't at all worried by your heavy lecture program." Frost had spent the last two days at Yale; in the coming week he'd address "the biggest crowd ever"—his friend Charles Feinberg had planned it all—in Detroit, with a *Life* photographer trailing him all day long. *Poetry's* birthday party—three full days in Chicago. A family visit in Greenwich for Thanksgiving, then a "brand new talk at Dartmouth." After *that,* back in New York for the National Arts Center. Had he memorized the dates? "Biggest schedule ever!—but why?" I asked, "Trying to rack up a record?" He laughed. "In case you have nothing to think about between engagements, here's something for you to consider."

"Oh, if it's still another book, the answer is *no*." I had reached for notes in my breast pocket, but dropped my hand. "Well, why don't you say what it is?" Frost asked.

I summed up the project quickly, only to have to reply and add as he pressed for specifics. I was ready with places and persons, including others ignored by the Nobel judges: Tolstoy, Hardy, Conrad, James, Zola, Proust, Strindberg, even Eliot's idol Valéry. Someone had remarked that the Nobels were like our National Institute: "more good writers outside than in," I said, before going into my list. Who, he asked, were the ones I could really count on besides Rebay and his friends in Paris and Rome? I showed him my outline: thirteen countries, with names of men and women I'd come to know from my work on *The Poem Itself* and my own publications in Athens and Belgium. There were also surprises: Mexico, Poland, Sweden where *North of Boston* had been translated forty-four years ago. Had he ever received his *Gesammelte Gedichte* issued in German in 1952? No, but was I aware that Japan had done the same with *A Boy's Will* in 1959? And what about England, Scotland, Ireland, not on my list? And how would I go about choosing the essays? I replied: a board of co-editors, international maybe. "No," he insisted, "Americans; three at the most, or you'll never agree. No collective!" I suggested Jarrell and

Fitts. "When do you want to get started?" The minute you say the word *go,* I explained. "Then consider it said—with pleasure! And write to Kay for the names in Japan. We can talk some more about this tonight at Joe's."

But as I feared, there was no chance to continue our talk. My wife, who had never listened to Frost, went with me to the Hunter College recital. The rites began with a speech by Aaron Copland, the MacDowell award, and a heap of telegrams. "If only my mother could see me now," said Frost, quoting Kipling without acknowledgment, as he'd done before to avoid an acceptance speech. Four or five minutes passed before he had hit his accustomed stride, and from then till the end, he recited and commented playfully, seriously, salting his words with hints which his hearers hardly expected from the lips of the aging bard who had "taken the measure of Krushchev"—a phrase later bandied about in the Blumenthal living room, while Frost, in his usual after-lecture routine, silently dined alone.

Among the guests were William Meredith and Franklin Reeve, poet, novelist, and Frost's Russian interpreter. It was Joe, however, with whom I spent most of the evening. Was Frost getting over Kennedy's "silent treatment"? Probably not. During their drive back from the Hunter reading, Frost took care to explain "at length that the President and the other men in the government simply failed to realize that during his talk with Krushchev he'd prepared the way and achieved some success in bettering relations between the U.S.A. and the U.S.S.R. . . . 'A conflict of magnanimities'—that was how he summed up the confrontation."

My wife, because of the busy work day awaiting her, wanted to leave before midnight. After thanking our hosts, we made our way to the poet to say goodnight. "We'll continue." He nodded. "I thought we might have some minutes here, but we both need more than minutes. Remember the date I gave you. And ask Kay the name of the Japanese poet."

A week passed before I heard from Rebay. He had started to work on the hundreds of letters between Giuseppe Ungaretti, the Italian poet, and Jean Paulhan, the editor of the *Nouvelle Revue Française:* Both men would be pleased to help with the Frost project. Ten days later: Ungaretti "might write the essay if given a year," though others (Eugenio Montale, Mario Praz) would be equally good. As for France: Paulhan expressed great admiration for Frost and would soon provide the names of writers to consider. Hence, when I set out to meet the poet on the afternoon of the 30th, I had news to report.

The cast of his face shocked me—but, then, hadn't he just completed the heaviest tour of his life? On top of which he had added yesterday's broadcast for the National Cultural Center! "Progress," I announced, waving a letter. He perked up at once, avid for news, wishing to hear all that Rebay had reported. How this led us to Horace Gregory's verse, I can't recall. His words on *A Further Range*— missing the finest poems—and his adulation of Eliot were known to us both; also that during the thirties, his critical views, though marked by the Left's blindness, preserved a basic integrity. What mattered now, I thought, was his "proud career as a poet"—Fitts's words, which seemed if "rightly taken" warrant enough for a book of collected poems. Bracing myself for the bruited Frostian vindictiveness, I asked how he felt about the idea. "Don't hold back for *my* sake! If the book lives up to Dudley's praise and your own, publish it, publish it—though it ought to come out *after* the Edward Thomas." He pushed aside the British edition of Thomas' poems I had shown him. "Somebody should be able to find the book that Holt once published. Send it to me as soon as you can?" He planned to compare the two tables of contents before making up his mind.

"Did you ever discuss Thomas' poems with Eliot?" Never, nor did he plan to. Besides, from everything Herbert Read had told him in Washington, it was just as I'd said: all Eliot talks about now is the theater. It seemed important while speaking of Frost projects to learn where *North of Boston* stood on his list. Not high up at the moment, he said. "Just as I hoped," I replied. When he asked my reason, I cited Jeffers on Frost: "a regional poet who is also universal . . . like Wordsworth, expressing the universal through the particular."

"Nobody talks of Jeffers, and now he's gone. We should *do* something. He just kept working his vein. Stayed in the West—succeeded. Good poetry isn't dependent on geography." While I glanced at my watch, noting his train's departure, he added, "Neither is real religion dependent on churches—but shouldn't we start to get started? . . ."

Standing outside close to the Holt building, he gazed back for a moment. Without a word, he grasped my arm. We moved along the one short block to our left, and then, at a leisurely gait, south on Vanderbilt Avenue. The top of the new Pan-American skyscraper standing above Grand Central Station glinted with the last rays of the sun. Holding our gaze, it struck us both with wonder. "Did you watch it go up?" he asked. "How could they pour the forms so high up there?" I described what the workmen had done: huge precast concrete window-walls swung into place by overhead cranes, then locked to the girders—probably bolted.

We strolled for minutes in silence. "Greatest city that ever was—the greatest." He kept gazing high at the buildings shadowing the pavements. Once inside his train and seated together, we spoke about epochs of history. I mentioned something I'd read of the way an era reflects itself in its building-shape—that civilizations reveal their visions of life in the way they design their roofs: the horizontal, flat ones count on down-to-earth living and those with spires reach out for something beyond. What about ours? Both? Could it be ourselves divided? He mused a moment, then looking at me: "I want to read more of your writing. Bring whatever you can when you come to Florida. This year we'll have all the time we want for talking. No pages to sign!" I was starting to speak when the coach conductor touched my shoulder. I had only a minute or two to say goodbye.

Two days later, at Jordan Hall, though admitting that he had been ill and had felt a bit tired, he stayed the evening through. It may be unwise to imagine that during this final public performance, he reached for a note of finality, yet no one could miss his determination to assign to poetry at last a place "apart." It was higher than things such as politics, religion, and other "contentions." It was something "in itself," "song in itself," virtually pure. "October," for example, published fifty years ago in *The Youth's Companion,* was "innocent of everything I know of." Leaping forward in time to his current book, he read an equally innocent one, "Questioning Faces." And in his very early "The Tuft of Flowers," the mower spared the flowers "just because he liked them." He also read his recent Christmas poem "Away!" in which, he said, he was being "somewhat poetical at the risk of my life." The full performance closed with "The Road Not Taken," but instead of leaving the hall, he answered questioners—easefully, even about his ill-starred Krushchev remark. Someone asked him to read "Two Tramps in Mud Time," whose final words had "worried" him. After the poem, he spoke at length about gambling: It was every man's inalienable right "to go to hell in his own way"; that one of the "sweetest" things a person could say was "I bet my sweet life on this." His last remark had an air of detachment. After a short laugh, he announced, "It's a wonderful world!" Then calmly, "To hell with it!" His listeners watched, unsure. * *

On the morning that followed, Kay found him much too ill to keep his physician's appointment. She called in a doctor at once. After considerable wrangling, Frost agreed to go to the Peter Bent Brigham hospital. The tests revealed more than chronic cystitis. On December 10th, the surgeon removed the prostate and the cancerous tissue within the bladder. The operation had been a success. Frost, now comfortable and healing well, looked toward an early recovery, only to be struck on Sunday, the 23rd, by a pulmonary embolism. I was told the news next morning: There had been some damage to the heart but the poet had come through well.

In the afternoon's mail, the first thing I opened was a packet from Paris. Rebay enclosed with his own letter one he had just received from a man suggested by Jean Paulhan to write on Frost for our international essay volume.

> I thank you for your letter of the 19th. It is not possible for me to accept your offer—for which I thank you—for the following reasons:
>
> 1) I do not believe that Robert Frost is a first-rate poet; he enjoys a glory which seems to me excessive and it is too bad that this misconception that has lasted so long continues. Americans—so slow, for example, in recognizing Emily Dickinson—are doing what they can to have the Nobel Prize awarded to Frost. There are over a dozen of us, European critics, who try to prevent that. We have succeeded, since the old monkey no longer has any chance.
>
> 2) Your letter—and I hope that it is only through some "gaucherie"—appears to wish to dictate to me what I ought to think of Frost; you will understand that it is impossible for me to accept in advance an attitude that would not agree with my own.
>
> 3) The money offered for this "directed" work strikes me as absurdly inadequate.

If you wish, you can write, on my behalf, to M. Henri Thomas, c/o Editions Gallimard. He is one of the few French writers with some indulgence for Frost.

Cordially,
Alain Bosquet * *

Then there *was* a cabal, as some of us long suspected. I studied the letter. *"Nous sommes une quinzaine de critiques en Europe"*—not just in France! Who, in fact, were these "European" critics so bent on preventing Frost from receiving the Nobel award? And how could this writer be sure that "they had succeeded"? Paulhan could instantly get to the facts by confronting Bosquet: His firm admiration of Frost should be reason enough to spur him to act. I also wrote in reply that Rebay might think of following the news I'd heard of a Frost book in the standard Seghers series (*Poètes d'aujourd'hui*). The editor, Roger Asselineau, would undoubtedly know of some critics to write for my project.

One week later, New Year's Day, Frost had another setback. Fortunately it was milder—so much so that within a few days he sent out word that he found himself "better than a little less bad." Soon he received the news of the Bollingen Prize, which most of us thought he'd "collected ages ago." His response would have seemed overgenerous if it hadn't been made on the day that his doctors rewarded him with "a virtual new lease on life." Letters and telegrams flooded his room, but the joyousness stopped on the night of the 7th—another pulmonary embolism. Once again he recovered well, and now the physicians changed his "social regime." Visits no longer need be confined to Kay and her daughter. Friends were allowed to come—at first, just a few, for a very short stay, then gradually more and more, among them Edwards, Udall, Reeve, Hyde Cox. After his first reprieve, Lesley arrived at the bedside. "I think of you as Robert Cœur de Lion," she wrote to him after their visit. He replied with a moving letter of praise.

During the time he was free from visits and medical calls, he was busy "thinking a sequel" to his Christmas poem. Edwards, overjoyed by this news, shared it with me while urging that I telephone Kay for an early visit; Robert was expecting me soon. On the 22nd, Louis had been at his bedside for more than an hour. Frost, talking on and on, ended by "ordering" him to be present in England for the "spring surprise." On the 23rd, three writers from the U.S.S.R. paid him a welcome visit. I left a message for Kay: I'd come at once—Friday, Saturday, Sunday. I had no reply; it was difficult, I was told, for her to keep track of appointments. But Pound's daughter had presented herself on the day that the Morrisons left for a rest in Goshen. At once I arranged to fly to Boston on Wednesday.

The hospital phoned Edwards on Monday morning. Frost, for some reason, hadn't been able to eat. Later that day a second hospital call reported sufficient improvement to allow him a visit with two of his Cambridge friends. I was looking forward to Wednesday, especially after a long phone conversation with Louis, who had visited with him on the 22nd: "His mind is as vigorous and his talk as pungent as ever. Unless there's an unforeseen setback, he should be up and around fairly soon."

Ten hours later, about 2:00 A.M., I awoke with a sudden dryness in my throat. I went to the bathroom to take a drink. As I walked toward my bed, I said to myself quietly, "Robert has died."

Minutes past 9:00 the next morning, I entered the Holt offices. "You've heard, I suppose?" I was asked by someone I don't remember. "Yes, that's what I said." She stared at me.

The dryness in my throat that had broken my sleep was now a choked-up head cold. And when John McGiffert of Channel 13 phoned to ask me to lead a television program that evening of the 29th, together with Wystan Auden and Thomas Johnson, I replied that I might not be able to speak clearly enough and to read Frost's poems.

The program began with a taped recording of "Provide, Provide," after which I defined the occasion: "Robert Frost died this morning at the age of eighty-eight," followed by the tribute from Kennedy. Briefly introducing myself and Auden and Johnson, I recited "For Once, Then, Something," after which the program proper began. It consisted of readings by each of us of one or two particular poems and of personal comments interspersed with recordings of Frost's own voice in "The Tuft of Flowers" and "The Road Not Taken." Some friendly remarks about Frost from each of us took up the next few minutes. Then Johnson, turning to me, half-questioned, "Didn't you say to me once that Frost taught you to *think* poetry?" Nodding but scarcely knowing what to say, I took refuge in words on the "sound of sense" and in Frost's advice about reading a poem carefully but not too carefully. Auden spoke of Frost as a poet of winter and night. I added a sentence, quoting some lines about "home" from "The Death of the

Hired Man." Cued by the program director that our time was nearing an end, I turned to the script of "The Lesson for Today." I recited the five-line coda slowly:

> I hold your doctrine of Memento Mori.
> And were an epitaph to be my story
> I'd have a short one ready for my own.
> I would have written of me on my stone:
> I had a lover's quarrel with the world.

Johnson, having to teach next morning, rushed for his train. Auden and I sloshed through the snow to a tavern across the street. I was finally losing my voice, but Auden more than made up for my nods and coughs. I wanted to know why he'd chosen to read "The Middleness of the Road." He was eager, I thought, to chatter along till the place closed down; but suddenly, halfway through a long sentence, he stopped, leaped from his stool, and dashed to the street. I knew better than to ponder why.

Tributes from all over the land and from far-off countries marked the death of the poet. Two days later, in Harvard's Memorial Church, thirty friends and relatives attended a private service, followed on the afternoon of February 17th by a public ceremony in the Johnson Chapel of Amherst College. Some 700 guests listened as Mark Van Doren read the eleven Frost poems he had chosen. The Right Reverend Henry Wise Hobson, who conducted the service, and Amherst President Calvin H. Plimpton, delivered, in turn, "Meditations" and "Reflections" of the kind, I believed, that the poet might have approved. For me, however, the most impressive of tributes appeared on February 23rd: the Robert Frost issue of the *Saturday Review*, prepared by its poetry editor, John Ciardi—"Robert Frost" by Charles R. Anderson; "The Classicism of Robert Frost" by John F. Nims; "Robert Frost: Teacher-at-Large" by John S. Dickey; two paragraphs from President Kennedy's broadcast on Frost's "courage, towering skill, and daring"; a holograph reproduction of Frost's Christmas poem "Away!"; and seven photographs taken at various times in the poet's career. The centerpiece of the issue was Ciardi's own contribution: "Robert Frost: To Earthward," a one-page "editorial" which remains to this day the indispensable approach to a knowable Frost (242).

With the road to "understanding" Frost suddenly thrown open, choices had to be made from an ever-enlarging list of proposed memoirs, anthologies, essays, selections, picture albums, biographies, and so on. Edwards, the Executor of the Frost Estate, moved slowly and cautiously. Some of the projects were out of his range but permission to quote from the poet's writing lay within Holt's firm grasp. Four books mainly or largely composed of letters were already approved: *The Letters of Robert Frost to Louis Untermeyer; Selected Letters of Robert Frost* edited by Lawrance Thompson; *Robert Frost and John Bartlett: The Record of a Friendship* by Margaret Bartlett Anderson; and *A Swinger of Birches: A Portrait of Robert Frost* by Sidney Cox. The first two would be issued by Holt, and as early as possible.

On the morning of March 25th I arrived at Newtown. Before I could step from my car, Louis approached: "Would it be too vulgar to ask what you think of my manuscript?"

"It most certainly would." I nodded. " 'No friend,' " I began, quoting from Frost, " 'has ever released me to such letter-writing.' And I *too* wondered why you kept keeping him running 'on to such lengths, extravagantly and hell-for-spelling.' In case you've forgotten, you'll find those words in his letter of August 9, 1947, from Ripton." Within ten minutes we were reading the editor's foreword and short introduction. "Approve?" asked Louis.

"Do I have to answer? Not one penciled query, as I needn't remark. But I urge that we go through every word together, just to make sure."

From the opening page to the one marked 629A there were nothing but minor queries, typewritten errors, and so on. But here—the third of the bawdy poems included a word that in A.D. 1963 would not be allowed to appear, at least by Holt. Poems 1 and 2 could remain untouched, but the third? Louis had been prepared, having scrawled at the bottom: "See next page for possible alternate."—which we used without great loss to Frost or his readers. From that point on we sailed to the last: the postscript added by Louis after his final visit. I repeated what I had said before: "The best biography Robert will ever be *given*. The best self-portrait. And the end of Frost as the white-haired saint. Robert's shade should be grateful." Bryna Untermeyer, herself an editor, asked why it took us so long. "For one thing, we're looking at every word; for another, we've still the end to discuss."

"What end to discuss?" Louis demanded.

"The index, of course. The safest thing is for you to do it yourself. Otherwise—" But what had got into me? Louis cried. How could I dare to want to add such a thing to this *intimate personal* book? "For the sake of readers, who'll want to know what he says about Elinor, Carol, Marjorie, Kay, even Bryna . . . and his comments on poems, revisions, titles, politics, God, humor, grief-grievance—need I go on?" Louis kept shaking his head. "But it isn't as though you've left the letters *inviolate!* You've censored a bawdy poem and in spite of Robert's request that you 'please burn it,' you include the letter about Elinor (36f.). Not that I disagree. It's one of the most affecting parts of the book." He continued to shake his head, hoping, I guessed, that I'd stop. "Do me one favor, please," I said. "Promise to weigh the pros and cons, especially the pros! And—if you won't do it, I'll make the index myself." He perked up suddenly. "I assume, then, that I have your promise? . . ."

Edwards, eager to hear how the day turned out, listened to all I said. Most important, I added: I learned some things that I couldn't have otherwise known. In spite of the difference in temperament, attitude, politics, taste, and the rest, Robert and Louis were not only fond of each other; they trusted each other through almost fifty years. "They'd never have used the word, but they really loved each other— which didn't blind them one bit to each other's failings. Louis doesn't hold back, and a good thing too. As for his comments and notes, they're neither too long nor too short, and a few—for me at least—are revelations. It really is, as his foreword says, 'an unguarded autobiography.' But there's one thing still to be settled: the index. Louis is against it—thinks it doesn't belong. But to publish this book without any index at all would be unforgivable. There isn't a single important collection of letters without one. And this collection's invaluable. I can't think of anything like it. If all goes well, books should be ready by August."

"You missed Larry Thompson by minutes," Frances remarked as I made my way to my office. "The manuscript's on your desk." It was truly enormous—and prepared with skill and industry by a writer who knew how to make me appreciate the size of his task. I began with the table of contents. In addition to the letters themselves, Thompson had added a long chronology of Frost's career, divided into ten periods, each one forming a chapter with a special preface. As a curtain-raiser, the first dealt with the poet's background through five letters by his father and mother. There were also two appendixes "designed primarily to clarify certain oblique references in the letters": (1) a selective genealogy beginning with Nicholas Frost, born *c.* 1595 in

England, and concluding with Elinor Bettina, dead two days after birth in 1907; (2) a not very moving poem, "Genealogical," Frost's "Whitmanism" of 1908. From my first impression, the project promised to offer the needed complement to the separate books of letters from Frost to a single person—Cox, Untermeyer, Bartlett.

Thompson had chosen 466 letters *from* Frost to 123 correspondents; in addition, 40 letters sent *to* Frost from 34 people and 55 *about* the poet from 13 others. But a hasty count suggested that more than 100 had already appeared. Although I was rather dismayed by the large number of dull impersonal letters—dealing with autographs, bibliophilic concerns, manuscript collectors, teaching positions, honorary degrees, lecture engagements—some of the items more than made up for the waste: notably, the 38 letters by Elinor Frost; 10 or so to Bernard DeVoto; 15 to G. R. Elliot, one of his oldest friends; and a lengthy and important one from Frost's sister Jeanie. There were also omissions—not one to Mark Van Doren.** And then there was Wade Van Dore. Thompson chose from the many that he had been shown, one only and, from what I knew, not in the least representative of what he himself had defined as "one of RF's most unusual and lasting friendships." I made a note of Mark and Wade along with other suggestions that required revision. One of these had to do with the publisher Thomas Bird Mosher, to whom many readers were greatly indebted for printing in his *Bibelot* series foreign writings they couldn't have otherwise known. Thompson's headnote begins "A picturesque gourmet, dilettante, and book collector, with a taste for blue-china poetry, fine printing, and pornography . . ." What was "blue-china poetry"? No explanation. What were the grounds for calling the man a pornographer? This wasn't merely questionable; it was slander which might bring the authorities down on the head of Thompson and, by implication, being a Mosher admirer, of Frost. One of the leading bookmaking experts found the words "absolutely false if not libelous. Nowhere is there even the slightest evidence of pornography. As for the 'blue-china' poetry . . ." The headnote appeared on page 46[6] (letter 34); and nothing up to this point had called for the smallest query. Now I wondered what lay in store.

But not for long—the answer (pp. 50–51) was clear in Preface IV: "London, Beaconsfield, and Gloucestershire. 1912–1915." The two brief pages worried me. Once having landed in England, the Frost

---

[6] For the reader's convenience, page numbers refer to the printed book.

pictured by Thompson spared no efforts in driving himself and everyone else he corralled on a personal public-relations campaign that the
shrewdest professional would have found hard to equal. In fact, according to Thompson, the whole voyage to London was nothing but
a self-promotional plot to advance his career as a poet. Had I now
come on "the real Thompson"—at least that part of the man from
which Frost had implored protection?

When Thompson arrived to work on the preface, I asked if he'd
stopped to gauge the effect that his words would produce. "You really
should, for your *own* safety. In any case," I added at once, "the letters
by Frost do *not* bear out your charges. If anything, they do the opposite. Please take these pages back and reread Frost's letters and Elinor's
(p. 53). You'd be laughed at for charging that Frost had 'coached'
Abercrombie (p. 127). Just remember that your job in the preface is
merely to give the background; it's not to attribute motives. Frost's
letters speak for themselves. Better not force your interpretations on
the readers." I laughed. "Quite a few will remember your Birthday
piece in the *Saturday Review*—your 1959 love-letter to Robert. If
they'd see these pages, they'd—what should I say? After reading your
first three prefaces, which seemed to me exactly right, in clear un-
obtrusive prose, I knew how well you could play the part. Preface and
letters were all of a piece. I remarked to myself, 'a very good job.' But
Preface IV . . ."

I had no way of knowing what to expect—surely not the speedy
revision that he placed in my hands. I put it aside. "Now you've leaped
to the other extreme and it's just as false—all sweetness and light when
you know that it isn't the truth, when we *all* know that Frost must
have harbored a hope. Louis puts it quite simply: 'Frost had gone to
England *partly* to try himself against another background and *partly*
because his wife had said she wanted to live under thatch.' Wouldn't
you, in your thirty-ninth year as a poet *without* an audience, hope that
there might be people in the country where English verse was born
who might give your poems the hearing denied them at home? Frost
didn't know a soul when he landed in England. Naturally, when the
man at *TP's Weekly* urged him to try the publisher David Nutt, whose
name he had never heard, he took a chance. What did he have to lose?
And when Flint urged him to call on his 'fellow countryman Pound,'
why shouldn't he go—but he went *after* his book appeared. Not to
solicit endorsement. As we both know, as a matter of fact—" Larry
waved me aside. "What I asked for," I corrected myself, "what is

needed now is a balanced statement based on a hard, plain view. Let the letters do the convincing. Yours is not the unguarded autobiography that Louis published, nor a Bartlett account of a friendship. This is your particular choice of 380 new letters along with 100 already published. Frost supplies the text; you're to supply the plain chronological facts. And the reader will draw conclusions, matching your words with Frost's."

I dropped into Edwards' office to report progress. I explained that Larry either didn't know what he thought, or that there was something fishy. We would have to wait to see what he did with his third version of Robert's voyage to England. His first two tries were unacceptable—one too black, the other too white. I was making notes and would keep him informed.

"Any day now" I expected the altered preface. It failed to arrive. Instead, a telephone message informed me that Larry soon would be coming in with everything else for the book, which meant the general introduction, the revised preface I asked for, and the index, "which was something out of the ordinary." An extremely long, unexplained delay; then all at once—why? Would he overwhelm me with so many things I could never agree to that we'd reach an impasse? And in order to find a solution, would he offer to temper the most negative parts in exchange for which I would also give ground, so the end result would be far from the book I hoped for but one that *looked* like a genuine compromise? And the published work would be close to his hoped-for version.

Larry busied himself with notes of his own while I studied the new preface and the twelve-page introduction. I'd listed my queries and had added a few from what I'd just read, so we'd get all the obstacles over at once. "Roll up your sleeves for *la lutte finale,* if you don't object to my quoting the Marxist theme song for the final conflict." He smiled. "But give me a moment before we start." He smiled again. "First, for me your book is a real contribution. No doubt about that. Second, you've made no pretense at hiding your very personal critical view of Frost as a man. Third, *you* have every right to insist that the picture of Frost the public saw wasn't the truth; and therefore, holding the view that you have, you feel impelled to 'unmask' Frost, as you say and most certainly do in your introduction. *But*—you have no right to *overdo* your unmasking, to discover a mask where there isn't any mask at all. Louis once and for all disposed of Frost-as-the-white-haired-saint but he never went overboard. I'm being as honest with you as you say you're being with Frost. Sometimes"—I picked up my notes and clippings—"when you let yourself lose control, you produce a picture that shows *unreasonable* distrust and suspicion. This happened once before—the Inauguration. You were saying what 'really' happened: Frost had determined to steal the show from Kennedy; it was simply a put-up job. You do the very same thing in a number of manuscript pages, and *these* are the things I query. You're entitled to give your negative view, *except where it is uncalled for* or *not borne out by the facts.*"

There weren't too many examples and I hoped we could clear them away. Otherwise, he'd force his readers to think that Frost's official biographer, his trusted friend who had sent him a birthday valentine—I pointed to the *Saturday Review* clipping—suddenly turned against him, that instead of taking Frost at his word, he looked for devious schemings, mischievous plots, falsifications. "You'll be undermining your *own* credibility," I warned. "This is much too important a book to suffer because you and I disagree about Frost as a fallible mortal. And don't make the error of telling the reader he can 'roll his own' biography with the makings you offer him *here,* since there's vastly more to the life of Frost than appears in your pages—as everyone knows." He stared at me. "Shall we start, then?"

"Fair enough, but *after* you look at my index. It's a *real* innovation; you'll see." Spreading it over my desk, he beamed. "And it's all complete. When the page proofs come, I'll fill in the blanks after each entry."

The opening listings (A, B, C, D, E) seemed careful and clear, and the first few under F, impressively ample: Marjorie Fraser, Willard, Carol, and Elinor in particular. Then came the innovation. Immediately after "FROST, ROBERT LEE [26 Mar. 1874–29 Jan. 1963]: a pile of typewritten pages alphabetized into forty-three topical subheads starting with "Accounts, Biographical" and ending with "Suicide." Apart from entries on writing (books, poems, poetic practice, themes, theory, sentence sounds, style) there were twenty-seven sections, each with a brief title and each composed of Thompson's comments and Frost's phrasings. "The quotations cited," the introduction stated, "are representative, and are those which the editor considers of special interest."

"I thought you said this Index is all complete." Thompson nodded. "Maybe complete as a *negative* view, but where is the rest of the person, the *positive* Frost? You couldn't offer readers *this* as the valid picture of Frost, for of course it isn't. *They* know that. You said it plainly here in your Birthday essay." I showed him the Birthday clipping. He drew himself back.

"It's *all there,* I tell you." He shook his head.

"All there, is it?" Flipping the pages, I read out: "Cowardice, Enemies, Fears, Masks and Masking, Punishments, a whole page on Resentments, Running Away, two pages on Self-Indulgence . . . Now, where is the Generous Frost who gave $100 to Wade Van Dore to buy a farm for himself—Wade told me you read that letter. What about Frost's long-lasting friendships that your headnotes refer to? And his joy and grief as a father—Marjorie's death, Carol's, the pain over Irma? What about Frost the husband, from the year of Dismal Swamp and the secret wedding down to his season of blackness after Elinor's death? And I haven't yet mentioned his reticence or his famous Puritan restraint, which would balance your 'Self-Indulgence.' And his politics—all through the letters! His deep-felt sense of America, 'The Gift Outright.' And the humor, the wonderful playfulness known to thousands of listeners?"

I stopped in hope of an answer. Silence instead. "Not *one* word to add to *this* index?" I shook my head. "It's all there, you said. But it isn't. Listen to Larry Thompson's picturing Frost in the *Saturday Review*—only yesterday for thousands of readers. March 1959." I quoted from his Birthday essay:

[D]uring the past ten years, he has extended his value to us in so many new ways and with such characteristically saucy wit and seriousness as to bring new glory not only to himself but also to his country . . . He has never lost his knack for seeing beyond . . . He has remained a steadfast witness-tree to that kind of traditionally guarded Yankee optimism and confidence that we have so largely lacked and needed. . . . He has served his nation with distinction . . . has proved himself native to the grain of the American idiom. So with gratitude as well as love we salute him on his eighty-fifth birthday as our most renowned and our most cherished poet.

"Your index topics exclude Courage, yet you quote him twice. Shall I read it?" I set the page down on my desk top. "I'll start to compile the missing person—using your very own words as well as Frost's. I'm flying abroad, you know—February till April. I've plenty of time to do what is needed to 'correct'—let me be as polite as I can!—the distorted picture you've made. Every word I cite will be given the source."

I gathered the manuscript pages. "Here's something more: my queries. Each is fully explained. Tomorrow I'll mail you my notes on the big introduction and your third preface revision. Xerox copies of everything listed will go to Al Edwards along with my explanations. I'll keep a second set, to check with the proofs when I'm back—before press. One thing more, have you scanned your index for names of writers mentioned at length by Frost? I don't recall any entry on T. S. Eliot, but maybe I looked too quickly."

"Every writer who mattered to Frost is there. You can take my word for *that,* at least; but I'll check it again. Thanks."

I hurried to see Edwards. "This won't take long but you *have* to listen. Larry and I have just gone over his manuscript, and I've told him—politely as possible—all that I'm *positive has to be done* so the published book won't embarrass you and Holt—but especially you as Executor of Robert's estate. You not only have the *final* say as his publisher; you're also his friend—and much as I hate to remind you, his protector up to a point." I gave him a capsule report. "Glance at this list of Robert's qualities here in the index. He says they are 'representative of Frost as a person.' " I showed him the words.

"I think I've had some effect but just as a start, since I forced him to listen by reading aloud his very own words of 1959 in the *Saturday Review*. He promised to add 'a balancing page' for the introduction. It's hard to know how much of this Larry believes and how much of it is . . . Well, not that it makes a difference. What matters is the book as it finally stands and later—God help us—the official biography." I stopped. "I'll make a copy, if you want to glance at my notes."

"I'll do that." He nodded, though his mind was on other matters. "Tell me again the date of your flight!" I repeated: "Lincoln's Birthday." "Good—that gives us a month."

Unfortunately his new duties as Executor of the Frost Estate took up more and more of his crowded hours. Not until late afternoon of the April day I returned from London, was he able to make the time to hear my report. I gave it quickly. First, the *Encyclopedia Judaica*: It had run into serious obstacles, fiscal *and* editorial; the safest course for Holt was to bid it goodbye. Agreed? . . . Second, Horace Gregory's *Collected Poems*: Sad as I was to miss the publication day party, I'd already heard through the grapevine that a fine review would appear quite soon in the Sunday *Times*. Third, Christina Stead's *The Man Who Loved Children*: We could now proceed to republish it. Simon and Schuster had granted permission, and two close friends of Jarrell told me he'd surely write an Introduction. But my main business was Thompson's *Letters*. I was told that the proofs were on the way.

I assumed wrongly. The work was already in pages: both printing and binding scheduled so that books would be mailed to reviewers late in May or early June for July publication. Obviously, it was now too late to make changes.

Facing the huge bundle, I turned at once to the positive words I had virtually forced Thompson to add. I sighed, "Well done," then looked at my list of notes. A quick check forced me to doubt that my notes and suggestions had ever been read—even my passing remark about index entries: "T. S. Eliot," in spite of letters 440 and 440a, was not to be found (616), nor the proper date for Elinor's death (lix, 468). But how could the poet's biographer present the London years (50 ff.) without even hinting that Frost had wavered between Great Britain and Canada? How could he stand by the "topical index" portrayal which he knew he could remedy, at least in part, by adding affirmative entries? Why did he cling to his headnote slander on Mosher (46) which would reap the contempt of experts? Loaded words ("tactics," 157f.), slurs ("mutual admiration society," 160 f.), "malice" used three times in two pages (xvi f.), missing identifications ("Mr. Skinner," by now a scholar of world-wide fame [326]). Small errors of fact might warrant forgiveness, *e.g.*, citing the wrong poem ("Build Soil" for "Christmas Trees," 545). But one omission (528, headnote) hid from the reader Frost's fury at Thompson for giving a false view of the poet's thoughts on religion (above, my page 146).

How would the critics respond to a work most of whose words (Frost's) clashed with the person portrayed by the Topical Index? Would they see through the editor's pretense of showing Frost "as he was"? Some of them might be daring enough to gaze on Thompson plain: self-unmasked by his poorly concealed biases. But from most reviewers *the letters alone* would draw a positive verdict, with Thompson merely a guide. Few would compare the volume with the Untermeyer and Bartlett collections. *Selected Letters* would surely be well reviewed.

It was—with qualifications. Jarrell, in a touching tribute to Frost, never mentioned the editor's name.** *Newsweek,* while noting the virtues, warned readers that only part of the truth would be found in the book's pages. The *Atlantic* criticized Thompson for not providing for the letters "a detailed background," and declared as unwarranted his invitation to readers to use the book "to roll their own" biography. For the *Yale Review,* Thompson's "failure to respect the crucial distinction between life and art" marred the work; also the fact that, despite his disclaimer, he "suggests that Frost is *always* artful in using rhetorical strategies" (reviewer's italics). Most perceptive of all was a long critique by Leon Edel, an acknowledged authority on literary biography and the correspondence of writers (*Saturday Review*). Judging the range and nature of Thompson's additions to the Bartlett and Untermeyer books, Edel regretfully noted the absence of early letters and the "artificiality" of the many examples dealing with business, degrees, bibliography, and so on. Edel gazed at Frost, also at Thompson—the poet "master of badinage . . . toys with ideas, life, the world, chuckling all the while in letters that make us feel the vitality, the richness of his inner being." As for the editor's work, "the annotation is sparse, books and persons are not identified, useful dates are missing . . . [The] strange self-indulgent index . . . fails to record the names of many persons discussed in the letters. . . . T. S. Eliot, Shakespeare, Edna St. Vincent Millay." Because the review touched on various points I also had queried in the course of editing—matters I had cited to Edwards while reading the manuscript *months* before publication—Thompson charged me with having conspired with the critic to attack his achievement.

To believe that Leon Edel might have joined in any such plot was the height of absurdity, of course, yet Thompson repeated his accusations, and in so doing, created a welcome predicament: In view of Thompson's charges of my "complicity," all hope of our ever working together on any project had become unthinkable. Frost's repeated phrase—"I'm counting on you to protect me from Larry"— pounded my ears as I warned Edwards once more of the dangers ahead. I urged him to use the same person who had worked with the manuscript of *Selected Letters.* "Hold fast to Louise Waller—she's all we have." He made no reply, waiting. "By the way, I've spoken with Fitts—some questions about Robert's *Complete Poetry* project. There are more problems than I'd thought of before. A truly definitive book, it *has* to be—once we've made up our minds what 'definitive' means. . . ."

Meanwhile Edwards asked my opinion of a dramatization by Donald Hall, Michigan's poet-in-residence: *An Evening's Frost.* I read it twice and gave it my blessing. The work had been planned to play at Ann Arbor in January (1965). Marcella Cisney, Artistic Director of the University of Michigan Professional Theatre Program, had persuaded Hall to write the text, having conceived the project after watching one of the actor-stars of the thirties, Will Geer, in a Twain program. Like the Michigan group, I hoped that the work would appear all over the country.[7]

In addition to *An Evening's Frost,* two films had been made of the poet, neither of which I had seen. The first, twenty-six minutes long and in color—described as "Robert Frost at home reading his poems against the pictorial background of New England"—had been done for the United States Information Agency by Sidney J. Stiber and released in 1960. A year later the United States Office of Education made it available to schools. Before long a second project arose. Edward Foote, like Frost a luncheon guest on President Kennedy's yacht, set his heart on a feature-length documentary. Shirley Clarke, his director, who was known favorably for *Skyscraper* and other avant-garde films, planned to produce the work in sixteen months or so, at intervals, in Washington, Hanover, Cambridge, and Ripton. The initial footage was filmed toward the end of January (1962) at Amherst; the last in Vermont after the poet had settled in for the summer. *Robert Frost: A Lover's Quarrel with the World* was not released until 1963. Produced by the Boston WGBH Educational Foundation, the film was later acquired by the U.S.I.A., which distributed it to embassies as well as some other outlets.[8]

I counted at least eleven "Frost items" already published or due to appear. There were two critical studies—Reuben Brower's, Radcliffe Squires'—three letter collections—Untermeyer's, Bartlett's, Thompson's—four portrait biographies—by Sidney Cox (*Swinger of Birches,* 1957), Jean Gould, Daniel Smythe, Louis Mertins—a book of *Interviews* edited by Edward Connery Lathem, and *Selected Prose* edited by Hyde Cox and Lathem. Bookstores soon would be loaded with more of Frost than tables and shelves could display. And additional works, some of them of outstanding importance, were in preparation—

---

[7] New York in 1966; a national campus tour (Vassar to San Francisco) in 1967; a West Coast tour in 1968.

[8] Apparently a re-release was made by Holt in 1967; also a Pyramid Film release in 1971. A documentary entitled *Robert Frost's New England,* made by DeWitt Jones, was released by Churchill Films in 1976. In April 1984, Burgess Meredith was said to be making a film of his own on Frost.

Lesley Ballantine Frost's *New Hampshire's Child;* the *Family Letters of Robert and Elinor Frost;* Reginald Cook's *A Living Voice;* the first of the three *Centennial* volumes edited by Jac Tharpe. The conspicuously missing item—the "definitive" *Poetry of Robert Frost*—I hoped to be able to arrange for soon, with the help of Dudley Fitts.

Frost and books about Frost were not my only concern at Holt in the first few days after New Year's 1965.

I kept close watch on the nine-month-old poetry volume by Gregory, and the almost finished Trilling anthology planned for colleges. One evening, while dining with a friend, I was traced through a series of messages by a hotly excited Gregory. He had just been told he had won the Bollingen Prize. Seconds later, I tracked down Edwards at home to tell him the news. "Bollingen *again?*" he shouted into the mouthpiece. "How *about* that! Two in a row for Holt! Sounds like some kind of record. Is it?"

"Ask Horace! He'll probably know. His number is 914-EL9-4362, and it's not too late to call. Add, if you will, that I'll be there tomorrow—*carrying* an Irish congratulation. I think you know how it tastes. . . ."

The Stead novel couldn't win any such prize—reissued books were usually not considered—but I hoped for the kind of response it had long enjoyed from scores of distinguished writers. The "impossible" task, as always, was to make the critics aware that *The Man Who Loved Children* was in fact a neglected "classic" (Lowell), "a work of absolute originality" (Elizabeth Hardwick), which "*must* be listed among the best American novels of the century" (Peter Taylor).

"Are you free to talk with ACE, I mean Mr. Edwards?" Frances asked. . . .

"Kay just phoned," he began. "She wants you to know she's selling Pencil Pines, and she says you're 'the logical person to have it.' " He beamed. "Why don't you and your wife fly down—look it over? She'll keep it off the market till you decide. *Think* about it! You know Florida; you know the place."

I knew the place and we both knew Florida. My wife and I had spent a month in the Rinehart house nearby. But remembering how I'd described the two little cottages, she saw no sense in making the trip. I couldn't explain to her why, but I felt that somehow I owed myself the chance to see it again. Of course we would have to make changes. As a start, we could move the houses together and add what we wanted. With that grove of beautiful fruit trees, the Florida birds, and the towering pines, it might turn out to be for us the winter retreat it had been for Frost. Besides, the trip would take only a day. We'd be there for lunch and home that night, with plenty of time to take a good look and decide.

Entering Pencil Pines with Kay and Ted as the hosts strangely confused me. We arrived, as planned, at noon; and over a splendid seafood lunch prepared by Kay, the five of us—including Ted's classmate Marshall Best, whom I'd known for years—chatted of everything in the world but Frost. It was difficult to feel at ease. I saw from the look on her face that my wife could never agree to Pencil Pines—the shadiness, the closed-in feeling: "It's precisely 1.9 acres," Kay remarked as she served the coffee. "Why don't you tour the land before you work with your measuring tapes." We toured the land, then entered the smaller cottage. With obvious zeal, we marked the size of each room on a roughed-out floor plan, then crossed the court and started to do the same in the larger cottage—then stopped. Kay, eyeing our moves, approached us at once. "Oh, what a shame! What a dreadful shame! I'm so used to the place as it is, I forget how much must be done. And of course, compared to your spacious Rinehart house . . ."

I shook my head. "People should form some sort of group to save the place—as a landmark. Have you thought about Metro's Historic Preservation Board?"[9] We thanked them as we started to leave. "We're sorry too. It was kind of you to have us. I couldn't have ever forgiven myself, if we hadn't come down. But you realize . . ."

On our way through Coconut Grove, we stopped to greet our Sunshine Realty friends, who had found us the Rinehart house. We were here, I explained, to consider the lovely impossible place that belonged to Robert Frost. It's up for sale. "When must you leave? There's something we can't allow you to miss. . . . Perfect for you from November till May, with the rest of your time on the Vineyard. . . ."

Neither of us felt certain when my wife and I made the decision to move, though the fault—as we later would call it—had been mainly mine. I had always planned my time at Holt as I pleased—would the new arrangement ask for more than any business could tolerate?

[9] Privately purchased in 1985, "Pencil Pines" was designated a landmark to be so listed in the National Register of Historic Places.

Edwards, however, raised no objection. I arranged to work in New York each month for a ten-day period—time enough to follow my special projects. Trilling's anthology was nearly ready to set in type, and his new idea—a "reader" of literary criticism—was about to enter the planning stage. Yet nothing had been finally done with *The Poetry* volume. I was counting on Fitts to accept the task. We had planned to go over the problems on March 31st, after his Harvard reading, but this was also "MacLeish Night" at Hunter College, a birthday tribute by four poets, and I was one.**

Often during the summer months I asked myself why I remained at Holt. There was one sure answer only: I had given my word to see the poetry book to completion. By now I had brushed aside all hope of finding "the ideal editor." Fitts, I knew I could work with—a trusted friend, also admired by Frost, a man of impeccable scholarship, classic *and* modern, whose attitude toward sound and its role, Frost would have found congenial. School problems canceled our date for November. We should have to wait.

"Florida was a mistake. We've put the place on the market." Edwards looked up, surprised. "I'll be in New York till Thanksgiving—ten days at your beck and call." He nodded, waiting, I guessed, to hear me out on the Thompson biography. "You've read the reviews?" He nodded again. "What will be done about Volume Two?" A long-distance telephone call saved us both.

Before my flight to New York, I received Louis' letter dated November 9th: "By this time you have seen my piece on Larry Thompson's first of his three projected mayhems." The rest was partly I-told-you-so about Florida, partly apology for failing to speak his mind about *Robert Frost: The Early Years* (in the *Saturday Review*). But someone, thank heaven, of critical consequence, had said what all of us knew should be said: Richard Poirier in *The New York Times Book Review*. Although Benjamin DeMott had also pointed to Thompson's "defects of composition and a troubling uncharitableness," like most reviewers he gave himself up to superlatives (*Book Week*). Poirier, on the other hand, saw no reason to be impressed by Thompson's zeal at piling "fact" on apparent fact: "For the story of Frost can only be penetrated by the most speculative and compassionate analysis" for which the "banalities of Thompson's prose and the orderliness of his schemes" were simply inadequate. Moreover, "moralistic attitudes inform the organization of much of the book." Indeed, "there is reason to be skeptical" of what this biographer does with "important materials"—of how he interprets "facts." I was not surprised to read in the same pages Poirier's remark that *The Letters of Robert Frost to Louis Untermeyer* was "the most important revelation we have had so far of Frost's career and personality."

The sales people at Holt were not elated. Of the many reviews of *Robert Frost: The Early Years,* the one most influential by far was also the most disparaging—and yet it probably would have been "worse" if Louise Waller had not, in some degree, been able to draw in the reins on Thompson. We arranged to talk during my New York stay. It had been, she sighed, a harrowing experience. By the time their work was finished, they were both on tight-lipped terms. I asked about Volume Two. There were problems, she said, personality problems within her department—the sort that couldn't be solved; but in any event "the pleasure of editing Volume Two" will be given to someone else. I disagreed: Surely Edwards couldn't allow this to happen. Once he heard, he'd simply insist that Louise do the job, even against her wishes.

But, she said, Edwards already knew. He *must* have approved and probably, from what he was told, felt that the person could handle it. I had started to ask the name of "the person" when, as had happened before, a long-distance call from Dudley Fitts stopped our discussion.

His words ended my hope of his doing the *Poetry* volume. Reading the pages approved by Frost for the purpose of spotting what he missed and adding a comma where needed to keep to his meaning—this was no problem at all; it might even be fun. But the job ahead? Pure drudgery—finding, then ploughing through all the journals—dozens at least, probably scores—that had first printed the poems. True, there were photocopy machines and research assistants, *but* they would have to compare *every* poem in *every* printing in *every* volume by Frost, including *every Collected* and every *Selected* and then record *each* variant. Had I any idea of the time such labors required? I should try with an early example; good old "Death of the Hired Man," not to mention "Kitty Hawk" or, if they demanded too much, the 1953 Christmas card: "One More Brevity." It was probably true that a good many poems had very few changes, but to do the definitive book, one must do the definitive job, which—much as he loathed to admit after all his delaying—was plainly impossible now. Yet college English departments were loaded with scholars who'd leap at the job, though their work would have to be checked not less than once by a colleague. Did I want him to canvass the field? He would do so at once to atone for his ghastly behavior.

During my New York visits I saw less and less of Edwards. Was he too "involved" these days to follow the plan that had always marked our relationship—asking to hear my views in advance of making some policy change? As THE PRESIDENT of a thriving firm, he was living his cherished dream with a gusto that made him glow in spite of its nightmare moments. "Big changes, long overdue—for the best" had become his great concern. What if some of these moves struck me as ill-advised? Was I honor-bound, duty-bound to tell him? It was one thing for me to be close to the scene, as I'd been before, but now?—after my Florida move, seldom readily reachable? Much of the time, he would have no choice but to act alone and regret or savor the outcome which—until now—rarely touched on his work as Frost's Executor. But his twofold role as the business chief of Holt and the intimate friend of Frost in whom the poet had placed his trust would soon compel him to choose where choice-without-anguish would not be possible. Warning signs had already appeared, tied to the books published and yet to be published by Thompson. Even my quite unofficial life had been troubled by intimations of the pain in store for Edwards. Some of my friends and some of my Frost acquaintances bluntly demanded why, in view of "the slurs in the Thompson *Letters* and its horrible index," I had failed to remove my name from those to whom the editor gave his "particular thanks." It was still too soon to be challenged about *The Early Years,* but what would I answer after the second of "Larry's three projected mayhems" appeared?

There would be no need to explain: nothing blocked me from quitting Holt whenever I pleased. Of the three "in house" non-Thompson Frost projects, the *Selected Prose* and the *Interviews* had been issued, yet despite my failure to launch the third—*The Poetry*—my conscience was clear, having found a feasible way to achieve a solution: Louise Waller and I, independently, would fine comb *In the Clearing* and the current *Complete* (1949) and *Selected* (1963) for typographical errors, missing commas, and so on; and Dudley Fitts would propose some dependable scholars to prepare the "variants" section. I would play no part in anything done by Thompson or in anything done by Holt to promote the Thompson books. Edwards, on the other hand, as the head of a firm that depended on making profits, would *have to* authorize, for as long as it brought in sales, advertising aimed at persuading readers to purchase books that defamed the poet-and-friend who had vested his trust in him.

Thoughts of leaving Holt had been with me for years, waiting, it seemed, for something to force the issue. On a long drive back to his home in New Canaan, Edwards had sought my response to the notion of Holt's joining a huge corporation, "CBS, for example." Now, three years later, with rumors of purchase and mergers filling the air of the publishing world, enough was known to prophesy what would happen when Holt was "absorbed." Experts in "the management field" dispatched by the new ownership would take over at once. What could they make of the work-as-you-please arrangement I had had from the start? It was merely a matter of waiting. Edwards, facing unpredictable pressures, would have to safeguard himself. Soon enough I should have what I had always longed for: "time for myself"; and whatever the phrase might come to mean, I welcomed the unforeseeable burdens of freedom.

IV
_____

THE FABRICATION OF THE "MONSTER" MYTH

This book opened with comments by Denis Donoghue on the problems that faced a biographer who had come to loathe his subject. The words appeared almost thirty years after he had met with Thompson, at a Dublin party shortly before the close of Frost's 1957 "good will" mission. "Larry and I got on very well," Donoghue wrote to me three days after his essay appeared. "I sent him later a typescript of my proposed Frost chapter for *Connoisseurs of Chaos*: it was vaguely hostile, making much (too much, I now think) of the Social Darwinist aspect of Frost's poems. Thompson wrote back a long 'By God, how right you are! I'll tell you the REAL [sic] truth about that monster' letter, giving me a relentless account of Frost's dealings with his family, and the horrific consequences of his being a monster. And so forth."

Less than two years after mailing this letter, Thompson saluted Frost in the *Saturday Review*. This 1959 "Birthday Letter" proclaimed that:

> . . . during the past ten years, he has extended his value to us in so many new ways and with such characteristically saucy wit and seriousness as to bring new glory not only to himself but also to his country. . . . So with gratitude as well as love we salute him on his eighty-fifth birthday as our most renowned and our most cherished poet.

Thus begins "A Native to the Grain of the American Idiom." In the course of three packed pages, Thompson hails Frost's "Yankee optimism" as well as the "courage and daring and action and skill" with which he "answered and overcame" the challenges that had troubled his long career. In fact: "His entire life might be taken as a gathering metaphor of confronting and overcoming difficulties." After piling praise upon praise, the essay concludes: "We can take pride in extending to him once again, and with ever increasing gratitude, the felicitations of the nation he has served so well" (199).

A rare tribute, all the rarer for having been written two years after his "monster" letter to Donoghue and two before declaring to me that Frost had contrived his Inauguration performance "so as to steal the show" (148f.). It is difficult *not* to speculate. Did Thompson believe what he wrote to Donoghue in 1957? What he said in the *Saturday Review* in 1959? What he told me of the reading of "The Gift Outright" in 1961? What he "showed" to the world in *Selected Letters* and the three biographical volumes? . . .

One should be able to make a judgment once one has learned of the Frost-Thompson relationship. I have traced its course by drawing on various sources: intimate friends of Frost; Roy H. Winnick, Thompson's co-author of Volume Three, *The Later Years, 1938–1963*; the poet himself; his letters; the biographer's own account in the "Notes on Robert Frost by Lawrance R. Thompson: 1939–1967," housed at the Alderman Library of the University of Virginia.[10] The importance of these "Notes" to anyone seeking to understand the official biography, its author, and its impact on the public's vision of Frost cannot be overstated.

An excerpt from Thompson's " 'Introduction' to his 'Notes,' " as revised by Winnick (Appendix to *Robert Frost: The Later Years, 1938–1963*), chronicles his meetings with Frost, from his junior year at Wesleyan University to July 1939, when the poet asked him to serve as official biographer. Thompson's fourteen pages, marked by affection and charm, testify to the faith of Frost in a devotee who had gone so far as to plan, with Wilbert Snow, a book of *Selected Prose* with the poet's blessings. In the year that followed (1937), Frost "was deeply

---

[10] The "Notes" were transcribed at Thompson's request before his death in 1973 and sold by his widow in 1975. Since 1980 they have been available for reading in the Manuscript Department. Hereinafter referred to as "Notes."

touched" to learn that this son of a Methodist minister from New Hampshire, now employed by Princeton, was writing a graduate dissertation on Longfellow. The ties between Thompson and Frost grew steadily closer, culminating in Frost's request that Thompson "act as honorary bearer" at the service for Elinor Frost in 1938. It was held at Amherst, and while he was there, Thompson by chance met Professor Robert S. Newdick of Ohio State University, who with Frost's permission was writing the poet's biography. On July 5, 1939, Newdick suddenly died. Twelve days later Frost invited Thompson to come to Ripton. He arrived on the afternoon of the 29th and before the evening was over, he was made the official biographer.

Though Frost (sixty-five) was almost twice the age of Thompson (thirty-three), their relationship began quite comfortably, so far as the public knew, and continued to flourish. Frost was proud when the young man went to war—"the only soldier I can call my own at the front. He is on . . . a merchant vessel gunning for submarines." In the same letter (to Sidney Cox), he referred to *Fire and Ice: The Art and Thought of Robert Frost* (1942), urging Cox not to read it until he had written his own. To Thompson, he confessed to having

> read enough of the book to see I am going to be proud of it. I take now and then a dip into a chapter, gingerly. I don't want to find out too much about myself too suddenly. You gave me an anxious moment about my "golden mean." I should hate to get stuck in the golden mean. You make it all right in the end. . . .

Frost "felt loyal to Larry," one of his friends explained. "He was kindly about his efforts," though not enthusiastic about "the results" in *Fire and Ice*. Forty years later his judgment totally changed—or Thompson recorded a wholly imaginary hurt at the Washington birthday party "when he had stung me with such cutting remarks about *Fire and Ice*."

Frost said little to me about the volume, in contrast to his response to *The New York Times* review of *A Masque of Reason* (1945). He was not only troubled by Thompson's failure to grasp the poem; he was deeply concerned with the ways by which his biographer might misrepresent his sense of God, faith, and religion. The review had "infuriated" Frost, Thompson's "Notes" record; it had "said in part that the masque was an 'unholy' play, and that RF would inevitably 'catch hell from his more orthodox admirers because he has dared to make light of sacred themes.' RF soon after took LT aside to assert the piety, if not the 'orthodoxy,' of his play." But Frost continued to worry. Three years later he wrote a detailed letter in the hope of enabling Thompson to present the religious beliefs fairly and clearly. He still felt far from assured. As late as September 1953, Frost made an urgent call on the Thompsons while they were busy packing to drive from Ripton to home. "He had not finished all he wanted to say, the day we took our last drive, about *A Masque of Reason*," whereupon he made clear *his* views about good and evil and the question of virtue rewarded. "It had been a bad review, admittedly," Thompson adds in recording the visit, "based on a misunderstanding of the *Masque*. But Frost seemed to have the feeling that I was still a child of darkness, and here he was to straighten me out with the true gospel." Frost then talked about fear. "All religions, he said, were based on fear," and God hadn't let men know what the "Big Plan" is. "At about this time," wrote Thompson, "I was getting ready to yawn," though Frost had more to say, some of it indispensable to anyone striving to understand his thought. Here, perhaps, the subject of Frost's religion should end, but Thompson was still unclear. In 1971, eight years after the poet's death, while working on Volume Three, he asked his collaborator Winnick to call on Rabbi Reichert "to help Professor Thompson unravel Frost's complicated set of religious beliefs by writing down some of your recollections concerning the degree to which Frost was a religious believer."

In 1946 Janet and Larry Thompson spent the first of nine consecutive summers at the "Euber Place" in Ripton, while Thompson worked on the biography. His relationship with Frost, so the "Notes" report, flourished so well that of one of their talks in 1948, he wrote, "I feel better about our relations now than at any time since I've known him. . . . Now I know where I stand with him, and all's well." One problem, however, worsened with every summer, owing to "Kay's violent dislike of Janet. . . . So long as I was the carefree bachelor, with a bit of a record for being related to Don Juan and Lothario, Kay thought I was 'charming.' But as soon as I married [1946], the trouble started . . . inseparately related to her cumulative habit of treating the Thompsons as 'poor relations.' " Since "Janet's dislike of Kay was never concealed," the continuing "tension inclined Kay to poison Frost against me. . . . The wonder is that Frost and I are even on speaking terms."

These words, written in 1962, led to an all but unbelievable statement. Through the six long summers of 1949–1955, Thompson made few notes of his talks with the poet: "I was convinced that Frost had shot his bolt; that the latter years of his life would become compressed into very few pages; that nothing more of importance would happen." Comment would be superfluous were it not for the fact that soon after being "convinced," Thompson was writing a book that he ought to have known would create new problems between himself and the poet.

Melville's Quarrel with God appeared in March 1952. Frost said almost nothing in public that told its effect on his thoughts, and his letter to Thompson could hardly have been more evasive. After some cordial words about Melville's reasons for hating evil, he admits, "As I jump to the last chapter of a love story to see if 'she got him,' so I began with your summary to see if you got Melville. Having made sure of that I can take my time with the rest of your exposition." Whether he read each page or not, Frost said enough to show that he knew how Thompson "handled" his victim. That the book was not to his taste, I wasn't surprised to learn from an intimate friend, nor that Frost "may even have been alarmed for fear that Larry would subject him to a similar analysis with somewhat similar conclusions." There can be no doubt that the fear arose out of Thompson's tendency to oversimplify when facing a person too complex to be understood and accepted in all his complexities. Possibly Frost may not have read reviews, yet he probably heard that the book had "failed" because of "the super-subtlety of its author, who perceives a bear where there is but a bush." Or because, in the view of another Melville scholar, Thompson's method was "indefensible." Or another critique that Thompson accused Melville of "literary deception," of writing "at different levels to introduce his anti-Deist philosophy and yet not offend the reading public of his day." Might Melville's basic rejection of God somehow inspire Thompson to suggest the same about Frost? Would the "writing at different levels" charge be turned around to explain away Frost's successful appeal to all types of listeners?

To judge from his "Notes," Thompson was quite unaware of any such questions or of Frost's deepening dread of the way he would be portrayed in the still unwritten biography. But the days at Ripton in 1953 led to the following words: "This ended the summer in which I have been on terms of intimacy with Frost greater than at any time since we were at Key West [1940]. I had hoped that some of the tensions of the past might be buried. But now I know that the tensions will never stay buried, and that Kay Morrison will keep them operative, if nobody else does." Later (1962) he would name the summers of 1949 through 1953 as "the period during which the relationship between Frost and myself took its first decidedly downward trend, from which it has never recovered, and can never recover."

In trying to follow the course of the next ten years, it is best to view them first from the vantage point of the poet before looking from Thompson's. Frost was not merely aware of the countermeasures against the expected blow. He agreed to prepare a special preface for Sidney Cox's *Swinger of Birches: A Portrait of Robert Frost* (1957). He had also promised Elizabeth Sergeant both time and help with *Robert Frost: The Trial by Existence* (1960). Books of this kind were all to the good; and he already may have known or suspected that similar works would appear in time—by Daniel Smythe, perhaps, Louis Mertins, and others. None, however, would bear the official endorsement of the Thompson biography. None would be able to undermine its stigmatic effects. Only one writer could neutralize the dangers. "Al Edwards is still hoping," he told his old friend Untermeyer over lunch one day in (March) 1954, that "you'll write my biography, and so do I." He had said this before. He would say it again. That Louis might finally change his mind, was at least possible.

Something with reason to hope for—unlike a turn of the tide in relations with Thompson or in Thompson's "gift" for understanding his work. I was not surprised to learn that Frost had "nothing good to say" about his biographer's 1959 pamphlet that appraised his poetic stature. Later that year, he had all but taken my breath away when he shouted, "I'm counting on you to protect me from Larry" (116).

Two years later, thanks to the State Department, Frost and Thompson traveled to Israel together. When the plane took off, they were sitting apart, and from what Professor Sholom Kahn reports of their days in Jerusalem, the tension between them rarely escaped their hosts. (Frost had been unaware of Thompson's anger after attempting to make a date with the El Al stewardess: "If there's anyone I would care to have dinner with," she said, "it is Mr. Frost.")

Many engagements awaited the poet after returning home. There was *In the Clearing* to put into final form, in addition to other tasks that were always part of his program. His last full year, 1962, started and ended with illness, yet he gladly accepted assignments that were much too large for a person half his age. They were capped by the most ambitious and stirring of all when President Kennedy asked him to visit the Soviets as part of a cultural exchange. This time he made the decision: no more dissembling. He would not subject himself to the troublesome presence of the man from whom he had asked protection. "I want a variety in the followers on my trail," said his letter to Thompson, "and I want some of them to be not too critically intent on who I am and what I am. I didn't want to be made too self conscious in this momentous decision."

In Thompson's eyes Frost had broken his promise to include him on important visits abroad, yet this was no mortal sting compared to some other hurts he had suffered. Frost frequently "invented"; he gave him conflicting accounts of events; he reinterpreted meanings. "Don't let me fail to explain," he would say, but didn't explain; and then to soften the blow, he would add: "We're both trying to understand me." As early as 1948, when Thompson felt they were reaching their highest accord, Frost advised, "Don't pay attention to what I say." "Don't let me throw any dust in your eyes"—precisely what he'd been doing. "Mythologizing," critics hostile to Frost had been calling it; Thompson branded it "lies." In fact it was neither, for what do you tell a person you cannot trust and from whom you feel you must gain protection? You befuddle him, give him conflicting accounts, force him to rage with confusion, make him unable to sort the true from the false. You know that your fate is endangered, that you cannot reach out from the grave.

Not till the final years did Thompson come to fear that Frost had often "held back" and had given him "differing versions" because *he* had failed to live up to expectations. Hadn't the poet conveyed as much in the guise of a question—"Don't you think you should drop the biography?"—reinforcing his hope with a reason—"You know too much about me"—which he knew Thompson would recognize as the opposite of the truth. Surely Kay must have "pressured Frost into saying that," Thompson decided. The episode passed; bafflement reigned; the biographer's anger vented itself in hate and resentment—and in playing antipodal roles. In public: Frost's affable friend, the devoted praiser of poems, the man most avid to herald in print the eighty-fifth birthday. In private: the knowing revealer of Frost-the-monster (to Donoghue); of the nation's deceiver on the day of Inauguration; of countless slurs, gratuitous charges, hostile interpretations, and so on throughout the "Notes." He admits having given the poet "plenty of chance[s] to build up resentments against me."

And yet as late as March 1962, Thompson could speak of their recent visit "as one of our best." But from that date on their relations worsened. They met only twice, and briefly: in July and October. Thompson telephoned (December 8th) three days after Frost had entered the Peter Bent Brigham hospital. "Was he mad at him?" Frost asked. "Was anything wrong?" Three loud shouts of "no-no-no" came the answer, closing their last conversation. Five weeks later Thompson set down in "a note from the heart": "Here I am, pretending that I'm anxious to see Frost when the truth of the matter is that I really don't care whether I ever see him again, alive or dead."

★   ★   ★

Having already dealt with events from the poet's death through the publication of Thompson's *Robert Frost: The Early Years,* I need only recapitulate the sequence. *The Letters of Robert Frost to Louis Untermeyer* appeared at the end of August 1963 and Thompson's *Selected Letters of Robert Frost,* one year later. I have detailed how I had striven to cleanse the book of the worst of its biases—though my efforts achieved rather small success. The *Selected Letters* was well received but with qualifications, especially by Leon Edel in the *Saturday Review.* Because he raised a number of editorial points I had earlier made in the hope of improving the volume, Thompson held me responsible for "Edel's hostile review." Thus it became impossible for me to play any part in preparing Volume One of Frost's official biography.

"Although our relations had been very pleasant while doing the *Letters,* and thus began pleasantly with the biography, we completed the book in a stiff-lipped state"—begins one of Louise Waller's letters to me that record what occurred after she had received the almost completed manuscript that Thompson and Holt were equally eager to publish quickly.

> My first reading upset me [her letters continue]. Larry's picture of Frost was negative—always the worst interpretation of Frost's behavior—and my own experience with Frost had been quite the contrary. Instances of Larry's jealousy of Frost—minor and not so minor—startled me from the beginning. One in particular [see parenthentical sentence, p. 215 above] helped me to see how Larry's competitiveness with Frost had influenced his writing.

And so I found myself explaining to him that much of the tone of the book as originally written would cause Thompson himself to be seen in a negative light by critics and readers.

Our relationship deteriorated because of my efforts to neutralize his interpretations of the poet's character and his background. And I did manage to rid the ms. of some of the petty backbiting. Not all, of course, for Larry was very reluctant to make changes.

I warned him many times to delete negative interpretations that were obviously unwarranted or arbitrary. In any case, most of the types of negative reactions to Frost's personality which occur through Volume II and contribute to its sourness, I succeeded in excising from Volume I. And for that much, at least, I take credit, especially because his cutting was never done without some insistence on my part. Stormy reactions to any sort of criticism were not unique—both to my tentative and later more demanding requests for changes. By the time my labors were over, I was thoroughly sick of Larry's tantrums and of Larry himself, and probably he of me.

Although she could not prevent him from adding another topical index (198f.), her success in removing biases was wholly beyond compare with whatever was done for *The Years of Triumph, 1915–1938*. Despite my efforts and those of others who knew her at Holt, the woman assigned to edit Thompson's second volume chose to ignore all problems. Holt had employed her to "traffic" books through the press, which was not an editing job; and from all I learned, she had little training for editing. By the time she was given the manuscript, Thompson's stature, because of the wide attention won by *Selected Letters* and *The Early Years, 1874–1915*, well might have made an inexperienced editor hesitate to go "all out" as Louise Waller had done with Volume One. And to judge from the *Years of Triumph* as published—the only means that we have—she failed to "edit out" the portrayal of Frost that made the "monster-myth" possible.

To understand the course that this myth had taken, a reader should realize there are four separate agents who together account for the influence that a book exerts on the public—the author; the publishing house whose editor/editors, charged with preparing "satisfactory" manuscripts, have the right, when they judge it important, to insist and enable the author to change the work for the better; the book review whose editor/editors select the critic, accept or reject his or her submission, or agree to print it provided that small, large, or moderate revisions are made; the reviewer who may or may not bring to the book the requisite competence, objectivity, critical judgment, and taste. For simplicity's sake, we may use *The New York Times Book Review* (henceforth: *TBR*) as epitomizing the third and the fourth. In the eyes of authors, critics, bookstores, and publishers, its influence upon readers exceeds by far that of any other medium.[11]

To begin with, two reviews of *Robert Frost: The Years of Triumph, 1915–1938,* appeared in *The New York Times.* A tone of regret hovered above the first, but the second charged into battle. Its author, Helen Vendler, an academic reviewer of verse, had, at the time, the kind of standing that led many readers to listen seriously to what she said. "A disastrous life" (from her second paragraph) headlines the family photograph that all but fills page 1 of the *TBR.* After deriding Thompson for the book's subtitle, she proclaims to the world that Frost was "a monster of egotism" who "left behind him a wake of destroyed human lives." On what does she base this statement? Frost-family tragedies: cholera (Elliott, dead at four); septicemia (Marjorie at twenty-nine); mental illnesses (Carol, Irma); even "ill-fated marriages," none of which (needless to say) had been caused by the poet, save in a wild denunciation of Frost by his daughter Lesley as summarized by Thompson. Vendler, however, does not inform her readers that Lesley changed her tune.** Lesley's *current* book *New Hampshire's Child* (1969) pays tribute to *both* her parents. These are errors of omission indeed for any responsible scholar or critic . . . or reader.

How, then, was Vendler able to find the "monster" and the "wake of destroyed human lives"? Strangely enough, by taking as gospel the very book that she damns as "intellectually superficial," "embarrassing often and tedious at worst"—the work of a writer "capable of criminal blandness." And this is her *only* source: "a biography which hides behind an affectation of fairness."[12]

---

[11] Conceded even by those who deplored the fact. According to the *Literary Market Place* of 1978, the *TBR*'s circulation was 1,456,000; that of the *Washington Post's* book section, 741,000. A buyer is not necessarily a reader; those who read the reviews may be fewer or more. Those who finally *hear* what reviewers say surely outnumber readers. Some books which were never or even negatively reviewed—exceptions proving the rule—have acquired widespread readership.

[12] Her list of Thompson's failings, too long to quote, mentions among other things his "siding with Frost against all comers when it suits him" and "abandoning detachment" at other times; his "maddening habit of relegating to the notes facts which

One should assume that the *TBR* editor(s) would have urged her into making a more balanced attempt, in which her charge against Thompson would not undermine—as it does—her attack on Frost, and to ask her to cite, if only in fairness to readers and acceptable scholarship, the existence of differing portrayals of Frost. Unfortunately, this teacher showed no knowledge of them; the only other book on Frost with which she appears familiar (Munson's) was forty-three years old. Yet not only Vendler: All reviewers I read had shown themselves ignorant of the other current books by people who knew him longer and better than Thompson had known him (Cox, 1957; Cook, 1958; Sergeant, 1960; Untermeyer, 1963)—books that portray Frost as a credible, fallible human being and dependable friend.

One may wonder why Thompson, Holt's editor, the *TBR's* editor(s) and critics all combined to create the "monster" myth. One year later, two reprintings and the Pulitzer Prize reinforced its effects. Was the legend here to stay? Many people displayed almost perverse delight when assured that their erstwhile idol had feet of clay. Very few published objections, but how could the public know when the only protest printed (but not in full) by the *TBR* was written by—of all people—Lesley Frost, this time denouncing Thompson for hating her father and for gullibly parroting tales that Frost had fed him while warning: "Trust me on the poetry, but don't trust me on my life." Up to this time no one had publicly questioned the "facts" in *The Years of Triumph* or its ways of interpreting "facts."

Two new books, however, were to cut the ground from under much that Thompson had written and Vendler had stressed. In 1972 the *Family Letters of Robert and Elinor Frost* appeared, edited by Professor Arnold Grade with Lesley Frost's introduction. These purely personal documents—which, of course, had never been intended for print—made a travesty of Vendler's "family portrait" and her "Frost's disastrous life" and of much in Thompson's biography. In spite of their indispensableness to an understanding of Frost, the *Family Letters* failed to affect the book-reading world, thanks to reviews and reviewers. Much the same must be said about Kathleen Morrison's memoir that followed, *A Pictorial Chronicle* (1974). Based

belong in the text"; the "crudeness of [his] categories" in discussing Frost's religion; his utter failure to do justice to Frost's "stunning lectures," "conversational energy," his "asides of genius."

on the author's daily association with Frost over twenty-four years, its judgments and interpretations—of identical episodes—differ sharply from Thompson's. Yet her book was ignored by the *TBR,* to the mystification of scholars, since those in quest of a first-hand knowledge of Frost cannot help but regard it, with the *Family Letters,* as an unreplaceable document—which is not to suggest that her judgments are always convincing.

Her book was warmly dedicated to Thompson, who had died in April 1973 after a long illness, but not before providing for the completion of Volume Three of his Frost biography. Shortly after receiving a Pulitzer Prize in May 1971 for *The Years of Triumph,* he suffered a stroke. One of his graduate students, Roy Winnick, then on leave from Princeton, heard the news in August. He also learned that Thompson had undergone brain surgery and that, despite some paralysis caused by the stroke, the prognosis was hopeful. In visits and letters over the next several months, Winnick asked if there was anything he could do to help his friend and mentor resume his work on Volume Three. He called again at Thompson's house in the spring of 1972. Thompson intimated that he could use a research assistant. Winnick might wish to consider undertaking that role, and, if he liked, a spare room in the house would be his to use. Two weeks later, before any definite arrangements had been made, the services of an amanuensis became a matter of urgency. After suffering another stroke, Thompson again underwent surgery and was found, this time, to have a malignant brain tumor. Asked by Janet Thompson if his services were still available, Winnick replied that they were and agreed to begin working with Thompson immediately. He moved back to Princeton the very next day.

On June 17 [I quote from Winnick's letter to me, October 18, 1983, as slightly expanded by him in June 1985], I drove with Mrs. Thompson to the Harkness Pavilion at Columbia Presbyterian Medical Center in New York, and spent two hours talking with Thompson about his illness, our work together, and Frost—an honest-to-God working session with a man just out of surgery—and fully aware that he was dying. Thompson's bravery was remarkable. Before this second operation, he had ordered his doctors to preserve his mind at all costs—even if that meant leaving him terminally ill. All he asked was enough time and mental faculties to make possible the completion of his Frost biography. And that was precisely what he got. Although his reading and writing skills remained impaired, as they had been since the first stroke, he could *think* and coherently express his thoughts.

Having moved into the Thompson house, the first thing I did was to read and reread Volumes I and II, then the unpublished 2000 page document called, I believe, "Notes from Conversations with Robert Frost," the hundreds of chronological notecards, the letters and clippings in Thompson's files, anything I could lay my hands on. When Thompson returned from the hospital we spent three or four hours a day talking about Frost. I was struck, as I said, by Thompson's bravery and determination—but also, I must add, by Thompson's evident animus toward his subject. This was reflected both in his comments to me and in the conversation notebooks he had written over a period of many years.

I knew early on of what my work with Larry would consist: writing copy based on our conversations and his research materials, then reading it to him for his corrections and comments. As the work progressed, I realized that what Larry did in large part was to give back to me, almost word for word at times, accounts and interpretations already recorded in his notebooks. He didn't really add very much beyond what was already there—which was, of course, a great deal. So our conversations helped keep his mind occupied, his spirits up, but didn't do much directly to get Volume III written. Fortunately, I had the resources I've just described, and in addition Larry's *Selected Letters of Robert Frost,* the Untermeyer *Letters,* and the *Family Letters.* And I had enough information at my disposal bearing Larry's personal stamp to write an account that was demonstrably close to what he had set out to

For the first five or six months after the second operation [June 1972], Larry was in pretty good shape. He went for chemotherapy once or twice a week and these sessions knocked him down for a day or two. But we talked at length about Frost, and when he was not up to talking, I was reading or writing. Gradually the periods of lucidity became shorter, the pain greater, and he slowly lapsed into coma. After ten months, on April 15, 1973, he died. We had produced a crude, partial draft totaling less than 200 typewritten pages.

Although some of those close to the situation seemed to feel that I was the logical person to complete the biography, I was only 25 years old and perfectly green. I'd never written anything longer than a 43-page term paper and had certainly never been published. So it behooved me to ask if some more nearly qualified and competent person were available to take over the job of finishing Volume III. I put forth two obvious candidates: Carlos Baker and Edward Connery Lathem, each of whom had been devoted to Larry and each of whom had known Frost. Both men declined, saying I was the one who should complete the book. It was then, I suppose, that the enormity of what I was up against first hit me. . . .

I was in an odd position for a first-time author: terrified not that my publisher would reject my manuscript, but that my publisher, in order to complete the trilogy, would *accept* it—only to have it found egregiously defective. After three readings of Volumes I and II and continuous immersion in the conversation notebooks, I think it reasonable to assume that I had mastered Larry's prose style and, more important, his way of looking at Frost. It thus seemed at least theoretically possible that I could write in something approximating Larry's voice and tell the Frost story in a way approximating what a healthy Thompson would have done himself. So I plodded ahead, writing sometimes several pages a day, more often a paragraph or two, often nothing usable at all. Dreading the consequences of a job badly done, I fought an almost daily battle against depression. Eventually I had a manuscript that took Frost's life from 1938 to his death in 1963.

Carlos Baker was most generous with encouragement and advice. Ed Lathem sent meticulously detailed commentaries. By about 1974 I had produced a "complete" manuscript that at least one reader considered ready for publication. But I was unconvinced and spent another year rewriting—for perhaps the fourth time. Hyde Cox read the manuscript, as did Kay and Ted Morrison. All three made many constructive comments. In December 1975, as a result of these readers' favorable reaction to the complete final draft, I felt for the first time that the three-and-a-half years I had put into the work might, after all, result in a book of which no one, living or dead, need be ashamed. . . .

How much of Volume III is Thompson, how much Winnick? I suppose the only writing that can be said to be by Larry, verbatim, is the opening section of Chapter One, the English Diary chapter, and a few other passages scattered throughout. About half the book, as a guess, is my writing based closely on Larry's from notebooks or elsewhere. I wrote on my own when there was no choice—for example, about the two masques, Carol's suicide, Frost's death, his friendship with Hyde Cox. I might add that Larry had also drafted a table of contents before his illness and that the organization of the book—which we discussed at considerable length—is close to what he all along intended.

I was very conscious always of who I was—and who I was not. I wanted only to tell the story Thompson wanted to tell, as nearly as possible in the way he would have told it. I went out of my way *not* to form independent opinions about what Frost was like, why he did what he did, what particular poems signified, etc. I wanted only to be a conduit, an alter ego for Thompson. Not his successor as biographer, not a full-fledged collaborator. Himself.

On October 31, 1983, in reply to my letter, Winnick wrote:

I would not say that I never interjected my own perceptions into the writing of Volume III. Of course I did, all the time—inevitably. My perception of Frost was so much less extreme than Larry's as set forth in his conversation notebooks and in his comments to me that I had to temper Larry's verbally expressed and written but off-the-record sense of Frost with my own—and with the sense of Frost as a somewhat mellower and more attractive individual that Larry had assured Hyde Cox he intended for Volume III. ("To those who say I was too hard on Frost in Volume II," Larry had written Cox in a letter I quote from memory, "I say 'Stick around. Frost is going to win in the end.'") I regarded the capturing of that "other" Frost, so little seen in Volumes I and II, as an essential part of my work on Volume III—essential in fairness to Frost *and* to Thompson. I really had to walk a tightrope in that respect (as in others), being fair to Larry's more objective perceptions of Frost and fair to the objective reality of Frost's life to the extent that I could determine it (or, rather, them). . . .

Thomas Wallace, who managed the Trade division at Holt, found the manuscript "readable and interesting," made some minor suggestions, sided against Janet Thompson's efforts to name it "The Years of Glory" (her husband's announced intention), and saw the work through the press. It appeared on December 13, 1976, more than six years after Volume II, during which time nine works essential to critics of Frost had been issued: *Selected Prose* and a book of *Interviews* (both 1966), *New Hampshire's Child,* Reginald Cook's *Robert Frost: A Living Voice* (1974), *A Pictorial Chronicle, Centennial Essays I* and *II* (1974, 1976), William Sutton's *Newdick's Season of Frost* (1976). No reviewer, in all good conscience, could deny that the data contained in these works existed, or ignore them as irrelevant to any respectable judgment of Volume III.

The *TBR* assigned *The Later Years* to a man whose entire critique described in detail a person he could not have known, having been twelve years old when the poet died. The portrait, he said, derived from his reading of Thompson's trilogy—not even a hint that some five totally different (positive) portrayals existed—yet even his reading of Thompson had been less than competent, as Winnick quickly made clear to the *TBR*. Yet it should be noted that the featured appearance of this review in the most influential journal devoted to books reinforced Vendler's "monster" distortion of Frost. The review called forth so many horrified protests from people it could not ignore that the *TBR* had to take the unusual step of allowing them five packed columns of print (March 6, 1977). Winnick, enraged by the falsifications that the critic (David Bromwich) set forth, sent the *TBR* a letter to straighten the record. At least some part of it needs to be made available:

> That Frost is vulnerable to attack for misconduct in a number of instances, even the most devoted of Frost's many friends would scarcely deny. But two of the episodes Mr. Bromwich selects as examples of Frost at his very worst are in reality nothing of the kind. I refer to Frost's actions before, at the time of, and following, first, the suicide of his son Carol in 1940 and, second, the commitment of his daughter Irma in 1947. In the first instance, Frost did all that he could for a period of many years to help Carol get on his feet psychologically and economically, an effort of fatherly concern that was never greater than at the time of his son's death. The caring extended equally to Carol's wife and son, whom he helped to support both emotionally and financially long before and long after Carol's end. The letter of Frost to his

grandson from which Mr. Bromwich quotes is hardly proof of Frost's "badness." On the contrary, it is a mark of Frost's high esteem and commiseration for the brave youngster whose maturity and courage are so unaccountably disparaged by Mr. Bromwich as "heroics."

As for Irma's commitment, Frost spent endlessly of his pocketbook and of himself seeking to arrange his daughter's life so that she might continue to remain on her own despite her growing insanity. Frost hardly "gave up" on Irma, and thirty years later she continues to benefit from his fatherly generosity.[13]

How could the eminent *TBR* permit itself to be part of this literary defamation. Here is a typical excerpt: "after reading [Thompson's] volumes one feels that to stand in the same room with a man about whom one knew a quarter of the things one now knows about Frost would be more than one could bear." Why did the *TBR* neither acknowledge nor print the letter with the pivotal facts that Winnick cited but Bromwich omitted? Whatever the answer,[14] publication of the Bromwich review raised doubts in the minds of many, not only of those dismayed by the attack on Frost. To be sure, book-review editors, like all other people, Frost included, shouldn't be damned forever for occasional bad behavior. The *TBR* has survived its mistakes and the image of Frost has survived its despoilers. Yet one cannot keep from wondering—what might have happened if, for example, William H. Pritchard's *Frost: A Literary Life Reconsidered* (1984) had appeared at the time of *The Later Years* and the *TBR* had assigned Bromwich to deal with them both.

★   ★   ★

"Frost was no saint (he never claimed to be) but neither was he, as misreaders of the Thompson biography have claimed, a monster. Frost was a complex, contradictory man, at times worth hating (as

---

[13] Excerpted from photocopy of Winnick's unpublished letter of January 18, 1977, to Harvey Shapiro, the editor of the *TBR;* by permission. Irma died in May 1981.

[14] Shapiro's reply (April 18, 1984) to my inquiry: "Was I in fact there? Was I on holiday? Was I sick? How do I know? I must have assigned thousands of books in those 8 years as editor, and I remember many assignments fairly well. Richard Poirier's is the only Frost book I can recall being concerned with during my

few did who knew him), at times worth loving (as many did who knew him) but always only too human in his response to experience," Winnick reminded Shapiro. To much of which I say "amen" but with one proviso: These are Winnick's words, not Thompson's.

Not until 1940, when he went with Frost to Key West, did the poet's biographer start to make notes with an "intimacy of detail." And not until 1961 was his "higgledy-piggledy note-taking" given the form of a single typewritten work now known as the "Notes on Robert Frost by Lawrance R. Thompson." Housed in the Alderman Library of the University of Virginia, they were purchased on February 17, 1975, and opened for public use in 1980. The "Notes" begin with a thirty-eight-page introduction written July 21, 1962, followed by more than 1,000 pages of text, from 1 through 1862, some of which bear unusual numbering (*e.g.*, N. 678–aaaa through N. 678–jjjj). Though the entries are not chronological, they do establish, as Thompson had hoped, "some kind of continuity," but with notably little on 1949–1955, since Thompson believed "that Frost had shot his bolt; that the latter years . . . would become compressed into very few pages" (see above, p. 214). After reading page 965 of the "Notes," I was given the final folders. They began with page 1425. In spite of the efforts of Robert Hull of the Manuscripts Department, pages 966 through 1424 could not be found. That these pages exist or existed cannot be doubted in view of the index listings (*e.g.*, "Edwards, N. 1156, N. 1261, N. 1345–49; Elinor Frost, N. 1190, N. 1203, N. 1366, N. 1400–08; as well as eight entries under "Religion" and "Skepticism".)[15]

Though a fourth of the pages are missing, any person concerned with facts, the truth, the *dependability* of Thompson's official biography cannot in all good conscience ignore the official "Notes" now available—most assuredly, no critic, no scholar, no disaffected reader. Up to this time, no writer on Frost as a person has taken account of the

tenure."—not even after sending to print five columns of protests (from Alfred Edwards, Dorothy Van Doren, Kathleen Morrison; March 6, 1977).

[15] Quoted words in this paragraph are from Thompson's "Notes," which appear on 8 $1/2''$ x $14''$ sheets with some thirty lines per page, in Boxes 5 and 6, Item No. 10,444, Rare Book Department. In reply to my inquiry, Joan St. C. Crane, Curator of American Literature Collections, states: "We can only conclude that 966–1424 were removed before the archive was deposited in Virginia. Possibly they contained sensitive material that Lawrance Thompson or Mrs. Thompson thought best to remove" (November 16, 1984). Winnick writes: "Pages 966–1424 were missing, I'm quite sure, even while I was working on volume three" (December 6, 1983).

fact that these "Notes" on which Thompson largely based his books are sometimes at odds with the published volumes on important matters. A reader need only compare what the "Notes" set forth on thirty-four separate pages with the words on the same subject in *The Later Years:* the "Notes" and the published biography present two very different accounts of "the most important motivating factor in all of Frost's later years, from 1938 onward [N. xxxi]." Thompson's phrase is no overstatement. Frost himself said as much many times— to his daughter Lesley and to friends, both in conversation and letters—on the role of Kathleen Morrison. [16] This example, with its manifest implications, offers more than enough evidence to convince the most skeptical reader, who will see at once that reviewers who praise the official biography as a treasure house of dependable facts have been misleading themselves and their readers out of ignorance that no longer can be accepted. The "facts" as implied by reviewers go beyond the listing of times and events into motives, vices, virtues: interpretations and judgments which project the biographer's biased version of Frost as a human being. [17]

Thompson recorded his "Notes" as would many other writers of detailed biographies, and although the Virginia archive is far from complete, it contains an abundance of data on times, places, public and private events, travels, occasions of honor, letters, talks, and the like. But for readers and critics of Frost, its main significance rises out of its treatment of men and women involved in the poet's life. There were more than a few of more than passing importance, but for reasons of space and proportion, we should deal with those of major interest only, with merely a word or two on some of the others.

Frost, to be sure, is the centerpiece of the "Notes." That some of the poet's acts and words would incite Thompson to seize every negative word he could to assuage his hurt, anger, horror, or blackening hope,

[16] I have placed on file with my publisher the numbers of thirty-four pages at various points in the "Notes" that support my statements. Frost's remarks can be found, for example, in *The Letters of Robert Frost to Louis Untermeyer,* pp. 312 (italic), 314; *Family Letters of Robert and Elinor Frost,* to Lesley, December 1938; *Newdick's Season of Frost,* p. 358; Mertins' *Robert Frost: Life and Talks-Walking,* p. 233.

[17] That Thompson's books, as Pritchard says (xi), are "essential for the reader who wants to follow the [bare] events of Frost's life from year to year," there can be no doubt, provided one realizes they have their share of erroneous items, some of which were corrected in the one-volume *Robert Frost* by the editor, Edward Connery Lathem (1981), whose task was limited mainly to that of condensation.

should surprise no reader, once the unhealable break had occurred, once the biographer feared he had failed to live up to the poet's faith, once he apparently saw he no longer could cope with the powers his subject possessed. Since the official Frost biography had become his *raison d'être*, the dread of being dismissed forced him to act with a desperation fueled by fear—and more. For even after the point of no return, he could find himself wavering. As he strove to understand this "complex, contradictory man" who was also "psychotic" (N. 598-f), he could hope that in spite of all they had suffered, the two of them might still recapture the trust that had marked their first few years. Frost was at times "a madman, a liar, deceiver" (Thompson's words) and so on, but also a person haunted by fears, who had suffered tragedies; a prodigy of thought, of physical vigor, of great poetic achievement—he was this and more: one who would always elude him, whose "apparent inconsistencies can be explained as being all a part of a larger consistency" (N. 307). Thompson convinced himself he had found the key in Horney's *Neurosis and Human Growth: The Struggle Toward Self-Realization* (1950). He devotes almost 100 pages to summarizing his "discovery of a kinship between my approach to Frost's psychodynamics and Horney's" (N. 1518). That this "key" helped him to view Frost with uncharacteristic detachment is evident when he tries to apply Horney's text to his problem. A telling example:

> It's easy enough to get mad at that old bastard . . . [but] The point is that here was a man who actually achieved a well-deserved and lasting fame as an artist-poet; a man who, in spite of his flawed human qualities, was at times extremely lovable; a man who, in spite of all his meanness to so many people, really went out of his way to help certain people—and did help them. I must keep reminding myself of this. (N. 1614)

Unfortunately he did not always heed his own precept. As a consequence, the picture of Frost that his volumes gave to the world led, with the aid of reviewers, to the monster-myth.[18]

In the early part of this chapter, while speaking of Frost's relation-

---

[18] In the making of which Thompson's topical indexes played a decisive part. In applying Horney's text to Frost's views on a number of subjects (*e.g.,* religion, science), he reaches conclusions that contradict the poet's straightforward statements.

ship with Thompson, I quoted lines from the "Notes" on Kathleen Morrison (see above, p. 213)—five sentences only. In more than twenty-six instances throughout the archive, Thompson speaks of this problem, for a problem it was from the time he became the official biographer. Why? One is strongly tempted to speculate, though telling reasons are set forth often and sharply, out of which a uniquely triangular tension evolves. "I am caught," said Thompson in confidence to a friend, "in a conflict of loyalties which cut in three directions. First, my loyalty to Frost, then my loyalty to Kay, and finally, Frost's loyalty to Kay (N. 637)."

Thompson, however, was not a part of the problem when in 1939 the poet, deeply in love with Kay and certain that she was in love with him, hoped they would marry. Though weeks, months, and a year passed by, Frost held fast to his faith in the wished-for outcome. At about this time, the poet's chosen biographer and trusted friend wrote a letter "pleading" with Kay not to do what Frost proposed: to divorce her husband. The "Notes" say nothing of Kay's response; they merely add that she kept the letter and "placed it under wraps in the Dartmouth safe" (N. 1683).[19] Was Frost ever told of the letter's existence?

The relationship between Kay and Thompson involved much more than interpersonal attitudes. At stake were the practical publishing rights to everything the poet had put on paper: not only to works whose publication raised no problem—poetry, letters, lectures, talks, and the like that would form the public canon—but strictly private writings in verse and in prose that some of his friends might strive to withhold from the world. Who would be given control? Frost hadn't said, nor would the verdict be known so long as he lived. Those who for personal reasons were much concerned watched and behaved with caution. The relationship between Kay and Thompson continued to be, to outsiders' eyes, helpful and cordial, camouflaging suspicion and dislike. In time they would have to come to terms with each other, work out arrangements. If Thompson's "Notes" are reliable, both were playing a game (N. 964f.).

Reading the "Notes" from beginning to end makes a distasteful experience. Few people, not even some of Thompson's close friends (N. 961f.), escape censure. Others are viewed with overwhelming antipa-

---

[19] The text of the letter does not appear in the "Notes."

thy ranging from doubt, fear, and suspicion to hatred and fierce contempt, though the author wavers at moments. There are also a good many errors of fact.[20] Though not in themselves important, their presence makes one doubt the truth of much of the rest of the work. But these are the least of the troublesome parts of the "Notes," less troublesome even than its racist remarks (N. 629, N. 1507), its savage attack on Sergeant (N. 654e), its garbled quotation of Frost's pornographic quatrain (N. 650), its fearsome account of Kay's disposition of the manuscript of "The Silken Tent" (N. 1680–1685). Typical of the "Notes" at their most extreme, yet faithful to the author's approach, are the statements on note page 598-f.: Robert and Elinor Frost are "good examples of psychotics"; their son Carol "went insane"; their daughter "Irma went insane"; "Lesley is insane although still at large";[21] and "the best of the four children (Marjorie) had her own nervous breakdowns." When, if ever, had Thompson known Elinor Frost? Long enough to support any psychiatric diagnosis? Why is Jeanie omitted? And Elliott (1896–1900), was it only *cholera infantum* without so much as a trace of his parents' psychoses? Elinor Bettina, dead soon after birth, free of the taint?

I am drawn at times to the often striving, sober Thompson, who occasionally arrives at an insight. This, for example: On Frost's whole life as one of "pleasurable resistance to the assertions of mind, not because he opposes them but rather because he opposes the assertiveness or the positiveness of those assertions, knowing that this assertiveness represents only one of many ways of stating imponderables." Not the most lucid of phrasings, yet an effort to see why Frost had said that "he never had wanted to know anything exhaustively . . . too well" (N. 470).

Though no one may hope to summarize 1,500 pages in ten, the archive's nature and what it explains of Thompson's approach must

---

[20] I cite these personal examples of Thompson's mistakes because they concern my physical presence at specified times and places: I did *not* visit Boston during Frost's final illness (N. 866); I was *not* in Michigan at any time in the twenties (N. 1505); I did *not* ever make an offer for Pencil Pines, which has houses built of wood and *not*, as Thompson states, of cinder or coral block (N. 1510, etc.).

[21] But when it furthers his purpose, Thompson presents this "insane" person's words as true; *e.g.,* her penny-dreadful revolver story ("Take your choice. Before morning one of us will be dead.") in *The Early Years,* p. 308—told at length by Thompson, who most uncharacteristically omits all evidence.

by now be clear. They reveal a writer whose feelings for Frost changed from admiring devotion to a loathing that could nonetheless waver at times toward the "first fine raptures." The "Notes" were intended to help dissolve the mystification that Frost continued to be to Thompson in spite of their numberless talks, visits, letters—in spite of the poet's efforts to help his interpreter understand his beliefs on matters of grave concern. One more example: Though time and again he strove to make clear his special approach to religion, Frost never felt sure that his words had in fact been grasped.

Thompson's unresolved problem—to understand this man of elusive complexities—grew larger with time as his strivings became less rewarding. The wall between them thickened. The poet's faith in his young devotee turned into doubt, distrust, suspicion, fear, and a cry for "protection." The biographer—restless, unsure—reached out in all directions, ever in hope of seizing the key to the artist's person. He could never succeed, blocked as he was by a deepening dislike and a need (conscious or not) for assuaging frustrations by resorting to a highly respectable mode of retaliation: telling "all" "in the name of scholarly truth."

It is helpful, if shocking, to realize that in more than a thousand pages Frost's poems as poems are virtually ignored. I doubt that Thompson was ever aware that, as Poirier says, "he did not know how to read them." He was sure of his gifts as a critic, but his main concern in the "Notes" was the poet's person. And because of his constitutional bent for "perceiving a bear where there is but a bush" (as one scholar remarked of his Melville book), the "Notes," like the volumes they fostered, for the most part amount to an endless attempt to "unmask" the man and to show what he "really" was. In public he would bow and scrape before Frost; in private he could safely fashion his posthumous revelation of the public's idol. But the revelation tells more of Thompson than of Frost, in the "Notes" and in the biography with its page after page of hostile interpretation. And the irony—or the pity, perhaps—is that Thompson himself was enraged when critics of *The Years of Triumph* spoke of Frost with the very same word he had used: "monster." They had simply misread his book! How he could say this is hard to imagine in view of the topical index he insisted on placing into *Selected Letters*. He enlarged the device in his subsequent volumes. How could reviewers miss seeing this clue to the author's intention after the positive portraits of Frost in the books by Sergeant, Untermeyer, Cook, and Cox? There were few exceptions—Karl Miller in the *New York Review of Books,* Calvin Bedient in *The New Republic,* both writing on Thompson years after the monster-myth had been born.[22]

As for the lingering notion of Thompson's reliability in providing all the important factual truths of the poet's career, readers need only turn to page 231 above. Yet the term "factual truths" raises questions to which we must presently turn.

Though out of print, the official biography is revered even in recent reviews as the irreplaceable source of facts about Frost—"truthful facts." But what are truthful facts—and "What is history?" Edward Hallett Carr in his classic by that title asks and explains: "The facts of history never come to us 'pure,' since they do not and cannot exist in a pure form. They are always refracted through the mind of the record-er. It follows that when we take up a work of history, our first concern should not be with the facts which it contains but with the historian who wrote it [p. 24]." Frost implied as much: "Though historians are my favorites they can disturb me with a tendency to be novelists . . . till I lose my confidence that there is any such thing as a fact." Neither Carr nor Frost questions any event on which there is total agreement (the date of the Frosts' secret marriage; when Elinor died; the time of Carol's suicide). And the writer of any biography has to offer facts of this type to build a chronology. But everything else is "always refrac-ted through the mind of the recorder."

What does this tell readers and critics of Thompson's biography? One, he is totally dependable in stating that John F. Kennedy was in-augurated January 20, 1961; two, he is totally undependable in declar-ing to me that Frost had intended to steal the show from the President and "had it planned from the start—everything" (see above, pp. 148f.). Crude though it be, the example draws the line between factual truths and events "refracted through the mind of the recorder"—which is to say the biased interpretation that *typifies* Thompson's biography. The work *as a whole* sets forth an unmistakably hostile image of Frost as a person. Not that every page attests to this claim; the work has a good many plain documents and letters unmarred by interpretation and many plain citations of dates, places, and similar "neutral" items

---

[22] Miller, suspecting "some suppression of Frost's kind actions and common humani-ty," cites almost half the entries of the topical index in Volume II only: "it reads like a character assassination, and its most startling item is 'murderer,' " for which the author's "supporting pages" are absurd (November 19, 1977). Bedient: March 5, 1977.

(some of which are erroneous).** As for the rest—the three books as an entity—it exemplifies all that *What Is History?* establishes *and* its caveat: "Study the historian before you begin to study the facts" [p. 26]. But after all we have seen of the topical index and the "Notes," no great study is needed.

Because the trilogy cannot be found in bookstores, readers must count on libraries, and, if unavailable there, on Lathem's condensation of 1,880 pages into 546. The omission of all three sections of Thompson's "Notes" that follow the original text creates an insoluble problem, for Thompson's 391 pages supplied—along with much that belonged in the text—sources, documentation, and other essential data (*e.g.,* "as told to LT by . . ."). Hence it is now very difficult for a reader not only to check the letters and other reference materials but also to tell where Thompson offers his own opinions, "explains" what others have said, or lets them speak for themselves. As for the text itself, Lathem holds to its point of view and its image of Frost.

True though it is that the negative view of the poet prevails, there are signs of change. And yet—as late as 1983, Alfred Kazin, who "knew Frost well enough, was astonished" that Thompson's portrayal "had become the definitive picture"—echoing another note—written by Elizabeth Kray (who knew Frost when directing the Y Poetry Center) from a far-off western campus: "It's very fashionable here to dismiss the poet as a mean old man"; to which I may add remarks about Frost as "a bad person" from a scholar who had neither met the poet nor read his biography. One year later, however, William H. Pritchard's *Frost: A Literary Life Reconsidered* forced reviewers to "reconsider" Frost and the Thompson picture of Frost they had flaunted. One of them, who in 1970 (in the *TBR*) had launched the monster-myth, did a somersault: "Pritchard's damning account of Thompson as a biographer is convincing." She "would now send any reader, for a first knowledge of Frost," to Pritchard rather than Thompson. The poet's humor, mischief, irony, teasing, and playfulness are all happily rendered, and as Poirier says in the most discerning critique, "Pritchard's balance and moderation serve the life very well indeed," which is all that a reader could want as a first stage in the turn of the biographical tide. A second, in process of publication, *Robert Frost and Wade Van Dore: The Life of the Hired Man,* is invaluable for its first-hand account by a man with whom the poet "probably spent more time than with anyone else outside his family."

A third book, of unusual charm, is precisely entitled *Robert Frost: A Friend to a Younger Poet*. Focusing on two years only (1934–1936), the author, Henry Dierkes, brings new and welcome light to Frost's relationship to other poets.**

A widespread myth about someone famous dies hard; and the more demeaning it happens to be, the longer it tends to survive. Thompson's official biography, though now condensed to a fourth of its almost 2,000 pages, will remain part of the record; but so will a number of totally different works which reviewers largely ignored. I cite them briefly as reader-reminders, for each in its way is unique and its offerings important. Of six volumes (some of them mentioned before), only two are, strictly speaking, biographies: Elizabeth Shepley Sergeant's *Robert Frost: The Trial by Existence* (1960) and Kathleen Morrison's brief *A Pictorial Chronicle* (1974). Two other works—Sidney Cox's portrait, *A Swinger of Birches* (1957), and William Sutton's *Newdick's Season of Frost* (1976)—incomplete at the time of Newdick's death—like Reginald Cook's *The Dimensions of Robert Frost* (1958) and *Robert Frost: A Living Voice* (1974), record many years of the poet's life combined with abundant quotations, the last including transcripts of twelve major talks by Frost at the Bread Loaf School of English.

Of the letter collections, three are indispensable: *The Letters of Robert Frost to Louis Untermeyer* (1963), Thompson's *Selected Letters* (1964), and Arnold Grade's *Family Letters of Robert and Elinor Frost* (1972). The first and third also provide unique biographical data.

Essays on Frost's poetry are too numerous to list. Beginning with parts of Randall Jarrell's *Poetry and the Age* (1953), they include Reuben Brower's *Robert Frost: Constellations of Intention,* Radcliffe Squires's *The Major Themes of Robert Frost* (both 1963), and—most important and challenging—Richard Poirier's *Robert Frost: The Work of Knowing* (1977). Brief sections of critical writings appear in college paperbacks: edited by R. A. Greenberg and J. G. Hepburn (1961), J. M. Cox (1962), James L. Potter (1980).

A rich diversity of essays on Frost-as-writer and/or Frost-as-person distinguishes the *Centennial Essays* volumes (1974, 1976, 1978), prepared by people who knew the poet personally or studied his work with care—John Ciardi, Victor Reichert, Marice C. Brown, J. Donald Crowley, James Dickey, Stearns Morse, to name just a few. "Whatever happened to the image of the quick-witted sportive Robert Frost, jesting and teasing, ebullient and artful?" asks one contributor (Reginald Cook, in discussing Thompson's biography), and he offers some answers.

A handful of Frost anthologies round out the list: a small book of *Selected Prose* edited by Hyde Cox and Edward Connery Lathem (1966); *Interviews* with the press, chosen by Lathem (1966); a limited edition of *Prose Jottings of Robert Frost,* drawn from his notebooks and miscellaneous manuscripts and edited by Lathem and Cox with an introduction by Kathleen Morrison (1982). Finally, *Robert Frost: Poetry and Prose* edited by Lathem and Thompson (1972), 460 pages composed of "some of his best and best-known poems, against a background of his other writings, many of them little known and some, indeed, heretofore unpublished." The text of the verse in this Frost "reader" raises a serious question that *cannot* be ignored. The italicized word barely suggests my discomfort in having to discuss a work by a man to whom I am deeply indebted and deeply grateful, who has been unfailingly generous with aid and time and counsel: Edward Connery Lathem.

In the summer of 1967 he was asked by Holt to prepare a new edition of Frost's *Complete Poems*. The 1949 volume, then available, not only failed to include *In the Clearing* (1962); it also was marred by errors in need of attention. After two years of zealous laboring, *The Poetry of Robert Frost* appeared (1969), the official collection bearing a "Publisher's Note" which referred to the current need for a volume "scrupulously edited for textual accuracy." The book was reviewed by a number of poets and critics. Two years later, in his introduction to the same work published by the Imprint Society, Lathem discussed the differences between the text of the books by Frost issued with his approval during his lifetime and that of the 1969 alteration. He also explained its genesis. Not long after *In the Clearing* appeared, Frost had "requested [Lathem's] assistance with parts of the overall task" of preparing "a new major collection of his verse." The Frost Estate asked Lathem "to prepare an edition that would serve both general readers and scholarly users" and "to include within its notes section precise indication of all textual emendations by the editor . . . (dealing mostly with punctuation, and including some reversions to earlier correct forms of what were in effect corruptions within the two basic copy-texts)"—the 1949 *Complete Poems* and *In the Clearing*.

Lathem's discussion of "differences" starts with three examples, to each of which Frost, upon having them called to his attention, willingly added the needed comma ("To err is human, not to [,] animal"; "Well[,] they remind me of the hue and cry"; "One each of everything as in a showcase[,]/ Which naturally she doesn't care to sell"). He was eager, Lathem also reports, to replace British spellings with American forms, but he doesn't tell us whether the poet asked that all proper names be corrected or that all the words be spelled consistently or— most important of all—that his punctuation be changed where no room for confusion exists. We are therefore left to conclude that these three types of emendations were made by Lathem because he believed it essential for spelling and punctuation to follow the mode of usage that he thought best. And, given *carte blanche,* he decided upon his own set of rules for copy-editing poetry, such as many journals and publishing houses use in the copy-editing of prose. Spelling presents no problem; choose an acceptable dictionary and follow it always or with certain stated exceptions. But punctuation in *poetry?*—with its question marks, long dashes, short dashes, hyphens, commas, and so on? Their use profoundly influences not only the sound and the meaning but also a host of other, "subtler" effects for which we have no names.

Lathem gives examples to justify his changes. One of these, despite his supporting logic, raised indignant protests. The well-known line from "Stopping by Woods . . ." he repunctuates:

The woods are lovely, dark, and deep,

Frost's copy-text used by Lathem omits the comma after "dark," so that it reads there just as Frost revised it for his *Complete Poems:*

The woods are lovely, dark and deep,

But, says Lathem, no commas are found in what appears to be a first-draft manuscript, nor in its first publication in *The New Republic.* He might have added that when it appeared in *New Hampshire,* it differed from the later *Complete Poems* only in placing a period after "deep." What, then, "had to be" done? Lathem added a comma to "dark" be-cause on recorded recitals he heard Frost "give the three adjectives ap-proximately equal stress." But as any number of frequent listeneners knew from his platform readings, in "saying" his poems Frost was as inconsistent as he was in other respects, sometimes racing through verses as though over-anxious to end the performance quickly.

Angered remarks have been made on this change by Lathem, none more pointed than Poirier's: "The woods are not, as the Lathem edition would have it (with its obtuse emendation . . .) merely 'lovely, dark, and deep.' Rather, as Frost in all the editions he supervised intended, they are 'lovely, *i.e.* dark and deep'; the loveliness thereby partakes of the depth and the darkness which make the woods so ominous."

Lathem, in explaining other changes, often relies on the oral evidence drawn from recordings "to remove ambiguity or bafflement." And he cites some examples "which unpunctuated would be potentially troublesome," as perhaps they might have been if the words had been run together as prose and not as divided by Frost: into separate lines, each producing a pause, no matter how slight, at the end. Lathem also inserted space to provide for stanza divisions omitted from earlier volumes, and he standardized single and double quotations marks—changes well worth making. Before releasing his manuscript, he consulted several people with "special qualifications to advise, so that although the responsibility is squarely the editor's, the result is hardly idiosyncratic."

More than a few poets and critics disagree strongly, among them William Pritchard, Gerald Burns, Frank Bidart, Richard Poirier, Richard Wilbur, Peter Davison, Denis Donoghue, Richard Ellmann, Christopher Ricks. On the other hand, Hyde Cox and Walter Havighurst approve strongly. And no doubt there are others on both sides of the issue. Of all the published accounts I have read, the most extensive by far appears in Donald Hall's *The Weather for Poetry*.[23]

Frost did not keep to himself his views on punctuation. He prided himself on writing a fifty-word telegram without once using "Stop." To Professor L.W. Payne, whose list of supposed errors in the 1930 *Collected Poems* taxed his patience, he wrote in part, "I indulge a sort of indifference to punctuation. I dont mean I despise it. I value it. But I seem rather willing to let other people look after it for me. . . . You must remember I am not writing school-girl English." Twenty-one years later he told a Dartmouth audience, "I hate to depend on

---

[23] ". . . The editor makes by my count 1,364 emendations, of which his notes justify 247 by reference to earlier printings. Thus he makes 1,117 changes for which he offers no textual sources." Among other statistics cited—additions: 443 commas, 13 colons, 156 long dashes, 22 semicolons, 3 parentheses, 12 question marks, 81 hyphens; deletions: 101 hyphens, 2 ellipses; etc. University of Michigan Press, 1982, pp. 140–159.

punctuation at all." And as Lathem points out, "Frost did not actually relish having individuals challenge him regarding the punctuation of his verse."

Since 1969 Frost's publisher has replaced his final (1949) edition of *Complete Poems* with *The Poetry of Robert Frost* edited by Edward Connery Lathem, from whose "Editor's Statement" these sentences are drawn:

> *Complete Poems* and *In the Clearing* have been chosen as possessing prime textual authority and are followed in *The Poetry of Robert Frost*. Departures have, however, been made from these copy-texts, both for the correction of errors and for achieving greater textual clarity. All editorial changes have been recorded (as EMENDATIONS) in the notes [pp. 529–582] except those associated with standardizing the employment of double quote-marks for the setting off of quotations and single quotes for quotations within quotations. Although an effort has been made to normalize spelling, in order to attain a degree of uniformity for the volume as a whole and to conform to present-day usage, no attempt has been made to impose upon the text strict consistency in capitalization, since to do so would risk occasional conflict with the poet's intentions of emphasis or with other of his deliberate stylistic practices [p. 526].

The statement makes clear to the reader much that was done in editing. It does not, however, speak in detail of either the kind or extent of the alterations in punctuation, though a reader will find, by comparing the 1949 *Complete Poems* with *The Poetry of Robert Frost,* that the editor for the most part followed the copy-editing principles that are commonly used for prose. Hence, I believe, the refusal by certain critics and anthologists to use the Lathem versions despite the publisher's unwillingness to grant any other permissions.

The Frost Estate and Henry Holt and Company, Inc. owe both a debt to their poet and an obligation to "do something."[24] They might start with a brief question to poets, critics, and scholars: "How do poets punctuate?" Or, if disinclined to take such a course, they might choose to examine the verse of such varied writers as Eliot, Cum-

---

[24] Although Lathem himself regards his edition as "an interim provision," his data on the successive revisions made by Frost surely must be retained (pp. 529–582).

mings, MacLeish, Robinson, Yeats, Dickey, Williams. Eliot, perhaps, said it all in a letter to the *Times Literary Supplement* some sixty years ago in response to a critic's review of Herbert Read's *English Prose Style:* "verse, whatever else it may or may not be, is itself a system of punctuation, the usual marks of *punctuation* themselves are differently employed."

TOWARD THE "KNOWABLE" FROST

After a busy twelve-day stay with his biographer Newdick, Frost (for the first time calling him "Dear Robert") sent him a warning word:

> I'll never forget my visit with you—what I read to you and what you said to me. The point I tried to make was that I was a very hard person to make out if I am any judge of human nature. I might easily be deceiving when most bent on telling the truth.
>
> *(December 2, 1938)*

The words differ in tone and context from those that he typically made to Thompson: "I grow curious about my soul out of sympathy for you in your quest for it" (1948); "I trust my philosophy still bothers you a little. It bothers me." (1959). Frost was aware of the problems he presented to biographers, and his private professions of badness helped no more than his words to the press—"I contain opposites" or "I'm not confused. I'm only well mixed." To dismiss such words as meaningless play would make no sense with a man deeply aware of his "moods" and their cost to himself and others. When his friend Rabbi Reichert quoted a well-known play on words from the Talmud, he quickly accepted the sting: "I'd have no trouble with the first two. It's the last, 'temper,' I have to watch":

> By these three things is a man recognized as worthy (is a person's character determined): by his cup, his purse, his anger—*Koso,*

Kiso, Ka-a-so. B'koso—if his wisdom is in equilibrium; B'kiso—if he acts with his fellow-men with integrity; B'ka-a-so—if he is not more hot-tempered (quick to anger) than needed.

Urging Frost to reform was far from the rabbi's intent; his friend was no normal mortal. Sidney Cox hadn't even approached the truth when he called him the "original 'ordinary' man."

It was John Ciardi who saw Frost plain:

Robert Frost was a primal energy. There were serenities in the man as time brought them to him, but there was in him a volcano of passion that burned to his last day. . . . To be greatly of the earth earthy demands the bitter sweat and scald of first passions. That heat could erupt into cantankerousness at times, and even into the occasional meanness of which violent temper is capable. But the splutters of cantankerousness and the violences of temper were only surface bubbles on the magmatic passions of the man, part of the least traits that accompany intensity. . . .

It is just that passionate intensity that must be realized before the man can be loved, mourned—and read—in his own nature. . . . His genius, wild and ardent, remains to us in his poems. It is the man we lose, a man salty and rough with the earth trace, and though towering above it, never removed from it, a man above all who could tower precisely because he was rooted in real earth.

There seemed nothing to add, yet the picture led many people to think of examples that glossed the passage above, attesting to the "more than usual" will and desires, powers and needs, of this surely "excessive man"—to his conversations that might have gone on forever: part of his hunger for people, which was balanced at the other extreme by a need to be wholly alone ("Desert me, desert me!"[151]). His "contradictions"—mocked by hostile critics, mis-taken by others—dealt with so many received ideas as to brand him perversely rebellious despite his desire to hold close to a commonsensical center. But not to moderation—"I should hate to get stuck in the golden mean," he forewarned Thompson (212). Yet he knew as well as anyone else from Emerson's "Experience" that "The line he must walk is a hair's breadth," that "The wise through excess of wisdom is made a fool." Few could do better than Frost in walking the hair's-breadth line through the beckoning maze of ideas, seeking out and treasuring "the least display of mind," while never losing sight of the limited reach of human thought.

Twenty-four Augusts ago the Unitarian Church of Martha's Vineyard asked me to speak on the poet. I named my talk "The Unknowable Frost"—not out of false modesty: the better I'd come to know him, the more I found him immense-in-complexity. The date was August 1962, long before I had read one word of *The Letters of Robert Frost to Louis Untermeyer,* of Thompson's *Selected Letters; even* longer before I would go through the *Family Letters of Robert and Elinor Frost,* the *Selected Prose,* the *Interviews,* the lectures in Cook's *Robert Frost: A Living Voice.* The *Vineyard Gazette's* report—"Burnshaw Sees Robert Frost as the Most Elusive and Subtlest Poet"—was accurate to the letter, and its headline faithful to what I believed at the time—and still believe. But if asked to speak about Frost today, I should have to qualify "unknowable." Would Frost approve? The reply would be no more predictable than the poet himself, who defied at times all efforts to enter his privacy but at others confessed with astounding candor "facts" he had kept from the world. The bluntest observers spoke of the man as a "bundle of contradictions"; others, using the gentler "paradoxical," threw up their hands, though the contradictory aspects might have been born out of wholly acceptable premises. For me, Frost's "baffling" behavior asks to be seen in terms of Carlyle's discussion of symbols, that "wondrous agency," because, as he said, it contains not only concealment but revelation as well.

"I have written," wrote Frost in an early note to Cox, "to keep the over curious out of the secret places of my mind both in my verse and in my letters." Thus could he chide a friend and would-be-biographer. A poem might bear the same warning: "any eye is an evil eye/ That looks in onto a mood apart." On the other hand, writes Theodore Morrison, "When the mood was on him, he could spill out confidences with a recklessness the very opposite of the man who made himself a place apart and hid his tracks." Mere contradiction or a twofold need? No one was more aware of this question than Frost, in spite of his letter to Cox, for as Jarrell safely observed, "anyone who has read his *Collected Poems* and *Selected Letters* has entered some of the secret places of his mind." And as Frost himself confessed of his poems to a Dartmouth audience, on a subject he liked to avoid, "So many of them have literary criticism in them—*in* them. And yet I wouldn't admit it. I try to hide it." This was late in his last November.

But the same need to be known-and-unknown had been part of his earliest book. In "Revelation" the speaker is drawn toward opposed positions, both of which he must take:

> We make ourselves a place apart
>   Behind light words that tease and flout,
> But oh, the agitated heart
>   Till someone really find us out.
>
> 'Tis pity if the case require
>   (Or so we say) that in the end
> We speak the literal to inspire
>   The understanding of a friend.
>
> But so with all, from babes that play
>   At hide-and-seek to God afar,
> So all who hide too well away
>   Must speak and tell us where they are.

The poem asks to be rightly read, with full concern for every word (lines 3, 4, 5, 6, 11, 12 in particular), and the final phrase—not "who" nor "what," but "where." Paradox or a constitutional urge toward divergent "goods"—desiderata, each ministering to a need of the total self. So in his wish for protection from being "found out" in matters too private for most people, he could say that he sometimes hoped to be misunderstood. Yet, with a very limited few, he might show a glimpse of part of himself which he yearned to conceal, as occurred with a letter to Untermeyer. Within twenty-four hours he wrote: "Please burn it. Be easy on me for what I did too emotionally and personally"—an appeal we might have expected from one for whom excessive response was the norm (26.). A man who feared he had bared too much could also enlarge small insults into causes for rage or remark at the close of his last public performance: "It's a wonderful world . . . To hell with it."

Such incidents—except for those who, with Eliot, separate the person who suffers from the mind that creates—stand in the way of comprehending Frost's total achievement. Like others who understood its range, he viewed the prose and the verse as parts of a whole. "Most of my ideas occur in verse. But I have always had some turning up in talk that I feared I might never use because I was too lazy to write prose." Some, however, that turned up in talk were used—and not in prose. Peter Davison, who had listened with him for years, tells about one:

> He tried on the sounds of words to see if they would fit his ideas, his jokes, his turns of wit. Often you could watch him working out a poem in conversation, testing an idea in different suits of clothes. I heard him, over many months of playing with the contrast between tools and weapons, finally come up with a couplet which had been solicited by the United Nations for their Meditation Room . . . : "Nature within her inmost self divides/ To trouble men with having to take sides."

Lazy though he called himself about writing prose, he "produced" four books of letters; a number of prefaces, introductions, and other works besides the *Selected Prose*. And vastly more of his "talk" than he might have suspected found its way into print: public lectures, interviews with the press, personal conversations with various friends. One of the most assiduous, Reginald Cook, found that: "The difference between Frost as poet and Frost as talker is more a matter of method than of style. In the run of his talk, I heard passages in cadences as moving as any of those in his poetry," some of which can be heard in the first of Cook's two Frost volumes. As for the lectures, many of which he recorded, they invariably "*sound* better than they read." For "the voice on the sound track, with its pauses, hesitancies, repetitions, and stresses, enlivens the talk and evokes a remarkable presence."

He had moved far from the poet of 1909 who, after painful trials, learned to lessen his fear of facing an audience—filling his shoes with pebbles, dousing the back of his neck with ice-cold water. Biographers need not say why a man driven to writing poems can also be husband, father, teacher, farmer; but how explain the "remarkable Frostian presence," described by Cook, who, when asked to recite a poem to a group in Derry in 1906, had to implore a friend to read in his place. The bare facts cannot provide the answer as they follow from birth the body's genetic uniqueness—a uniqueness making for differences in development, since no organism long responds with the full capacities with which it was born. From its earliest moment, some are inhibited, some diminished, others lost in the course of its meeting events—the accidents and effects of what it encounters. The organism responds with the functional remnant of all it at first possessed; and as it learns and grows and changes, makes its unforeseeable ways of responding-behaving, drawing on powers and weaknesses that outer events may lead, at best, into seeming self-transcendence.[25]

As early as his eighteenth year Frost confessed that he found even in his failures all the promise he needed "to justify the astonishing magnitude of [his] ambitions." "Into My Own," the first poem of *A Boy's Will,* offered a hidden answer—"They would not find me changed from him they knew—/ Only more sure of all I thought was true." A manifesto of fixity?—if wrongly taken. "One of the greatest changes my nature has undergone is of record in To Earthward," he professed to DeVoto, "and indeed elsewhere for the discerning." Of the last words of "Into My Own" he explained in 1959, "The new thing with me has always included the old. Those lines are really about loyalty." Loyalty?—to what he knew that he was, which the world would never learn? Biographers who searched or pried would be thrown off track, but he might have guessed, in spite of his willed concealments, that all his "talk, mythologizing, or lies" would fail IF one could finally know how to read his writings: to "discern" the poems and the prose. A crucial, decisive IF. Yet a twentieth-century John Keble whose skill as perceiver matched his insight as critic might be able to "see" the work for what it must be: "unconscious autobiography."[26] Not, of course, of the total person: parts of the life, parts of the self which lie "too deep for tears" never might find their words. Yet a man whose work seemed to ask to be read biographically promised more than enough: the "subtlest and most elusive poet" might, with lucky discerning, prove to be, to some degree, knowable.

Frost had been writing poems for twenty-three years before he gained recognition. Sudden fame awaited and, despite the vicissitudes of taste, it seemed to grow wider. Much as the public's praise helped his faith in himself, no one's approval meant so much to him as Elinor's. Yet this was only one of her contributions which, when added together, formed so great a part of his life that to *know* Frost is

---

[25] Stanley Burnshaw, *The Seamless Web,* Braziller, 1970, pp. 32f., 36.

[26] M.H. Abrams, *The Mirror and the Lamp,* Oxford, 1953, pp. 259ff., quoting George Lyman Kittredge as well: "Unquestionably the man is there, the real Shakespeare is somehow latent in his plays. . . ."

impossible unless one knows something of Elinor. Comments by certain biographers offer us glimpses: striking, candid, for the most part brief, limited by times and places of meeting—a "vital part of his picture . . . inscrutable in many ways, shy" and "untamed, and fiercely watchful" (John Holmes).

All who saw her speak of her physical presence—her fine head, with its coiled braids and classic Puritan features, an "arresting New England beauty purified . . . into an almost desperate calm" (Sergeant's words, much like my own impression [21]), to which she adds: "a hint of melancholy and somber pessimism." Part of the time. Not always—even after the grief over Marjorie's death. Sitting with both Frosts in The Gulley kitchen, Reginald Cook and his wife chatted at ease, the poet in the corner, his chair tilted back, his wife close by. "Mrs. Frost, an animated talker, had as pleasant a voice as I have ever listened to, and her warm, friendly smile quickly overcame any constraint we might have felt." Henry Dierkes' account of a luncheon visit adds another dimension: "Mrs. Frost had probably become accustomed to sitting in the shade of her illustrious husband, but when the conversation turned to poetry she entered into it and spoke with a confident authority."—phrases that would have seemed quite just to Van Dore, who, after years as part of her household, offered a two-word summary: "sweet-severe."

I had a good number of hours alone with her, because Rob almost never got up before 10, while she usually was about by 7 or half-past. Many times just the two of us had breakfast together. Often she was the first in the kitchen. I would find her quietly sitting smoking a cigarette—a habit she had picked up from the wives of their friends in England. I doubt she smoked over two a day through 1925–35 when I was with her the most. Very seldom would she be reading a newspaper or book. From what she called her "sitting room" she didn't need to look out a window. She just sat there—one-third dreaming and two-thirds thinking of or planning for her family. That seemed to be her role. When it looked as if he might succeed as a poet, I'm sure she wanted that to happen—without having faith that it would. Constitutionally she had become a pessimist, but she didn't enjoy suffering or sadness. . . . Elinor felt that she truly owned her Rob and she wasn't keen about sharing him with anybody. When I describe her as "sweet-severe" I mean her overall kind, mild manner. . . . She had piercing black eyes. One liked just to look at her.

Through their first six months at Derry she could get along without curtains, even an indoor pump; but Frost at times had to be "forced" into working. "Rob!"—he was deep in talk with Sidney Cox—"It's after nine o'clock, and you *must* go milk. It's not good for her to wait so long." Frost preferred to delay the chores; Elinor hated housework. Most of the time they could take each other's ways without apology.

Not until 1964, in *Selected Letters,* could we gain a sense of another Elinor Frost. And eight additional years would pass before the *Family Letters of Robert and Elinor Frost* provided the nearest thing we have to a full-length portrait of a thoughtful, sensitive woman who lived for the present, her family, her home. To the poet's large correspondence her fifty letters added acute variations, counterpointing his judgments. Their views often collided; she was scarcely less opinionated than Frost. As Arnold Grade remarks, the "influence of this firm, intuitive, highly intelligent woman who brought order and discipline to the farmhouse of art was enormous"—not only in family matters and in shaping the work of the writer but, most important of all, in their man–woman relationship. "F is as considerate of Mrs. F," reads one of Newdick's research entries of 1935, "as a lover in his teens. And her eyes shine from their depths as they rest on him." Some forty years later, Poirier would declare that Frost was not only "a great poet of marriage, but maybe the greatest since Milton, and of the sexuality that goes with it." And in several important poems, he explores the subject—which others approach with unwarranted confidence, usually through "The Subverted Flower," with its "clear" biographical basis, its long-delayed publication, the purported tension between the maiden's reserve and the male's animal wildness. More to the point is the implication of Poirier's earlier statements, remarking upon: "The magnificent clarity of his love for his wife which is full of a critical respect for her individual separateness." I do not know of any body of English verse that brings to its treatment of women the perceptiveness, the compassion, the respect, the attributive wisdom that we find in Frost's.

Nor do I know of a poet so eager to give the woman who shared his life all he considered her due: "She has been the unspoken half of everything I ever wrote, and both halves of many a thing from My November Guest down to the last stanzas of Two Tramps in Mud

Time." The words hold true of more than his writings. It was Elinor who went alone to speak to Grandfather Frost when her household lay in crisis, winning his promise to help them start their life anew at the farm in Derry (27). It was she who wrote to every absent child (two or three times weekly); who tried to protect Frost before, during, and after his frequent attacks of illness (35). Months after Marjorie's death, though hardly able to "go on living from day to day," she saw no choice: "Robert depends on me, and the other children do to some extent," she confessed to a friend. "I *must* keep up." Not only was she able to "keep up"; she displayed surprising resilience. She took delight in Marjorie's "bright, forward, exceptionally merry" daughter. She relished the prospect of choosing a permanent house for their Florida winters (37). She was still the woman who lived for her home, for her family, for the present.

And not, to be sure, for any posthumous glory. The gifted high-school girl whose poems and essays praised "the ideal . . . as surely the best of life" had long since disappeared. It might have been years before the death of their first-born in July 1900 with its shattering grief that kept her speechless for days. Frost, unable to bear the torment, burst into self-accusations. It was God—God's wrath come down on his head for failing to summon a doctor in time to save the young life. Elinor, when she finally spoke, lashed at his wild self-punishing talk and his "senseless belief" in a God concerned with human affairs. Living was hateful; the world too evil to bear—yet bear it she must, with a second child in her arms. There were four more offspring to come—three would survive.

In his letter to Untermeyer of March 21, 1920, Frost doesn't explain the cause of his sudden announcement: "Elinor has just come out flat-footed against God." To his playful countering arguments—"How about a Shelleyan principal or spirit coeternal with the rock of creation"—she replied bluntly, "Nonsense and you know it's nonsense, Rob Frost, only you're afraid you'll have bad luck or lose your standing in the community if you speak your mind." But in fact his "mind" was not what her words assumed, nor what he wished it might be. Their thoughts on faith would keep moving farther apart till the rift would become unbridgeable. And yet, if as Frost told Lesley after Elinor's death, she had "colored" his thought "from the first," through the rest of his days her atheistic certainty never quite left his mind despite his determined self-dedication to faith and belief.

In the same letter (March 1, 1939), he goes on to remark: "She dominated my art with the power and character of her nature"—a phrase implying very much more than it states. That she stopped him from publishing "The Subverted Flower," has long been known (were there others also?). That he counted on her to judge his poems, we learn from a letter he sent with her list of titles to Untermeyer, who was making a new anthology. "Domination" of a different sort comes to light in another intimate letter: "Pretty nearly every one of my poems will be found to be about her if rightly read . . . they were as much about her as she liked and permitted them to be." With a number of friends he gladly spoke of her gifts as a critical reader and how they affected his work. She "could hurt him" by saying what she wouldn't let pass in a poem, he had told John Holmes. He explained to Mertins: "an imperfect line, or flash of beauty spoiled, hurt her worse, both physically and spiritually, than I ever knew. This was the only goad I needed. . . ."

"Domination" welcomed and prized—but not always: the "Roosevelt" poems, for example ("To a Thinker," "Build Soil"), that she pleaded with him to withhold.** To which must be added other species of fear. Frost tried hard to make light of the fact that as early as 1917 she had grown "especially wary of honors that derogate from" what he mockingly called "the poetic life she fancies us living." She was no less wary of "reputation, that bubble"—what if Newdick, his early biographer, were left one day with the sudden eclipse of "his" poet? There was also the deep, half-hidden fear of the plight of Frost as triumphant public performer for the harm it might do to the poet-artist.

In the letter that said she was "wary of honors" Frost added: "She wouldn't lift a hand or have me lift a hand to increase my reputation or even save it." Had she changed? Were the words untrue? After *A Boy's Will* appeared, she was "somewhat disappointed": The reviewers should have done better, for how could "they help seeing how exquisitely beautiful" were some of the poems. Moreover, Yeats had said that the book was "the best poetry written in America for a long time. If only he would say so publicly," she added. Some twenty years later she made no attempt to hide her elation at Frost's success: "It is certainly *grand* about the Book-of-the-Month Club" choice of *A Further Range,* she wrote to her publisher's wife. She probably felt the same of "The Critics and Robert Frost," a paean by DeVoto in the *Saturday Review,* based on Holt's recently issued *Recognition of Robert Frost.* She read it aloud—"I sat and let Elinor pour it over me," he said in a letter of thanks to the author on December 29, 1937. Within three months the one about whom "pretty nearly every one of [his] poems had been written" died. For more than forty-five years the finest gift he could make was a poem that fulfilled her hope. There were more than a few. When, after *Mountain Interval* appeared, the widow of an Amherst colleague, assisting her in preparing sandwiches, asked, "Don't you think it's beautiful yourself?" Elinor dropped her knife and clasped her hands. "Beautiful," she said in a voice close to tears. The place and time was Franconia, 1917, twenty-five years since the poems that each had been writing brought them together.

Not long after, their quietsome world of two had become a house of childhood bustling with four young lives. By now, however, the special delights of the early years—that readers can live in *New Hampshire's Child: The Derry Journals of Lesley Frost* and the book of *Family Letters*—had long since passed. Gone, the Christmas parties or made-up stories or tales about elves and fairies; no more morning winters piled with snow too high for walking which they watched their father shovel clear from the house to the barn to the mailbox, from the pump to the maple they christened the woodpecker tree. As Frost recalled, rather wistfully in his aged years, "I played with them more than most fathers," showing them how to read the tracks of foxes, rabbits, and squirrels, of chickadees and partridges, asking their help each spring with the garden beds and the plants they discovered together, tramping the woods. Elinor spoke to an Amherst friend of a Christmas Eve when Rob was carving small wooden animals for the children. One was a pig for Carol, but at 2:00 A.M. he decided it needed a pen. He sat there, whittling till daylight, and "I sat there with him. I went to sleep as I rocked and woke at dawn. . . . Rob had just finished the pen!"

The cherishing hope of the early years gave way to worry and fear for three of the children. Carol, now in his sixteenth year, "has absolutely no one to play with," his mother wrote to Lesley. "He just does nothing a good deal of the time and that drives me almost distracted." Irma's actions at times foreshadowed her problems, alienating Frost from a former student for a fancied sexual advance. "Take the way with her that will keep the peace," Frost urged Lesley a few years later. "Her strictness is part of her nature. Don't try to make her over. Some of it she will outgrow, but not all." Marjorie, the youngest, frailest, lonely now and discouraged, was intermittently plagued by illness, overwork, and "nervous prostration." Her parents did all they could, but they strained to do more, whatever the cost (31). Elinor's death saved her the grief over Carol's suicide and Irma's fate (74). Frost had striven to help his son by reinforcing his self-assurance in writing, going so far as to call his "Stratton" poem "powerful and splendid," "written with a man's vigor," "richly attractive," "with so much solid truth, such condensation and intense feeling." Two months later: "That was another good poem. . . . Your way is certainly your own." And in 1935, the highest praise he could give: Your "apple-crating poem . . . has a great deal more of the feeling of real work and country business than anything of mine could ever pretend or hope to have." Nothing availed. As he wrote to Untermeyer after the suicide, "I tried many ways and every single one of them was wrong. Some thing in me is still asking for the chance to try one more."

What would become of Irma? He had shielded her from Marjorie's death: "Irma is in no condition to face the terribleness" of the news, he had warned her brother. Twelve years later, John Cone, her husband, wrote to her father to explain why, after close to two decades, he felt forced to end the marriage. Frost wasn't greatly surprised to learn of his daughter's jealousy, prudery, of her frequent hysterical outbursts, of her fears of being persecuted. Once the divorce was final, she was quite unable to try to fare for herself. Frost sought to find a suitable place where she could live. After a number of failed attempts, he knew she would have to be placed in an institution. On the day of her formal commitment in Concord, New Hampshire, he strove to make her see that her stay would help her recover. "Get out of here," she replied. On the day after Christmas, 1947, he wrote to his friend Margaret Bartlett of "the sad ending to Irma's story. She is at once too insane to be out of an institution and too sane to be in one. So she suffers the sense of imprisonment where she is."

He was used to tragedy; by now he had gained a composure and strength that none of his intimates would have dreamed possible after Elinor's death. No one could talk again, as Hervey Allen had done in 1938, of a powerful engine "wracking itself to pieces from running wild after the loss of its flywheel." Frost had resolved to survive. Four months after Elinor's loss he "refused," he wrote to a friend, "to be bowed down as much as she was by other deaths," though the forms this refusal was taking appalled both friends and foes. Then the hoped-for change began: Untermeyer and others could see: "By December the worst of his long period of blackness was over." His friends the Morrisons helped in essential ways, with Kay's agreeing to serve as his secretary-manager. Installed in a Boston apartment, the man who throughout his marriage had lived in thirty-five houses or more was about to be settled down and "watched" for the rest of his days. In 1939 he bought the Homer Noble Farm in Ripton, Vermont, for the summers; in 1940, Pencil Pines in Florida, for the winters; in early 1941, the house at 35 Brewster Street for the other months of the year. A "diastolic-systolic motion," Sergeant had termed the decades ahead, taking him forth to read, teach, talk, take part in the world at large, then return to one of his homes. More and more friends were replacing his family losses. There were also more and more writings, lectures, interviews; good-will missions (Brazil, Britain, Israel, Greece); honors, medals, degrees, awards, birthday dinners; calls from posts of political power, topped by the invitation to read the Inaugural poem and President Kennedy's bid for a special mission to Russia. The older he grew, the more commitments he welcomed and kept, till the morning after his final public speech and the doctor's hospital orders he couldn't refuse.

His final public speech betokened a basic change. "The poem," he now made clear, was "the song itself," and poetry stood above the world of "contentions"—politics, education, and even above religion. In 1956, in three consecutive talks in New York, he had made some specifications:

> I reached a point lately where I could finally divide life into three parts, the three greatest things in human thought: Religion, Science, Gossip. At the top, the exaltation part, they are close together. . . .

> Science . . . first for glory, not for use. The top is discovery for discovery's sake.

> Gossip. I venture to say that the greatest of the three is Gossip. It may be defined as our guessing at each other in journalism, novels, poetry in that order. Gossip exalts in poetry. Poetry is the top of our guessing at each other. . . . The beauty of gossip is that it is the whole of our daily life. It has flashes of insight. The height of imagination is there.

On a much more telling note in a talk two decades before, he spoke of his years of writing after "My Butterfly" (1894), "the first poem that I got any personal satisfaction from. Twenty years of it when I was out and in and didn't know what I was and didn't know what I wanted, nor what the feeling was that I wanted to satisfy. Not having anything in mind, no formula, just seeking, questing."

The last two words can serve for the years that followed, for the poet *knew* that "seeking, questing" goaded him on till the end. Do these words offer the clue to the knowable Frost? All his days and nights were marked by the quest. It reflected itself as he strove with the great "three things in human life," clearly in the words he wrote and uttered, but vividly also at times in his acts—public or privately known—in the things he feared, dared, risked, played with, loved, hated, believed, and hoped he would finally know.

"Writing, teaching a little, and farming. The three strands of my life," he told a reporter in 1960. Teaching "a little"? If his interviewer had scanned his career, he would have smiled: "Educating" for Frost had been second only to writing. "I taught every grade"—kindergarten, at home, school, college, he said to me once, smiling, with bittersweet pride (168), "And I like the academic in my way . . . and I know, up to a certain point, that the academic likes me." He didn't care to stop to say why, nor did I ask, though the academic seemed less than half of what he had been as a teacher. "It takes all sorts of in- and outdoor schooling" from a couplet of *In the Clearing* rose to my mind. I was now in the midst of the second ("To get adapted to my kind of fooling."); the first, I hoped, would someday come to light through those of his colleagues who might be helped by indoor students who had seen him perform.

Meanwhile we have data enough to follow his teaching career after he gave up study at Dartmouth (in 1892, before completing his first semester) to help in his mother's private school in Methuen, Massachusetts. From there he taught in a district school in Salem, New Hampshire; then, after marriage, joined his mother again. He became a special student at Harvard in September 1897; he left in March 1899. Not until nine years later did he finally give up poultry-raising and farming to earn his living by teaching:[27]

[27]1906–1911: Pinkerton Academy, Derry, New Hampshire.

1911–1912: New Hampshire State Normal School, Plymouth.

1917–1920: Amherst College.

1921–1923: University of Michigan (Poet-in-Residence, then Fellow in Creative Arts).

1923–1925: Amherst College (Professor of English).

He planned, he said, to write a book about teaching and schools. He never did. But words by Frost (and by others on Frost) abound on the subject. It would be no large undertaking to gather enough for an essay or at least a full report of his sayings. For example:

[T]he only education worth anything is self-education. All the rest consists of schoolwork, textbooks, training, aids to help distinguish one fact from another without helping us to tell true values from false. But that doesn't mean I don't believe in people learning as well as learned people. I'm for educated humanity all the time—except in an undiscriminating way. All men are born free and equal—free at least in their right to be different. Some people want to mix the weak and the strong of mankind; they want to homogenize society everywhere. . . . I want the cream to rise.

I ought to have been poet enough to stay away [instead of returning to Amherst in 1923]. But I was too much of a philosopher to resist the temptation to go back and help show the world the difference between the right kind of liberal college and the wrong kind.

I never taught long enough to carry anything out. I was a symbolical teacher. After giving a class a chance to say if there was anything in the bunch of themes on my desk they wanted to keep and satisfied myself there wasnt I threw them unread into the waste basket while the class looked on. If they didn't care enough for the themes to keep them I didnt care enough for the themes to read them. I wasnt going to be a perfunctory corrector of perfunctory writing.

I have long thought that our high schools should be improved. Nobody should [enter them] without examinations—not aptitude tests, but on reading, 'riting, and 'rithmetic. . . . A lot of people [want] to harden up our education or speed it up. I am

1925–1926: University of Michigan (Fellow in Letters).
1926–1938: Amherst College (under various arrangements, including his Charles Eliot Norton Lectures at Harvard 1936).
1939–1940: Harvard University (Ralph Waldo Emerson Fellow in Poetry).
1943–1949: Dartmouth College (Ticknor Fellow in Humanities).
1949———: Amherst College (Simpson Lecturer in Literature).

interested in toning it up, at the high school level. . . . establish-
ing named chairs . . . to create tenure and prestige for teachers.

"I'm going to leave you with the motto: 'Don't work, worry!' " he
said to his Harvard class before a fortnight's absence. He had hoped
they would understand the point of his thought: "worry about ideas."
But as often happened, he expected too much.

Pronouncing himself, with a twinkle, "the greatest living expert"
on education, he could also speak with gratitude of the institutions
that have been "so patient with my educational heresies." As to how
extreme these heresies were, we have various comments from first-
hand observers: scattered in books most of which can be found in libraries only. Many are well worth reading—for example, a Normal
Training School student's remarks as of 1911; Dorothy Tyler's
"Robert Frost in Michigan"; Gardner Jackson's "Reminiscences"; recollections by several Dartmouth colleagues in the *Southern Review,*
October 1966; Frost's own "Education by Poetry" in *Selected Prose.* **

As much of this book has shown, many ideas important to Frost
came out in his conversations. Did he hit his stride at midnight? Some
of his listeners thought so, but not all—witness his endless hours of
daylight talk at the Phillips Academy and "The Master Conversationalist at Work" in Ciardi's report of his 1959 visit to Pencil
Pines (134f., 109).

"In twenty years I have walked many miles with Frost—always in
conversation, entertaining ideas"—I quote Hyde Cox from *You Come
Too.* "We all speak of having ideas but entertaining them is an art. . . .
It is almost the heart of education." For hearers, of course; but also for
Frost himself—"self-education" as noted by numerous listeners, trying out sounds of words, turns of wit, notions, testing, viewing-
reviewing long-past moments for possibly hidden meanings.

How many people alive today were lucky enough to have heard
"the very best talker I've ever known"—the usual phrase one meets in
accounts of his listeners. To help re-create the experience for those to
whom it smacks of the mythical, more is required than a list of topics
combined with attempts at describing bodily gestures, tones of voice,
glances, twinkles, and so on. Frost had spoken of in- and outdoor
schooling as "education by presence." The presence is gone, yet a
sense of what it could mean for a listener can in part be recaptured
with the help of people with whom he had often conversed. Reginald

Cook, for example, who talked with Frost intimately over a period of forty years:

His talk-spiels were legendary; marathon nocturnal sessions, continuing from two to four or five hours. He could talk anywhere, anytime, and with the greatest of ease. Yet the length of the talks was hardly more remarkable than the range. Once he launched into a diatribe on doctoral dissertations, shifted key to the reading of poetry, alluded to prize fighting, and reacted vigorously to the current popularity of the anti-Keynesian Adam Smith. Another time—October 4, 1952—he covered the spectrum, talking about baseball, the presidential campaign, education, poetry, language, the Greeks (notably Herodotus), Shakespeare's songs, Russia, slavery, loyalty, and writers (Jesse Stuart, Robert Penn Warren, Ernest Hemingway, William Faulkner, and Erle Stanley Gardner). After a formal lecture, he unwound in the house of a stranger, talking about witches, politics, great Americans, and words with three n's in them, like *noumenon*. Following another formal lecture and reception, he talked from eleven o'clock until three in the morning, discussing en route Morgan horses, psychiatry, Catullus, politics, Tung oil, spun-glass fishing rods, philosophy (categorizing philosophers into two groups—the annalists and the analysts), education, Generals Lee and Grant, the Imagists F. S. Flint, T. E. Hulme, and Ezra Pound. He wrapped up the nocturnal session, expressing a preference for Immanual Swedenborg's "Heaven" to Dante's "Hell."

Frost's talk is not pyrotechnic or febrile. On the contrary, it is social, genial and expansive. There are few unintended pauses in it. One thought starts another, and he rambles on while the deep-set blue eyes, the blunt nose, the expressive lips, the formidable chin and the shock of white hair all help to pin a point down. . . . He always seems at random like a bluebottle fly on a hot midsummer day. . . . His voice is medium in pitch, rather low than high, but not gutteral; and it registers sensitively shades of feeling. . . . Just as the charm of the man comes to focus in his talk, so the total force of the poet comes to focus in the resonant voice . . . readily able to reproduce the brogue of Irish speech tones, or nuances in colloquial idiom and the accent of a countryman, or blank-verse paragraphs of Miltonic eloquence. . . . In Frost's poetry the meaning is partly in the tone. Similarly, in his conversation one has to hear the voice intonate the thought to catch the total meaning.

The aim of all education, for Frost, was self-cultivation, as everyone knew who read "Build Soil," his Phi Beta Kappa poem that created a storm in the thirties (46ff.) Twenty years later his solicitude for "the individual" above "the group" was, if anything, firmer: "The best things and the best people rise out of their separateness." He took pleasure in telling the tale of the chunk of iron from Sweden and the poem the United Nations asked him to write for it—and then rejected (245). He also spoke of his welfare-minded granddaughter Robin's challenge: "Don't you believe it's important to do good?" "It was more important," he said, "to do well." Yet he didn't quote her reply, nor say how he answered her, if he had—a clash of wills that the advocate of "the individual" ought to have relished and doubtless did, at least in part, knowing the risks involved: "the individual," the core problem of all societies, old and new.

Whitman, democracy's dauntless advocate, saw and stated it plain: "the big problem, the only problem, the sum of them all—adjusting the individual to the mass" (65). But the dangerousness implicit in Whitman's fear, for Frost was a challenging virtue. "Democracy means all the risks taken—conflict of opinion, conflict of personality, eccentricity. The tone is freedom to the point of destruction." These words announced in his eighty-sixth year almost repeat a notebook jotting of unknown date: "A nation should be just as full of conflict as it can contain, physically mentally, financially. But of course *it must contain*. The strain must be short of the bursting point—*just short*" (italics added). And indeed, as he told a reporter: "I like all this uncertainty that we live in, between being members and individuals." Although he was deeply opposed to "everything and everybody that want people to rely on somebody else," he declared that for reasons of "the public health,/ So that the poor won't steal by stealth/ We now and then should take an equalizer." The seeming contrariety is one of a number encountered before, at the time when Frost was attacked as a rockbound New England conservative (65). He was fully aware of having been "too much one way and then too much another through fifty years of politics," as he told a Bread Loaf audience in 1961. The poem that he read—"Take Something Like a Star"—was one in which he "hated" himself for his shifting about. "Maybe I'm one who never makes up his mind," he had said to a friend a decade before.

"Maybe?" It was one of his needs and necessary strengths in his life-long seeking, questing: Keep open to change. "It's well to have all kinds of feelings; for this is all kinds of a world," he'd told Sidney Cox. It is even better, he came to believe, to be able to welcome growth and change and to let it be known to friends and to "the discerning" (246). His statements about poetry and the "great issues were continually growing and changing," to quote from the introduction to *Selected Prose*. "Great issues were among the things he loved most and lived with most intimately." They were one of his long addictions—trying out new ideas, playing with them, hoping to learn by stating what he believed at the time and might find to be less than the waiting truth it seemed. If seeking, questing led him to self-contradiction, it was part of the costly process of self-education.

No more striking example is known than the letter he wrote to Norman Thomas but did not survive to complete. "I yield to no one in my admiration for the kind of liberal you have been, you and Henry Wallace." The letter explains what he hoped to tell Krushchev in person:

> . . . we shouldn't come to blows till we were sure there was a big issue remaining between us, of his kind of democracy versus our kind of democracy, approximating each other as they are, his by easing downward toward socialism from the severity of its original ideals, ours by straining upward toward socialism through various phases of welfare state-ism. I said the arena is set between us for a rivalry of perhaps a hundred years. Let's hope we can take it out in sports, science, art, business and politics before ever we have to take it out in the bloody politics of war. It was all magnanimity—Aristotle's great word.
>
> *(September 28, 1962)*

Magnanimity? An odd word for Frost to use, his critics would say. Jealousy, rather; competitiveness, campaigning—noisome parts of the poet's career which even admirers conceded. Few had attempted to look at the under-surface. They could turn the other way, pretend that they hadn't heard him say that "jealousy is a passion I approve of and attribute to angels." Or when he explained to an Oberlin audience in 1937: "What is jealousy? It's the claim of the object on the lover. The claim of God that you should be true to Him, and so true to yourself. The word still lives for me." Twenty-two years before he had hoped to avoid "the odium of seeming jealous of anybody," but by then he had entered the fray. As the author of *A Boy's Will* and *North of Boston,* he was part of the writers' world. Could he close his eyes to the rivalries, the politics, the thirst for success all about him? "I wonder," he asked his friend the poet Kreymborg after his third book appeared, "do you feel as badly as I do when some other fellow does a good piece of work?" Kreymborg peered at me sadly as I listened many years later: "Frost had hopes for *Mountain Interval* but it failed badly, badly. The reviews simply missed the wonderful poems. He was hurt and of course he was jealous—but worse: *worried*—worried about the future." He shrugged. "Even now, with all his successes, he's secretly worried. I could tell from something he said and the way he said it—afraid the bubble might burst."

In his 1960 interview for the *Paris Review* a seemingly different Frost let himself go on the theme of performance. "The whole thing is performance and prowess and feats of association." But for Poirier, the most revealing statement of all was "Scoring. You've got to score. They say not, but you've got to score—in all the realms." Few people possessed the gift to hear what Poirier heard in those seventeen words:

> Frost even in his mid-eighties still had to remind himself that he was tough enough to live. Of course no man really tough would be so sententious about it, or so lovably anxious to dispel the guilt of having had to be so fiercely competitive in order to live at all.

The words appeared in a double review of *Robert Frost: The Early Years* and *The Letters of Robert Frost to Louis Untermeyer* (206). In discussing the second, Poirier points to some of the ways in which Frost resorted to playfulness "to keep his image from solidifying even for himself:

> He mocks his own foxiness . . . and describes nearly all his meetings and relationships with rival poets as if he were a kind of shrewd buffoon. . . . Being at once fiercely ambitious and genuinely contemptuous of literary politics, Frost was at times close to nervous collapse "from the strain of competition." His efforts at creating a benign public image were motivated less by cynicism than by the emotional necessity of escaping the wear and tear of such competition by seeming to be above it.

Escape was not always possible; the wear and tear could be wounding enough to force him to break a commitment (180). But most of the time he could gather strength for a challenge. "The object in life is to win—win a game, win the play of a poem," one of his notebooks reads. "Obviously," he might have added, for how could competing be wrong? It was Nature itself. "I divide my talks," he explained to Cook, "into two parts, both in this world. First, there is the basic animal faith which leads me to believe in playing to win. And, secondly, at a higher level, there is a lift or crest where . . . you hope you don't make too much of a fool of yourself in the eyes of *It*."

In the eyes of the less exalted, the hope sometimes failed, sometimes succeeded. Four years after Eliot's speech in praise of Frost at the Books Across the Sea dinner in London and Frost's graciously thankful reply, he could still cry out in resentment: "Did any government ever send Eliot anywhere?" And yet he wholly approved the inclusion of "rival poets" in the Untermeyer anthologies; and he fostered the series of Michigan poetry readings in 1922 by Padraic Colum, Amy Lowell, Vachel Lindsay, and that "most artificial and studied ruffian" Carl Sandburg. He publicly lauded the work of Robinson, Ransom, and Moore. Although he "hated" Masters, he couldn't "say for certain" that he didn't "like Spoon River. I believe I do like it in a way." In 1951, when Sandburg won the Pulitzer Prize, Frost quickly agreed he deserved it. The "fiercely competitive" Frost who maintained: "There's only room for one at the top of the steeple" bowed to Yeats as "undoubtedly the man of the last twenty years in English poetry." And so on and so on. . . .

There would be no point in trying to reconcile the Elinor Frost of her husband's letter of 1917 ("She wouldn't lift a hand or have me lift a hand to increase my reputation") with the woman who "only" hoped that Yeats, having praised the poems of Frost as "the best written in America for a long time," "would say so publicly." Frost's concern with gaining readers is vividly clear in the published letters, which also reveal an Elinor Frost striving for and taking delight in the poet's success. No less anxious than Whitman to be read by a very large audience, he had made a start even while living in England, *vide* his letters to Sidney Cox and to John Bartlett. Pound, the master promoter, and Pound's behavior, good and bad, had "told" him what could be done, but Pound never advised him how or where to begin.

On February 22, 1915, all six Frosts and Edward Thomas' son Mervyn landed at Ellis Island. An unfamiliar magazine, *The New Re-*

public, caught his eye on a newsstand as he sauntered about 42nd Street near Grand Central Station. To his great surprise, the contents page listed a review of *North of Boston* by Amy Lowell, one of the movers and shakers of the famed Imagist movement. He hastened to read her response. Some of her reservations struck him as wrong; others as almost absurd; yet her review was impressively long and her verdict highly favorable—"certainly one of the most American volumes of poetry which has appeared for some time." A happy sendoff for Elinor and the children, who were going by train to New Hampshire as paying guests at the home of friends in Bethlehem! Frost would remain in New York. He had Mervyn's immigration problems to solve. And how could he possibly leave without paying a call to his newfound publisher, Henry Holt?

The call was the first of numberless visits Frost would make in the course of his long career. Greeting him with surprising warmth, his editor Alfred Harcourt, chief of the Trade division, told him at once how *North of Boston* came to be published: it was Mrs. Holt's discovery. He also gave him a check from *The New Republic:* $40 for "The Death of the Hired Man," published some weeks before. It would be worthwhile, Harcourt went on, for Frost to make the acquaintance of various people who might prove of help in the future. Frost agreed to follow his mentor's counsel—to attend an open meeting of the Poetry Society, to lunch with the staff of *The New Republic:* Walter Lippmann, Herbert Croly, Francis Hackett, Philip Littell. Neither Harcourt nor Frost, however, had been aware that the poet's work had been sharply attacked at a Poetry Society meeting two months before, or that Frost's conservative views would be quite at odds with those of his luncheon hosts.

What mattered most was the tie he had made with Harcourt and the latter's concern with arranging "helpful relationships." With this in mind, he decided to try the *Atlantic Monthly,* though every *North of Boston* poem he had sent them always came back with: "We are sorry we have no place in the *Atlantic Monthly* for your vigorous verse." Why, Frost started to reason as he fidgeted in the reception room, would the editor, Ellery Sedgwick, one of Boston's cultural greats, put aside his tasks to talk with a man whose work he rejected? But before he could think of leaving, Sedgwick suddenly stood in front of him, holding out both hands in an effusive greeting. Amy Lowell, he said, had told him of *North of Boston,* but would the poet himself consent to tell him the story now? . . . Before the visit was over, Frost agreed to join the dinner party that night at the editor's home and to stay as his overnight guest. A round of literary meetings followed—at the Boston Authors' Club, with Nathan Haskell Dole, Sylvester Baxter, and William Stanley Braithwaite of the Boston *Transcript.* "If you want to see what happened in Boston," Frost wrote from Bethlehem to Sidney Cox, "look me up in the Boston Herald for Tuesday March 9 under the heading Talk of the Town." Baxter had written: "The homecoming of Robert Frost has been the sensation of the day. . . ."

Alfred Harcourt's advice had led not only to "helpful results" but also to troubles. Amy Lowell and Frost—in spite of their effort to bear with each other's difference in taste, theory, and manner of person— never arrived at a sympathetic relationship. In William Stanley Braithwaite, the magazine-verse anthologist, Frost hoped to find a poetry critic unreserved in support and in admiration. Pritchard's summary words on Frost's behavior are a model of kind restraint: ". . . in the case of Braithwaite and Lowell there was a large disparity between the way he dealt with them publicly and what he said about them in the privacy of letters to people he trusted." The lines one reads in the letters, although they form a dismaying picture, call for the reader's awareness that Frost knew that his earning abilities depended on his reputation as poet, reciter, and "presence." And not with "the critical few" alone. On the contrary: "to arrive where I can stand on my legs as a poet and nothing else I must get outside that circle to the general reader who buys books in their thousands." This was his goal, he explained to Bartlett from Beaconsfield in November 1913. He might not succeed but he wanted his friend to realize how much he "believed in doing it—dont you doubt me there. I want to be a poet for all sorts and kinds. . . . I want to reach out."

Frost, of course, succeeded, helped by readers, editors, teachers, believers, reporters, by reviewers and critics, none more zealous than Untermeyer, from the time he discovered "The Fear" and "A Hundred Collars" (December 1913). Frost welcomed and sometimes asked support in the face of attacks, but alongside Whitman and Melville, he makes a most unimpressive sight as a self-promoter.[28]

---

[28] Thompson termed Frost "a campaigner" (*The Years of Triumph*, p. 718). Whitman planted anonymous reviews written by himself. Melville "followed the fortunes of *Typee* with zest, and even wanted to manipulate the controversy through a planted newspaper review of his own." *Publishers Weekly*'s recent charge against Frost for

However amateurish Frost as a self-promoter may appear today, as a "poet-speaker-performer" he was unsurpassed. From years of barding around, he learned that not only "everything written is as good as it is dramatic" (279) but also everything said in a hall of listeners. "I have myself all in a strong box where I can unfold as a personality at discretion," he wrote about publishing poems; but the words apply to his platform presence as well. In the early days of success (1916), he had grown aware of his problem: how to prepare a "face" to present to an audience. The solution probably called for introducing some acting, some pretending, some masking of what he considered his frailties. The poet of 1909, who learned to lessen his fear of facing an audience (245), sought to meet the need of his listeners or what he thought it to be. And, inevitably, at certain times before some groups, "something" differed in Frost. I quote the negative view of Randall Jarrell:

> I want to appreciate more than his best poems, I want to exclaim over some of the unimportantly delightful and marvelously characteristic ones. . . . But first let me get rid, in a few sentences, . . . of what might be called the Peter Pan of the National Association of Manufacturers, or any such thing . . .

Jarrell's words on the "public self" that "gets in the way of the real Frost, of the real poems" can neither be shrugged off nor accepted. For the "platform self" of any writer, teacher, or other performer varies with time, place, mood, and numberless other conditions. The public Frost of his famous Norton lectures obviously bears no relationship to Jarrell's Peter Pan of the N.A.M. "Frost had us all in the palm of his hand," wrote one of his critic-poet-listeners at Harvard, "simply by being himself . . . But what a self!" Or to make the phrase just and precise, *which* public self?

He had the audience in the palm of his hand, but at what personal cost? Questions keep crowding in about winning, scoring. "They say not, but you've got to score—in all the realms" (260). What if it took too great a toll at times? Were his efforts at building a public image— to return to Poirier's words—motivated mainly by his need to escape

publicity-seeking makes ludicrous reading in the 1980's, when the serious writer V. S. Naipaul blandly refers to visiting Oslo to promote his current book; the scholarly Italian professor Umberto Eco does the same speaking of his "autumn promotion tour of the U.S.A."; and so on.

264

the wear and tear of competing by seeming to stand above it, being both fiercely ambitious and truly contemptuous of having to show some part of his private self to strangers who had come to be pleased, carried away, entertained, held in the palm of his hand? And what— beneath their laughter and applause—did they think and feel him to be? He had long ago "found" the answer in "fourths"—those he worried about were the "25% who hated him for the right reasons" (89). How did he feel about *them?* "The best audience the world ever had" could be found in the little college towns all over the land. There he could talk in earnest—they would weigh the words. He could tease— they would take it as play. He might test their reading by "saying" poems they had missed, and thank him for it. As for those who came "for the wrong reasons," he would have to judge, guess, ready himself to act the parts that would hold them till the end. Once when Cook approached as he left the stage to say how well he had spoken, he glowered: "That's what *you* would say, anyway."—hurrying off without giving a clue as to why he "knew" he had failed. What had he done or said to have caused five or six people to leave before he'd finished? The thought might pain him for days or fade, only to reappear at a worried moment. Every time he stepped to the podium, he knew that, however sure he might feel at the start, the outcome would be uncertain.

Once a performance was over, he could give himself to the person-to-person relationships that became his life. "I have come to value my poetry almost less than the friendships it has brought me," he volunteered eight months after Elinor's death. Among such friends were many whose work-a-day lives were not involved with the writing of poems—a physician (Jack Hagstrom), a teacher (Howard Mumford Jones), a printer (Joseph Blumenthal), a painter (Andrew Wyeth), a rabbi (Victor Reichert), a cultural leader (Hyde Cox). There were also farmers, librarians, men in business, scientists, journalists, government people—the list runs on and on. Two of his deepest friendships—the short-lived one with Edward Thomas, the tie that lasted till death with Louis Untermeyer—are now quite widely known. But something needs to be said of other relationships, largely unknown, which widen our knowledge of Frost as poet and friend.

Thompson's thirteen pages on "Encouraging Younger Poets" offer little beyond six summarized sketches and long quotations from Frost's lectures on writing and his introduction to a student anthology. Two of the writers "encouraged" by Frost wrote prose: Lawrence

Conrad and B. F. Skinner. For one of the four poets, Joseph Moncure March, author of *The Wild Party* and *The Set-up,* Frost entertained high hopes, till he turned from verse to creating Hollywood scripts. Two others—Kimball Flaccus, Clifford Bragdon—seemed to gain from Frost's guidance, but also gave up poetry. All but Wade Van Dore ceased to be writers; four became teachers and scholars. Hence, according to Thompson, Frost had but one success and—in Thompson's account, which Van Dore derides as false—success of a very odd kind. I refer to the two poems (22) that led to the making of "The Most of It."

In a 1928 interview, Frost, though known to be frankly jealous of rivals, willingly named four younger poets as likely to win importance: among them, Robinson Jeffers, Archibald MacLeish, Stephen Benét, and Raymond Holden. Twenty-six years later he told another reporter that among the "individuals of great worth in the younger generation" were Elizabeth Bishop, Karl Shapiro, Robert Lowell, Richard Wilbur, and Leonard Bacon." He also expected to see "good things of others," including Delmore Schwartz. But who the "others" had been turns into guesswork, except where records exist. From my own conversations with Frost, from private letters and books, I can list as some of the poets encouraged or helped or praised by Frost: John Holmes, Donald Hall, Charles Foster, Robert Francis, William Meredith, I. H. Salomon, Peter Davison, Theodore Roethke, E. Merrill Root, Wade Van Dore, Henry Dierkes, Robert Lowell, Richard Wilbur, Thomas Hornsby Ferril, James Hearst, Charles Malam, Peter J. Stanlis, John Ciardi, Melville Cane, David Schubert. These are merely the names I happen to know; others can doubtless be added.

Frost on occasion contributed introductions to new anthologies, some by students, some by young published poets. The unexpected excitement he felt in reading *Poetry's* special issue of verse by living Israelis moved him to send the editor the gift of a warm response (142). One even more surprising was made by Frost when he learned that a former student, Reuben Brower, was starting a little poetry journal and also planning to marry. He wired at once: 1934 SEP 4/ STOP PRESS YOU'VE GOT ONE COMING TO YOU TOMORROW. The "one coming" was the manuscript of "Provide, Provide" accompanied by a letter: "Accept the enclosed for the New Frontier as a wedding present. I owe it to you anyway for a day in class made memorable by your reading of the falling out of faithful friends./   Ever yours/ R.F."

Frost's encouragements varied from spoken praise to counting on friends to repeat his comments. They could also take other forms: a testing challenge, a sharp demand to revise "defective" passages, a reasoning "plea" to remove the kind of self-indulgent imbalances he abhorred. Rarely were his words allowed to appear on a book jacket. Rarely would he speak as he did to Wilbur—"The Puritans" was "the best little poem" he had seen in a year or so. A useful book could be made to present Frost in his varying roles as helper. There are surely records to draw on. One of them, by Hugo Saglio, on file at Amherst, quotes the considerate excuse of Frost to save a blind student the problem of making his way to his house: "Why don't I come to *your* room? People keep coming here and the telephone keeps ringing. We can talk better there. . . ."

Meanwhile we can turn to three new books that provide a beginning of sorts. I have already drawn on *Robert Frost and Wade Van Dore: The Life of the Hired Man,* a first-hand account of unique value for everyone concerned with the poet-as-person. Unlike Van Dore, Dierkes was close to Frost for three years only (1934–1936), but they bore unusual fruit; witness his *Robert Frost: A Friend to a Younger Poet:*

> We swapped poems for a while [I quote from his letter] before he suggested that I should have a book and from that point on he was most helpful in the decisions about which poems should be included or left out. What is really remarkable is that Frost had very little use for free verse because he said he wouldn't know how to break off the lines without doing it "hocus-pocusly." What Frost didn't know was that when I lacked half a dozen poems to fill out the book manuscript I sneaked in some of what I considered my best sonnets by typing them as if they were free verse. I didn't tell him and he never discovered it.

The title poem of Dierkes' book, *The Man from Vermont,* points not only to peace and the end of wars but to poets as the agent of the change. Milton Hindus believes that Frost may have attempted "a dialectic refutation" of Dierkes' optimistic view of the future—"What roused the everlasting 'oppositionist' in Frost . . . may be surmised" from his 1957 Christmas poem, "The Objection to Being Stepped On." Whether Hindus is right or wrong in his introduction to Dierkes' book matters much less than the comments by Frost to specific poems. For the first time (I believe) we can read about some of

the ways in which the teaching-poet guided writers in whom he believed: glimpses of Frost at work as critic-and-helper.

In the midst of a New York reading at the New School in the winter
of 1930, Frost spotted the face of an Amherst student, David
Schubert. Expelled in his sophomore year for missing chapel, cutting
classes, and similar failings, he was now living from hand-to-mouth
and trying to write. After the lecture, Frost walked with him to his
boarding-house cell and listened to his poem on Faustus. They talked
together for hours. Before leaving, Frost promised to urge Amherst
to take the young man back; he also gave him some money and offered
to send the same amount each week (in the thirties, $3.00 could help
one survive). Schubert was readmitted, then dropped for good in December 1932.

Frost sent him to meet with another former Amherst student, Peak
Crawford, who was selling books at Brentano's. Within five minutes
they were friends. Frost heard nothing more from Schubert himself,
but he came upon some of his poems in the *Saturday Review,* the *Yale
Review,* and *Poetry,* which in 1936 gave him a prize. Five years later
Frost read him again in the New Directions' volume *Five Young Amer-
ican Poets.* That was the last till the evening after his lecture at Bard
College in the forties. He and his host, Theodore Weiss, talked about
universities and writing and Frost started to reminisce about young
poets he had known. Suddenly he quoted: "Atta boy Jesus Christ
Professor." To his great amazement, Weiss replied: "O, yes, David
Schubert." The two proceeded to talk of publishing a book of
Schubert's poems. Frost applauded the project and offered to help in
spite of his age. Time passed. In the summer of 1946 the Weiss's *Quarterly Review of Literature* featured a large group of Schubert's poems.
Frost quite probably learned from friends who had read the issue that
the author he had striven to help had died in April.

"Generosity" does not appear in Thompson's topical indexes.
Frost, to be sure, never regarded himself as "a nice person." No one
was more aware than he of the "terrible things" he might possibly do
or had already done (as his letters reveal). He could even hide in a clos-
et the morning after some act that he gravely regretted ("I was too
ashamed to face you . . ."). As in other respects—one is tempted to
say, in almost all—he would overreact, over-blame. But sometimes
even extreme self-punishment failed to assuage the pain—"I'm the
kind that can't get over things[.] I have to say they have never been.
Annul[,] not divorce." And yet he knew he was not alone in self-

entrapment: "You want to believe that great writers are good men," he said to Van Wyck Brooks. "It's an illusion that dies hard." To which Maxwell Perkins added, "They are all sons of bitches."

Can "badness" stand as the norm, or—to be more specific—did Frost in dealing with people, for the most part act in reprehensible ways? The question sounds absurd to ask of a person known for his numerous friendships—and yet, on certain occasions, Frost behaved in ways deplored by even his warmest admirers. I offer three examples of the supposedly "worst," based—so far as possible—on data given by those who were either on the scene or part of it.

The "search" for a fit biographer brought on problems years before the poet selected Thompson. In 1926 there were three possibilities: Edward Davison, an English poet who called at Bread Loaf during the Writers' Conference; Wilfred Davison, Dean of the School of English; Gorham B. Munson. Edward Davison's opening chapter troubled Frost by its sharply negative treatment of Louis Untermeyer. At once the writer agreed to prepare a revision, assuming, since nothing else had been said, that all was well. Frost, however, had other ideas, stirred by an essay he read in a March issue of the *Saturday Review* which named him "the purest classical poet of America." In the fall he took a train to New York, reached the author, Munson, by telephone, and proposed that he write a monograph for the series edited by John Farrar. The project, discussed over dinner that evening, moved so fast that the writing was done by June and sent to the printer. Frost's many suggested corrections arrived too late to be made. *Robert Frost: A Study in Sensibility and Good Sense* appeared November 1, 1927.

Its closing chapter led reviewers to mistake Frost for a follower of Irving Babbitt, chief of the "New Humanists," whose harsh attacks on William James and Henri Bergson were more than the poet could stomach. His relationship with Munson came to an end, but not the relationships with the two Davisons. The Dean's "disappointment was great," Farrar informed Frost, who, so far as I know, did nothing. With the English poet, however, he tried to make reparations, and in minor ways succeeded, helping promote his lectures and enabling him to receive a Guggenheim grant. Davison, in turn, was more than generous. "Let's not have the biography between us always as our reason for meeting or avoiding each other," Frost proposed. "Let's consider it dropped." Davison agreed, and the two remained friends.

Another case of Frost's unseemly behavior also involved an English poet, but one of a special brand. The scene: St. Botolph's Club,

November 1932; the occasion: a dinner in honor of Eliot, currently Harvard's Norton Professor of Poetry. Sergeant's "possibly mythical composite" derived from witness accounts from Frost, Ferris Greenslet (who chose the date so that Frost could attend), and David McCord.** Frost "began the evening a bit antipathetic—with a touch of the old jealousy," he remarked years later with some contrition. But as things moved on, he had all he could do to control his disgust with the way that Eliot, then at the height of his fashion, patronized his questioners, who approved with pious solemnity every last word he said. At a certain point, "Eliot announced that Burns could not be considered a poet at all—in fact no poetry had been written north of the River Tweed except for Dunbar's gloomy 'Lament for the Makers.' "

"Eliot sounds like a Border name," said Frost, his Scotch blood rising.

"We were Somerset Eliots."

"Might we consider Burns a *song writer?*" Frost countered ironically. Eliot finally conceded "One might grant that modest claim." By then, Frost had had enough, but one of the guests, holding the text of "The Hippopotamus," proposed that each of them read a poem of his own.

> He offered [wrote Frost to Untermeyer] to read a poem if I would read one. I made him a counter-offer to *write* one while he was reading his. Then I fussed around with place-cards and a borrowed pencil, pretending an inspiration. When my time came I said I hadn't finished on paper but would try to fake the tail part in talk when I got to it. I did nine four-line stanzas on the subject "My Olympic Record Stride." Several said "Quite a feat." All were so solemn I hadn't the courage to tell them that I of course was lying! I had composed the piece for my family when torn between Montauk, Long Island, and Long Beach, California, the summer before. So be cautioned. They must never know the truth. I'm much to blame, but I just couldn't be serious when Eliot was taking himself so seriously. . . .

Another "poetry competition" occurred at the Bread Loaf Writers' Conference on August 27, 1938, an evening lecture and reading by Archibald MacLeish, whose growing importance and warm reception proved too much for Frost to accept with civility (110):

Early in the proceedings [I quote from Wallace Stegner's account]
Frost found some mimeographed notices on a nearby chair and
sat rolling and folding them. . . . Now and again he raised the
roll of paper, or an eyebrow, calling the attention of his seat mates
to some phrase or image. He seemed to listen with an impartial, if
skeptical, judiciousness. About halfway through the reading he
leaned over and said in a carrying whisper, "Archie's poems all
have the same *tune*." As the reading went on, to the obvious
pleasure of the audience, he grew restive. The fumbling and rus-
tling of the papers in his hands became disturbing. Finally
MacLeish announced "You, Andrew Marvell," . . . a favorite.
Murmurs of approval, intent receptive faces. The poet began.
Then an exclamation, a flurry in the rear of the hall. The reading
paused, heads turned. Robert Frost, playing around like an idle,
inattentive schoolboy in a classroom, had somehow contrived to
strike a match and set fire to his handful of papers and was busy
beating them out and waving away the smoke.

There was more to come. Charles H. Foster, a former Amherst
student then living at Bread Loaf on a scholarship in memory of
Elinor Frost, wrote an account in his *Journal*:

Frost did not take kindly to Archie's talk, I found out, when I met
him in the kitchen. He was mixing himself a drink of a tumbler of
whiskey. . . . Ted Morrison asked him to be good and he said
he'd be all right when he put what he had in his hand where it
should go. When we went into the living room everyone felt the
tension and Benny DeVoto was pacing around. . . . "God–damn
it to hell, Charlie. Robert's acting like a fool. Archie wasn't talking against him." . . .[MacLeish now read *Air Raid* which
provoked a heated discussion between Morrison and DeVoto]. I
went over to see how Frost was stirring the waters. I sat next to
Frost on a davenport and after a time Archie came over and sat on
the arm of it. Frost had one arm around me and as more drinks
were drunk and the discussion arose, Archie balanced himself
with an arm around my shoulder. . . . Frost said that it made him
mad when "a young squirt" like Spender gave what he had
worked on all his life a phrase, and tried to take the credit for
it. . . . "Jesus H. Christ, Robert," said Archie. . . . "You're the
foundation and we all know it." "I'm an old man. I want you to

say it, to say it often. I want to be flattered." . . . Archie then tried to make the conversation less personal and Frost said "God-damn everything to hell so long as we're friends, Archie." "We are friends, Robert." . . .

One week before, according to Foster's *Journal,* Frost called himself "a God-damn-son-of-a-bitch, a selfish person who had dragged people roughshod over life. People didn't understand who wanted to make him good." Elinor had been dead since March; his long "period of blackness" had not yet ended. "I've been crazy for the last six months," he wrote in September to Untermeyer. "I haven't known what I was doing. . . . Do you think I'm still living in this world? Tell me the truth. Dont spare me."

What of the decades after the poet's recovery? Having never witnessed a burst of his bad behavior, I approached various friends who had long been close to the poet—only three were able to give examples. The first—from Professor Robert N. Ganz, who in 1956 or 1957 drove Frost across Vermont to a party near Dartmouth:

I showed up at the Homer Noble Farm about 20 minutes late. He hated people to be late, a sign to him of disrespect. He showed this feeling by speaking with disdain of my Volkswagen. Perhaps he may also have been disappointed that his chariot was not to be more comfortable. In any case, he said, as he descended into the seat—anything but a throne—"I wouldn't trust *you* in a war with the Germans." (I might have replied, "When we have wars with the Germans, I go and you don't." But I didn't.) In addition to being a rebuke, Frost's comment, of course, was funny. Still, I'm sure, he regretted his show of temper. Near the end of our trip— we got a bit lost—he complimented my car's maneuverability. This was, obviously, a kind of apology. Then, because the car didn't have a fuel gauge, we ran out of gas—at the foot of a large hill or small mountain. He was *very big* about this as we started to trudge up the road. We were soon picked up by other guests and Frost continued to comfort me, to be gentle with my ego. I recall his saying, as we approached the house, there were better men outside than in—another effort to minimize my embarrassment. He did the same at another time when a driver rudely honked. Leaning out of the window, he yelled in a burst of loyal belligerency, "What's the matter with *you?*"

My second reply came from Alfred Edwards—he had been at Holt since 1945—who had seen "very few examples of Frost's 'bad behavior' ":

For the most part he was considerate with almost everyone though occasionally very short with Thompson when Larry's probing questions made him feel the "official" biographer might slant RF's image to fit *Thompson's predetermined image* of the poet.

Only once was I victim of a tantrum. RF was one of very few American authors of his time to be paid a 20% royalty on all copies sold. When I negotiated a contract with him in 1958 for *You Come Too,* I lowered the royalty to 15% as children's books carry lower royalty scales and are priced accordingly.

RF's pride was hurt, he was furious. Over the telephone he gave me a tongue lashing including some colorful language. He would not listen for my answer so I dropped the receiver terminating his call.

Several hours later he called back to apologize, later signing the offending contract. Neither ever mentioned the incident thereafter. Years later Kay told me Frost admired my guts and was glad he named me sole executor and trustee in his will, a fact I did not know until after his death.

My third reply was made by Joseph Blumenthal, who states that the incident he reports "should be stressed as being the only time in our 30-year association when Frost ever blew his top with me":

The setting was early January, 1962, when I was visiting the Howard Mumford Jones' in Cambridge for the weekend. At the end of the evening I told Robert that I had an extra set of proofs of *In the Clearing,* that his OK was imperative if the book were to be completed in time for the dinner in Washington for his birthday in March. Robert asked me to call at Brewster Street "tomorrow at two."

Promptly I rang the bell. He opened the door, his eyes angry, shook his finger in my face, said "Damn you!" and barred the way, indicating that something was wrong. It was the first time

273

in a thirty-year friendship that I had encountered him in such a state of agitation. I knew no reason for his anger with me unless he felt that I was putting undue pressure on him to release the proofs I had under my arm. I offered to leave for New York at once and take the proofs back with me. But he said no, to "come on in." Mrs. Morrison was already there. We three sat around his dining table, each with a set of proofs, and the agitation quickly subsided. Frost read the proofs aloud and made a number of corrections as he went along. After three or four relaxed and harmonious hours, he handed me his set with "OK as corrected" and invited me back for breakfast next morning.

Something more must be said about Frost: first, as a "racist," and second, as a "mythologist." From all I have learned, the racist charge hangs on his use of *nigger*. "The world hates Jews and despises Blacks. I'd rather be hated than despised," he remarked, typically, to Reichert, for whom the poem "The Black Cottage" demonstrates Frost's "puzzlement" on the whole subject of race (lines 61, 75–83, 105–110). Frost was "acceptance personified" when compared with such other poets as Stevens ("Who's the lady coon [Gwendolyn Brooks]?" "I don't like this place. Too many Jews come in here.") and MacLeish ("I find race feeling runs pretty hot in my veins.") To say nothing of words by Pound, Eliot, Auden, Tate, Williams, Lowell. None of which erases the fact that Frost on occasion muttered or shouted "nigger" in anger over some petty event, imagined slight, discourteous act, or similar provocation. But Frost didn't say "nigger" only in anger. At my house, at our breakfast table, he used it to test my wife's and my daughter's reaction, knowing I saw through his game, since he'd spoken warmly to me of Sterling Brown and knew of our intimate friendship—the Browns had been guests at our daughter's wedding and Sterling would attend the party for Sergeant's biography (137f.).** But whether spoken in anger or play, "nigger" remains a racist word. Hyde Cox holds a different view on the whole subject:

> I don't think the word should be applied to Frost at all. I could go on at length to prove that he was not basically anti any race. *He relished diversity.* There were—we both know—occasions when he seemed to be using race difference to vent his frustration with an individual (he was highly competitive) but such behavior in him had no root. "We love the things we love for what they are."

The line quoted by Cox applies in a curious way to Frost's recollections. "Mythologizing" his past not only served when needed to confuse biographers; it could also cause him concern, as with Pound's review of *A Boy's Will* in *Poetry* (18). The line between deliberate reshaping of one's past and simple forgetting often cannot be marked. "Trust me on the poetry, but don't trust me on my life" may be a "way of admitting that he couldn't always trust himself to tell—or even to see—the entire truth about himself"—so Thompson believed. How can anyone find "the entire truth"? That Frost tried to recall events as they had happened hardly needs to be stressed: nor that he sometimes failed (*vide* "A Minor Bird," 129f.); nor that he felt compelled to insist about "certain things" that "they never have been": to "Annul[,] not divorce."

This phrase from his *Prose Jottings* more than all others involving the past points to his need for maintaining a view of his life he could bear. Seen in this light, his contradictory statements—on time, place, people; on what he had or hadn't done, loved, or hated—bespeak his concern that the place he had earned might be lost to him, not of his doing but out of the workings of chance, fashion, taste—forces beyond control or foreseeing. Or to use the vast, encompassing word: fear. One might make an anthology of instances of varying sorts and intensities, from mild insecurity to darkest dread, from the early days with his reckless idolized father to the final words uttered in public that, whatever else they intended, voiced a defiant life-without-hope misgiving (188f.).

Some twenty years ago James Dickey "felt sure" that "the motivating emotion in Frost was fear." Randall Jarrell remembered that the poet "could never seem to forgive people" who scared him "within an inch of his life." In his comments about *King Jasper,* Frost stressed two fears: the fear of God; the fear "that men won't understand us and we shall be cut off from them." Years before, he had taken especial care with Sidney Cox to explain that he "didn't believe it did [him] the least good to be told of the enemies he had had to defend [him] from." Out of hearing, out of mind, and, if possible, out of sight: He stayed away from Pound on his Washington visits to avoid confronting those who were out of their senses. "We all have our souls—and minds—to save, and it seems a miracle that we do it, not once, but several times. He could look back and see his hanging by a thread," John Bartlett noted after a talk with Frost. Page after page could be filled with acts observed, friends' quotations, lines of prose and verse, whole poems—

on fear. In counter-response, Frost celebrates daring, courage, taking risks.** ("I'd rather be taken for brave than anything else," he told Lesley.) Or hides, shielded by humor. "Be careful how you offer to take care of me in my last days," he teased Van Dore. "You never can tell about a poet's future." And yet, though "any form of humor shows fear, . . . [b]elief is better than anything else." And of all beliefs, even the most exalted, belief in one's self must come before all others, whatever one is stirred to do or say or imagine to assure its safety.

If fear is this poet's motivating emotion, and if humor in *any* form shows fear, what is one to think of the "serious" Frost? Ironically, as Sidney Cox has written, Frost frequently said: "It's a funny world."

> If he said it once, he has said it a thousand times. He said it sadly, he said it mockingly, he said it calmly as he slowly shook his head at the solemn explanations of the great minds, and he said it smiling as he made an opening for more truth. . . . Seriously, it's funny. It's seriously funny. And it's funny because it's serious. You often have to wait a while before you are amused. And even then most good smiles have a disappearing trace at least of ruefulness.

Untermeyer was quick to stress Frost's "extraordinarily playful spirit," but his book of *Letters,* though rich with examples, merely implies its range. At the "lowest" extreme: puns, good, bad, brilliant, sometimes "impossible" (Schenectady-synedoche). At the "highest": looking hard at the meanings of "you bet your sweet life" or, in the closing quatrain of "Two Tramps in Mud Time," joining "love and need" with "work [as] play for mortal stakes." Better than high and low would be breadth of kinds, which offers a world in itself— reveling in baseball talk; challenging the Poetry Society of America audience with a famous Davies poem (he had bet they would miss); insisting "I'm never serious except when fooling"; testing a reader's "rightness" by saying "My truth will bind you slave to me"; quoting his fee for a sonnet to an ex-world heavyweight champion ("because the last two lines . . . don't mean anything anyway"); taking "oppositionist" stands in an argument without concern for where they might leave him stranded; testing an audience after receiving a medal with "Oh, if my mother could only see me now" without acknowledging Kipling as its author; trying the patience of friends with comments he hoped would lead to a battle of wits; starting a punning contest he knew he might lose . . . To which one could add dozens of better examples. More to the point is Frost himself on the subject:

I own any form of humor shows fear and inferiority. Irony is simply a kind of guardedness. So is a twinkle. It keeps the reader from criticism. . . . Belief is better than anything else, and it is best when rapt, above paying its respect to anybody's doubt whatsoever. At bottom the world isn't a joke. We only joke about it to avoid an issue with someone to let someone know that we know he's there with his questions: to disarm him by seeming to have heard and done justice to his side of the standing argument. Humor is the most engaging cowardice. With it myself I have been able to hold some of my enemy in play far out of gunshot.

When the question comes up . . . what in the world are we to do next, the answer is easily either laugh or cry. We have no other choice. It takes wit to supply the laugh, yes and the tears too I guess.

[S]tyle is the way the man takes himself; and to be at all charming or even bearable, the way is almost rigidly prescribed. If it is with outer seriousness, it must be with inner humor. If it is with outer humor, it must be with inner seriousness. Neither one alone without the other under it will do.

Play no matter how deep has got to be so playful that the audience are left in doubt whether it is deep or shallow.

Pritchard considers this last sentence "perhaps his deepest word on the subject." He never professed to be giving the whole of the truth in any assertion; how could he possibly do so, convinced as he was of the limiting power of thought, all human thought? Everything he says about play, for all its sureness of tone, is a grain of truth—large, probing, provocative, beyond any sensible doubt at times but only at times; or, to make him witness against himself: earnest acts of playing with truth, playing for truth, which can take the mind as far as mind can go in its "seeking, questing." So he is able to write that "The way of understanding" with its outer or inner seriousness is always "partly mirth."

The *Centennial Essays II* devotes six of twenty-two chapters to "play." "Acceptance in Frost's Poetry: Conflict as Play," by Professor Marjorie Cook, argues "that Frost finds balance through his ability to see conflict as play. Serious play," in fact, "is the crux of Frost's poetics," which calls to mind Pritchard's belief that "everything he did or wrote could be thought about in the light of the [fact that one] of Frost's favorite words for poetry was 'Play,' " and poetry means "not just the poems but also the prose reflections: essays, interviews, notebooks—above all, the letters," to which I should add the talks and conversations.

With a poet of Frost's complexity, readers do well to look from a number of vantage points, to consider other assumptions. For example, Poirier's words "To the Reader":

Frost is a poet of genius because he could so often make his subtleties inextricable from an apparent availability. The assumption that he is more easily read than are his contemporaries, like Yeats and Eliot, persists only in ignorance of the unique but equally strenuous kinds of difficulty which inform his best work. He is likely to be most evasive when his idioms are so ordinary as to relax rather than to stimulate attention; he is an allusive poet, but in a hedging and off-hand way, the allusions being often perceptible only to the ear, and then just barely—in echoings of earlier poets like Herbert or Rossetti, or in metrical patternings traceable to Milton; he will wrap central implications, especially of a sexual kind, within phraseologies that seem innocent of what they carry. The conclusion of "The Need of Being Versed in Country Things"—"One had to be versed in country things/ Not to believe the phoebes wept"—sounds like a formula ready made for the delectation of critics who can then talk, as indeed I do, about poetry in nature, nature in poetry. But the proffered interpretation is compelling enough to mask other possibilities which would greatly enrich it. . . .

His poetry is especially exciting when it makes of the "obvious" something problematic, or when it lets us discover, by casual inflections or hesitations of movement, that the "obvious" by nature *is* problematic. . . .

He leads us toward a kind of knowing that belongs to dream and reverie. . . .

His practices derive from his passionate convictions about poetry as a form of life. . . .

"Most folks are poets. If they were not," Frost told a reporter, "most of us would have no one to read what we write." Nothing was said about critics and how they might help, for the date was 1921, years before the land was flooded with New Critics who could hardly wait to proffer the *real meanings* of any poem they happened to have at hand. Classrooms echoed with interpretations—brilliant, wild, clear, obtuse—but rarely without some technically provable basis. In 1958 Professor M. H. Abrams put "Five Ways of Reading *Lycidas*" into an essay which also included his own critique so that readers could know what was going on all around them and judge for themselves. By now the anything-goes approach (182) has been driven away by others equally doomed—while the poems remain unchanged, to be used by newcoming readers and critics to minister to their wishes; that is, to respond to the temper of each. One reads according to one's ability *and* one's needs. For example, Professor Helen H. Bacon delivers a lecture on "In- and Outdoor Schooling: Robert Frost and the Classics." And others do the same: They view the poems in the light of their own inclinations and knowledge. Thus, in limiting ways, does Frost, "the subtlest and most elusive of poets" (243), come to be "known" *at the start,* and so remains unless readers seek the help of a "world" that is waiting to open their ears and eyes. And a world it is. By now the poems have been studied, discussed, brooded upon by so many writers that specialists find it difficult to encompass them all. Such riches are not without hazards, but a reader can guard himself by reviewing essentials, many of which Frost provided in comments, letters, talks.

"Everything written is as good as it is dramatic." The test holds true of many, possibly most, of Frost's poems—notably in "Mending Wall" and "The Death of the Hired Man," household items for years. Two "contradictory" speakers, both of them "right" up to a point, and only when they are joined is the poem resolved—and then in an "open-endedness." As much holds true of "Provide, Provide" (55): though "sung" by a single speaker, the contradictory voice is heard through implications that cannot be missed; and again the poem says all that is needed without an overt "conclusion." "Life sways perilously at the confluence of opposing forces. Poetry in general plays perilously in the same wild place. In particular . . . between truth and make-believe." A duality, as one might suppose, commonly forms the base of the poet's dramatics, but not always: witness poems marked by more than two forces, attitudes, "voices" living in conflict ("Directive," "Two Tramps in Mud Time," "The Draft Horse"); or in which the opposing "something(s)" are hypothesized ("I Could Give All to Time," "Acquainted with the Night," "The Most of It").

Though open-ended "conclusions," like works which ask the reader to add what the writer omitted, are considered typically modern, often other critical touchstones are used. For example, if the twentieth-century vision is characteristically bleak, pessimistic, Frost as "a poet who terrifies" must be rated "modern." And so he is for more than a few critics. Not, however for Rexford Stamper, who holds that "the juxtaposed interpretations of facts reveal Frost's modernity." Nor for Lloyd N. Dendinger: Yeats, Eliot, Stevens, "the poets most often held up as the most modern," all follow the nineteenth-century pattern of " 'replacing' what has been lost to the poet as a result of the scientific, industrial, and political revolutions," the loss "lamented as early as Wordsworth's cry" in "The world is too much with us," in Arnold's "Dover Beach" and "Stanzas from the Grande Chartreuse," in Eliot's "Prufrock." Frost's "modernity rests primarily in the fact that . . . he turns neither to Eliot's 'chambers of the sea' nor to Yeats's prophetic vision of some 'rough beast' . . . but rather to the 'real' world [that Howells described] as the 'poor real life' of the largely impoverished countryside of New England." James Dickey, however, notes that "through this stealthy rusticity" Frost is able "to say the most amazing things without seeming to raise his voice . . . that the modern poet is trying to express—bewilderment and horror, wonder and compassion, a tragic sense of life, which he . . . suggests without bitterness or whining." Frost's innovations in verbal texture are too apparent to need attention ("let what will be, be"; "stay us and be staid"; "Back out of all this now too much for us"), or his openness to revolutions in syntax. What he valued in Christopher Smart's "Where ask is have, where seek is find" was the "cavalierliness with words." Indeed, "The height of poetry is a kind of mischief."

In letters, speeches, and conversations—everywhere—Frost talked about his art:

The sound is the gold in the ore. . . . We need the help of context—meaning—subject matter. That is the greatest help toward variety. All that can be done with words is soon told. So also with meters—particularly in our language where there are virtually but two, strict iambic and loose iambic. . . . The possibilities for tune from the dramatic tones of meaning struck across the rigidity of a limited meter are endless. . . .

Then there is this wildness. . . . it has an equal claim with sound to being a poem's better half. If it is a wild tune, it is a poem. Our problem then is, as modern abstractionists, to have the wildness pure; to be wild with nothing to be wild about. . . . so the second mystery is how a poem can have wildness and at the same time a subject that shall be fulfilled.

It should be of the pleasure of a poem itself to tell how it can. The figure a poem makes. It begins in delight and ends in wisdom. . . . It begins in delight, it inclines to the impulse, it assumes direction with the first line laid down, it runs a course of lucky events, and ends in a clarification of life—not necessarily a great clarification, such as sects and cults are founded on, but in a momentary stay against confusion.

No tears in the writer, no tears in the reader. No surprise for the writer, no surprise for the reader. . . . [L]ike giants we are always hurling experience ahead of us to pave the future with against the day when we may want to strike a line of purpose across it for somewhere. . . . Like a piece of ice on a hot stove the poem must ride on its own melting.
—"The Figure a Poem Makes," 1939

Everything written is as good as it is dramatic. . . . Sentences are not different enough to hold the attention unless they are dramatic. . . . All that can save them is the speaking tone of voice somehow entangled in the words and fastened to the page for the ear of the imagination.
—Preface to "A Way Out," 1929

[Metaphor]: saying one thing and meaning another, saying one thing in terms of another, the pleasure of ulteriority. Poetry is simply made of metaphor. So also is philosophy—and science, too. . . .

Every single poem written regular is a symbol small or great of the way the will has to pitch into commitments deeper and

281

deeper to a rounded conclusion and then be judged for whether any original intention it had has been strongly spent or weakly lost. . . . Strongly spent is synonymous with kept.

—*"The Constant Symbol,"* 1946

Poetry begins in trivial metaphors, pretty metaphors, "grace" metaphors, and goes on to the profoundest thinking that we have. Poetry provides the one permissible way of saying one thing and meaning another.

—*"Education by Poetry,"* 1931

A poem . . . begins as a lump in the throat, a sense of wrong, a homesickness, a lovesickness. It is never a thought to begin with. It is at its best when it is a tantalizing vagueness. It finds its thought and succeeds, or doesn't find it and comes to nothing. It finds its thought or makes its thought. . . . It finds the thought and the thought finds the words.

—*Letter to Louis Untermeyer, January* 1, 1916

Poetry—it's the ultimate. The nearest thing to it is penultimate, even religion. It's a thought-felt thing.

—*Oxford Lecture, June* 4, 1957

Earlier than any of these statements is the one Frost made to Bartlett (July 4, 1913) on the audile imagination. Convinced that Swinburne, Tennyson, and others whose effects arose largely from assonance were on "the wrong track or at any rate on a short track," he felt confident enough to write:

I alone of English writers have consciously set myself to make music out of what I may call the sound of sense. Now it is possible to have sense without the sound of sense . . . and the sound of sense without sense. . . . The best place to get the abstract sound of sense is from voices behind a door that cuts off the words. . . . The sound of sense . . . is the abstract vitality of our speech . . . pure sound—pure form. . . . [but] merely the raw material of poetry. . . . [I]f one is to be a poet he must learn to get cadences by skillfully breaking the sounds of sense with all their irregularity of accent across the regular beat of the metre. [Eight months later he added:] A sentence is a sound in itself on which other sounds called words may be strung. . . . The sentence-sounds . . . are as definite as words. . . . They are gathered by the ear from the vernacular and brought into books. . . . *The ear does it*. The ear is the only true writer and the only true reader. . . . [T]he sentence sound often says more than the words.

So much, then, for theories. What of his practice? "Perfection is a great thing," he said at his 1954 birthday dinner. He "determined to have it" for Elinor's sake as much as his own, but long before (six months after her death), he not only "ceased to expect it [but] actually crave[d] the flaws of human handwork." Such craving isn't evident in his writing. As late as 1959 his "utmost ambition" was still "to write two or three poems hard to get rid of." That he strove for perfection, I knew from watching him try out last-minute changes with the proofs of his final book. None, however, approached the depth of difference in the two versions of "A Minor Bird" (129) or "Design" (entitled in 1912 "In White," published in 1922 with all lines changed but four). A full account of Frost's revisions is as useless to hope for as the composition dates of the poems. But his borrowings are sometimes easily traced. J. Donald Crowley cites a few ("A Drumlin Woodchuck," "Neither Out Far nor In Deep," "Desert Places") in his essay "Hawthorne and Frost" that stresses the source of "The Wood-Pile," together with Frost's "confession that it was his habit to make deliberate borrowings." Speaking in 1955 of the reader's need to give himself over completely to his book, he declared that "every single one of my poems is probably one of these adaptations . . . taken" from what he was "given." Things dropped into his mind to come back on their own or were consciously drawn from Emerson, James, Santayana, and who can say how many more, knowing the "smokeless powder" source of "The Wood-Pile" (164).

Many of Frost's beliefs about critics and theory I have cited before—poetry as "correspondence" (172), the role of the New Critics (182), what is truly lost in translation (123), to name but three. One "idea" which he seldom mentioned but to which he had given much thought was the "inappropriateness" of being termed a "Symbolist" poet. "If my poetry has to have a name, I'd prefer to call it Emblemism," not "Symbolism, [which] is all too likely to clog up and kill a poem." I know of only one writer to cope with this difference, Samuel Coale, who considers the early "Stars" the clearest example:

The stars "congregate" above "our tumultuous snow" as if they were symbols of some more permanent meaning, as if they symbolized a "keenness for our fate." Frost, however, rejects such personification of natural objects, rejects the "symbolism" he describes, and prefers to take the stars *as they are* "with neither love nor hate." They are significant by virtue of their permanence as natural objects, by their very existence and distance from us . . . ; they remain not allegoric or symbolic but in Frost's terms emblematic of man's encounter with the very presence of existence itself. . . .

No attempt is made to force the stars to reflect a mood of the poet, to humanize and incorporate it into some allegorical mirror of the human soul. Nature remains a permanent "other" beyond our comprehension, yet significant since people and nature both are part of some great cosmic encounter. Thus each natural fact is emblematic of "something" whose existence we can know only in the thing itself. Not every poem by Frost conforms to this principle. "Stopping by Woods . . . ," (he named it his "best bid for remembrance") succumbs to the very poetic Symbolic reverie that the emblematic encounter purports to deny. Yet Emblemism is what he hoped his work as a whole would embody and be understood as portraying.

"My poems—" he said in his early fifties, "I should suppose everybody's poems—are all set to trip the reader head foremost into the boundless." Thirty years later, when questioned about some proffered meanings of "Stopping by Woods . . . ," he replied, "Now, that's all right; it's out of my hands once it's published," which didn't stop him from saying of its being a death-poem, "I never intended that but I did have the feeling it was loaded with ulteriority." He often talked of specific poems, occasionally of how they were written, most often of when or where. Did the comments help? To speak for myself only: A poem is a virtual object added to the landscape—virtual because it cannot be touched or seen; the experience it offers is never actual as the warmth of the sun is actual. The poem speaks to readers indirectly in a mode of dramatized speaking addressed to their own experiences, their own desires. Response depends on what they bring to the poem and what they are able to "hear." At best they may think that they hear it all. If they hear little, they may search for help.

For me, at times, merely a passing word or part of a friend's tale of a talk with the poet has opened my ears to meanings. But many comments (including some of Frost's) have hindered or seemed irrelevant. I gained nothing at all from being told that "The Road Not Taken" involved Edward Thomas; that "Into My Own" was "really" about loyalty; that England was the birthplace of "The Sound of the Trees"; that the heroine of "The Lovely Shall Be Choosers" was the poet's mother. In any event, how is one helped to "know" "The Subverted Flower" by being informed that Elinor White was part of the scene? Whether "The Silken Tent" was "about" Mrs. Frost (as Lesley recalled) or Mrs. Morrison (as Thompson insisted) may matter to Frost's biographers, but not to a reader involved with the poem itself. Yet with certain writings, background help is essential. Few readers can fail to benefit from Pritchard's discussions of *North of Boston* and *A Witness Tree*.

Frost's poems, as everyone knows, are sometimes difficult, always subtle, and in some degree elusive. By saying that "The poet is entitled to all the meanings the reader can find in his poem," he not only stressed the likelihood of clashing interpretations but also proposed its rightness and, by implication, fostered repeated encounters with the very same poem. He could sometimes play a game by keeping readers off balance. Of "The Most of It" he might say dryly, "It's another one people have bothered around about—the meaning of—and I'm glad to have them get more out of it than I put in. . . . I do that myself as the years go on." Throwing dust in the eye was almost a pastime, Cook implies, quoting some of his comments—"Neither Out Far nor In Deep" was a "rhymy little thing," "a joke on microscope and telescope." And although with "Kitty Hawk" he took great care to state what it meant, most of the time he chose to insist that his poems were clear if rightly taken—if he had wanted to make them clearer, he would have used different words. And, in any case, a poem should not "be pressed too hard for meaning." True, certain ones had to be "taken doubly," others singly (as he wrote in *A Further Range*); but most of his poems could and would be taken in multiple ways. At times the most perceptive of critics and readers emerge from identical poems with thoughtfully differing judgments—with apparently irreconcilable recognitions. **

Which amounts to saying in a somewhat oblique paradoxical way that much of Frost is "obscure." That "His subject was the world that is so familiar and that no one understands"—true though it be—doesn't lead to an answer. Nor that his poetry fails to be helped by the kinds of explication that help readers of Eliot, Yeats, or Stevens.

There are no adducible fixed-and-findable treasures at the end of the analytic rainbow: no Eliotic neo-Christian myths, no "systematic" Yeatsian *Vision,* no ascending steps on Stevens' stairway of imagination. Frost's poetry calls for more than the tracking down of allusions, ambiguities of language, echoes from other writings, and the other "strategies" which, once exhausted, end the need to explore. Eliot, Yeats, Stevens (as others also have found) are "easier" writers than Frost. There would be no imperative point in saying of them that "The poet is entitled to *all* the meanings that the reader can find in his poem"; whereas with Frost this seemingly evasive remark showed the way toward "the answer." Read, for example, "I Could Give All to Time," then see what such thoughtful critics as Poirier, Jarrell, Brower, Pritchard, and Cook have to say. Does any one of these comments satisfy a reader avid to know the meaning of *every line?* Hyde Cox, with whom Frost often discussed his work, waives the question aside: "The poem suggests more than one can specifically nail down, and that is as it should be." Which leads back to Frost's assertion that poetry was "the one permissible way of saying one thing and meaning another" *and its hazards;* for it presupposes being "rightly taken," which cannot be counted on when a crucial part—or parts—of the rest of the meaning is missing. (As noted above, "Don't work, worry!" he told his Harvard students, only to be forced to add later: "I meant worry about ideas.")

"Rightly taken"—Frost "explains"—holds the key to his meaning. "They say the truth will make you free./ My truth will bind you slave to me." What does the couplet say? "You can talk by opposites and contraries with certain people because they know how to take you," he told a college audience. What if they do not know? What happens to the meaning? And what led Frost, within a month, to hint at the couplet's missing part by urging a different audience: "Having thoughts of your own is the only freedom"—*telling* them how to take his poems. One might hope that everyone knew by now. But more must be taken into account than his talking by opposites or omitting parts of implicit meanings. To understand a Frost poem calls for putting together "*all* the meanings that the reader can find"—those that are clearly stated, others plainly or even vaguely implied, still others only suggested—then drawing out of all that is found, intimations of the *poem's* intention. For the meaning itself rises out of the mixed totality which most surely includes the seeming contrarieties that themselves form much of the "message," as they well might do in the work of a poet for whom "everything written is as good as it is dramatic." To take rightly a poem by Frost is to open one's ears, eyes, and all other senses to the indefinably subtle ways with which he played his language in the hope that the "thought-felt thing"[29] he created would find continuing life in the life of his reader.

A thought-felt thing: "Poetry is the thought of the heart. I'm sure that's what Catullus meant by *mens animi*." Though "feeling is always ahead of thinking," "poetry must include the mind as well . . . The mind is dangerous . . . but the poet must use it." Use it with "fear and trembling"; use it with full concern for the limits of knowledge: "there is nothing anybody knows, however absolutely, that isn't more or less vitiated as a fact by what he doesn't know." Granted—yet thinking is a gift to treasure. "No one can know how glad I am to find/ On any sheet the least display of mind." No one can know how he felt by "gradually [coming] to see" that in his poem "Give All to Love," Emerson meant "Give all to meaning. The freedom is ours to insist on meaning." On meaning and more. On the freedom to "stay" as Emerson stayed throughout his life: like the hero of " 'Uriel,' the greatest Western poem yet," to look with "cherubic scorn," with "contempt for a person that had aged to the point where he had given up newness, betterness." One could—and should—remain immune from cherubic scorn without forgetting that few blessings, if any, come unmixed.

Those of science—to take the clearest case of Frost's concern with thought and its ceaseless searching—"It's the plunge of the mind, the spirit, into the material universe. It can't go too far or too deep for me." Lost in admiring science (179), he let nothing stop him, given his lay limitations, from learning enough to be able to follow some of its great explorers. Niels Bohr went out of his way to tell the host of a dinner discussion that the poet's questions were more incisive than those of any professor-scientist present. Frost not only was overjoyed by all that science had learned; he also mocked the fear of its possibly robbing existence of mystery or romance—at the same time, loathing the smallness of mind, the arrogance, the "cocksuredness," of many professional scientists he encountered. "It is not given to man to be omniscient." After so many years of remarkable searchings, they're

---

[29] One may take a Frost poem rightly and still not learn its meaning. Pritchard may be correct: Some of the poems may be "ultimately not quite understandable." Frost "likes at times to be misunderstood—in preference to being understood wrongly," Sidney Cox assured Newdick.**

still unable to do much more than ponder three great questions: where we came from, where we are going, what the steering principle of human living has been. And Darwinism, great as its founder was, seemed in its fixed determinist form to be marked by an all-explaining pretentiousness ruling out everything else—"passionate preference," Bergson's *élan vital,* Jamesian free will—that made of our lives far more than mechanical applications of ordained behavior. Evolution itself, moreover, confirmed the basic belief in progress, about which Frost held strong reservations: "The most exciting movement in nature is not progress, advance, but the expansion and contraction, the opening and shutting of the eyes, the hand, the heart, the mind."

If science, with its ceaseless testing of all it learns of the world outside, brings no light to the three great questions, what of philosophy, which is based on nothing beyond our mind's self-knowledge? "Logical systems [are] nonsense," Frost maintained, for "even the most impersonal processes [are] determined largely by influences controlling the logician but altogether excluded from the system and ignored." Thus in 1915; twelve years later: "I'm less and less for systems and system-building. . . . I'm afraid of too much structure. Some violence is always done to wisdom you build a philosophy out of." For example, the systematization of science which proceeds by assuming it possible to find all the answers when the most it can find are "pieces of wisdom," grains of truth. Much the same for politics, for here also the answers, if any exist, lie past the reach of the human mind—which didn't keep him from weighing the proffered solutions. "Communism, democracy, socialism . . . all complex problems of our time . . . have to be examined seriously." "A deeper understanding of socialism" was what he was wishing to "get" in Russia, he informed *Izvestia* in September 1962. Eight years before, after attending the World Congress of Writers in Brazil, he declared: "I'm a nationalist and I expect other people to be." Yet during World War II, he had called himself "a Lucretian abstainer from politics."

Frost's beliefs on politics, many of which I have quoted, appear to some as a model of contradictions. But to others his contrarieties result from observing the same phenomena from differing points of vantage, each of which leads to a different perception possessed of its own validity (98). Various pages set forth the poet's response to the Great Depression and the government's efforts to save the system by methods that some considered a threat to their freedom. Pages 79–83 above may be worth rereading, especially pages 81–83, which move past the New Deal programs and into the system itself. Where did the poet "really" stand at the time of ferment, and why (88)? More important: What was his stand on social justice after the thirties had passed into World-War conflict and emerged to confront the peace? His effort to set forth answers would have to appear in works such as the *Masques,* for the problems basic to politics were basic as well to religion.

Frost, with what seemed like a quip, refuted the charge that he contradicted himself: "I'm not confused; I'm only well-mixed." "I *am* the conflicts, I *contain* them." He was deep in his eighty-fifth year, having often in letters and talk and some of his best-known poems given the source of his contrarieties. For example, on the meaning of "Mending Wall," he denied that he had any allegory in mind other than

. . . the impossibility of drawing sharp lines and making exact distinctions between good and bad or between almost any two abstractions. There is no rigid separation between right and wrong.

The Emersonian idea of being pleased with your own inconsistency I never had. I always hoped that the thing would tie together some way. If I couldn't make it, that was up to God.

All truth is a dialogue.

All a man's art is a bursting unity of opposites.

Hegel taught a doctrine of opposites, but said nothing about everything's having more than one opposite.

But even where . . . opposing interests kill,/ They are to be thought of as opposing goods/ Oftener than as conflicting good and ill.

Everything in life contains a varying blend of order and riot, from the individual to nations.

We look for the line between good and evil and see it only imperfectly[,] for the reason that we are the line ourselves.

You'll have plenty to do just keeping honest—that is to say[,] reporting your position truthfully from phase to phase.

If "Frost appears to contradict himself, the explanation," says Tharpe, "is simple: he tried to tell the truth. In the everyday world, a thing appears at times to be true, and at times its opposite appears to be true." Though such contrariety was an ever-beckoning mystery and necessity, it was not beyond transcending. In 1926 he wrote to Sidney Cox:

> Having ideas that are neither pro nor con is the happy thing. Get up there high enough and the differences that make controversy become only the two legs of a body, the weight of which is on one in one period, on the other in the next. Democracy monarchy; puritanism paganism; form content; conservatism radicalism; systole diastole; rustic urbane; literary colloquial; work play. . . . I've wanted to find ways to transcend the strife-method. I have found some. . . . It is not so much anti-conflict as it is something beyond conflict—such as poetry and religion that is not just theological dialectic.

We are into a subject that needs a book in itself. What did he *really* believe? How far did his faith take him? We have bits and pieces from others, as well as his works to guide us. Do they offer enough? To avoid being wrongly taken, he took unusual care, at times, in his public use of "spirit" and "soul," equating the first with "mind" and the second with "decency" or "integrity." But "God" he used unglossed, in spite of or maybe because "The thought it suggests to the human mind," as Shelley had warned, "is susceptible of as many varieties as the human minds themselves."

> I despise religiosity. But I have no religious doubts. Not about God's existence, anyway.

> [God] is that which a man is sure cares, and will save him, no matter how many times or how completely he has failed.

> I never prayed except formally and politely with the Lord's prayer in public. I used to try to get up plausible theories about prayer like Emerson. My latest is that it might be an expression of the hope I have that my offering of verse on the altar may be acceptable in His sight Whoever He is.

[T]he self-belief, the love-belief, and the art-belief, are all closely related to the God-belief . . . the relationship we enter into with God to believe the future in—to believe the hereafter in.

My fear of God has settled down into a deep inward fear that my best offering may not prove acceptable in his sight. I'll tell you most about it in another world.

My approach to the New Testament is rather through Jerewsalem than through Rome and Canterbury.

Is that agnosticism? [he asked after reading from Sir John Davies' "Man" (163)]. [T]he rest of the poem would show you that it's very religious. What fills up the knowing is believing.[30]

The God Question. Religion is superstition or it is nothing. It is still there after philosophy has done its best. . . . [P]hilosophy is nothing but an attempt to rationalize religion.

[Religion] is a straining of the spirit forward to a wisdom beyond wisdom. . . . And the fear of God always has meant the fear that one's wisdom, one's own human wisdom is not quite acceptable in His sight.

Greatest of all attempts to say one thing in terms of another is the philosophical attempt to say matter in terms of spirit, or spirit in terms of matter, to make the final unity. That is the greatest attempt that ever failed. . . . But it is the height of poetry, the height of all thinking.

Why will the quidnuncs always be hoping for a salvation man will never have from anyone but God? . . . How can we be just in a world that needs mercy and merciful in a world that needs justice. . . . If only I get well, I'll go deeper into my life with you than I ever have before.

---

[30] I know my soul hath power to know all things,
  Yet she is blind and ignorant in all;
  I know I'm one of Nature's little kings,
  Yet to the least and vilest things am thrall.

  I know my life's a pain and but a span;
  I know my sense is mock'd in everything;
  And to conclude, I know myself a Man—
  Which is a proud and yet a wretched thing.

To these citations more could be added without implying the sort of coherence that several scholars and friends have sought to provide. I find the most rewarding pages in Cook's *The Dimensions of Robert Frost* (188–194) and the three *Centennial Essays,* especially Reichert's (415–426, I) and Hall's (325–339, III). Of the other works that may yet appear, one of especial import would result if the poet's friend Hyde Cox were to put in writing some of their talks on God. It might offer more of revelation than concealment, though the two in Frost seldom are found apart.

Take, for example, "something," the most significant single word in the poems. Forty years ago McGiffert, in three close pages filled with examples, speculated about its use and suggested answers. Two more books were still to come, also a verse concordance that lists 135 lines for "something," sixty-eight for the closely related "someone," and eight for "somehow." Of all these uses, sixty-five exemplify what McGiffert calls Frost's "refusal to define the indefinite [by] creating his special blend of fact and implication." It refers to the tangible or, as he notes, the intangible; more often to both. In "The Grindstone," the speaker is "all for leaving something to the whetter." Leaving what? In "Maple," the search for the secret of the girl's odd name was in vain, but "it proved there was something" rewarding in the search itself. This is not the "something" of line twenty-one in "The Code," which is followed by clear defining; nor the wife's partial attempt (in "The Death of the Hired Man") at explaining "home" as "Something you somehow haven't to deserve." Nor even the menacing implications in the "something" the waters "thought of doing . . . to the shore" in "Once by the Pacific." It is rather the ineffable-elusive at the close of "For Once, Then, Something," the intimation of knowledge beyond human grasp in "A Passing Glimpse," the unaccountable "someone" whom the killer had to obey in "The Draft Horse." It is present also behind the words of the "altogether remarkable poem" of Poirier's altogether remarkable study of "A Star in a Stone Boat," in which the speaker explains that he goes about "as though/Commanded in a dream" by something or someone that somehow "promises the prize/ Of the one world complete in any size/ That I am like to compass, fool or wise."

In a speech to the American Academy of Arts and Sciences on receiving its Emerson-Thoreau medal, Frost ascribed his religious beginnings to his Scotch Presbyterian mother. Reading Emerson made her a Unitarian, until, reading on into *Representative Men,* she became a Swedenborgian. "I was brought up in all three of these religions . . . [b]ut pretty much under the auspices of Emerson." What happened to Frost's beliefs from this point on has been studied by too many writers to call for more than a few remarks on his meeting with three other thinkers: William James, Henri Bergson, Henry Thoreau. From all he learned of their thoughts, he proceeded to draw what became his unique composite of principles, beliefs, predilections, meanings, and convictions. James and Thoreau reinforced his inherent drive to confront "the essential facts of life" unveiled and without any turning away from its hard realities. But James went on to provide him with vastly more—all he could need—from his first encounter in 1897 at Harvard with the *Principles of Psychology* on to *The Will to Believe,* to *Pragmatism,* and then to whatever else he may have decided to study.[31] That James was his greatest teacher, Frost was proud to proclaim, and critics and scholars have zealously shown the indebtedness. Readers have only to turn to Poirier, Brower, Squires, Cook, Pritchard, and the three *Centennial Essays* for extensive examples, some of which also discuss the relation of Frost to Emerson, Hawthorne, and others, including Bergson, whose crowning work, *L'Evolution créatrice,* he found in 1911 when it first appeared in English. There is more to life than intellect can explain. By *intuiting* experience from within, we learn that its essence is an *"élan vital":* a life-force that thrusts, pushes, flings itself on, and expands outward in a ceaseless struggle against the decline of nature in a reaching back toward the Source. Like James, Bergson interpreted human experience in both down-to-earth and metaphysical terms based on neither science nor Christianity but the individual's knowledge.

[31] James expanded Charles Peirce's pragmatic idea of meaning into an instrumental theory of the mind as serving our lives. The basis is sense experience: a continuous flowing consciousness, varied and multiple, which likes some feelings and dislikes others, rejecting, neglecting the rest. Hence the world of things is largely made of our *choosing.* And the same selectiveness operates with our ideas. We attend to and promote whatever gives our total nature the most satisfaction, which is to say that the nature of truth is pragmatic—for something to be true, it must "work." Reality is nothing but experience borne on the stream of consciousness which expands and contracts and interacts with other human streams. But man has always felt around and about him the presence of a different experience, sympathetic, akin to his own striving for good over evil. The true way of interpreting this psychological experience, which is also metaphysical, calls for believing that it comes from another consciousness: one like our own, with which we commune, which loves and wishes to help us. We may conceive of God as limited (the world being visibly imperfect and

By the time that Frost was arranging poems for his first book, *A Boy's Will,* he had come to a view of faith and God that prepared the pattern of all that he later learned through seeking, questing. He defined himself as "an Old Testament believer." He confessed having had revelations: "Call them 'nature's favors.' An owl that banked as it turned in its flight made me feel as if I'd been spoken to . . ." Although he publicly called it "a curse to be an agnostic," he feared that certain remarks he had made might be misconstrued as a skeptic's; hence, he "commissioned" an intimate friend to convince Thompson that he truly believed in God. The couplet-prayer "Forgive, O Lord, my little jokes on Thee . . . " would probably only seldom be wrongly taken, but what of his shrugging off sectarian theology, churchly trappings, even some venerated Christian tenets as "froth"? How many people would know that his kind of belief drove him to draw the line "between trivialities and profundities"? Yet there can be no doubt that at times he felt less than sure. Seven months after Elinor's death he suddenly turned on Newdick: "Where is this God I hear so much about? Where *is* he?" Thompson refers, ten years later, to Frost's having said "he [had] moved from skepticism to almost complete mystical faith and back again," but he does not quote a word to support his interpretation. Nor are we given a clue to the last of a trio of letters to Untermeyer, each with a verse beginning "To prayer." The first and second (July 7, September 26, 1921) seem easy to grasp, but the third (January 15, 1942)? "As your editor, Louis," I said, "may I read your comment?" He shook his head. I quoted the closing: " 'Oh, if religion's not to be my fate/ I must be spoken to and told/ Before too late!'—he says that he *had* been spoken to but adds 'I believe I am safely secular till the last go down.' No comment at all, Louis, not even on 'till'?" He smiled, handing me the next manuscript page. "This one's about my sixth revised—transgression."

full of real evils) and ourselves as striving by His side together to counteract these evils. There are obstacles: man's unwillingness to work with God, also the factor of chance (Peirce's "tychistic" view: the unpredictable element that may work against efforts of God-and-man). Existence is therefore a gamble, with enormous stakes and tremendous risks, but well worth taking. When no evidence is at hand or obtainable, it is permissible to believe; and a positive belief is more consonant with the health of mind and soul than a distrustful one. "God," James concluded in *The Varieties of Religious Experience,* "is the natural appellation . . . for the supreme reality, so I will call this higher part of the universe by the name of God. We and God have business with each other; and in opening ourselves to his influence our deepest destiny is fulfilled."

Frost defined a religious person as one who "can say he aspires to a full consent"—"All I do in [*A Masque of Mercy*] is reach for something." Aspiration: strong desire. "To believe is to wish to believe," wrote Unamuno, "to believe in God is, before and above all, a wish that there may be a God." More than once in intimate moments, Frost dwelt upon *Mark,* Chapter 9:23–24: "Lord, I believe; help thou mine unbelief." One thinks of his credo: Belief is "best when rapt, above paying its respects to anybody's doubts whatsoever." Doubts were as much a part of his trial by existence as his faith, aspiration, and all-too-human moods. "Play me some great music, something you think is great," he asked Hyde Cox in the course of a visit. His host played part of a Handel *Messiah* recording. As it closed with the aria, "I know that my redeemer liveth," Frost listened intently. "Hyde, do you know your redeemer liveth?" he asked half-teasing. "Sometimes I think so," came the reply, "do you?" "Oh, I don't know," Frost answered, "but I do know there's such a thing as redemption." In the autumn after his trip to Russia, at a party in Reichert's Ripton home, he asked out of nowhere, "Victor, what do you think are the chances of life after death?" "I teased Frost by reminding him that when you ask a Jew a question, you don't get an answer; just another question: 'What do you think?' I asked. He became deeply silent. Then he said to me, 'With so many ladders going up everywhere, there must be something for them to lean against.' " His words, echoing James ("The mutable in experience must be founded on immutability"), cannot be heard apart from all he had sought in his life of seeking. So Marice Brown—like others close to the poetry—sees Frost as "a spiritual explorer . . . not only driven to understand the *how* of God's ways but . . . also deeply concerned with the *why*. . . . The thread that runs through it all is the quest itself."

In his *Letter* of 1935 to *The Amherst Student* the ostensible subject was the special badness of the present age, but the heart of his message was "form." The "evident design" in the situation facing people "may vary a little" from age to age. Its background has always been "in hugeness and confusion shading away from where we stand into black and utter chaos." But . . .

There is at least so much of good in the world that it admits of form and the making of form. And not only admits of it, but calls for it. We people are thrust forward out of the suggestions of form in the rolling clouds of nature. . . . When in doubt there is always form for us to go on with. Anyone who has achieved the least form to be sure of it, is lost to the larger excruciations. I think it must stroke faith the right way. The artist, the poet, might be expected to be the most aware of such assurance. But it is really everybody's sanity to feel it and live by it.

For the maker he was, ever "seeking, questing," much that he learned became the stuff of poems and of other writings and talks that are virtual poems-in-prose. "Any little form [he was able to] assert upon the hugeness and confusion [had] to be considered for how much more it [was] than nothing, [also] for how much less it [was] than everything."

The thoughts foretoken "The Figure a Poem Makes," the preface to his 1939 *Collected Poems* (280f.). No words by Frost on "the poem" are so widely quoted: "It begins in delight, it inclines to the impulse, it assumes direction with the first line laid down, it runs a course of lucky events, and ends in a clarification of life—not necessarily a great clarification of life, such as sects and cults are founded on, but in a momentary stay against confusion." The last five words lead us to James (". . . if a reader can lapse back into his immediate sensible life at this very moment, he will find it to be a big blooming buzzing confusion") and to Frost's paraphrase ("The present/ Is too much for the senses,/ Too crowding, too confusing—/ Too present to imagine"/). Besides this assault on the senses, "There is always tragedy. That is what life is. . . . [N]othing," however "is so composing to the spirit as composition. We make a little order where we are. . . . We make a little form and we gain composure." "Each poem clarifies something. But then you've got to do it again" "because confusions keep coming fresh." Will there be no end? Can "what seems to us confusion" be "but the form of forms," as Job supposes in *A Masque of Reason?* "Directive" offers a promise: "Drink and be whole again beyond confusion." Moreover, "the good of the world" not only admits the making of form but demands it—"it is really everybody's sanity to feel and live by it." This is the human lot: to be called to achieve some form, some order out of the hugeness, buoyed upon faith in assurances that may bring acceptance.

No one can say what acceptance meant to the poet without bearing in mind certain "givens" of existence as he saw them:

(1) The human mind is limited; we do no more than we can, draw-

ing on every type of thought we are able to summon, from pure intuition and "passionate preference" to the fine complexities of reason. *All* are fallible: At one extreme, "The White-Tailed Hornet's" thought-by-instinct (aimed at a fly, "he swooped, he pounced, he struck;/ But what he . . . had was just a nailhead./ He struck a second time. And other nailhead"); at the other extreme, science, which by virtue of testing itself, "goes self-superseding on."

(2) Living entails freedom of choice with responsibility. We can choose to will to believe, to believe things into existence; we can even consider ourselves to be working with God to perfect the universe. At the end, we shall have to account for our lives, hoping that all we have done and all we have been will be deemed acceptable.

(3) Much that we do must be done solely by faith in the outcome: We must willingly dare, take risks, gamble our lives. ("You're always believing ahead of your evidence"—Frost; "It is only by risking our persons from one hour to another that we live at all"—James.) Fear, the obbligato of courage and daring, "is the great thing to exorcise; but it isn't reason that will do it" (James). Frost experienced fears too many and varied to name, from imagined slights to crucial doubt that his offering would prove "acceptable in the sight of God."

(4) "You are not safe anywhere unless you are at home with metaphor," hence the need to be educated by poetry; for "all there is of thinking is the metaphor whose manage we are best taught in poetry." "All metaphor," however, "breaks down somewhere." Even the greatest "of all attempts . . . to say matter in terms of spirit, or spirit in terms of matter [has] failed." And yet we must keep on striving to perceive in disorder new and profound unities. For Wordsworth, as *The Seamless Web* reminded readers, the necessity for such perceiving flows out of the depths of the organism. It is, as he wrote, "the great spring of the activity of our minds, and their chief feeder. From this principle the direction of the sexual appetite, and all the passions connected with it, take their origin; it is the life of our ordinary conversation. . . ." Wordsworth and Frost, as Poirier notes in a recent essay, "are nearly identical in their theories of poetic 'strain' and of the pleasures it affords."

(5) We learn not only through poetry: The study of nature at times yields knowledge too precious to miss. For Emerson, the "moral law lies at the center and radiates to the circumference." No such belief is found in Frost, although, as he wrote: "We throw our arms wide with

a gesture of religion to the universe." In his attitude toward nature, Frost resembled Thoreau,[32] who wished "to front the essential facts . . . [to] learn what [they] had to teach," for with all its moments of bleakness, a "true account of the actual is the rarest poetry." Frost never worshiped nature, yet some of his finest poems are prayers, petitions, "instructions to the season." One need only leaf through his books—from the early "Rose Pogonias," "A Prayer in Spring," "October," and on. The worlds of nature, which he never ceased to explore from both afar and up close, stirred him into reachings beyond the "reports" of the senses. "I'm always saying something that's just the edge of something more," he answered a man who called his work "a vast symbolic structure." More than that he avoided saying, aware that his brightest and darkest pages and those of neither extreme had been born in response to "somethings" seen or heard or imagined in the natural world.

(6) When questioned on some of his work in which sensitivity to nature's beauty is allied with poignant awareness of the suffering within the natural order, he replied, "Where is there any benevolence of purpose?" His words apply no less to certain poems on the human condition—"A Servant to Servants," "Out, Out—," "The Housekeeper," "Home Burial," and similar works that inspired Trilling to refer to Frost as "a poet who terrifies" (105). None that were known to Trilling had gone so far as "The Draft Horse." Written in 1920, it remained unpublished till 1962:

> With a lantern that wouldn't burn
> In too frail a buggy we drove
> Behind too heavy a horse
> Through a pitch-dark limitless grove.
>
> And a man came out of the trees
> And took our horse by the head
> And reaching back to his ribs
> Deliberately stabbed him dead.
>
> The ponderous beast went down
> With a crack of a broken shaft.
> And the night drew through the trees
> In one long invidious draft.

[32] Frost: "A poet must lean hard on facts, so hard, sometimes, that they hurt."

The most unquestioning pair
That ever accepted fate
And the least disposed to ascribe
Any more than we had to to hate.

We assumed that the man himself
Or someone he had to obey
Wanted us to get down
And walk the rest of the way.

No gloss can suffice. The poem reflects the "tychistic" belief that James shared with Peirce: the objective reality of pure chance as a central factor in all earthly existence (294fn.). The words speak to each other; they speak to the poem as a whole. Not a syllable about purpose—"a lantern that wouldn't burn," a grove "pitch-dark" and "limitless," and yet one word ("invidious") moves the poem out of the world of pure chance.

(7) One is tempted to read the poem as more than "A true account of the actual": as justice-mercy on a cosmic scale, unlike the equivalent in human affairs where at least in theory "solutions" at times are conceivable. Frost's most extensive effort at "explaining" justice-mercy was made in the *Masques*—with no greater success in resolving than explaining usually achieves. Could the conflict be traced to the nature of people, to the stuff we are made of, as the conflict of a different sort inheres in the metal chunk of "From Iron"—"Nature within her inmost self divides/ To trouble men with having to take sides"? Justice-versus-mercy troubled him till the end. Did he still believe it to be "a natural conflict built into the moral universe"?

(8) As natural, perhaps, as his need to be with people?—a need common to most mortals, but with Frost—like almost everything else—found in a heightened state. From infancy till Elinor's death, he had never lived by himself and then, with the help of the Morrisons, he was much of the time surrounded by people, and alone only by choice. In 1943 he invited Van Dore to "come up and help with the haying . . . and at least we can talk" (75). Not long after his visit, Wade was asked to "stay permanently" as his helper and companion. Van Dore had become deeply aware of the poet's "need never to be alone." He had often escaped from solitude into Wade's presence, and when not talking together—as they did each night till morning—he

was always companioned by his dog. His loneliness expressed itself in various ways. Obviously: when he wrote of "the fear that men won't understand us and we shall be cut off from them." Indirectly: in his poetry's most common situation—a man, or a man and wife, alone in a small isolated house—or in one of his "favorite" figures—a house abandoned, with ruin as an image of heroism "against hopeless odds."

(9) Hopeless odds—humanity's impotence within the world that engulfs him. In his Norton lecture ("Does Wisdom Signify?"), referring to problems of the universe, he declared, wagging a lively finger, "The surest thing you know is that we'll never understand. And we'll never lack resources to stay here, to hang onto the globe." "At Woodward's Gardens," a poem that was soon to appear, bore the subtitle "Resourcefulness Is More Than Understanding." Twenty-three years later the line disappeared. Why? So far as I know, he was never asked nor ever explained. It would seem, however—whatever "resourcefulness" signified—that his passion to understand had regained control. Not that any admitted change had driven him closer to "knowing." Nothing he said after dropping the line implied any notably new understanding. In that very year (1959) he said that his forthcoming book would be named *The Great Misgiving*. The final title, *In the Clearing,* failed to reflect the book as a whole (159ff.). Moreover, the poems defined by Joseph Kau as "creational" showed that Frost "metaphysically was never 'in the clearing.' " Frost continues to wrestle with faith and fear; he wills to believe. He places "The Draft Horse" after his "Cluster of Faith" section and ends the book with the group that he calls "Quandary." It was three months after *In the Clearing* appeared that he said he had always hoped that all the contradictions and inconsistences of life on earth would "tie together some way. If [he] couldn't make it," the problem "was up to God."

In 1953 Jarrell opened the eyes of a good many critics and readers to the greatness and profundities of Frost, "exclaiming" not only over "some unimportantly delightful and marvellously characteristic poems" but also selecting others that reveal him "for what he really is." Jarrell focused on poems that the modernist elite had missed, works "unique in the poetry of our century and perhaps in any poetry." The essay led to Trilling's birthday speech that likened Frost to Sophocles, the poet "his people loved most . . . chiefly because . . .

they felt, perhaps, that only a poet who could make plain the terrible things of human life could possibly give them comfort" (105). In spite of a controversial response, the ascription changed the course of critical views, the dark overshadowed the light, but not entirely and not for long. Within a year G.W. Nitchie published his "case against" Frost, which was followed by numerously varied studies, notably in the three *Centennial Essays.*

In the first volume, while Robert Rechnitz stressed "The Tragic Vision of Frost," Marjorie Cook, in Volume Two, maintained that the poet's view of existence is "ultimately affirmative and therefore comic." Neither term is adequate as a characterization of Frost, for the sense of "no harm being done" (epitomized by Miranda's speech in *The Tempest*) is the surely decisive sense of the comic that sets it apart from the tragic: that problems cannot always be solved; that even if evil is somehow destroyed, much good may be wasted also. The "ultimately affirmative" Frostian view may best be defined as "acceptance." But what kind of acceptance—gleeful, willing, reluctant, resigned? Could a gathering of some relevant lines point toward an answer?**

Heaven gives its glimpses to those
Not in position to look too close.

The fact is the sweetest dream that labor knows.

It had to seem unmeaning to have meaning.

The only certain freedom's in departure.

Earth's the right place for love:
I don't know where it's likely to go better.

Anything more than the truth would have seemed too weak . . .

Keep off each other and keep each other off.

And of course there must be something wrong
In wanting to silence any song.

And tell me truly, men of earth,
If all the soul-and-body scars
Were not too much to pay for birth.

The trial by market everything must come to.

But even where . . . opposing interests kill,
They are to be thought of as opposing goods
Oftener than as conflicting good and ill . . .

Let the night be too dark for me to see
Into the future. Let what will be, be.

The way of understanding is partly mirth.

. . . the utmost reward
Of daring should be still to dare.

Nothing gold can stay.

But power of blood itself releases blood. . . .
Oh, blood will out. It cannot be contained.

We dance round in a ring and suppose,
But the Secret sits in the middle and knows.

[W]hat seems to us confusion
Is not confusion, but the form of forms. . . .

I have it in me so much nearer home
To scare myself with my own desert places.

And forthwith found salvation in surrender.

We may take something like a star
To stay our minds on and be staid.

Standing alone, some of the lines seem to be pointing less toward affirmant light than to darkness. But within their poems they attest to knowledge-sought in probing the actual; and whether or not answers were found, naming itself asserts a truce that implies acceptance. Only two of the passages come from the *Masques,* though their stage-characters, as in all such works, are partly the writer. All the poems, however, large and small, mirror the poet's seeking-questing for momentary stays in a world confused with beauty and bleakness. It is ours to choose to live with; the decision to stay bespeaks acceptance of all that awaits in a huge and ruthless place we shall never quite understand any more than what we are. To explore these unintelligibles is also to learn "There are roughly zones whose laws must be obeyed" despite our thirst for the limitless.

What Frost valued, of course, were the ever-recurrent occasions to discover something or make "a new start." Nor would it matter when searching brought back only pieces, glimmerings: "If you see the little truths with sharp delight or pain, you will not be anxiously straining to do final justice to the whole of reality." And if wisdom consists of enduring the world and our limits just as they are, our ability to know the whole of reality demands our trust in ultimates out of our reach. It also insists on less-than-final statements, partial insights which can seem to deny others. Frost so often spoke in terms of "as if" that its bearing on contrarieties in some of his poems may be lost on readers. Radcliffe Squires remarks in this regard on Melville's complaint: It was unfair to hold a poet answerable forever for what was true for him only in the moment. In every case, the less-than-final statements cannot be said to arise from Frost's refusal to take a stand, as his 1937 letter to Sidney Cox makes clear.** Moreover, A Masque of Mercy (he called it his "Whole Bible") bewilders—by intention?—as forthright words and parody weave in and out, not to mention the contradictory words on courage. The effect of the lines approaching the end seems more than anything else to encourage uncertainty—which should not surprise us in Frost, an exemplar of Negative Capability, that Keats said Shakespeare "so enormously" possessed: "when a man is capable of being in uncertainties, mysteries, doubts, without any irritable reaching after fact and reason."

The Masque fails to reach a settled conclusion, yet changes occur, among them Jonah's conversion, which leads back thirty-four years to "the myth of 'The Trial by Existence.' In both poems," says Nitchie (who elsewhere censures Frost for the virtue lauded by Keats), "what really matters is . . . the joyfully, arduously willed acceptance of a world we never made." "A Lesson for Today," printed a year before the Masque, would have served him better. In 160 rambling lines on the world and its ages, Frost acknowledges much that might cause despair—"Earth's a hard place in which to save the soul"; "The groundwork of all faith is human woe"; the "belittled human race [is] either nothing or a God's regret"; ourselves, "the total race,/ The earth itself is liable to the fate/ Of meaninglessly being broken off." In view of which "No choice is left the poet . . . / But how to take the curse, tragic or comic." Acceptance demands both: He replies with words for his gravestone—"I had a lover's quarrel with the world."

But acceptance asks for more than a private epitaph. And of all his writings, one lyric alone dares hold up a mirror to the reader's eyes. "Neither Out Far nor In Deep" moves calmly in simple words. But who are these people? Where is this shore, this sea? What are the watchers doing? Why? And the poem—what can it be but the emblem of the human condition: mystified, seeking-questing:

> The people along the sand
> All turn and look one way.
> They turn their back on the land.
> They look at the sea all day.
>
> As long as it takes to pass
> A ship keeps raising its hull;
> The wetter ground like glass
> Reflects a standing gull.
>
> The land may vary more;
> But wherever the truth may be—
> The water comes ashore,
> And the people look at the sea.
>
> They cannot look out far.
> They cannot look in deep.
> But when was that ever a bar
> To any watch they keep?

In the year after the poet's death, Jarrell reviewed the *Selected Letters*. These are his words toward the close:

> In the end he talked as naturally as he breathed: for as long as you got to listen you were sharing Frost's life. What came to you in that deep grainy voice—a voice that made other voices sound thin or abstract—was half a natural physiological process and half a work of art; it was as if Frost dreamed aloud and the dream were a poem. Was what he said right or wrong? It seemed irrelevant. In the same way, whether Frost himself was good or bad seemed irrelevant—he was there and you accepted him.

The world was also there, and whether Frost thought his trial by existence worth the grief and scars, he had made the choice, had accepted the risks. In the end did it matter that the Secret could not be found, the Truth that would burn the eyes out? * * "All I would keep for my-self," he had said, "is the freedom of my material—the condition of body and mind now and then to summons aptly from the vast chaos of all I have lived through." What of the words others were taking as Truth—the Incarnation, "half guessed, half understood" (Eliot) or "that the final belief/ Must be in a fiction" (Stevens)? Earth's con-ditions and human nature scorned any more-than-human answer, pointing at best to intimations, hidden glimpses, to the momentary fulfillments of the will to know in a quest that itself was reward enough for one who had long accepted himself and the world.

CHRONOLOGY

1874 Born Robert Lee Frost, San Francisco, March 26, to William
Prescott Frost, Jr., and Isabelle Moodie Frost.

1885 Father dies (May); moves with mother and sister Jeanie (born 1876)
to Lawrence, Massachusetts.

1890 Begins to write verse; publishes first poem ("La Noche Triste") in
Lawrence *High School Bulletin.*

1892 Graduates from high school; Elinor Miriam White his co-
valedictorian. Studies for some months at Dartmouth College; continues a series of miscellaneous jobs (cobbler, hired hand, light-
trimmer, gate tender, bobbin-boy, etc.). Robert and Elinor conduct
their secret marriage ceremony (summer).

1894 His first poem purchased by *The* (New York) *Independent* ("My
Butterfly: An Elegy"). Offers a privately printed booklet of five
poems, *Twilight,* to Elinor. Rejected, he runs away to New York,
Virginia, and the Dismal Swamp.

1895 Teaches in his mother's private school (spring). Marries Elinor,
December 19, in Lawrence. They move into an apartment with his
mother and sister.

1896 First child, Elliott, a son, born (September). Frost begins his life-
long "botanizing."

1897 Enters Harvard College as a special student (September).

1899 Leaves Harvard (March). Daughter Lesley born (April). Poultry-farming, Powder Hill House.

1900 Elliott dies (July). Frosts move to Derry, New Hampshire, farm bought for Robert by his paternal grandfather (October). Mother dies (November).

1901 Grandfather dies (July), willing to Frost the Derry farm and an annuity.

1902 Third child, Carol, a son, born (May).

1903 Begins to publish prose in poultry journals. Frost family rents a New York apartment for one month (March). Fourth child, Irma, born (June).

1905 Fifth child, Marjorie, born (March). First of his annual trips north to relieve hay fever.

1906 Publishes several poems (including "The Trial by Existence," October). Teaches part time at Pinkerton Academy.

1907 Ill with pneumonia (March). Sixth child, Elinor Bettina, born (June); dies within two days.

1909 Frost family moves from Derry farm to apartment in Derry Village (September).

1911 Quits teaching at Pinkerton Academy (June). Moves with family to Plymouth, New Hampshire; teaches at its State Normal School (September).

1912 Frost family sails to England (September); moves to Beaconsfield. His first book accepted by London publisher (David Nutt, October).

1913 *A Boy's Will* (April). Ezra Pound reviews it for *Poetry*.

1914 Frosts move to London, then Gloucestershire (May). *North of Boston* (May).

1915 Return to U.S.A. (February); Holt publishes *North of Boston* (February), then *A Boy's Will* (April). Frost plans to buy Franconia, New Hampshire, farm. Phi Beta Kappa Poet, Tufts College (May).

1916 Beginning of literary fame. Phi Beta Kappa poet, Harvard College (June). *Mountain Interval* (November).

1917 Frost teaches at Amherst College (January, until May 1920).

1920 Frosts move from Franconia to South Shaftsbury, Vermont (October).

1921 Frost speaks at the Bread Loaf School of English, Ripton, Vermont (July). Frosts move to Ann Arbor, where Robert serves as "Poet in Residence" at the University (September).

1922 Continues at the University, but as "Fellow in Creative Arts."

1923 *Selected Poems* (March). Frost returns to Amherst College (November), to continue there until 1925. *New Hampshire* (November; awarded Pulitzer Prize, May 1924).

1925 Appointed a Fellow in Letters, University of Michigan (September).

1926 Returns to Amherst College as Professor of English (remaining there until 1938).

1928 Visits France and England with Elinor and Marjorie (August). *West-Running Brook* (November).

1929 Jeanie Florence Frost dies (September) after 9 years in a Maine mental institution.

1930 *Collected Poems* (November; awarded Pulitzer Prize, June 1931).

1932 Reads Phi Beta Kappa poem "Build Soil" at Columbia University (May).

1934 Daughter Marjorie dies of child-bed fever (May), having married Willard Fraser in June 1933. Robert and Elinor visit Key West, upon their physician's orders.

1936 Frost appointed Charles Eliot Norton Professor of Poetry, Harvard College (spring). *A Further Range* (May; awarded Pulitzer Prize, May 1937).

1937 Elinor undergoes surgery for breast cancer (October). She and Robert winter in Gainesville, Florida.

1938 She dies of heart attack (March 20). Robert moves to a Boston apartment (September).

1939 *Collected Poems* (February). Appointed Ralph Waldo Emerson Fellow in Poetry, Harvard University (May). Summers in his newly purchased "Homer Noble Farm" in Ripton, Vermont. Appoints Lawrance Thompson his official biographer (July).

1940 Hemorrhoidectomy (January). Buys acreage in South Miami (May). Carol Frost commits suicide (October, in Vermont).

1941 Buys year-round house, 35 Brewster Street, Cambridge, Massachusetts (spring).

1942 Builds "Pencil Pines," winter home, South Miami (February). *A Witness Tree* (April; awarded Pulitzer Prize, May 1943).

1943 Appointed Ticknor Fellow in the Humanities, Dartmouth College (autumn, remaining affiliated with Dartmouth until 1949).

1945 *A Masque of Reason* (March).

1947 *Steeple Bush* (May). *A Masque of Mercy* (September).

1949 *Complete Poems 1949* (April). Life appointment as Simpson Lecturer in Literature, Amherst College (October).

1954 80th birthday dinner. Serves as delegate to World Congress of Writers (Brazil, August).

1957 Good-will mission to Britain and Ireland upon request of the U.S. Department of State (May-June).

1958 Consultant in Poetry, Library of Congress (appointed in May).

1959 85th birthday: political interviews, evening dinner.

1961   Reads poem at Kennedy Inauguration. Visits Israel, Greece (March).

1962   *In the Clearing* (March). 88th birthday dinner. Good-will mission to the U.S.S.R. upon President Kennedy's request (August–September). Final series of public appearances. Enters Boston hospital (December).

1963   Dies January 29. Ashes interred in Old Bennington, Vermont, cemetery (June). *Letters of Robert Frost to Louis Untermeyer* (August).

1964   *Selected Letters of Robert Frost* (July).

1966   *Robert Frost: The Early Years, 1874–1915; Interviews with Robert Frost; Selected Prose of Robert Frost.*

1970   *Robert Frost: The Years of Triumph, 1915–1938.*

1972   *Family Letters of Robert and Elinor Frost.*

1974   *Robert Frost: A Living Voice; Robert Frost: A Pictorial Chronicle; Frost: Centennial Essays, I.*

1976   *Robert Frost: The Later Years, 1938–1963; Newdick's Season of Frost; Frost: Centennial Essays, II.*

1977   *Robert Frost: The Work of Knowing.*

1978   *Frost: Centennial Essays, III.*

REFERENCE NOTES

The numbers at the far left refer to pages in *Robert Frost Himself* and the abbreviations in italics to the books from which citations have been made. These citations appear in the text either within quotation marks or in passages marked with a double asterisk(**).

Ordin.   Sidney Cox, *Robert Frost: Original "Ordinary" Man,* Holt, 1929

Swinger   Sidney Cox, *A Swinger of Birches: A Portrait of Robert Frost,* New York University Press, 1957

Dimens.   Reginald L. Cook, *The Dimensions of Robert Frost*, Rinehart, 1958

Sergeant   Elizabeth Shepley Sergeant, *Robert Frost: The Trial by Existence,* Holt, Rinehart and Winston, 1960

Unterm.   *The Letters of Robert Frost to Louis Untermeyer,* Holt, Rinehart and Winston, 1963

Brower   Reuben A. Brower, *The Poetry of Robert Frost: Constellations of Intention,* Oxford, 1963

Bartl.   Margaret Bartlett Anderson, *Robert Frost and John Bartlett: The Record of a Friendship*, Holt, Rinehart and Winston, 1963

Sel. Lett. *Selected Letters of Robert Frost,* Lawrance Thompson, ed., Holt, Rinehart and Winston, 1964

Early Y.   Lawrance Thompson, *Robert Frost: The Early Years, 1874-1915,* Holt, Rinehart and Winston, 1966

Interv.   *Interviews with Robert Frost,* Edward Connery Lathem, ed., Holt, Rinehart and Winston, 1966

Prose   *Selected Prose of Robert Frost,* Hyde Cox and Edward Connery Lathem, eds., Holt, Rinehart and Winston, 1966

Poetry   *The Poetry of Robert Frost,* Edward Connery Lathem, ed., Holt, Rinehart and Winston, 1969

Triumph   Lawrance Thompson, *Robert Frost: The Years of Triumph, 1915-1938,* Holt, Rinehart and Winston, 1970

Fam. Lett. *Family Letters of Robert and Elinor Frost,* Arnold Grade, ed., State University of New York Press, 1972

P&P   Robert Frost/Poetry and Prose, Edward Connery Lathem and
           Lawrance Thompson, eds., Holt, Rinehart and Winston, 1972
Living   Reginald [L.] Cook, Robert Frost: A Living Voice, University of
           Massachusetts Press, 1974
Pictor.   Kathleen Morrison, Robert Frost: A Pictorial Chronicle, Holt,
           Rinehart and Winston, 1974
Centen.   Frost: Centennial Essays—Centen.-I, 1974; Committee on the
           Frost Centennial of the University of Southern Mississippi;
           Centen.-II, Jac Tharpe, ed., 1976; Centen.-III, Jac Tharpe, ed.,
           1978; all published by the University of Mississippi
Newdick   Newdick's Season of Frost: An Interrupted Biography of Robert Frost,
           William A. Sutton, ed., State University of New York Press,
           1976
Later Y.   Lawrance Thompson and R.H. Winnick, Robert Frost: The Later
           Years, 1938-1963, Holt, Rinehart and Winston, 1976
Poirier   Richard Poirier, Robert Frost: The Work of Knowing, Oxford, 1977
Jott.   Prose Jottings of Robert Frost, Edward Connery Lathem and Hyde
           Cox, eds., Northeast-Kingdom, Vermont, 1982
Pritch.   William H. Pritchard, Frost: A Literary Life Reconsidered, Oxford,
           1984
Notes   Lawrance R. Thompson, "Notes on Robert Frost: 1939-1967,"
           Manuscript Department, University of Virginia Library,
           Charlottesville

page
xi   When one writes about Frost": Randall Jarrell, "To the Laodiceans,"
      Poetry and the Age, Vintage, 1955
      "in talking": Living, 115
      "allows us to hear Frost's conversation": Philip Booth, May 15, 1958
xii   "I must say some things over and over": Sel. Lett., 152
   4 "national bard" etc.: Later Y., 346-48. See, for example, eulogy by Louis
      M. Lyons of Harvard broadcast on the night of Frost's death over
      WGBH (Boston) and printed by the Spiral Press for the Memorial
      Services at Amherst, Feb. 17, 1963.
   5 **: The first defense, by Nathaniel P. Willis, appeared Oct. 20, 1849; the
      second, by John R. Thomson (which accepted several Griswold
      canards), in the Southern Literary Messenger, November; the
      "irrefutable answer," in Graham's Magazine, March 1850
      "the speculations and activities": Unterm., Foreword
   8 "he is quoted as 'once having said'": 1922 edition, Harcourt Brace. The
      1921 edition presented eight poems; the 1925 edition, fifteen.
  11 "First about Thoreau": Sel. Lett., 278
  18 "talked and laughed": "The Golden Room," by W. W. Gibson, Atlantic,
      Feb. 1926

19 "Fine old boy": typical of Frost's penchant for using identical or similar words on a subject. See *Sel. Lett.,* 107-8.

22 "You won't need": Van Dore expressed surprise that Frost hadn't said of his trip to England, "Let's go find some little cottage where I can write this novel."

"the similarities of circumstance": *Poirier,* 162

28 "Marj is in hospital in Baltimore": *Sel. Lett.,* 359

29 "The police picked her up": *Unterm.,* 102-3. Jeanie died in 1929.

30 "I am so deeply smitten through my helm": *Unterm.,* 220 (Feb. 23, 1932)

31 "been overdoing too much": *Sel. Lett.,* 395, to Richard Thornton

32 "We are going through the valley": *Unterm.,* 240

"The noblest of us all is dead": *Unterm.,* 241-42. "Cadmus and Harmonia were changed into 'two bright and aged snakes,' transported to the hills, '...and there/Placed safely in chang'd forms, the pair/Wholly forgot their first sad life...'"—Untermeyer's note quoting Arnold's "Empedocles on Etna," lines 427-60, published separately (1853, 1854, 1857) as "Cadmus and Harmonia." Frost: "My favorite poem long before I knew what it was going to mean to us."—*Unterm.,* 240

"I long to die myself": *Sel. Lett.,* 412

"A crown dependency": *Sergeant,* 337

33 "range of temperature is between 70 and 80": *Unterm.,* 250-51

"Elinor is not fit for anything": *Unterm.,* 260

35 "Robert is awake so late at night": *Triumph,* 462

36 "I'm your bonfire that you started": *Unterm.,* 292

"I tried two or three times yesterday": *Unterm.,* 295-96

37 "Be easy on me for what I did too emotionally": *Unterm.,* 296

"I am gaining strength quite rapidly now": Dartmouth College Library (to Mrs. Richard Thornton)

"Everything went smoothly": *Sel. Lett.,* 453-54

41 "of deprivation": *Poirier,* 152, 147

42 "It remains to summarize": *New Republic,* Dec. 3, 1930

45 "'Truth? A pebble of quartz?'": *Poetry,* 225

46 "The end of May, for Phi Beta Kappa. 'Build Soil'": *Poetry,* 316

49 **: League of Professional Groups for Foster and Ford, with subsection:

"League for Professional Writers," which included artists

53 "On Taking Poetry": *Living,* 75

"To the Laodiceans": *op. cit.*

54 "Provide, Provide": (facing page) *Poetry,* 307

57 **: See *Letters of Archibald MacLeish,* R. H. Winnick, ed., Houghton Mifflin, 1983, p. 275

"You've just been immortalized": Wallace Stevens, *Ideas of Order,* Alcestis Press, 1935; Haniel Long, *Pittsburgh Memoranda,* Santa Fe,

1935; *The New Caravan,* Alfred Kreymborg, Lewis Mumford, Paul
Rosenfeld, eds., Norton, 1936, pp. 72-7

58 "'Seriously though,' said Mr. Frost": *Baltimore Sun,* Feb. 26, 1936, which
includes "To a Thinker," *Interv.,* 84

"If [Frost] implies that Mr. Roosevelt's thought": *Interv.,* 86

59 "I own I never really warmed/To the reformer": *Poetry,* 326

"expressive much more of the minor": Arvin, June 1936; Gregory and
Blackmur, June 23, 1936; Fitts, *New England Quarterly,* Sept. 1936

60 "Some of [Frost's] philosophical": *Books,* June 6, 1936; Humphries,
Aug. 11, 1936; Root, Oct. 1936

"Abuse from The New Masses": *Triumph,* 696, n.34, Feb. 12, 1938

"begged [him not to include]": *Sergeant,* 320

"as classicist in literature, royalist": *For Lancelot Andrewes,* Doubleday,
1929, p. vii

61 **: *After Strange Gods,* Faber, 1934

"We have it now. For socialism is": *Poetry,* 318

62 "Which, for no sordid self-aggrandizement": *Poetry,* 319

"Build soil. Turn the farm in upon itself": *Poetry,* 323

"The thought I have, and my first impulse is": *Poetry,* 323-24

64 "rude, lame, unmade": "Considerations by the Way," *Conduct of Life*

"I myself see clearly enough": Whitman, *The Poetry and Prose,* Simon
and Schuster, 1949, pp. 821-22

65 "Keep off each other and keep each other off": *Poetry,* 324

"We have no way of knowing that this age": *Prose,* 105-6

"That is the same old question": reported by Horace Traubel; see Stanley
Burnshaw, *In the Terrified Radiance,* Braziller, 1972, pp. 108, 148n

"No I'm not...I'm more radical": *Dimens.,* 39

66 "On Taking from the Top to Broaden the Base": *Poetry,* 298

"So that the poor won't have to steal by stealth": *Poetry,* 363

"Count me as in favor of reforming": *Unterm.,* 127

"It is not the business of the poet to cry for reform": *Silver and Gold,*
University of Colorado student newspaper, Aug. 1, 1933

"Sarah Cleghorn...[S]aint, poet — *and* reformer": *Three-Score: The Autobiography of Sarah N. Cleghorn,* Random House, 1936

"Pity me for not knowing what would set everything right": *Unterm.,* 86

"The national mood is humanitarian. Nobly so": *Unterm.,* 285

"Forgive, O Lord, my little jokes on Thee": *Poetry,* 428

"another prayer,...only this is": *Living,* 183

"O'Shaughnessy's poem ["Ode"] about us music-makers": *Unterm.,* 255

67 "They feared and hated the New Deal": Stearns Morse, *Southern Review,*
January 1973 (the title "Lament for a Maker" echoing Dunbar's poem
grudgingly praised by Eliot at St. Botolph's Club, see p. 270)

"[T]he awful state the labor situation": *Sel. Lett.*, 457

"Even outsiders, Amherstites, could see the rift": *Newdick*, 357

68 "The main attraction...was Hemingway": Arthur Casciato, *Citizen Writers*, (doctoral dissertation)

69 "It would take many shapes—between Stalinists and Trotskyites": Casciato *op. cit.*

"I am going to have you strike that blow for me": *Sel. Lett.*, 436

70 "would ever get up from the slaughterhouse floor": *Sel. Lett.*, 456

"a natural enemy [of Frost]": *Poirier*, 230

"his already published best. They were locked": *Poirier*, 237

"a testing ground. Only in those political": H. E. Barnes, *An Intellectual and Cultural History of the Western World*, Cordon, 1937, pp. 1213-14

72 "I should have remembered how much": *Bygones*, Harcourt, 1965, p. 145

"I'd rather there had been no war at all": *Unterm.*, 335-40

73 "I've been crazy for the last six months": *Unterm.*, 311

"I shall never be the scared fool again that": *Fam. Lett.*, 200

75 "to be with Frost for a little while": Van Dore's letter to me

"Perhaps if you knew exactly where I was": Van Dore, *Robert Frost and Wade Van Dore; The Life of the Hired Man*, Wright State University, 1986

"Lunch and dinner were taken with Frost, Ted, and Kay": letter to me

77 "reveals the fervent emotions of the mind": John Keble, *Lectures on Poetry*, Oxford, 1912, I, p. 47

78 "turning point in the poem": *Brower*, 236

81 "I was lunching with Robert yesterday": see *Bygones, op. cit.*, pp. 169-70

82 "You ask: 'Who are you to bring me to trial?'": Dartmouth College Library, July 22, 1953

"Just lunch with Louis, baring his soul": reproduced as typewritten, my errors included. I don't recall the "copy" referred to by Untermeyer.

83 "It has taken a long time for Robert to show": *Unterm.*, 368

89 "Mr. Frost seems": T. S. Eliot, "London Letter," *The Dial*, Apr. 1922

97 "The encounter was a wholly new experience": see Joseph Blumenthal, *Robert Frost and His Printers*, W. Thomas Taylor, Austin, 1985, and *Typographic Years*, Beil, 1982

98 "the two powers [U.S.A. and U.S.S.R.]": *Interv.*, 189

100 "Never saw it": Quoting "Moon Compasses," Fitts asks, "Is this not the fatal note of great poetry?" (*New England Quarterly*, Sept. 1936)

"My new project": *The Poem Itself*, Holt, Rinehart and Winston, 1960

102 "Poetry has always played": *Interv.*, 195-98, summarized

103 "We have come to think of him": Lionel Trilling, "A speech on Robert Frost," *Partisan Review*, Summer 1959

106 *"Fiat Nox"*: second section of *West-Running Brook*

109 "We had a good time together": John Ciardi, "Robert Frost: Master Conversationalist at Work," *Saturday Review*, Mar. 21, 1959

111 "You heard, I guess, what happened": Burnshaw, *Early and Late Testament,* Dial, 1952

113 "Dear Trilling: Not distressed at all": *Sel. Lett.,* 583. Upon Rigg's rejection of the trade rights to Trilling's *The Experience of Literature,* I turned them over to Doubleday with Trilling's approval.

116 "You've heard what I think of 'Uriel'": Thompson reviewed *A Masque of Reason* in *The New York Times Book Review*, Mar. 25, 1945. Thompson's *Fire and Ice: The Art and Thought of Robert Frost,* Holt, 1942

119 "Enormous Caf": see Keats, *Hyperion,* Book II, beginning with line 52

121 "And that Minnesota pamphlet by Larry": Thompson, *Robert Frost,* University of Minnesota Press, 1959

122 "A verse translation": see reference note above to p. 100

126 "A symbol. It stands for unity": "From Iron," *Poetry,* 468
"At the end of the row": *Poetry,* 450

130 **: of the YM-YWHA, 92nd Street and Lexington Avenue, New York, known for its program of poetry readings as the "Y Poetry Center"

134 "real reader knows good poetry doesn't depend on geography": Louis Mertins, *Robert Frost: Life and Talks-Walking,* University of Oklahoma Press, 1965, p. 261
"Frost was here indeed": letter to me

139 "a strong statement of a man's belief": "A Son's Return: Oh Didn't He Ramble," in *Chant of Saints,* M. S. Harper and R. B. Stepto, eds., University of Illinois Press, 1979. See *The Negro Caravan,* Sterling A. Brown, Arthur P. Davis, Ulysses Lee, eds., Dryden, 1941: "Rich man Dives," p. 436.

142 "I thought so well of it": *Poetry: A Magazine of Verse,* July 1958; see also *Sel. Lett.,* 579

143 "I know. Vassar wants him": *The Negro Caravan, op. cit.* Sterling Brown, *Southern Road,* Harcourt, 1932

144 "C. [Cornelia] and I": letter to me, Dec. 23, 1960

145 **Yigael Yadin. Eleazar Sukenik had died in 1953.

147 **: *Dimens.,* especially pp. 188-94

148 "to the President-elect John Finley": Professor of Classics at Harvard. See also *Centen-III,* 152-53

150 "Not much. But enough": for Whorf-Sapir, see Burnshaw, *The Seamless Web,* Braziller, 1970, pp. 114-18.

152 "How hard it is to keep from being king": *Poetry,* 462
"to give two lectures": *Interv.,* 255-58. Frost told the editor of the Yiddish daily *Der Tog* that he meant not political but spiritual affinity.
"It's the other fellow in the poem ["Mending Wall"]": *Interv.,* 257

154 **:see Rinna Samuel, *The New York Times Book Review*, Apr. 23, 1961
   "The way you turned on me": University of Virginia Library (not quite
   accurately quoted by Frost)
155 "innate propensity": James, *Principles of Psychology*, Longmans, 1890
158 "I've just received this essay": *Varieties of Literary Experience*, Stanley
   Burnshaw, ed., New York University Press, 1962
159 "Come up and see us": Frost's gratitude to Untermeyer for deferring
   publication was expressed in an airmail special delivery letter, Nov.
   4, 1961 (*Unterm.*, 382).
   "Remember my telling you": "Wallace Stevens and the Statue," *Sewanee
   Review*, Summer 1961
161 **: See Laurence Perrine, *Centen-II*, 96-7.
164 "That title line near the end": *Poetry*, 453, 462
   **: See *The Seamless Web.*, *op. cit.*, pp. 75-6.
175 "one of the master conversationalists": See note to p. 109
178 "Did you ever hear of": Stead, *The Man Who Loved Children*, Simon and
   Schuster, 1940; Holt, Rinehart and Winston, 1965
181 **: Frost to Thompson, *Sel. Lett.*, 590-91
   "bone tired": *The New York Times Magazine*, June 11, 1972
182 "Smile, if you will": *Understanding Poetry*, 1960; see its footnote p. 240
183 "Democracy is on trial": William James writing in 1908, quoted in John
   R. Harrison, *The Reactionaries*, Schocken, 1967, p. 26
184 **: Professor of Italian Literature, Columbia University
   "And you hated to take it back": Frost's 1959 Christmas poem, "The
   Prophets Really Prophesy as Mystics"; see p. 82
185 "brand new talk at Dartmouth": "On Extravagance," *P&P.*, 447
186 "If only my mother": Kipling's poem "M.I."
188 "Two Tramps": see *The Seamless Web.*, *op. cit.*, p. 74, note 20
189 **: see *Pritch.*, 257-61
   **: dated December 20, 1962; written in French
195 **: Mark Van Doren, *Autobiography*, Harcourt, 1958
   "blue-china poetry": Cook, *Centen-III*, 143, quoting Frost: "that is tea-
   cup stuff, like Lionel Johnson, Ernest Dowson, and the early Yeats."
199 "[D]uring the past ten years": "A Native to the Grain of the American
   Idiom," *Saturday Review*, Mar. 21, 1959
201 **: *Book Week*, Aug. 30, 1964
202 "Master of badinage": *Saturday Review*, Sept. 5, 1964
206 **: the others were Allen Tate, Louise Bogan, William Meredith.
   "For the story of Frost": *New York Times Book Review*, Nov. 6, 1966
210 "Larry and I": Donoghue's letter to me, Mar. 14, 1984
212 "the only soldier I can call my own": *Sel. Lett.*, 502
   "read enough of the book": *Sel. Lett.*, 503
   "He was kindly about his efforts": letter to me from Hyde Cox

"when he had stung me with such cutting remarks": *Notes*, 860

"infuriated [Frost]": *Later Y.*, 401, n. 17. The headnote in *Sel. Lett.*, 528–29, failed to inform readers about the review.

213 "It had been a bad review, admittedly": *Notes*, 532a–532e

"to help Professor Thompson unravel": *Centen.-I*, 415

"I feel better about our relations now": *Notes*, 427

"Kay's violent dislike of Janet [Thompson]": *Notes*, 435c, d, and a–d

214 "I was convinced that Frost had shot his bolt": *Notes*, 435e

"As I jump to the last chapter": *Sel. Lett.*, 553

"may even have been alarmed": letter to me from Hyde Cox

"the super-subtlety of its author": *New York Herald-Tribune Book Review*, June 22, 1952

"literary deception": Richard Chase, *Saturday Review*, May 31, 1952

"This ended the summer": *Notes*, 532h

215 "the period during which the relationship": *Notes*, 435b

"If there's anyone I would care to have dinner with": letter to me from Louise Waller quoting Thompson when she was editing *Early Y.*

216 "I want a variety in the followers": *Sel. Lett.*, 590

"Don't pay attention to what I say": *Notes*, 426

"Don't let me throw any dust in your eyes": *Sel. Lett.*, 529

"Don't you think you should drop the biography?": *Notes*, 651

"plenty of chance[s] to build up resentments": *Notes*, 1611

217 "as one of our best": *Notes*, 796

"Was he mad at him?": *Notes*, 861

"Here I am, pretending that I'm anxious to see Frost": *Notes*, 866

219 **: *Triumph*, 698, n. 4

220 "Trust me on the poetry, but don't trust me on my life" quoted in "Courage is the Virtue," *Newsweek*, Feb. 11, 1963. See Lesley Frost, *New York Times Book Review* "Letters," Sept. 27, 1970.

232 "he did not know how to read them": *New York Review of Books*, Apr. 25, 1985

233 "The facts of history": *What Is History?*, Vintage, 1961

"had it planned from the start": compare *Later Y.*, 277, 430, note 29, with Thompson's "explanation" to me reported on pp. 149f. See also Thompson's "Stick around until you can read Volume Three, because the old bastard is going to win in the end," *New York Times Book Review* ("Letters"), Apr. 3, 1977.

234 **: Van Dore (who, in Thompson's words, "has more firsthand knowledge of Frost as poet and farmer than I do," inscribed in one of his books, Jan. 25, 1964) in the course of reading *Triumph* noted mistakes and omissions. Curious as to their frequency, he skimmed 300 pages before giving up. Mistakes are almost sure to be made in so large a trilogy as Thompson's. How much does it matter, in *Triumph* for

example, that the automobile was not an "Overland" but an "Oakland?" that Frost was wearing not bedroom slippers but hiking shoes slit above the toe when he met Van Dore at the Littleton railroad station? that the two men never walked the Franconia countryside together? What *troubled* Van Dore was Frost's alleged discomfort from the "tension" Thompson speaks of between Van Dore and Lankes because "it didn't exist" any more than did Frost's supposed annoyance with Van Dore's "Man Alone" (which gave rise to "The Most of It"). To the foregoing items, two misleading inventions (at the very least) should be added: Trilling never dined with Frost, nor did Frost "go over the proofs of his last book in Miami." Untermeyer (and others) enjoyed the "howler" about "The Cow in Apple Time" (*Early Y.*, 605) and the implications. Dudley Fitts did the same with Thompson's citation of Milton when "any schoolboy cd've told him RF was quoting no one more exotic than Vergil" (*Early Y.*, 551). The statement that "Ciardi is dead" (*Early Y.*, 596) can be taken in stride by readers used to mistakes of this kind, but not the absence of key entries in the index, especially in *Later Y.* (Israel, *A Lover's Quarrel, You Come Too*, etc.). More examples perhaps should be added to edify those who continue to laud the official biography as the source of impeccable facts.

234 "knew Frost well enough, was astonished": Kazin's letter to me; also Elizabeth Kray's letter to me

"Pritchard's damning account": Readers should bear in mind in following Pritchard's pages on Thompson's "intentions" that Thompson's "I love you" letter was written Dec. 4, 1940, seventeen years before professing his loathing for Frost (see pp. 3, 210 above and *Pritch.*, xiii).

"probably spent more time than": *Christian Science Monitor*

235 **: Armstrong Press, Notasulga, Alabama, 1984

"Whatever happened to the image": Cook, *Centen.-III*, 132

238 "The woods are not, as the Lathem edition": Poirier, 181

"to remove ambiguity": *Poetry*, Imprint Society edition, Barre, Mass., 1971, editor's introduction, especially pp. xvii-xix

"special qualifications to advise": letter to me from E. C. Lathem

"I indulge a sort of indifference to punctuation": *Sel. Lett.*, 370

240 "verse, whatever else": *Times Literary Supplement*, Sept. 27, 1928

241 "I'll never forget my visit with you": Newdick, 218

"I grow curious about my soul": *Sel. Lett.*, 530

"I trust my philosophy still bothers you": *Sel. Lett.*, 584

"I contain opposites": *Interv.*, 271, 185

"I'd have no trouble with the first two. It's the last, 'temper,'": Reichert, *Out for the Stars*, Cincinnati, 1969, p. 6

242 "Robert Frost was a primal energy": *Saturday Review*, Feb. 23, 1963
243 "wondrous agency": *Sartor Resartus*, Book 3, chap. 3
"I have written to keep the over curious": *Sel. Lett.*, 385
"any eye is an evil eye/That looks in onto": *Poetry*, 385
"When the mood was on him, he could spill": *Atlantic*, July 1967
"anyone who has read his *Collected Poems*": *Book Week*, Aug. 30, 1964
"So many of them have literary criticism": *P&P*, 458
244 "We make ourselves a place apart": *Poetry*, 19
"Please burn it. Be easy on me": *Unterm.*, 296
"Most of my ideas occur": Frost to Sidney Cox, *Sergeant*, 311
245 "He tried on the sounds of words to see if": Peter Davison, *Half-Remembered*, Harper, 1973, p. 207
"the difference between Frost as poet and": *Living*, 5-6
"*sound* better than they read": *Living*, 30
246 "to justify the astonishing": *Sel. Lett.*, 20, to Susan Hayes Ward
"one of the greatest changes my nature": *Sel. Lett.*, 482
"The new thing with me": Ciardi, *Saturday Review*, Mar. 21, 1959
"talk, mythologizing, or lies": see letter to Sidney Cox, "Look out I don't spoof you." *Sel. Lett.*, 435
247 "vital part of his picture": *Newdick*, 194
"arresting New England beauty purified": *Sergeant*, xviii
"Mrs. Frost, an animated talker": *Living*, 9
"Mrs. Frost had probably become": Dierkes, *op. cit.*, 68-9
"I had a good number of hours alone with her": letter to me
248 "It's after nine o'clock, and you *must* go milk": *Swinger* 9
"influence of this firm, intuitive": *Fam. Lett.*, 275
"F is as considerate of Mrs. F": *Newdick*, 282
"a great poet of marriage": *Poirier*, 22
"The magnificent clarity of his love for his wife": *New York Times Book Review*, Nov. 6, 1966
"She has been the unspoken half of everything": *Unterm.*, 295-96
249 "Robert depends on me": *Sel. Lett.*, 410, to Edith H. Fobes
"Elinor has just come out flat-footed against": *Unterm.*, 101
"colored [his thought] from the first": see *Fam. Lett.*, 210
250 "Pretty nearly every one of my poems": *Sel. Lett.*, 471, to G. R. and A. Elliott
"could hurt him": See *Sergeant*, 293
"an imperfect line, or flash of beauty": Mertins, *op. cit.*, 229
**: *Sergeant*, 320
"especially wary of honors that derogate": *Unterm.*, 63
"reputation, that bubble": *Sergeant*, xix
"somewhat disappointed": *Sel. Lett.*, 78, to Margaret Bartlett
"It is certainly *grand* about the": *Sel. Lett.*, 429, to Nina Thornton

"I sat and let Elinor pour it over me": *Sel. Lett.*, 452

251 "Don't you think it's beautiful yourself?": *Sergeant*, 188

"I played with them more than most fathers": *Sergeant*, 77. See Frost's stories for his children, *P&P*, 216-24.

"I sat there with him. I went to sleep as": *Sergeant*, 78

"He just does nothing a good deal of": *Fam. Lett.*, 15 (Nov. 1917)

"Take the way with her that will keep the peace": *Fam. Lett.*, 102

252 "Stratton...powerful and splendid": *Sel. Lett.*, 390 (Mar. 1933)

"That was another good poem": *Fam. Lett.*, 153 (May 1933)

"apple-crating poem...has a great deal more of": *Fam. Lett.*, 183

"I tried many ways and every single one of them": *Unterm.*, 322-23

"the sad ending to Irma's story": *Sel. Lett.*, 528. Lesley removed Irma to a nursing home in Vermont, the expenses paid out of the income from Frost's will. See *Unterm.*, 345.

"wracking itself to pieces from running wild": *Unterm.*, 315

"to be bowed down": *Triumph*, 511, to J. J. Lankes, Aug. 3, 1938. See *Unterm.*, 103, end of letter, Apr. 12, 1920.

253 "I reached a point lately where I could": *Sergeant*, 408-9

"the first poem that I got any personal": *Swinger*, 85

254 "Writing, teaching a little, and farming": *Interv.*, 242

255 "[T]he only education worth anything": *Unterm.*, 376

"I ought to have been poet enough": *Sel. Lett.*, 293, to W. L. Cross

"I never taught long enough to carry anything out": *Unterm.*, 289

"I have long thought that our high schools": *Interv.*, 193, 181

256 "I'm going to leave you with the motto": see *Centen.-III*, 151

"the greatest living expert [on education]": *Interv.*, 193

"so patient with my educational heresies": *Interv.*, 101

**: *Newdick*, 317-19; Tyler, *Centen-III*; Jackson, *Triumph*, 100

"In twenty years I have walked": *You Come Too*, Foreword

257 "His talk-spiels were legendary; marathon": *Centen.-III*, 134

"Frost's talk is not pyrotechnic or febrile": *Dimens.*, 12-15

258 "Don't you believe it's important to do good?": *Unterm.*, 372-73

"Democracy means all the risks taken": *Interv.*, 194

"A nation should be just as full of conflict": *Jott.*, 109

"I like all this uncertainty that we live in": *Interv.*, 213

"everything and everybody that want people to": *Interv.*, 213

"the public health, / So that the poor won't": *Poetry*, 363

"too much one way and then too much another": *Living*, 183

259 "Maybe I'm one who never makes up his mind": *Living*, 200

"It's well to have all kinds of feelings": *Ordin.*, 16

"I yield to no one in my admiration for": *Pictor.*, 115

"we shouldn't come to blows till we": *Pictor.*, 115-16

"jealousy is a passion I approve of": Oberlin *Alumni Magazine*, May 1938

260 "the odium of seeming jealous of anybody": *Unterm.*, 18

"I wonder...do you feel as badly as I do": Alfred Kreymborg, *Troubadour, An Autobiography*, Boni, 1925, p. 336

"The whole thing is performance": *Poirier*, 294

261 "The object in life is to win": *Jott.*, 53

"I divide my talks into two parts": *Centen-III*, 165

"Did any government ever send Eliot anywhere?": letter to me from Robert Fitzgerald, see p. 155 above.

"say for certain [that he didn't] like Spoon River": *Unterm.*, 75

"There's only room for one at the top of the steeple": *Interv.*, 197

"undoubtedly the man": *Sel. Lett.*, 93, to Sidney Cox

263 "If you want to see what happened in Boston": *Sel. Lett.*, 156

"in the case of Braithwaite": *Pritch.*, 113. See *Triumph*, 535, note 53. When I edited *Unterm.*, the manuscript contained no hint of any such substitution, nor did Untermeyer mention a change.

"to arrive where I can stand on my legs as a poet": *Sel. Lett.*, 98

264 "I have myself all in a strong box": *Unterm.*, 29

"I want to appreciate more": *Poetry and the Age.*, op. cit., p. 37

"Frost had us all in the palm of his hand": Selden Rodman, *Tongues of Fallen Angels*, New Directions, 1974, p. 43

265 "The best audience the world ever had": *Interv.*, 161

"That's what *you* would say, anyway": *Centen.-III*, 170; see also 107

"I have come to value my poetry": *Unterm.*, 314

266 "individuals of great worth in the younger generation": *Interv.*, 140

"1934 SEP 4/STOP PRESS": letter to me from Helen Brower

267 "The Puritans [was] the best": letter to me from Richard Wilbur

"Why don't I come to *your* room?": *A Reminiscence of Robert Frost*, 1980, Special Collection and Archives, Amherst College

"We swapped poems for a while": letter to me

268 "Atta boy Jesus Christ Professor" letter to me from Theodore Weiss; see Schubert, *Work and Days*, the QRL 40th anniversary, 1983.

"I'm the kind that can't get over things": *Jott.*, 137

269 "You want to believe that great writers are good men": Brooks, *From the Shadow of the Mountain*, Dutton, 1961, pp. 180-81

"Let's not have": letter from Frost, Dartmouth College Library

270 **Sergeant*, 313-16

"He offered to read a poem if I would read one": *Unterm.*, 231 (*Poetry*, 294)

271 "Early in the proceedings Frost found": Stegner, *The Uneasy Chair: A Biography of Bernard DeVoto*, Doubleday, 1974, p. 206

"Frost did not take kindly to Archie's talk": quoted in *Later Y.*, 371

272 "I've been crazy for the last six months": *Unterm.*, 311

"I showed up at the Homer": letter to me from Robert N. Ganz

273 "For the most part he was": letter to me from Alfred C. Edwards
   "The setting was early": letter to me from Joseph Blumenthal
274 "The world hates Jews and despises": letter to me from Victor Reichert
   "Who's the lady coon?": Peter Brazeau, *Parts of a World: Wallace Stevens Remembered*, Random House, 1983, pp. 195-6 and 249
   "I find race feeling runs pretty hot in my veins": *The Letters of Archibald MacLeish, op. cit.*, p. 57
   **: Frost also knew that my wife worked in a children's clinic in New York City's Harlem; that I had published *The Negro Caravan;* etc.
   "I don't think the word should": letter to me from Hyde Cox
275 "way of admitting that he couldn't": *Early Y.*, xiv. See also note to p. 220 ("Trust me...").
   "[James Dickey] felt sure": in conversation with me, 1972
   "could never seem to forgive people": *Book Week*, Aug. 30, 1964
   "that men won't understand us and we shall be": *Prose*, 60
   "didn't believe it did [him] the least good": *Swinger*, vii
   "We all have our souls — and minds — to save": *Sel. Lett.*, 212
276 **: "the utmost reward/Of daring...": *Poetry*, 19; 497, line 106
   "I'd rather be taken for brave than anything else," *Sel. Lett.*, 595
   "Be careful how you offer to": letter to me from Van Dore
   "any form of humor shows fear": *Unterm.*, 166
   "It's a funny world": *Swinger*, 40-1
277 "I own any form of humor shows...inferiority": *Unterm.*, 166
   "When the question comes up": *Unterm.*, 366
   "[S]tyle is the way the man takes himself": *Prose*, 65
   "Play no matter how deep has got to be": Dartmouth College Library
   "perhaps his deepest word on the subject": *Pritch.*, xvi
   "The way of understanding is [always] partly mirth": *Poetry*, 306
278 "that Frost finds balance...Serious play": *Centen-II*, 223, 230
   "everything he did or wrote": *Pritch.*, xvi
   "Frost is a poet of genius because": *Poirier*, x-xii
279 "Most folks are poets. If they were not": *Interv.*, 32
   "Five ways of reading *Lycidas*": *Varieties of Literary Experience*, Stanley Burnshaw, ed., New York University Press, 1962
   "In- and Outdoor Schooling": *Robert Frost*, Lectures on the Centennial of His Birth, Library of Congress, 1975
   "Life sways perilously at the": *Sel. Lett.*, 467, to R. P. T. Coffin
280 "the juxtaposed interpretation of facts": *Centen.-I*, 82
   "the poets most often held up as": *Centen.-I.*, 273-74
   "through this stealthy rusticity": *Centen.-I.*, 55
   "cavalierliness with words": *Dimens.*, 50; *cf.* E. E. Cummings, *Poems: 1923-1954*, No. 34, p. 373, Harcourt, 1954
   "The sound is": first four quotations from *Prose*, 17, 13, 23, 33

282 "A poem...begins as a lump in the throat": *Unterm.*, 22
"I alone of English writers": *Sel. Lett.*, 79-80, 110-11, 113
283 "ceased to expect it [perfection]": *Sel. Lett.*, 482, to DeVoto
"utmost ambition": Ciardi, *Saturday Review*, Mar. 21, 1959
"Hawthorne and Frost": *Centen-I*, 288-309
"every single one of my poems is probably": *P & P*, 420-21
"If my poetry has to have a name": Untermeyer, *Robert Frost: A Backward Look*, Library of Congress, 1964, p. 3
284 "The stars 'congregate'": *Centen.-I*, 98. See also 89-107 passim.
"My poems": *Sel. Lett.*, 344, to Leonidas W. Payne, Jr.
"Now, that's all right; it's out of my hands once": *Interv.*, 188
285 "It's another one people have bothered around": *Living*, 248
"Rhymy little thing": *Living*, 303
"be pressed too hard for meaning": *Living*, 240
**: for example, comments on "Directive" (*Poetry*, 377) in Poirier, Brower, Pritch.
"His subject was the world": *Centen.-III*, 101
286 "I Could Give All": compare Poirier, 174-77, Jarrell, *Poetry and the Age, op. cit.*, p. 51; Brower, 232; Pritch., 234; *Living*, 257
"The poem suggests more than one can": letter to me from Hyde Cox
"the one permissible way of saying one thing and": *Prose*, 36
"Having thoughts of your own is the only freedom": *Centen.-III*, 150
287 "feeling is always ahead of thinking": *Living*, 207
"poetry must include the mind as well...The mind is dangerous": *Interv.*, 124. See also *Pictor.*, 47, interview in *The Scotsman*, May 1957.
"there is nothing anybody knows, however absolutely": *Unterm.*, 175
"No one can know how glad I am to find": *Poetry*, 358
"Give all to meaning.": *Prose*, 116
"cherubic scorn" *Living*, 130
"It's the plunge of the mind, the spirit, into": *Living*, 212
"It is not given to man to be omniscient.": *Interv.*, 64
"ultimately not quite understandable": *Hudson Review*, Summer 1976
**: Newdick, 219, to Sidney Cox. Frost or his editors could have supplied the English meanings of the Greek (*Poetry*, 427) or the Latin (*Poetry*, 394) that form parts of his poems. "Stopping by Woods..." was "the kind of poem he'd like to print on one page to be followed with forty pages of footnotes," he told Reichert, *op. cit.*, p. 13. Havighurst observed that certain poems were "so personal that [Frost] declined to read them on the platform": *Cent.-III*, 101
288 "The most exciting movement in nature is not progress": *Ordin.*, 21
"Logical systems [are] nonsense": *Swinger*, 12-3
"I'm less and less for systems and system-building": *Sel. Lett.*, 343
"A deeper understanding of socialism": *Interv.*, 286

"I'm a nationalist and I expect other people to be": *Interv.*, 121

"a Lucretian abstainer from politics": *Unterm.*, 335

289 "I'm not confused; I'm only well-mixed": *Interv.*, 185

"I *am* the conflicts, I *contain* them": *Sergeant*, 406

Nine quotations in order: (1) *Interv.*, 112; (2) *Living*, 190; (3) *Dimens.*, 177; (4) Frost's notebook quoted in *Early Y.*, 427 and often repeated in conversation; (5) *Jott.*, 65; (6) *Poetry*, 350; (7) reported in the Amherst *Journal*, May 2, 1947; (8-9) *Jott.*, 144, 91

290 "Frost appears to contradict himself": *Centen.-I*, 603

"Having ideas that are neither pro nor con": *Swinger*, 28-9

"I despise religiosity" and the ten quotations that follow: (1) Rodman, *op. cit.*, 41; (2) *Ordin.*, 36; (3) *Sel. Lett.*, 530; (4) *Prose*, 45-6; (5-6) *Sel. Lett.*, 525; (7) *Living*, 181; (8) Notebook, Dartmouth College Library; (9) Sermon, Rockdale Avenue Temple, Cincinnati, Oct. 10, 1946; (10) *Prose*, 41; (11) *Sel. Lett.*, 596 (Jan. 12, 1963)

292 "something": John McGiffert, *English Journal*, November 1945

"altogether remarkable poem": *Poirier*, 305-313

293 "I was brought up in all three of these religions": *Prose*, 112

294 "an Old Testament believer": *Dimens.*, 190

"Call them 'nature's favors'": *Centen.-I*, 424

"a curse to be an agnostic": *Interv.*, 194

"froth": *Dimens.*, 191

"between trivialities and profundities": *Notes*, 555

"Where is this God I hear so much about?": *Newdick*, 366

"he [had] moved from skepticism to almost complete": *Notes*, 426

"To prayer": *Unterm.*, 130, 136, 331

"This one's about my sixth revised—transgression": Untermeyer's characterization of his forthcoming poetry anthology

295 "All I do...is reach for something": *Dimens.*, 191

"To believe is to wish to believe": *The Tragic Sense of Life*, Dover, 1954, p. 114

"Lord, I believe": letter to me from Hyde Cox, Dec. 18, 1983

"best when rapt": *Unterm.*, 166

"Play me some great music": Hyde Cox quoted in *Later Y.*, 439

"Victor, what do you think": recounted to me in conversation

"a spiritual explorer": Marice Brown, *Centen.-I*, 4

"There is at least so much of good": *Prose*, 106

296 "It begins in delight, it inclines to the impulse": *Prose*, 18

"if a reader can lapse back into his immediate sensible life": *Some Problems in Philosophy*, Longmans, 1911, p. 50. See *The Seamless Web.*, *op. cit.*, p. 42, n8.

"The present/ Is too much for the senses": *Poetry*, 336

"There is always tragedy. That is what life is": *Swinger*, 174 "because confusions keep coming": *Times of London*, May 22, 1957

"Drink and be whole again beyond confusion": *Poetry*, 379

297 "he swooped, he pounced, he struck": *Poetry*, 278

"[science] goes self-superseding on": *Poetry*, 480

"You're always believing ahead of your evidence": *Interv.*, 271

"It is only by risking our persons from one hour to": *Philosophy of William James*, H. M. Kallen, ed., Modern Library, 1925, p. 25

"You are not safe anywhere unless" *Prose*, 39-43 (phrases reordered)

"The great spring": *The Seamless Web, op. cit.*, p. 183

"are nearly identical in their theories of poetic 'strain' and": *New York Review of Books*, Apr. 25, 1985, p. 34

"moral law lies at the center and radiates to": *Nature*

"We throw our arms wide with a gesture of religion": *Prose*, 71-2

298 "to front the essential facts...[to] learn what": *Walden*

"a true account of the actual is the rarest poetry": Thoreau, *A Week on the Concord and Merrimack Rivers*

"instructions to the season": *Poirier*, 200

"I'm always saying something that's just the edge": *Interv.*, 268

"Where is there any benevolence of purpose?": *Interv.*, 165

"With a lantern that wouldn't burn": *Poetry*, 443

"A poet must lean": *Swinger*, 10

299 "a natural conflict": Stanlis paraphrasing Frost, *Centen.-III*, 280

300 "the fear that men won't understand us": *Prose*, 60

"against hopeless odds": see W. H. Auden, *The Dyer's Hand*, Random House, 1962, pp. 345-47. Compare: "I never tire of being shown how the limited can make snug in the limitless": *Living*, 65n, with regard to *Walden* and *Robinson Crusoe*.

"The surest thing you know is": *Boston Herald*, Mar. 19, 1936

"creational": *Centen.-II*, 100 (phrases reordered)

"tie together some way": *Living*, 190

301 "case against [Frost]": *Human Values in the Poetry of Robert Frost*, Duke University Press, 1960

**: Quotations from *Poetry*: pp. 248, 17, 475, 460, 122, 17, 324, 251, 362, 106, 350, 249, 306, 19, 222, 254-55, 362, 485, 296, 348, and 403, respectively.

303 "There are roughly zones whose laws must be": *Poetry*, 305

"a new start": See Auden, *op. cit.*, p. 349

"If you see the little truths": *Swinger*, 80, paraphrasing Frost

"as if": Radcliffe Squires, *The Major Themes of Robert Frost*, Univ. of Michigan Press, 1963, p. 51

**: *Sel. Lett.*, p. 436 ("I refuse to explain my position on a lot of things we...left unsettled...Why should I press home my conclusions everywhere.")

"the myth of 'The Trial by Existence'": Nitchie, *op. cit.,* p. 223

"Earth's a hard place..." and the other quotations here: "The Lesson for Today," *Poetry,* 350-55

304 "The people along the sand": *Poetry,* 301

"In the end he talked as naturally": *Book Week,* Aug. 30, 1964

305 **: *Poetry,* 517, lines 629-30

"All I would keep for myself": *Prose,* 20

INDEX